Foreign Aid for Development

UNU World Institute for Development Economics Research (UNU-WIDER) was established by the United Nations University as its first research and training centre and started work in Helsinki, Finland, in 1985. The purpose of the institute is to undertake applied research and policy analysis on structural changes affecting developing and transitional economies, to provide a forum for the advocacy of policies leading to robust, equitable, and environmentally sustainable growth, and to promote capacity strengthening and training in the field of economic and social policymaking. Its work is carried out by staff researchers and visiting scholars in Helsinki and via networks of collaborating scholars and institutions around the world.

United Nations University World Institute for Development Economics Research
(UNU-WIDER)
Katajanokanlaituri 6 B, FIN-00160 Helsinki, Finland
www.wider.unu.edu

Foreign Aid for Development

Issues, Challenges, and the New Agenda

Edited by
George Mavrotas

A study prepared for the World Institute for Development Economics
Research of the United Nations University (UNU-WIDER)

OXFORD
UNIVERSITY PRESS

OXFORD
UNIVERSITY PRESS

Great Clarendon Street, Oxford, OX2 6DP,
United Kingdom

Oxford University Press is a department of the University of Oxford.
It furthers the University's objective of excellence in research, scholarship,
and education by publishing worldwide. Oxford is a registered trade mark of
Oxford University Press in the UK and in certain other countries

Published in the United States of America by Oxford University Press
198 Madison Avenue, New York, NY 10016, United States of America

British Library Cataloguing in Publication Data

Data available

Library of Congress Cataloging in Publication Data

Data available

ISBN 978–0–19–958093–4

To Eleni, for her continuous and unreserved support

Foreword

Foreign aid has been one of the most contentious topics in the history of intellectual thought on development issues. Many core questions remain the subject of intense debate. Does aid really work in promoting growth and reducing poverty in the developing world? Will a new 'big push' approach accelerate progress towards the Millennium Development Goals? What lessons can be learnt from half a century of aid giving? Answers to these questions are important for the construction of the new landscape in foreign aid, and for appropriate responses to the current financial crisis, which is expected to have far-reaching implications for both donors and recipients.

To assist planning for the future, there is a pressing need to assess the current state of knowledge, and to explore emerging issues and agendas. This volume brings together leading experts in this area to review the progress achieved so far, to identify the challenges ahead, and to discuss the emerging policy agenda in foreign aid. The papers emanate from the UNU-WIDER conference on 'Aid: Principles, Policies, and Performance' in 2006. It represents the culmination of almost a decade of UNU-WIDER research on development finance issues encompassing both external finance (aid, debt relief, foreign direct investment, private capital flows) and domestic resource mobilization (savings and financial sector development). The publications resulting from this research have had a significant impact within the international development community, and contributed to a vibrant discourse (with broad policy influence) that characterizes the UNU-WIDER mandate.

This book will be of special interest to policymakers involved in reforms of foreign aid policy, as well as an essential reference for students of development and international finance. A central conclusion is that—since development aid remains crucial for many developing countries—a huge effort is needed from both donors and aid recipients to overcome the inefficiencies and make aid work better for poor people. As global citizens we have a moral obligation to strive to raise people in the developing world out of poverty.

Anthony Shorrocks
Former director, UNU-WIDER

Acknowledgements

This volume emanates from a major international conference, 'Aid: Principles, Policies, and Performance', organized by UNU-WIDER and held on 16–17 June 2006 in Helsinki, which the editor had the honour and privilege to coordinate. The editor is indebted to the three anonymous Oxford University Press referees for their insightful and constructive comments and suggestions, of great benefit to the present volume, and to Sarah Caro, Commissioning Editor in Economics and Finance at the Oxford University Press, for helpful background discussions and extremely useful advice regarding the overall structure of the volume. He is also most grateful to Jenny Kimmis for truly outstanding editorial support and to Adam Swallow, UNU-WIDER Publications Assistant, for superb editorial advice. Special thanks to Anthony Shorrocks, Director of UNU-WIDER, for his strong support and encouragement during the preparation of this volume. Janis Vehmaan-Kreula, UNU-WIDER Conference Secretary, did a brilliant job providing exceptional assistance in running the conference, and Barbara Fagerman, Senior Programme Assistant at UNU-WIDER, provided excellent administrative support.

Chapter 2, 'Aid, Growth, and Development', by Finn Tarp is a shortened, revised, and updated version of 'Aid and Development' originally published in *Swedish Economic Policy Review*, 13 (2006), and included with their kind permission. Chapter 4, 'Reconstructing the Aid Effectiveness Debate', by Machiko Nissanke draws in part from her chapter 'Donor–Recipient Relationships in the Aid Effectiveness Debate', in *Aid Relationships in Asia: Exploring Ownership in Japanese and Nordic Aid*, ed. Alf Morten Jerve, Yasutami Shimomura, and Annette Skovsted Hansen (Palgrave Macmillan, 2007). Chapter 7, 'Aid to Fragile States: Do Donors Help or Hinder?' by Stephen Browne is based on chapter 5 of his book *Aid and Influence: Do Donors Help or Hinder?* (Earthscan, 2006) and is included with the kind permission of the publisher. An earlier version of Chapter 12 was released as Innocenti Working Paper No. 2007-02: 'International Support for the Realisation of Children's Rights: Aid Modalities and Accountability in Reporting and a Review of Aid for Basic Social Services' by Eva Jespersen and Julia Benn, UNICEF Innocenti Research Centre, Florence, Italy, from whom kind permission was granted to include herein.

UNU-WIDER gratefully acknowledges the financial contribution to the conference by the Finnish Ministry for Foreign Affairs. UNU-WIDER also acknowledges the financial contributions to the research programme by the governments of Denmark (Royal Ministry of Foreign Affairs), Finland (Ministry for Foreign Affairs), Norway (Royal Ministry of Foreign Affairs), Sweden (Swedish International Development Cooperation Agency), and the United Kingdom (Department for International Development).

Contents

Contents

III. Aid to Fragile and Conflict-affected Countries

IV. Aid Modalities

Contents

List of Figures

List of Tables

List of Tables

List of Abbreviations

ACP	[signatory countries of the Lomé Convention in] Africa, the Caribbean, and the Pacific
ADB	Asian Development Bank
APR	annual progress report
ARM	annual review meetings
ARPP	annual report on portfolio performance
ASEAN	Association of Southeast Asian Nations
BOP	balance of payments
BSS	basic social services
CAP	country assistance programme
CAS	country assistance strategy
CBA	cost–benefit analysis
CDF	comprehensive development framework
CDR	Council of Development and Reconstruction (Lebanon)
CDSF	contingency debt sustainability framework
CIDA	Canadian International Development Agency
CIS	Commonwealth of Independent States
CPIA	country policy and institutional assessment (World Bank index)
CPN-M	Communist Party of Nepal-Maoist
CPR	country performance ratings
CRC	Convention on the Rights of the Child
CRS	creditor reporting system (OECD-DAC)
CSO	civil society organization
DAC	Development Assistance Committee (OECD)
DCF	Development Cooperation Forum (of ECOSOC)
DFID	Department for International Development (UK)
DRC	Democratic Republic of Congo
DSA	debt sustainability analysis

DSF	debt sustainability framework
ECD	evaluation capacity development
ECOSOC	Economic and Social Council (UN)
EDA	effective development assistance
EIDHR	European Initiative for Democracy and Human Rights (EU)
ERBS	exchange rate-based stabilization
EU	European Union
EUDN	European Development Research Network
EVI	economic vulnerability index
FDI	foreign direct investment
GAVI	Global Alliance for Vaccines and Immunization
GBS	general budget support
GDP	gross domestic product
GFATM	Global Fund to fight AIDS, Tuberculosis, and Malaria
GMIF	Gender Mainstreaming Implementation Framework
GNI	gross national income
GPRS	Ghana poverty-reduction strategy
H&A	harmonization and alignment
HDI	human development index
HI	horizontal inequality
HIPC	heavily indebted poor country
HR	human rights
IBRD	International Bank for Reconstruction and Development
IDA	International Development Association (World Bank)
IFF	international financing facility
IFIs	international financial institutions
IGRs	international governance reviews
ILO	International Labour Organization
IMD	Institute for Multiparty Democracy (Netherlands)
IMF	International Monetary Fund
IRI	International Republican Institute (USA)
JRM	joint sector review mission
JSA	joint staff assessment
JSR	joint-sector review
LDCs	least-developed countries
LIC	low-income country
LICUS	low-income countries 'under stress'

M&E	monitoring and evaluation
MCA	Millennium Challenge Account (USA)
MDBS	multi-donor budgetary support
MDG	Millennium Development Goal
MDRI	Multilateral Debt Relief Initiative
MTBF	medium-term budget framework
MTEF	medium-term expenditure/budgetary framework
MTFF	medium-term fiscal framework
NAM	non-aligned movement
NBER	National Bureau of Economic Research
NDI	National Democratic Institute (USA)
NED	National Endowment for Democracy (USA)
NGDO	non-governmental development organization
NGO	non-governmental organization
NPV	net present value
O&M	operations and maintenance
OA	official aid
ODA	official development assistance
ODI	Overseas Development Institute (UK)
OECD	Organization for Economic Co-operation and Development
OEEC	Organization for European Economic Co-operation
OHCHR	Office of the High Commissioner for Human Rights
OPEC	Organization of the Petroleum Exporting Countries
PAF	performance assessment framework
PAMSCAD	Programme of Action to Mitigate the Social Consequences of Adjustment (Ghana)
PBA	performance-based allocation
PBA	programme-based approach
PEAP	Poverty Eradication Action Plan
PEFA	public expenditure and financial accountability
PEM	public expenditure management
PEMFAR	public expenditure management and financial accountability review
PER	public expenditure review
PFM	public finance management
PGBS	partnership general budget support
PPE	pro-poor expenditure

PRBS	poverty reduction budget support
PRGF	Poverty Reduction and Growth Facility (International Monetary Fund)
PRIDE	poverty reduction in difficult environments
PROGRESA	Programa de Educación, Salud y Alimentación (Mexico)
PRSP	poverty-reduction strategy paper
PSIA	poverty and social impact analysis
RBM	results-based management
SADC	South Africa Development Community
SAP	structural adjustment programme
SEE	South Eastern Europe
Sida	Swedish International Development Cooperation Agency
SLORC	State Law and Order Restoration Council (Burma)
SPA	Strategic Partnership with Africa
SPDC	State Peace and Development Council (Burma)
SPS	sector programme support
SWAP	sector-wide approach
TAS	Tanzania Assistance Strategy
TICAD	Tokyo International Conference on African Development
TRA	Tanzania Revenue Authority
UNDP	United Nations Development Programme
USAID	United States Agency for International Development
VAT	value added tax
WAEMU	West African Economic and Monetary Union
WFD	Westminster Foundation for Democracy (UK)
WSSD	World Summit on Social Development

List of Contributors

Richard M. Auty, Professor Emeritus of Economic Geography at Lancaster University, has advised many multilateral and bilateral agencies on economic development issues. His research interests include industrial policy, resource-driven development, and rent cycling theory. Recent books include: *Energy Wealth and Governance in the Caucasus and Central Asia* (Routledge, 2006), *Resource Abundance and Economic Development* (Oxford University Press, 2004), and *Sustainable Development in Mineral Economies* (Oxford University Press, 1998).

Julia Benn has worked in the Statistics and Monitoring Division of the OECD Development Co-operation Directorate since 1993 and is currently the manager of the Statistical Policy, Analysis and Outreach Unit. Before joining the OECD, she worked with the ILO and the Finnish Ministry of Foreign Affairs.

Graham Brown is Senior Lecturer in the Politics of Development at the University of Bath and Research Associate at the Centre for Research on Inequality, Human Security, and Ethnicity, University of Oxford. His research interests include the political economy of horizontal inequalities and conflict, with a regional focus in Asia, and the sociology of international aid policy.

Stephen Browne is Deputy Executive Director, International Trade Centre, Geneva. Trained as an economist at Cambridge and Sorbonne, he joined the United Nations in 1976. In Somalia, he coordinated the donor response to the humanitarian emergency in 1986. In Ukraine, as the first UN Representative, he started a resettlement programme for Crimea in 1993, and in Rwanda (1998–9) he was UN Coordinator for development and humanitarian assistance. He has written and published five books and many articles on aid and development.

Arjan de Haan is Social Development and Policy Adviser, UK Department for International Development, Beijing Office, and member of the faculty in the Institute for Social Studies in The Hague. During 2005–6, he was Visiting Professor at the University of Guelph, published *Reclaiming Social Policy* (Palgrave Macmillan, 2007), and started to work on a book on *How the Aid Industry Works* (Kumarian Press, 2009).

Ghassan Dibeh is Associate Professor of Economics in the Department of Economics at the Lebanese American University in Byblos. He is Editor of *Review of Middle East Economics and Finance*. His research interests include macroeconomics, political economy, financial economics, and econophysics. His research has appeared in *Physica A, Review of Political Economy, Energy Economics, Journal of International Development*, and *Middle Eastern Studies*.

Max Everest-Phillips is Senior Governance Adviser in the UK Department for International Development responsible for growth and investment issues. He has spent the last twenty years working both as diplomat and a development expert in Asia, Africa, and Latin America, addressing the political economy challenges in international development. He has written extensively on 'taxation as state-building', including a recent introductory guide for the World Bank Group on the political governance determinants of business taxation.

Sakiko Fukuda-Parr is Professor of International Affairs at the New School, New York. She works on development from the multidisciplinary human development and human rights perspectives. From 1995 to 2004, she was director of the UNDP *Human Development Reports*. Other recent publications include: *The Gene Revolution: GM Crops and Unequal Development* (main contributor and editor); *Readings in Human Development* (edited with A. K. Shiva Kumar); *Rethinking Technical Cooperation: Reforms for Capacity Building in Africa* (with E. Berg); *Capacity for Development* (edited with C. Lopes and K. Malik), and numerous papers and chapters on issues of poverty, gender, human rights, and technology. She founded and is co-editor of the *Journal of Human Development and Capabilities*, and is on the editorial board of *Feminist Economics*.

Patrick Guillaumont is Professeur émérite at CERDI, Université d'Auvergne, President of the FERDI (Fondation pour les Études et Recherches sur le Développement International), Director of the Revue d'Economie du Développement, and a member of the United Nations Committee for Development Policy. He is also a fellow of the Oxford Centre for Studies on African Economies (CSAE). His main research interests are development economics, foreign aid, human resources, and the least developed countries

Sylviane Guillaumont Jeanneney is Professeur émérite at CERDI, Université d'Auvergne, and a fellow of the Oxford Centre for Studies on African Economies (CSAE). She is also a member of the Conseil d'administration of the Agence Française de Développement. Her main research interests are development economics, foreign aid, exchange rates, monetary and fiscal policy, and, more recently, deforestation.

Nathalie Holvoet is currently a full-time lecturer at the Institute of Development Policy and Management, University of Antwerp (Belgium). Her main research areas are monitoring and evaluation in the context of development, gender budgeting, and intra-household resource allocation. She has published in, among other journals: *Evaluation and Program Planning, Evaluation, Development and Change, Feminist Economics, Journal of Modern African Studies*.

Michael Hubbard is Reader in Development Economics, International Development Department, University of Birmingham. He has collaborated in several studies of aid, sponsored by the African Development Bank, the Caribbean Development Bank, DFID, and OECD DAC, including the Joint Evaluation of General Budget Support (2006). His work on aid includes a special issue of *Public Administration & Development* (25: 5) on Reforming Aid Management.

Eva Jespersen joined UNDP in early 2009 as Deputy Director at the Human Development Report Office (HDRO) where she guides support to national Human Development Reports as well as contributes to the global HDR. At the time of the WIDER conference she guided UNICEF Innocenti research on social and economic trends and policies as they affect the realization of the human rights of children. She oversaw the release of flagship reports, Social Monitors and Report Cards, which consider child well-being in SEE/CIS and OECD countries, respectively.

Arnim Langer is Research Officer in Economics and Politics at the Centre for Research on Inequality, Human Security, and Ethnicity (CRISE) at the University of Oxford. His research focuses on the causes and consequences of violent conflict, post-conflict economic reconstruction, sustainable peace building, the persistence of horizontal inequalities, and the impact of macroeconomic policies on horizontal inequalities. He has consulted for the UNDP, World Bank, DFID, and UNRISD.

George Mavrotas is the Chief Economist of the Global Development Network (GDN), formerly a Senior Fellow and Project Director at UNU-WIDER and, prior to that, in the Economics Faculties of the Universities of Oxford and Manchester, UK. He is also a Visiting Professor at CERDI, University of Auvergne in Clermont-Ferrand, France. He is the author and co-author of more than 100 publications, including papers in leading peer-reviewed journals, chapters in edited volumes and books on a broad range of development issues. His other books include *Advancing Development: Core Themes in Global Economics* (Palgrave Macmillan); *Commodity Supply Management by Producing Countries* (OUP); *Domestic Resource Mobilization and Financial Development* (Palgrave Macmillan); *Financial Development, Institutions,*

Growth and Poverty Reduction (Palgrave Macmillan); *Development Finance in the Global Economy: The Road Ahead* (Palgrave Macmillan); *Development Aid: A Fresh Look* (Palgrave Macmillan) and *Commodities, Governance and Economic Development Under Globalization* (Palgrave Macmillan, forthcoming). He holds a PhD in Economics (DPhil) from Oxford.

Machiko Nissanke is Professor of Economics at School of Oriental and African Studies (SOAS), University of London. She previously worked at the University of Oxford, Birkbeck College, and University College London. She was Research Fellow of Nuffield College, Oxford and the Overseas Development Institute, UK. She has published numerous books and journal articles on financial economics and international economics, and has served many international organizations as adviser and coordinator of research programmes.

Gustav Ranis is the Frank Altschul Professor Emeritus of International Economics at Yale. He was Director of the Center for International and Area Studies, 1995–2003, Director of the Economic Growth Center, 1967–75, and Assistant Administrator for Program and Policy at USAID, 1965–7. He has authored more than twenty books and 300 articles on development.

Robrecht Renard is a full-time professor and currently Director of the Institute of Development Policy and Management, University of Antwerp (Belgium). His main research interest is the politics and management of the new aid modalities. He has also worked on cost–benefit and cost-effectiveness analysis. He has contributed to several international publications on aid and development and published in *Evaluation and Program Planning, Evaluation, European Journal of Development Research, Lancet*, among others.

Frances Stewart is Professor of Development Economics and Director of the Centre for Research on Inequality, Human Security and Ethnicity (CRISE). Her main interests include sources and consequences of conflict in poor countries, human development, poverty, and group behaviour. Books include *Horizontal Inequalities and Conflict: Understanding Group Conflict in Multiethnic Societies* (Palgrave Macmillan, 2008) and, with G. A. Cornia and R. Jolly, *Adjustment with a Human Face*, 2 vols (Clarendon Press, 1987).

Finn Tarp is Professor of Development Economics at the University of Copenhagen. He has thirty years' experience in academic and applied development research and teaching. His research interests include poverty, income distribution and growth, micro- and macroeconomic policy and modelling, agricultural sector policy and planning, international development assistance, household and enterprise development, and stabilization and structural adjustment. On 1 September 2009, Finn Tarp assumed the post of Director of UNU-WIDER.

Part I

Foreign Aid for Development

1

Introduction and Overview

George Mavrotas

Development aid has received a lot of attention since the implementation of the best known and probably most successful aid programme, the Marshall Plan, in Western Europe following the Second World War. Since then the aid landscape has changed many times and in recent years a number of key questions have emerged. Does aid work in promoting growth and reducing poverty in the developing world? Can aid buy reforms in recipient countries? Does aid affect governance in recipient countries? Will a new 'big push' approach accelerate progress towards the Millennium Development Goals (MDGs) or will another opportunity be missed? Can the lessons of almost half a century of aid be learnt? Indeed, aid is one of the few topics in the development discourse with such an uninterrupted and volatile history in terms of interest and attention from academics, policymakers, and practitioners alike. As Riddell (2007: 2) has put it, 'aid has managed, repeatedly, to reinvent and renew itself after repeated bouts of uncertainty, doubt and pessimism'.

In his influential study *Does Aid Work?*, first published more than two decades ago, Robert Cassen argued quite rightly that 'much of the public discussion of aid has been distorted by prejudice, ideology and selective glimpses of parts of the evidence' and that 'most aid does succeed in terms of its own objectives and obtains a reasonable rate of return; but a significant proportion does not' (Cassen 1994). Twenty years after the publication of this seminal study, aid issues are still dominated by politics and ideology in many cases. Yet the overall context in which development aid is now perceived and assessed is dramatically different. Kanbur (2006), in his comprehensive review of the economics of international aid, emphatically argues that 'if the historical evolution of the aid literature experience is anything to go by, it is unlikely that a survey of international aid in ten years time will have entirely and dramatically new policy issues from the ones highlighted here'.

What then might the next decades hold for aid effectiveness? In trying to answer this challenging question I would agree with Kanbur (2006), that 'the macro-econometric investigation of aid-growth regressions will no doubt continue into the next century. There are sufficient issues of data (how exactly is "aid" defined?), of econometrics (how can the truly independent effects of aid be identified from a mix of independent relationships?) and of development doctrine (what is "good policy"?) to keep the debate alive'.

The aid landscape has undergone important changes during the last two decades, pushing the aid agenda in new and interesting directions. In the early 1990s, following the collapse of the Soviet Union and the end of the Cold War, many observers predicted an 'end of history' for aid. It was assumed that a crucial motive for aid giving which had dominated the pre-1990 period, namely the political and strategic motives of the donor community, would lose its importance in the aftermath of the Cold War. Nevertheless, recent years have witnessed a revived interest in aid issues and the emergence of numerous studies on aid; many of which have been influential in policy circles. This dramatic change in the aid arena has mainly been the outcome of a number of important events. A milestone in this respect was the publication, in 1996, of the OECD-DAC report 'Shaping the 21st Century: The Contribution of Development Cooperation' which was instrumental in generating the new momentum on aid. By setting new priorities for aid, the report marked the increasingly widespread adoption of the international development targets and particularly the commitment to halve absolute poverty by 2015 as an important element in the rethinking of development aid, thus laying the foundations for the emergence of the Millennium of Development Goals.

Another important development was the publication in 1998 of the World Bank study *Assessing Aid*. Even though many of its empirical findings remain controversial (as do the assumptions upon which they were based), the study has been one of the most influential in shaping both the policy debate and the research focus since the publication of Cassen's *Does Aid Work?* A major contribution of *Assessing Aid* is that it managed to mobilize a new and still growing literature on the crucial nexus between policies in aid receiving countries, aid, and growth.

At the political level, the momentum has been built with the UN Conference on Financing for Development held in Monterrey in March 2002 and the widespread consensus among bilateral donors and multilateral agencies on the need to meet the MDGs by 2015. The consensus reached in Monterrey was a major step forward in revitalizing the aid agenda: there is now widespread agreement that more aid is required to meet the MDGs and that, at the same time, increasing aid effectiveness, mobilizing domestic resources, and exploring new sources of development finance beyond aid, are all crucial factors.

Following the important developments in Monterrey, mobilizing political will and building public support for further increases in aid have become central objectives. The international community is also exploring other possible sources of funding beyond aid; as doubling aid is likely to take donors some time.[1] Various proposals have been debated, including the UK proposal on the International Finance Facility aiming to 'frontload' aid through a securitization process in international capital markets so that the MDGs can be attained,[2] the US Millennium Challenge Account[3] that grants aid to countries that democratize their society and adhere to sound economic policies, and the UN Millennium Project Report (2005) and the Report of the Commission for Africa (2005) which call for a new aid policy with much larger aid contributions following the Monterrey consensus.

Initiatives designed to improve coordination among the donor community have also emerged.[4] The most important ones include the Declaration on Aid Harmonization by donors in Rome in 2003 and the Paris Declaration on Aid Effectiveness in 2005 which stressed the importance of ownership, harmonization, alignment, and managing for results for accelerating progress on aid effectiveness and MDG attainment. The year 2008 was also very special for development aid and development finance in general, in view of the Third High-Level Forum on Aid Effectiveness in September 2008, where heads of governments, multilateral institutions, and civil society organizations gathered in Accra to review the progress made in implementing the Paris Declaration. The Accra Forum was closely followed by the Follow-up International Conference on Financing for Development in Doha at the end of the year, which reviewed the implementation of the Monterrey Consensus. Add to these a lively group of rock stars and other celebrities who have recently joined those calling for substantial increases in development aid, and, more importantly, a series of influential books published by leading authorities in this area, and a new era for aid seems to have emerged (see, for example, Sachs 2005; Easterly 2006; Riddell 2007; Lahiri 2007; and Collier 2007).

The Accra High-Level Forum dealt with some key problems of the aid business, namely non-transparency, too many donor missions overstretching recipient capacities, the mix of (often incoherent) donor reporting standards, and so on. Devotees of such meetings noted a more robust language in the final communiqué than in the 2005 Paris Declaration on Aid Effectiveness. Yet, after Accra it is apparent that some donors intend to slack off, and do not take the process seriously enough. The emerging conclusion is that if the transaction

---

[1] See Atkinson (2004) for an excellent discussion.

[2] See Mosley (2004) for a detailed discussion.

[3] Clemens and Radelet (2003) and Radelet (2008) critically assess the MCA.

[4] Taken together, these altruistic initiatives indicate that strategic donor behaviour, where donors use their influence through foreign aid relations to achieve their own goals, has declined. Yet, as argued quite convincingly by Burnell (2004), issues related to strategic donor behaviour and *realpolitik* have not completely lost importance in recent years; See also de Haan and Everest-Phillips, and Browne in this volume as well as Mavrotas and Villanger (2006). It is fair to say, though, that aid is now more developmental and pro-poor compared with the Cold War era.

costs of official development assistance (ODA) do not come down further, then aid will be wasted (Addison and Mavrotas 2008b).

Recent years have also witnessed the continued expansion and increased complexity of the multilateral development finance system with the emergence of numerous donors, modalities, and instruments which make the system hard to manage. Indeed, there is growing evidence that multilateral development finance is no longer a 'system' but rather a 'non-system' with far-reaching implications for both donor and recipient communities. With multilateral complexity rather than aid levels being scaled-up, the capacity of the aid system to deliver is thrown into question. Maxwell (2006: 8) summarized the problem: 'Our main concern has been with the "architecture" of the aid system, especially the proliferation of bilateral agencies, international bodies, and special-purpose "vertical" funds. There are too many in total and too many in each country, with overlapping mandates, complex funding arrangements, and conflicting requirements for accounting and reporting.'[5] In addition, duplication, overlap, and fragmentation are creating substantial transaction costs for donors and recipient governments (Burall and Maxwell 2006; Roodman 2006; Knack and Rahman 2007; Mavrotas and Reisen, 2007; World Bank 2007). In 2007, forty-nine countries received roughly 14,000 donor missions. Donor fragmentation runs counter to the needs of developing countries and had a direct impact on how aid is delivered. In Tanzania, 600 projects are valued at less than US$1 million in implementation and Uganda had to deal with more than 600 aid instruments (Report of the 2008 Development Cooperation Forum).

While the Paris Declaration on Aid Effectiveness marked a positive change in articulating benchmarks for progress, the negotiations did not engage the full range of stakeholders. Furthermore, primarily occupied with monitoring aid delivery, the Paris Declaration has not demonstrated genuine ability to change donor behaviour or to link the aid effectiveness agenda with sustainable development results—concerns raised in the Development Cooperation Forum (DCF) of the United Nations Economic and Social Council (ECOSOC), which took place on 30 June and 1 July 2008 at the UN Headquarters in New York. The DCF particularly served to inform the Doha Review Conference and the Accra High-Level Forum. A particular feature of the DCF was that by giving voice to a wide range of stakeholders, including civil society, parliaments, local governments, and the private sector, it promised to become an effective global platform for representative, participatory, and multi-stakeholder dialogue on development cooperation issues. The DCF also recognized that the absence of consensus on a conceptual framework for 'aid effectiveness' is a major obstacle

---

[5] The 'non-system' has grown significantly in recent years, with the entry of new private and state actors, but with virtually no exit. There has been a strong growth in the creation of both public and private institutions financing development and public goods: the UNDP had counted 1,000 by 2004 (Kaul and Conceicao 2006).

to achieving sustainable development results. The DCF also stressed the importance of south—south and triangular cooperation as a growing dimension of international development cooperation through its complementary role vis-à-vis traditional bilateral and multilateral aid.[6] Finally, the DCF concluded that the aid effectiveness agenda should move towards broader agreement by setting measurable targets for untying aid, transforming technical assistance, reducing conditionality, maximizing concessionality, increasing multi-year predictability, and improving flexibility to deal with exogenous shocks (Report of the 2008 Development Cooperation Forum).

The Doha Conference on the other hand clearly stressed that the international context of aid has changed profoundly since Monterrey. In particular the Doha Declaration on Financing for Development emphasized that the international community is now challenged by the severe impact on development of multiple, interrelated global crises and challenges which include food insecurity, volatile energy and commodity prices, climate change, and above all, the global financial crisis. Indeed, the financial crisis changes the aid landscape in view of the implications that a global financial meltdown may have for aid budgets.

During these difficult times for aid budgets, honouring aid commitments remains a big challenge. At their 2005 summit in Gleneagles, the G8 committed to raise aid by US$50 billion, but they are still US$31.4 billion short. Aid fell by 8.4 per cent in 2007, after a 4.7 per cent fall in 2006. Debt relief under the Heavily Indebted Poor Country (HIPC) initiative and the Multilateral Debt Relief Initiative (MDRI) has dominated aid over the last two years. It is questionable whether this debt relief should even count as ODA since the debts are unlikely to have been repaid. At the Hokkaido summit in 2008, the G8 committed to raise ODA to US$130 billion by 2010. Again, it remains to be seen whether such a commitment will be materialized. The so-called 'new donors' such as India and China made their presence felt at Doha, and there is a drive to encourage them to become OECD-DAC members. Finally, the sharp rise in financial flows (not only aid, but also foreign direct investment) from Asia is one of the major changes in development finance in the years since Monterrey (Addison and Mavrotas 2008b).

Looking back on the impact of past economic crises on the scale of aid disbursements, Mold, Olcer, and Prizzon (2008) found that while gross domestic product (GDP) and aid flows tend to move together over long periods, there are instances in which aid disbursements have become 'decoupled' from economic growth in the OECD countries. They argue that what will most certainly happen as a result of the global financial crisis is a notable shift in the

---

[6] A central element of south–south cooperation is non-intervention in the internal affairs of partner countries which clearly emphasizes south–south cooperation as an additional option and not an alternative to north–south cooperation.

composition of resource flows towards multilateral contributions (as more funds are channelled through the International Monetary Fund (IMF) and the World Bank). In this context, there is a danger that much of the new resources will bypass the poorer and more vulnerable countries, and instead be destined almost exclusively for the emerging markets and middle income countries, to reduce systemic risks. Also of relevance here is the issue of public support for development aid. Recent polling data suggest that voters continue strongly to support aid to developing countries despite the financial crisis. It is also notable that public support for development aid has been consistently high across OECD countries over the past twenty years and it has never dropped below 70 per cent (Zimmerman 2008). What remains certain, however, is that the global financial crisis will seriously undermine the progress made so far on the MDGs. It is therefore absolutely crucial to increase ODA to poor countries (and improve its quality) since the focus should be on the number of poor people in this world, what to do for them, and finding where development aid fits into this bigger poverty picture (in view of the recent revised estimate of global poverty by the World Bank to 1.4 billion).

As expected, calls for scaling up aid generated a new interest among researchers and policymakers regarding the macroeconomic implications of such a 'big-push' approach. At the same time, there exists an ongoing debate over whether additional aid could be absorbed effectively. Issues related to diminishing returns to aid, the volatility of aid inflows, political economy aspects of aid, and the possible adverse effects of increased aid flows on real exchange rates in aid recipient countries have also been under scrutiny recently.[7] Similar attention is being paid to the possible crowding-out effects of new forms of development finance and debt relief, and policy coherence among the various sources of finance in connection with the overall effort to make progress with the MDGs. A central issue is the capacity of aid recipients to absorb such large amounts of development assistance and whether the right institutional mechanisms are in place to facilitate absorption.[8]

Has our understanding of the effectiveness of aid been improved over the last few years? The answer to this question is, undoubtedly, yes. Indeed, a plethora of empirical studies published over the last decade, employing better aid data and more robust econometric techniques, have clearly improved our

---

[7] On the important issue of the political economy of aid, see the 2006 Special Issue of the *Review of Development Economics*, ed. Lahiri and Michaelowa; in particular regarding the role of institutions within aid agencies and the conflicting objectives adopted in many cases, the delivery mechanisms involved, and the incentives which may affect the overall assessment of the various aid modalities adopted by donors.

[8] See Heller and Gupta (2002); Foster (2003); Addison, Mavrotas, and McGillivray (2005a); Addison, Mavrotas, and McGillivray (2005b); de Renzio (2005); Gupta, Powell, and Yang (2005); Collier (2006); Bourguignon and Sundberg (2007a); Killick and Foster (2007); Fielding and Mavrotas (2008); Kharas (2008); and Wood (2008) among others.

knowledge on the impact of aid on growth and poverty reduction. Although the literature on the empirics of aid remains far from conclusive, a substantial part of the new generation of aid studies suggest that aid has a positive impact on growth.[9]

Yet, various questions remain unanswered. Importantly, it is open to debate whether any verdict on the effectiveness of aid can be reached at all as long as the analysis is restricted to the aid—growth nexus—a point also made by Stewart in her critique of Griffin in 1971.[10] In this context, the small but recently growing fiscal response literature[11] provides a good example. Bourguignon and Sundberg (2007b) have also rightly argued that it is not surprising that the empirical literature on aid effectiveness has resulted in unclear results in view of the heterogeneity of aid motives, the limitations of the tools of the analysis, and the complex causality chain linking external aid to final outcomes. This has led to a situation, according to the authors, where the nexus between aid and development has been handled mostly as a 'black box'. And, opening that box is what is required to make further progress on aid effectiveness.[12] Finally, aid cannot 'kill all birds with one stone' in view of what donors have stressed repeatedly, namely that they pursue multiple, and frequently contradictory, objectives when granting aid (see, for example, Isenman and Ehrenpreis 2003). The specific purposes which aid is meant to serve according to the policy statements of donors—including poverty alleviation through better education and health, and institutional and participatory development—tend to escape analyses which focus narrowly on the aid—growth nexus (Mavrotas and Nunnenkamp 2007).

[9] It is beyond the scope of this chapter to review the vast literature on the aid—growth empirics; however, Chap. 2 in this volume by Finn Tarp does an excellent job. See also Tarp (2000); Beynon (2002); Beynon (2003); Hudson (2004); Dalgaard, Hansen, and Tarp (2004); Collier and Dollar (2004); Addison, Mavrotas, and McGillivray (2005a); Doucouliagos and Paldam (2005); Radelet (2006); McGillivray, et al. (2006); Easterly (2006); Easterly (2007); Bourguignon and Sundberg (2007b); Riddell (2007); and Lahiri (2007) on recent assessments of the aid effectiveness literature; see also Mosley (1987); Riddell (1987); White (1992); and Cassen (1994) on earlier reviews of the literature.

[10] Yet, the vast majority of the aid effectiveness literature has been devoted towards understanding the effects of aid inflows on economic growth (see Burnside and Dollar 2000; Hansen and Tarp 2000; Hansen and Tarp 2001; Dalgaard and Hansen 2001; Lensink and White 2001; Chauvet and Guillaumont 2004; Dalgaard, Hansen, and Tarp 2004; Easterly, Levine, and Roodman 2004; Rajan and Subramanian 2005; and Antipin and Mavrotas 2006, among others).

[11] The term is attributed to White (1992). The seminal contribution in this area is Heller (1975). Early fiscal response studies include Gang and Khan (1991); Khan and Hoshino (1992); and Otim (1996). In recent years the literature has blossomed with contributions by Franco-Rodriguez, McGillivray, and Morrissey (1998); Franco-Rodriguez (2000); McGillivray (2000); Mavrotas (2002); Gupta, et al. (2004); Mavrotas (2005); McGillivray and Ouattara (2005); Mavrotas and Ouattara (2006a); Mavrotas and Ouattara (2006b); Mavrotas and Ouattara (2007); Ouattara (2006a); Ouattara (2006b).

[12] This echoes White (1992), thus indicating a lack of substantial progress in the literature.

A central message emanating from recent work is that it is not sufficient to double aid efforts by raising and transferring more money (Killick and Foster 2007; Bourguignon and Sundberg 2007a). At least part of the reason for not making more progress with the MDGs is insufficient targeting of sector-specific aid; unless aid is better targeted, doubling aid is unlikely to have the desired effects (Thiele et al. 2007). And this issue is also related to the neglect of the heterogeneous character of aid in the vast literature of the aid empirics.[13] Furthermore, as Patrick Guillaumont and Sylviane Guillaumont Jeanneney argue in this volume, the 'big push' and 'absorptive capacity' approaches cannot be reconciled without reforms to the aid architecture associated with recent calls for scaling up aid. This also echoes Maxwell (2002) who suggests that it would be a missed opportunity to increase aid without considering the apparatus for delivering such large amounts of money. Finally, the ultimate measure of aid effectiveness is how aid affects the lives of poor people in developing countries. The voluminous literature on aid's macroeconomic impact has remarkably little to say on this topic; and less still in terms of practical advice to government officials and aid administrators on how to improve the effectiveness of development aid. Thus, focussing on impact evaluation studies might be the right avenue for practical and policy-focused research in this area (White 2009).

Against this shifting aid landscape, there is a pressing need to evaluate progress to date and shed light on emerging issues and agendas. This volume, emanating from a 2006 UNU-WIDER conference on 'Aid: Principles, Policies, and Performance', brings a review of the progress achieved so far, identifies the challenges ahead, and discusses the emerging policy agenda in foreign aid.

The 2006 conference was a culmination of several years of UNU-WIDER research on aid—and on development finance issues more broadly (Addison, Mavrotas, and McGillivray 2005a; Addison and Mavrotas 2008a). Areas researched have included external finance (for example, Odedokun 2004a, 2004b), aid (McGillivray and Morrissey 2004; Fielding, McGillivray, and Torres 2007; and, specific to sub-Saharan Africa: Addison, Mavrotas, and Mcgillivray 2005), debt relief (Addison, Hansen, and Tarp 2004), foreign direct investment (Addison, Guha-Khasnobis, and Mavrotas 2006) and short-term private capital flows (Griffith-Jones, Montes, and Nasution 2000; Ffrench-Davis and Griffith-Jones 2003), as well as domestic resource mobilization (Mavrotas 2008; Guha-Khasnobis and Mavrotas 2008). See also Addison, Shorrocks, and Swallow 2005 for further details.

The UNU-WIDER project and resulting volume *Development Aid: A Fresh Look* (Mavrotas and McGillivray 2009) investigated the effectiveness of different types of aid, in particular the impact on growth and poverty (and on key intervening macroeconomic variables), and developed ways to bring poverty more efficiently into the allocation of aid across countries.

---

[13] See the Special Issue of the *Review of World Economics* (*Weltwirtschaftliches Archiv*) in 2007 for a detailed discussion of the aid heterogeneity issue.

Issues related to aid heterogeneity and disaggregating aid flows in order better to understand aid effectiveness are covered in a special issue of the *Review of World Economics* (Mavrotas and Nunnenkamp 2007) and a broad range of foreign aid issues are also discussed in a special issue of the *Review of Development Economics* (Mavrotas 2009).

Various proposals on new sources of development finance were assessed in a UNU-WIDER study led by Sir Anthony Atkinson (2004), undertaken in cooperation with the UN Department of Economic and Social Affairs (UN-DESA) following a UN General Assembly resolution which called for a rigorous investigation of the advantages and disadvantages of new and innovative sources of funding.

The rest of the present volume consists of thirteen chapters. The next chapter in Part I provides the broad contextual setting, with a predominant focus on the overall nexus between aid, growth, and development. Part II looks at ways to enhance aid effectiveness; Part III investigates aid to fragile and conflict-affected countries; and Part IV addresses aid modalities. Finally, Part V examines issues related to the management of aid flows. The following discussion briefly summarizes each of the chapters.

Foreign aid looms large in the public discourse, and ODA remains squarely on most policy agendas concerned with growth, poverty, and inequality in Africa and elsewhere in the developing world. Against this background, Chapter 2 by Finn Tarp examines how foreign aid has evolved since the Second World War in response to a dramatically changing global political and economic context. The chapter opens by defining exactly what foreign aid is and looking at trends in aid flows. It then provides a rich review of the historical discussions on aid, before examining the evidence on whether aid has been effective in furthering economic growth and development. The chapter goes on to discuss the current aid and development debate and ends by highlighting some of the main unresolved issues.

More effective aid will be essential for reducing poverty in developing countries and meeting the MDGs. The three chapters in Part II, 'Enhancing Aid Effectiveness', tackle various aspects of the aid effectiveness debate. In Chapter 3, Gustav Ranis argues that at the very time professional scepticism about the effectiveness of foreign aid has reached new heights; donors appear to be willing to commit to large increases in aid. The chapter addresses this paradox by first examining the record of aid in the past, distinguishing between cross-country regressions and select country experience. The chapter then proposes the establishment of a new modus operandi for foreign aid, based on a much more passive, banker-like role for donors. Under such a system, recipients would approach donors once they had designed their own reform initiative, complete with self-conditionality.

Chapter 4 by Machiko Nissanke argues for a shift in the aid-effectiveness debate away from conventional perspectives of viewing aid as leverage for donor-inspired policy and institutional reforms. The chapter provides a detailed critique of performance-based allocation (PBA) methods, particularly the use of the Country Policy and Institutional Assessment (CPIA). The chapter goes on to discuss alternative approaches to evaluating aid effectiveness, namely the need for the introduction of state contingent aid and debt agreements and a stronger focus on institution building. A central conclusion emerging from the analysis is that aid will contribute to economic development only through establishing and nurturing productive donor–recipient relationships based on true partnerships and ownership. In this way, performance assessments could be made in an environment conducive to nurturing mutual trust and respect on the basis of transparent and free flows of information between donors and recipients.

Chapter 5 by Graham Brown, Frances Stewart, and Arnim Langer argues for a stronger focus on horizontal inequalities—inequalities between culturally defined groups—in aid policy. The chapter begins with a review of horizontal inequalities, followed by an analysis of how aid policy affects such inequalities. The chapter argues that donors run the risk of exacerbating problems if horizontal inequalities are not taken into account. The chapter then looks at how aid might be redirected to contribute to a reduction in horizontal inequalities. It shows how this would change aid allocation across countries, leading to more aid to heterogeneous countries relative to homogeneous ones—the opposite of the existing bias in aid distribution.

A substantial part of the aid literature in recent years has focused on the role of aid in war-affected countries and whether aid can be effective in fragile states. The chapters in Part III, 'Aid to Fragile and Conflict-affected Countries', aim to improve our understanding of the role of aid under these circumstances. Chapter 6 by Sakiko Fukuda-Parr argues that greater attention should be given to conflict prevention in the allocation and disbursement of aid. The chapter shows that violent conflict is a major obstacle to achieving the MDGs. The chapter also shows how development policy priorities and their support with aid can be deployed to reduce the risk of conflict. Conflict prevention, it is argued, is an important policy objective as a means to achieving MDGs as well as an end in itself since security from violence is an essential aspect of human well-being and human security. The chapter reviews the adjustments that would be needed to the aid architecture if conflict prevention were adopted as a policy priority.

In Chapter 7, Stephen Browne argues that the record of aid to fragile and poorly performing states is the real test of aid effectiveness. Rich countries can justify aid to fragile states through both altruism and self-interest. But, with some exceptions, donors have appeared at the wrong times and with the wrong attitudes, even sometimes undermining development progress, the chapter argues. State failure has dimensions of both will and capacity. Failure demands constructive engagement by donors, in some cases to save people in weak states from their leaders, and in all cases to save the states from circumstances which they cannot control. The chapter concludes with eight principles for donors to observe in engaging more productively with fragile states.

In Chapter 8, Ghassan Dibeh examines the Lebanese experience of foreign aid in the post-war era and reflects on the lessons for other post-conflict societies. The chapter describes how aid in post-war Lebanon passed through two phases with distinct features that have had far-reaching implications for development. In the first phase (1992–7), aid was mainly channelled towards reconstruction projects. The second phase (from 1997 to the present), witnessed a qualitative shift in foreign aid towards debt relief and financial stability. This allowed the government to strengthen the economy and avoid financial and currency crises. However, the chapter shows that the cost of such a qualitative shift was large in terms of fiscal management, diversion of funds from reconstruction, and the increased dependency of the Lebanese economy on foreign aid for stabilization purposes.

It is well known that aid is not homogeneous and this takes us to the next issue: the modalities through which aid is delivered. The four chapters in Part IV, 'Aid Modalities', aim to increase our understanding of how different types of aid and modalities work. Chapter 9 by Arjan de Haan and Max Everest-Phillips examines the politics of aid. Specifically, the chapter questions whether recent donor commitments sharpen the potential dilemma between increased aid and the political processes and changes that accompany this. The chapter examines the partnership enshrined in the Monterrey consensus, budget support and poverty-reduction strategy papers (PRSP) approaches, and assistance directly targeted to the poor. The chapter also discusses approaches to the role of aid in economic growth, current work on governance and institutions, and the relationship between domestic revenue generation and foreign aid. The chapter ends by showing how a better understanding of political context and changes can inform the aid agenda.

In Chapter 10, Nathalie Holvoet and Robrecht Renard argue that enhancing monitoring and evaluation (M&E) in the aid-planning process is essential. The chapter explains how the shift towards programme-based approaches has required donors and recipients radically to review their M&E policies: recipients have been expected to improve their embryonic M&E arrangements, while donors have been expected to wind down their M&E mechanisms and instead rely on those of recipients. The chapter does not question the underlying rationale for a shift towards recipient-led priority setting and control over implementation of aid resources, but argues that donors cannot let themselves off the hook so easily with respect to accountability. A twin-track process which balances the need to align as much as possible with recipients' M&E with the demands of accountability is proposed.

Chapter 11, by Michael Hubbard, examines budget support as an aid modality. It discusses the implications for practice and theory of a recently completed Joint Evaluation of General Budget Support 2004–6 based on case studies in Burkina Faso, Malawi, Mozambique, Nicaragua, Rwanda, Uganda, and Vietnam. The chapter begins by looking at the effects of partnership general budget support (PGBS) on government in recipient countries and finds that there are small but positive impacts. The chapter also discusses the implications of the evaluation findings for understanding the nature of PGBS and the behaviour of actors within PGBS. The chapter concludes that the operating environment for PGBS should become less uncertain as the capacity of recipient governments increases and donors make more reliable and predictable commitments.

Chapter 12 by Eva Jespersen and Julia Benn reflects on the use of the OECD-DAC creditor-reporting system, and interprets the results with regard to aid in support of children's rights. The chapter shows how the growth in new modalities for delivering aid presents challenges for aid-reporting systems, particularly from the perspective of international reporting on aid for children. The chapter also analyses ODA trends for basic social services, showing a clear upward trend over the last decade. The chapter argues for a system better to track aid to children outside basic social services in order to assess impact, draw lessons, and stimulate policy discussions. It also stresses that donors need consistently to apply a child and human rights approach in their development assistance.

How might a new 'big push' approach in aid-giving affect recipient countries? What might the implications be for absorptive capacity and overall management of aid inflows? And what might this imply for macroeconomic policies in the countries concerned and for the overall effectiveness of aid? The two chapters in Part V, 'Managing Aid Flows', address these crucial questions. In Chapter 13, Patrick Guillaumont and Sylviane Guillaumont Jeanneney examine whether absorptive capacity limitations imply that the 'big push' proposal should be abandoned. The chapter shows that the probability of a poverty trap exists for many countries, particularly the least developed countries, and that an increase in aid for these nations is important. Moreover, it shows that the decrease in marginal aid returns is slower in vulnerable countries, which should make these nations a priority in aid allocation. The chapter examines the main obstacles to absorptive capacity, such as disbursement constraints and short-term bottlenecks, macroeconomic problems, and institutional weakening. The chapter argues that a 'big push' will be needed to remove these obstacles. However, a 'big push' will only be feasible if aid policies are appropriately designed.

Finally, Chapter 14 by Richard M. Auty looks at aid as a form of rent (a revenue that can be captured by rent-seekers). More specifically, the chapter characterizes aid as a geopolitical form of rent and applies rent-cycling theory to the post-colonial development trajectories of Mauritania, Kenya, and Mozambique in order to distinguish the conditions under which aid is detrimental to sustained economic recovery from those where it is beneficial. The chapter finds that aid can reinforce the inertia of rent-seeking and retard economic restructuring (as was the case in Mauritania and Kenya). However, the chapter also argues that the selective deployment of aid as part of a dual-track reform strategy can improve outcomes.

The contributions to this volume suggest that although aid remains important for many developing countries, a huge effort is needed from both donors and aid recipients to overcome the inefficiencies and *make aid work better for poor people.*

References

Addison, T., and G. Mavrotas (eds) (2008a) *Development Finance in the Global Economy: The Road Ahead.* Basingstoke: Palgrave Macmillan for UNU-WIDER.

————(2008b) 'Development Finance: New Opportunities for Doha'. *WIDER Angle,* Nov.

——and A. Roe (eds) (2004) *Fiscal Policy for Development: Poverty, Reconstruction and Growth.* Basingstoke: Palgrave Macmillan for UNU-WIDER.

——H. Hansen, and F. Tarp (eds) (2004) *Debt Relief for Poor Countries.* Basingstoke: Palgrave Macmillan for UNU-WIDER.

————and M. McGillivray (2005a) 'Aid, Debt Relief and New Sources of Finance for Meeting the Millennium Development Goals'. *Journal of International Affairs,* 58: 113–27.

————(2005b) 'Aid to Africa: An Unfinished Agenda'. *Journal of International Development,* 17: 989–1001.

——A. Shorrocks, and A. Swallow (eds) (2005) *Development Agendas and Insights: Twenty Years of UNU-WIDER Research.* Helsinki: UNU-WIDER.

——B. Guha-Khasnobis, and G. Mavrotas (2006) *UNU-WIDER Special Issue on FDI to Developing Countries: The Unfinished Agenda. World Economy,* 29(1). Oxford: Blackwell.

Antipin, J. E., and G. Mavrotas (2006) 'On the Empirics of Aid and Growth: A Fresh Look'. UNU-WIDER Research Paper 2006/05. Helsinki: UNU-WIDER.

Atkinson A. B. (ed.) (2004) *New Sources for Development Finance.* Oxford: Oxford University Press for UNU-WIDER.

Beynon, J. (2002) 'Policy Implications for Aid Allocations of Recent Research on Aid Effectiveness and Selectivity'. In B. Mak Arvin (ed.), *New Perspectives on Foreign Aid and Economic Development.* Westport, Conn.: Praeger.

——(2003) 'Poverty Efficient Aid Allocations: Collier/Dollar Revisited'. *Economic and Statistics Analysis Unit Working Paper.* London: Overseas Development Institute.

Bourguignon, F. and M. Sundberg (2007a) 'Absorptive Capacity and Achieving the Millennium Development Goals'. In G. Mavrotas and A. Shorrocks (eds), *Advancing Development: Core Themes in Global Economics.* Basingstoke: Palgrave Macmillan for UNU-WIDER.

————(2007b) 'Is Foreign Aid Helping? Aid Effectiveness—Opening the Black Box'. *American Economic Review,* 97: 316–21.

Burall, S., and S. Maxwell (2006) 'Reforming the International Aid Architecture: Options and Way Forward'. Overseas Development Institute Working Paper 278. London: ODI.

Burnell, P. (2004) 'Foreign Aid Resurgent: New Spirit or Old Hangover'. UNU-WiDER Research Paper 2004/44. Helsinki: UNU-WIDER.

Burnside, C., and D. Dollar (2000) 'Aid, Policies, and Growth'. *American Economic Review,* 90: 847–68.

Cassen, R. (1994) *Does Aid Work?* 2nd edn. Oxford: Clarendon Press.

Chauvet, L., and P. Guillaumont (2004) 'Aid Effectiveness in an Unstable Environment'. Mimeo. Clermont-Ferrand: CERDI.

Clemens, M., and S. Radelet (2003) 'The Millennium Challenge Account: How Much is Too Much, How Long is Long Enough?' Working Paper 23. Washington, DC: Center for Global Development.

Collier, P. (2006) 'What Can We Expect from More Aid to Africa?'. Unpublished.

——(2007) *The Bottom Billion: Why the Poorest Countries are Failing and What Can Be Done About It.* Oxford: Oxford University Press.

——and D. Dollar (2004) 'Development Effectiveness: What Have We Learnt?' *Economic Journal*, 114: F244–F271.

Commission for Africa (2005) *Our Common Interest: Report of the Commission for Africa.* <http://www.commissionforafrica.org/english/report/introduction.html>.

Dalgaard, C.-J., and H. Hansen (2001) 'On Aid, Growth and Good Policies'. *Journal of Development Studies*, 37: 17–41.

————and F. Tarp (2004) 'On the Empirics of Foreign Aid and Growth'. *Economic Journal*, 114: F191–F216.

de Renzio, P. (2005) 'Can More Aid be Spent in Africa?'. *ODI Opinions*. London: ODI.

Development Cooperation Forum (2008) *Report of the First Development Forum.* New York: Economic and Social Council, United Nations.

Doucouliagos, H., and M. Paldam (2005) 'The Aid Effectiveness Literature: The Sad Results of 40 Years of Research'. University of Aarhus Department of Economics Working Paper 2005.05. Århus: Aarhus Universitet.

Easterly, W. (2006) *The White Man's Burden: Why the West's Efforts to Aid the Rest Have Done So Much Ill and So Little Good.* New York: Penguin Press.

——(2007) 'Was Development Assistance a Mistake?' *American Economic Review*, 97: 328–32.

——R. Levine, and D. Roodman (2004) 'New Data, New Doubts: A Comment on Burnside and Dollar's "Aid, Polices and Growth (2000)" '. *American Economic Review*, 94(2): 253–9.

Ffrench-Davis, R., and S. Griffith-Jones (eds) (2003) *From Capital Surges to Drought: Seeking Stability for Emerging Economies.* Basingstoke: Palgrave Macmillan for UNU-WIDER.

Fielding, D. and G. Mavrotas (2008) 'Aid Volatility and Donor-Recipient Characteristics in "Difficult Partnership Countries" '. *Economica*, 75(299): 481–494.

Fielding, D., M. McGillivray, and S. Torres (2007) 'A Wider Approach to Aid Effectiveness: Correlated Impacts on Health, Wealth, Fertility and Education'. In G. Mavrotas and A. Shorrocks (eds), *Advancing Development: Core Themes in Global Economics.* Basingstoke: Palgrave Macmillan for UNU-WIDER.

Foster, M. (2003) 'The Case for Increased Aid'. Report to the Department for International Development. London: DFID.

Franco-Rodriguez, S. (2000) 'Recent Advances in Fiscal Response Models with an Application to Costa Rica'. *Journal of International Development*, 12: 429–42.

——M. McGillivray, and O. Morrissey (1998) 'Aid and the Public Sector in Pakistan: Evidence with Endogenous Aid'. *World Development*, 26: 1241–50.

Gang, I., and H. Khan (1991) 'Foreign Aid, Taxes and Public Investment'. *Journal of Development Economics*, 34: 355–69.

Griffith-Jones, S., M. F. Montes, and A. Nasution (eds) (2000) *Short-term Capital Flows and Economic Crises.* Oxford: Oxford University Press for UNU-WIDER.

Guha-Khasnobis, B., and G. Mavrotas (eds) (2008) *Financial Development, Institutions, Growth and Poverty Reduction*. Basingstoke: Palgrave Macmillan for UNU-WIDER.

Gupta, S., B. Clements, A. Pivovarsky, and E. R. Tiongson (2004) 'Foreign Aid and Revenue Response: Does the Composition of Aid Matter?' In S. Gupta, B. Clements, and G. Inchauste (eds), *Helping Countries Develop: The Role of Fiscal Policy*. Washington, DC: IMF.

——R. Powell, and Y. Yang (2005) 'The Macroeconomic Challenges of Scaling Up Aid to Africa'. International Monetary Fund Working Paper 05/179. Washington, DC: IMF.

Hansen, H., and F. Tarp (2000) 'Aid Effectiveness Disputed'. *Journal of International Development*, 12: 375–98.

————(2001) 'Aid and Growth Regressions'. *Journal of Development Economics*, 64: 547–70.

Heller, P. S. (1975) 'A Model of Public Fiscal Behaviour in Developing Countries: Aid, Investment and Taxation'. *American Economic Review*, 65: 429–45.

——and S. Gupta (2002) 'More Aid: Making it Work for the Poor'. *World Economics*, 3: 131–46.

Hudson, J. (2004) 'Introduction: Aid and Development'. *Economic Journal*, 114: F185–F190.

Isenman, P., and D. Ehrenpreis (2003) 'Results of the OECD-DAC Development Centre Experts' Seminar on "Aid Effectiveness and Selectivity: Integrating Multiple Objectives into Aid Allocations"'. *DAC Journal*, 4: 7–25.

Kanbur, R. (2006) 'The Economics of International Aid'. In S. Christophe-Kolm and J. Mercier-Ythier (eds) *The Economics of Giving, Reciprocity and Altruism*. Amsterdam: North-Holland.

Kaul, I., and P. Conceicao (eds) (2006) *The New Public Finance*. Oxford: Oxford University Press.

Khan, H. A., and E. Hoshino (1992) 'Impact of Foreign Aid on Fiscal Behaviour of LDC Governments'. *World Development*, 20: 1481–8.

Kharas, H. (2008) 'Measuring the Cost of Aid Volatility'. Wolfensohn Centre for Development Working Paper No.3. Washington D.C.: The Brookings Institution.

Killick, T., and M. Foster (2007) 'The Macroeconomics of Doubling Aid to Africa and the Centrality of the Supply Side'. *Development Policy Review*, 25: 167–92.

Knack, S., and A. Rahman (2007) 'Donor Fragmentation and Bureaucratic Quality in Aid Recipients'. *Journal of Development Economics*, 83: 176–97.

Lahiri, S. (ed.) (2007) *Theory and Practice of Foreign Aid*. Amsterdam: Elsevier.

——and K. Michaelowa (2006) 'The Political Economy of Aid'. *Review of Development Economics*, 10: 177–344.

Lensink, R., and H. White (2001) 'Are There Negative Returns to Aid?' *Journal of Development Studies*, 37: 42–65.

McGillivray, M. (2000) 'Aid and Public Sector Behaviour in Developing Countries'. *Review of Development Economics*, 4: 156–63.

——S. Feeny, N. Hermes, and R. Lensink (2006) 'It Works; It Doesn't; It Can, But That Depends: 50 Years of Controversy over the Macroeconomic Impact of Development Aid'. *Journal of International Development*, 18: 1031–50.

——and O. Morrissey (2004) 'The Fiscal Effects of Aid'. In T. Addison and A. Roe (eds), *Fiscal Policy for Development: Poverty, Reconstruction and Growth*. Basingstoke: Palgrave Macmillan for UNU-WIDER.

——and B. Ouattara (2005) 'Aid Debt Burden and Government Fiscal Behaviour in Côte d'Ivoire'. *Journal of African Economies*, 14: 247–69.

Mavrotas, G. (2002) 'Foreign Aid and Fiscal Response: Does Aid Disaggregation Matter?'. *Weltwirtschaftliches Archiv* 138(3): 534–59.

——(2005) 'Aid Heterogeneity: Looking at Aid Effectiveness from a Different Angle'. *Journal of International Development* 17(8): 1019–1036.

——and E. Villanger (2006) 'Multilateral Aid Agencies and Strategic Donor Behaviour'. UNU-WIDER Discussion Paper No. 2006/02. Helsinki: UNU-WIDER.

——and H. Reisen (2007) 'The Multilateral Development Finance "Non-System"', paper presented at the Experts' Workshop on *Performance and Coherence in Multilateral Development Finance*, Berlin, January.

——(ed.) (2008) *Domestic Resource Mobilization and Financial Development*. Basingstoke: Palgrave Macmillan for UNU-WIDER.

——(2009) *UNU-WIDER Special Issue on Foreign Aid: Theory, Policies and Performance*. *Review of Development Economics*, 13(3). Oxford: Blackwell.

——and M. McGillivray (eds) (2009) *Development Aid: A Fresh Look*. Basingstoke: Palgrave Macmillan for UNU-WIDER.

——and P. Nunnenkamp (2007) 'Foreign Aid Heterogeneity: Issues and Agenda'. *Review of World Economics*, 143: 585–95.

——and B. Ouattara (2006a) 'Aid Disaggregation, Endogenous Aid and the Public Sector in Aid-Recipient Economies'. *Review of Development Economics*, 10: 434–51.

————(2006b) 'Public Fiscal Behaviour and Aid Heterogeneity in Aid-recipient Economies'. *Journal of Developing Areas*, 39: 1–15.

————(2007) 'Aid Modalities and Budgetary Response: Panel Data Evidence'. *Review of World Economics*, 143: 720–41.

Maxwell, S. (2002) 'More Aid? Yes—and Use it to Reshape Aid Architecture'. *ODI Opinions*. London: Overseas Development Institute.

——(2006) 'Aid Architecture: A Blueprint for the Future'. *ODI Opinions*. London: Overseas Development Institute.

Mold, A., D. Olcer, and A. Prizzon (2008) 'The Fallout from the Financial Crisis: Will Aid Budgets Fall Victim to the Credit Crisis?'. OECD Development Centre Policy Insights 85. Paris: OECD.

Mosley, P. (1987) *Overseas Aid: Its Defense and Reform*. Brighton: Wheatsheaf Press.

——(ed.) (2004) 'The International Finance Facility: Can it Deliver?'. Policy Arena, *Journal of International Development*, 16: 863–95.

Odedokun, M. (ed.) (2004a) *External Finance for Private Sector Development: Appraisals and Issues*. Basingstoke: Palgrave Macmillan for UNU-WIDER.

——(ed.) (2004b) *UNU-WIDER Special Issue on Development Financing*. World Economy, 27(2). Oxford: Blackwell.

Otim, S. (1996) 'Foreign Aid and Government Fiscal Behaviour in Low-income South Asian Countries'. *Applied Economics*, 28: 927–33.

Ouattara, B. (2006a) 'Aid and Fiscal Policy in Senegal'. *Journal of International Development*, 8: 1105–22.

——(2006b) 'Foreign Aid and Government Fiscal Behaviour: Panel Data Evidence'. *Economic Modelling*, 23: 506–14.

Radelet, S. (2006) 'A Primer on Foreign Aid'. Center for Global Development Working Paper 92. Washington, DC: CGD.

——(2008) 'The Millennium Challenge Account: Transforming US Foreign CGDEV Assistance Policy?' In T. Addison and G. Mavrotas (eds), *Development Finance in the Global Economy: The Road Ahead*, Basingstoke: Palgrave Macmillan for UNU-WIDER.

Rajan, R., and A. Subramanian (2005) 'Aid and Growth: What Does the Cross-country Evidence Really Show?' International Monetary Fund Working Paper 05/127. Washington, DC: IMF.

Riddell, R. (1987) *Foreign Aid Reconsidered*. Baltimore, Md.: Johns Hopkins University Press.

——(2007) *Does Foreign Aid Really Work?* Oxford: Oxford University Press.

Roodman, D. (2006) 'Aid Project Proliferation and Absorptive Capacity'. UNU-WIDER Research Paper 2006/04.

Sachs, J. D. (2005) *The End of Poverty: Economic Possibilities for Our Time*. London: Penguin.

Stewart, F. (1971) 'Foreign Capital, Domestic Savings and Economic Development' Comment, *Oxford Bulletin of Economics and Statistics*, 33: 138–49.

Tarp (ed.) (2000), *Foreign Aid and Development: Lessons Learnt and Directions for the Future*. Routledge Studies in Development Economics, 17. London: Routledge.

Thiele, R., P. Nunnenkamp, and A. Dreher (2007) 'Do Donors Target Aid in Line with the Millennium Development Goals? A Sector Perspective of Aid Allocation'. *Review of World Economics*, 143: 596–630.

UNDP (United Nations Development Programme) (2005) 'Investing in Development: A Practical Plan to Achieve the Millennium Development Goals'. New York: United Nations Millennium Project.

White, H. (1992) 'The Macroeconomic Impact of Development Aid: A Critical Survey'. *Journal of Development Studies*, 28: 163–240.

——(2009) 'Evaluating Aid Impact'. In G. Mavrotas and M. McGillivray (eds), *Development Aid: A Fresh Look*. Basingstoke: Palgrave Macmillan for UNU-WIDER.

Wood, A. (2008) 'Looking Ahead Optimally in Allocating Aid'. *World Development*, 36(7): 1135–1151.

World Bank (1998) *Assessing Aid: What Works, What Doesn't, and Why*. Oxford and New York and Washington, DC: Oxford University Press/World Bank.

——(2007) *Aid Architecture: An Overview of the Main Trends in Official Development Assistance Flows*. <http://web.worldbank.org/WBSITE/EXTERNAL/EXTABOUTUS/IDA/ 0,,contentMDK:21351637~pagePK:51236175~piPK:437394~theSitePK:73154,00.html>.

Zimmerman, R. (2008) 'The Fallout from the Financial Crisis: The End of Public Support for Development Aid?'. OECD Development Centre Policy Insights 87. Paris: OECD.

2

Aid, Growth, and Development[1]

Finn Tarp

2.1. Introduction

Foreign aid and its effectiveness in promoting growth and development in developing countries has been an area of intense controversy ever since Rosenstein-Rodan (1943) advocated aid to Eastern and South-Eastern Europe. Early optimism and confidence in the impact of foreign aid have been tempered with time. In the first edition of his *Leading Issues in Economic Development*, Meier (1964) dedicated some eighteen pages to the issue of foreign aid. He started by asking, 'How much aid?' By the time of the sixth edition (Meier 1995), the treatment of foreign aid had been cut in half and the questions raised were: 'Why official assistance?' and 'Does aid work?' In the 2000 edition (Meier and Rauch 2000) 'foreign aid' is not listed in the index.

Meanwhile the debate about the usefulness and design of foreign aid has continued unabated. Some insist aid is a waste of resources and even harmful to aid-receiving countries (Dichter 2005). They point in particular to Africa and scores of failed projects and swiftly conclude that aid has been an outright disaster. Others are disappointed and sceptical, a prominent example being Easterly (2001, 2003, 2008), who highlights aid's inability to buy growth.

[1] This chapter is a shortened, revised, and updated version of a paper originally published by the *Swedish Economic Policy Review* (see Tarp 2006). I am grateful to Christoffer Sonne-Schmidt for research assistance and to colleagues from the University of Copenhagen, especially Channing Arndt and Sam Jones, for comments and collaboration. Thanks for good comments are also due to Phil Abbott and to participants at the UNU-WIDER Development Conference on Aid, 'Aid: Principles, Policies, and Performance', held on 16–17 June 2006 in Helsinki. Finally, I would like to acknowledge expert advice from three anonymous referees. The usual caveats apply. In preparing this chapter, I rely on both field experience and a variety of academic outputs. They include Tarp 2000 and several articles published over the past seven years, including in particular work with Dalgaard, Hansen, and Roland-Holst. Please see Arndt, Jones, and Tarp (2006) for a companion paper to the present study, focusing on what can be said about aid and development in a specific country context, that of Mozambique.

Birdsall, Rodrik, and Subramanian (2005) view the potential impact of aid as seriously circumscribed, but remain largely supportive. A complementary approach in the middle ground is that aid has worked in the past in furthering growth and development, but aid is not equally effective everywhere and much remains to be learnt about how aid impacts in theory and practice (see Tarp 2000). Given this, the focus should be both on ways and means to improve the effectiveness of foreign aid disbursements and on increasing the total flow of resources. A final approach is to emphasize that a doubling of worldwide aid flows is our generation's challenge, a moral obligation of rich countries that will send forth 'mighty currents of hope' and lead to 'the end of poverty' (see Sachs 2005).

The analysis of aid's impact on growth became dominated by modern panel data macroeconometric frameworks during the second half of the 1990s.[2] Much of this debate has focused on whether the effectiveness of aid is conditional on policy, or whether aid can be expected to have a separate and positive impact independent of policy. This has involved a mixture of concerns. They range from technically demanding econometric modelling issues, to fundamentally different approaches, to the design and implementation of development strategy and policy. Overall, a substantial body of literature has emerged which suggests that aid works in promoting growth and development.[3] However, others remain sceptical and disagreement is characteristic in assessments of the necessary and sufficient conditions for aid to have a positive contribution on the development process. The same goes in relation to (i) different views on what constitutes 'good' economic policy and how economic policy and deeper structural characteristics interact with the efficiency of foreign aid; and (ii) the institutional framework through which aid is channelled.

Widespread calls have also been made for a 'big push' or a Marshall Plan for Africa. Sachs (2005) is a passionate spokesman for this approach, which is set out in the UN Millennium Project Report (2005). Also the World Economic Forum (2005) and the Commission for Africa (2005) reports can be consulted. The Commission for Africa was launched by the former British Prime Minister Tony Blair in February 2004, with the aim of taking a fresh look at Africa's past and present and the international community's role in its development path. These initiatives have attracted both praise and criticism, with Sachs and Easterly appearing to occupy opposing ends of the spectrum. Viewing their assessments from the perspective of historical developments in foreign aid on the one

---

[2] To be sure, general macroeconometric analysis of aid impact has been very influential since the 1970s, a prominent contributor being Prof. Paul Mosley and his co-authors; see Hansen and Tarp (2000) and sect. 2.5 where I discuss how the literature evolved in the 1990s.

[3] See Clemens, Radelet, and Bhavnani (2004). I will revert in what follows to selected contributions to this literature, which is ignored by Easterly (2008). According to his Google Scholar counting methodology (see his nn. 15 and 16), positive interpretations of the aid–growth link have been more extensively cited than Easterly leads the reader to believe.

hand, and the analytical literature on aid effectiveness on the other, is a general aim of this chapter.

The remainder of this chapter is structured in six parts. In section 2.2, I define what is meant by foreign aid (or more precisely Official Development Assistance (ODA)) and provide selected data on amounts and trends involved. Section 2.3 contains general historical background, while sections 2.4 and 2.5 turn to the allocation and impact of ODA. In section 2.6, I discuss the current debate, while section 2.7 concludes.

2.2. What is foreign aid?

What is foreign aid? For a precise definition it is useful to turn to the Development Assistance Committee (DAC) of the Organisation for Economic Co-operation and Development (OECD). The DAC is the principal body through which the OECD deals with issues related to cooperation with developing countries. According to the DAC, the term 'development assistance' refers to financial flows that qualify as official development assistance (ODA). ODA is defined as the sum of grants and loans to aid recipients that are (i) undertaken by the official sector of the donor country; (ii) with promotion of economic development and welfare in recipient countries as the main objective; (iii) at concessional financial terms, where the grant element is equal to at least 25 per cent.[4] In addition to financial flows, technical cooperation costs are included in ODA; but, grants, loans, and credits for military purposes are excluded, and transfer payments to private individuals are in general not counted. The same goes for donations from the public, commercial loans, and foreign direct investment (FDI).

Only aid to 'traditional' developing countries counted as ODA until 2005. For these (Part I) countries there is a long-standing UN target from 1970 that they should receive 0.7 per cent of donors' gross national income (GNI) as aid. Assistance to the 'more advanced' Eastern European and 'more advanced' developing (Part II) countries was recorded separately by the DAC as 'official aid' (OA), not included as part of ODA. DAC countries have over the years accounted for some 95 per cent of all aid flows, but the distinction between Part I and Part II countries is no longer used.[5]

---

[4] Conventionally the market rate of interest used to assess a loan is taken as 10 per cent. Thus, while the grant element is nil for a loan carrying an interest rate of 10 per cent, it is 100 per cent for a pure grant, and lies between these two limits for a soft loan. In calculating total ODA, no adjustment is made to take account of the smaller grant element of loans. The value of grants and the nominal value of loans that qualify are simply added up.

[5] The present DAC classification of countries is with a few exceptions consistent with World Bank practice, distinguishing between the least-developed countries (LDCs), other low-income, lower-middle-income, and upper-middle-income recipients of ODA.

In 2006 the total amount of foreign aid disbursed by donors to developing countries and multilateral organizations reached US$113.6 billion; see Table 2.1, which also shows that the average citizen in the donor countries contributed less than US$112 as ODA in 2006. This can be compared to a figure of around US$64 in 1960–73 and US$99 in 1992. It is equally clear from the table that the UN target of 0.7 per cent of GNI is with few exceptions very far from being reached. In this perspective, it is hardly surprising that Sachs (2005) and many others find present levels of aid unacceptably low. It can also be noted that donors in 2006 disbursed 25.7 per cent of total foreign aid to multilateral organizations. Some 84 per cent of this flow was disbursed to developing countries, with the European Union and the International Monetary Fund (IMF) and World Bank (including the International Development Association (IDA)) as the main sources followed by the UN and the Regional Development Banks (Table 2.2).

Table 2.3 gives an overview of aid per capita and aid as a percentage of GNI in aid-receiving countries with a population of more than two million. It is a widespread perception that foreign aid amounts to a very significant resource, in both absolute and relative terms, and aid is indeed not an insignificant flow measured relative to developing country production and income. At the same time, aid does not appear that sizeable when measured in relation to GNI or government budgets in the donor countries or in comparison with, for example, population size of aid receiving countries. Figure 2.1 presents ratios of total ODA to GNI and population in aid-receiving countries. ODA per capita almost doubled in real terms from 1970 to 1990; but perhaps the most revealing aspect here is the downturn from 1991 to 1992 after the steady increase in the previous decade. It is also evident that aid as a share of GNI in recipient countries has been on a declining trend since the early 1990s.

Figure 2.2 shows that the allocation of aid from 1996 to 2005, as measured by the aid to GNI ratio in aid-receiving countries, is highly skewed. Most recipient countries received aid to the order of 1.8 per cent of their GNI per year with a median of 3.2 per cent. This corresponds to a distribution of aid per capita with a mode of US$17.9 per year and a median of US$31.5. Illustrative country examples have been added to Figure 2.2. They demonstrate that the relative size of the aid inflow varies significantly among countries such as Vietnam, Bolivia, Tanzania, and Mozambique.

The 13.2 per cent size of the aid to GNI ratio in, for example, Tanzania may seem high. It should be kept in mind, however, that this share reflects not only the size of the aid flow but also the very low level of income. Income per capita in Tanzania has only recently grown to more than US$300 per capita, and Tanzania received about US$35 per capita per year in foreign aid from 1996 to 2005. With this background, modest expectations are advisable when analysing the overall impact of past aid on growth. Many constraints have hampered growth in Tanzania and elsewhere, and aid has been used for a multitude of purposes. These are, in many cases, only indirectly related to generating economic return.

23

Table 2.1. Net ODA disbursements by donor

	ODA 2006 prices (US\$ billion) (ODA as percentage of total)				
	1960–73[1]	1992	1998	2002	2006
USA	16.3	15.8	10.6	14.9	23.5
	(42.2)	(20.0)	(15.8)	(18.6)	(21.5)
Japan	2.6	10.8	10.8	9.5	11.2
	(6.9)	(13.7)	(16.0)	(11.9)	(10.2)
France	5.7	10.3	7.4	7.9	10.6
	(14.7)	(13.1)	(11.0)	(9.8)	(9.7)
Germany	3.8	8.8	6.7	7.3	10.4
	(9.9)	(11.2)	(10.0)	(9.2)	(9.5)
UK	4.3	4.8	5.2	6.7	12.5
	(11.2)	(6.1)	(7.8)	(8.4)	(11.4)
DK, L, NL, NO, and SE	1.9[3]	10.3	11.0	12.8	14.9
	(4.9)[3]	(13.1)	(16.5)	(16.0)	(13.6)
Other DAC	4.0	16.2	13.9	16.6	21.3
	(10.3)	(20.5)	(20.7)	(20.8)	(19.5)
Non-DAC	—	1.8	1.4	4.3	5.2
	—	(2.3)	(2.1)	(5.3)	(4.7)
Total[4]	38.6	78.9	67.0	80.0	109.6
of which:	(100)	(100)	(100)	(100)	(100)
Bilateral	32.9	53.7	44.9	56.1	81.4
	(85.2)	(68.0)	(67.0)	(70.0)	(74.3)
Multilateral[5]	6.2	24.7	22.1	24.0	28.1
	(16.0)	(31.3)	(33.0)	(30.0)	(25.7)

	ODA per capita (2006 prices, US\$) (ODA as percentage of GNI)				
	1960–73[1]	1992	1998	2002	2006
USA	83.2	62.0	39.2	51.6	78.6
	(0.4)	(0.2)	(0.1)	(0.1)	(0.2)
Japan	25.9	87.2	85.0	74.6	87.6
	(0.2)	(0.3)	(0.3)	(0.2)	(0.3)
France	116.3	179.6	126.6	132.4	167.2
	(0.8)	(0.6)	(0.4)	(0.4)	(0.5)
Germany	64.5	109.7	81.5	89.1	126.6
	(0.4)	(0.4)	(0.3)	(0.3)	(0.4)
UK	79.4	83.1	87.7	113.7	207.0
	(0.5)	(0.3)	(0.3)	(0.3)	(0.5)
DK, L, NL, NO, and SE[2]	59.5[3]	306.5	370.0	432.8	488.2
	(0.3)[3]	(0.9)	(0.8)	(0.9)	(0.9)
Other DAC[2]	38.7	87.9	75.6	93.1	124.1
	(0.2)	(0.3)	(0.3)	(0.3)	(0.3)
Non-DAC	—	—	—	89.3	56.1
	—	(0.3)	(0.1)	(0.3)	(0.2)
Total	64.1	99.0	80.2	88.0	111.9
	(0.4)	(0.3)	(0.2)	(0.2)	(0.3)

Notes:
[1] Average over the years.
[2] Average over the countries.
[3] Excluding Luxembourg.
[4] Sum of DAC- and non-DAC countries, total. Discrepancies due to averaging and rounding.
[5] Disbursements by donor countries to multilateral aid organizations. Denmark (DK) since 1978; Luxembourg (L) since 2000; Netherlands (NL) since 1975; Norway (NO) since 1976; and Sweden (SE) since 1975 have all had ODA as percentage of GNI above 0.7.

Source: OECD (2008: table 1); ODA by donor: <http://webnet.oecd.org/wbos/Index.aspx?DataSetCode= ODA_DONOR#>.

Table 2.2. Aid disbursements by multilateral organizations

	2006 prices (US$ billion)					Percentage of multilateral (total)				
	1960–73[1]	1992	1998	2002	2006	1973[2]	1992	1998	2002	2006
Multilateral, total *of which*:	3.5	20.4	19.2	22.8	23.6	100.0	100.0	100.0	100.0	100.0
United Nations	1.0	6.1	3.2	4.1	3.3	28.9	29.7	16.5	17.9	14.2
IMF and WB	1.0	6.9	6.6	8.7	6.4	29.6	33.7	34.2	38.0	27.0
European Commission	0.9	5.4	6.7	7.4	9.5	26.2	26.4	34.8	32.6	40.2
Regional Development Banks	0.5	2.1	2.5	2.3	2.9	15.2	10.3	12.8	10.2	12.2
Other Multilateral Institutions	0.0	0.0	0.3	0.3	1.5	0.0	0.0	1.6	1.2	6.5

Notes:
[1] Annual average over 14 years.
[2] In percentage of the total period's disbursements.

Source: OECD (2008: table DAC2a); ODA disbursements: <http://stats.oecd.org/wbos/Index.aspx?DataSetCode=ODA_RECIPIENT_REGION>.

Table 2.3. Average annual (1996–2005) aid shares for countries with populations larger than 2 million

Aid as percentage of GNI, increasing by country				Aid per capita, increasing by country			
-0.03	Azerbaijan	3.59	Korea, Rep.	-3.1	Egypt, Arab Republic	22.3	Korea, Rep.
0.00	Kenya	3.65	Hong Kong, China	0.7	Burundi	24.0	Malaysia
0.01	Zimbabwe	4.05	Singapore	0.8	Azerbaijan	24.5	Saudi Arabia
0.01	Vietnam	4.31	United Arab Emirates	0.9	Hungary	24.5	Hong Kong, China
0.01	Côte d'Ivoire	4.35	Saudi Arabia	1.0	Moldova	25.0	Mexico
0.01	Yemen, Rep.	4.45	Kuwait	1.2	Tajikistan	25.1	United Arab Emirates
0.02	Macedonia, FYR	5.19	Mexico	1.2	Sri Lanka	25.2	Singapore
0.04	Cameroon	5.22	Malaysia	1.2	Central African Republic	25.5	Brazil
0.04	Angola	5.23	Brazil	1.4	Czech Republic	26.8	India
0.04	Togo	5.46	Costa Rica	1.5	Tunisia	26.8	China
0.05	Moldova	5.71	Venezuela, Republic of	1.6	Niger	27.3	Libya
0.05	Jordan	6.38	Argentina	1.7	Chad	28.0	Kuwait
0.05	Serbia and Montenegro	6.75	Turkey	1.8	Poland	29.1	Costa Rica
0.10	Georgia	7.08	Chile	2.0	Côte d'Ivoire	30.2	Venezuela, Republic Bolivarian
0.11	Nepal	7.27	Uruguay	2.0	Slovak Republic	30.3	Myanmar
0.12	Albania	7.35	Iran, Islamic Republic	2.3	Guinea	31.5	Iran, Islamic Republic
0.13	Papua New Guinea	7.66	China	2.6	Angola	32.3	Argentina
0.16	Guinea	7.74	Panama	3.1	Cambodia	32.5	Turkey
0.25	Haiti	8.00	Oman	4.7	Uganda	33.5	Belarus
0.25	Bolivia	8.66	Thailand	5.6	Tanzania	34.7	Thailand
0.27	Honduras	8.81	Belarus	5.8	Madagascar	34.8	Chile
0.30	Central African Republic	8.87	Central African Republic	6.0	El Salvador	35.0	Korea, Democratic Republic
0.31	Benin	9.76	India	6.1	Cameroon	36.1	Cuba
0.36	Armenia	9.98	South Africa	6.4	Haiti	36.1	Uruguay
0.40	Senegal	10.27	Croatia	6.7	Benin	36.3	Uzbekistan
0.42	Cambodia	10.55	Colombia	6.7	Ghana	38.2	Indonesia
0.42	Ghana	10.92	Czech Republic	6.8	Mali	38.5	Nigeria
0.43	Congo, Republic	10.96	Russian Federation	7.0	Liberia	38.6	Turkmenistan
0.44	Chad	11.63	Jamaica	8.2	Malawi	39.0	Iraq
0.48	Tajikistan	12.17	Hungary	8.4	Burkina Faso	39.2	Philippines

Country	Value	Country	Value	Country	Value	Country	Value
Algeria	0.50	Ethiopia	13.08	Colombia	8.5	Bulgaria	40.8
Dominican Republic	0.60	Tanzania	13.22	Pakistan	8.6	Latvia	42.2
Poland	0.61	Uganda	13.27	Ukraine	8.8	Lithuania	45.9
Slovak Republic	0.69	Burkina Faso	13.69	Russian Federation	8.9	Kyrgyz Republic	47.0
Philippines	0.76	Madagascar	13.94	Syrian Arab Republic	8.9	Sierra Leone	48.8
Peru	0.77	Kyrgyz Republic	14.24	Algeria	9.1	Rwanda	49.4
Kazakhstan	0.80	Niger	14.33	Bangladesh	9.1	Papua New Guinea	51.9
Ecuador	0.82	Bosnia and Herzegovin	14.62	Panama	9.2	Senegal	52.2
Indonesia	0.83	Mali	14.74	South Africa	12.0	Lao People's Democratic Republic	54.7
Israel	0.88	Lao People's Democratic Republic	16.47	Dominican Republic	12.3	Georgia	56.3
Syrian Arab Republic	0.89	Zambia	17.31	Paraguay	12.7	Eritrea	58.8
Turkmenistan	0.90	Mauritania	17.64	Jamaica	12.9	Zambia	61.1
Paraguay	0.97	Mongolia	19.71	Kazakhstan	13.0	Mozambique	61.9
Romania	1.03	Congo, Democratic Republic	19.80	Sudan	14.4	Armenia	73.5
Ukraine	1.05	Nicaragua	19.91	Ecuador	14.6	Lebanon	74.4
Guatemala	1.18	Rwanda	21.44	Nepal	16.2	Congo, Republic of	74.8
Lithuania	1.20	West Bank and Gaza	22.07	Togo	16.3	Honduras	78.0
Latvia	1.21	Burundi	23.96	Kenya	16.3	Bolivia	82.2
Tunisia	1.22	Malawi	24.16	Peru	16.7	Mauritania	87.0
Nigeria	1.28	Sierra Leone	27.06	Ethiopia	16.8	Mongolia	92.5
Uzbekistan	1.35	Liberia	28.34	Oman	17.3	Albania	97.6
Lebanon	1.44	Mozambique	28.62	Vietnam	18.2	Macedonia, Republic of	104.5
Morocco	1.50	Afghanistan	31.61	Somalia	19.2	Serbia and Montenegro	107.5
Pakistan	1.65	Eritrea	32.60	Yemen, Republic of	19.5	Jordan	117.5
El Salvador	1.72	Myanmar	—	Zimbabwe	19.8	Israel	147.4
Egypt, Arab Republic	1.78	Korea, Democratic Republic	—	Morocco	20.0	Nicaragua	150.9
Bulgaria	2.21	Cuba	—	Congo, Democratic Republic	20.7	Bosnia and Herzegovina	197.1
Bangladesh	2.37	Iraq	—	Croatia	21.0	West Bank and Gaza	276.4
Sri Lanka	2.77	Somalia	—	Romania	21.2	Afghanistan	—
Sudan	3.08			Guatemala	21.6		

Notes: Aid per capita is constant (prices in year 2000) US$ and aid as percentage of GNI are averages of annual observations.

Source: World Bank (2007).

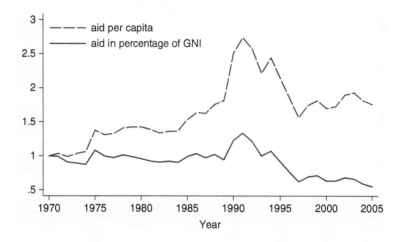

Figure 2.1 ODA per capita, and as a percentage of GNI in the recipient country

Notes: ODA and GNI in constant 2000 US$, and shares normalized to 1 in 1970.
Source: World Bank (2007).

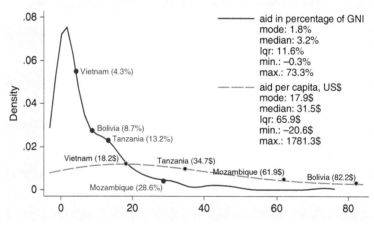

Figure 2.2 Density of average annual (1996–2005) ODA shares

Notes: Kernel density using Gaussian kernel. The height of the graph reflects the (weighted) average number of observations in an interval around the midpoint.
Source: World Bank (2007).

2.3. Historical background

Foreign aid in its modern form dates back to the early 1940s and intensified after the disruption that followed the Second World War. The international economic system had collapsed, and war-ravaged Europe faced a critical shortage of capital and an acute need for physical reconstruction. The response was the European Recovery Programme, commonly known as the Marshall Plan. During the peak years the USA transferred some 2 to 3 per cent of its national income to help restore Europe. The motives behind US aid were multifaceted, ranging from the selfish to the generous. Containing communism around the Soviet bloc and trying to secure access to raw materials and gain a leading role in the global trade and investment system were critically important nationalistic concerns. Altruistic aims, on the other hand, helped mobilize support from a wide spectrum of political opinion. The Marshall Plan, which was administered by the Organisation for European Economic Co-operation (OEEC), the predecessor of the OECD, was implemented on schedule, and its success fuelled highly optimistic expectations about the future effectiveness of foreign aid.

After the success of the Marshall Plan, the attention of industrialized nations turned to the developing countries, many of which became independent around 1960. Economic growth in a state-led planning tradition became a key objective during the 1950s and 1960s, and it was widely believed that poverty and inequality would be quickly eliminated through growth and modernization ('trickle-down'). The major part of the rapidly increasing bilateral flows during the 1950s came from the USA. New bilateral donor agencies (other than the USA) were mainly established in the 1960s, with the Commonwealth-inspired Colombo Plan from 1950 being an exception.[6] A transition toward more independent, multilateral relations also began to emerge during the 1960s. This created a constituency for foreign aid, and the non-aligned movement gave for some time an articulated developing country focus to this voice,[7] as did the various organs of the UN. They accounted for close to 30 per cent of multilateral assistance during 1960 to 1973 as shown in Table 2.2. The UK resisted the idea of institutionalizing these flows until nearly the mid-1960s, even after the creation of the OECD-DAC in 1961. The International Bank for Reconstruction and Development (IBRD), established at the Bretton Woods Conference in 1944, came to play a central role in multilateral development assistance, especially following the creation of the International Development Association in 1960. IDA channels resources to the poorest countries on 'soft' conditions alongside the regional development banks, formed during 1959 to 1966.

---

[6] See <http://en.wikipedia.org/wiki/Colombo_Plan>.

[7] The first official non-aligned movement (NAM) summit was held in Sept. 1961. Among the prominent developing country leaders who helped NAM get off the ground were Tito of Yugoslavia, Nehru of India, Nasser of Egypt, and Sukarno of Indonesia. Formally speaking, the non-aligned movement is an international organization of over 100 developing countries, which consider themselves not formally aligned with or against any major power bloc. While influential during the 1960s and 1970s, NAM started losing influence in the 1970s.

The original Marshall Plan was built around support to finance general categories of imports and strengthen the balance of payments (that is, programme aid), but from the early 1950s project aid became the dominating aid modality. Some donors continued to supply programme aid, but aid was increasingly disbursed for the implementation of specific capital investment projects and associated technical assistance.

The multilateralism of aid became somewhat more pronounced after the mid-1970s. Multilateral channels were at the time seen as more efficient and less political than bilateral aid, so the UN, World Bank, and other multilateral agencies expanded their activities quite considerably. The 1970s also saw an increased focus on employment, income distribution, and poverty alleviation as essential objectives of development and foreign aid. The effectiveness of trickle-down was widely questioned, and new strategies referred to as 'basic human needs' and 'redistribution with growth' were formulated. Nevertheless, the typical project aid modality remained largely unchanged; and microeconomic project evaluation, also referred to as cost–benefit analysis (CBA), was expanded and widely relied on in the aid debate. After the first oil crisis in 1973, commercial banks started playing a large role in international lending by recycling OPEC petro-dollars and issuing general purpose loans to developing countries to provide balance of payment support and expand exports. The oil countries bilaterally and multilaterally provided up to 30 per cent of all ODA at the peak of the oil price rises, so bilateral DAC donors and the international financial institutions (IFIs) were no longer alone on the lending scene. International lending surged, and this permitted high growth with little debt servicing difficulty.

The 'golden era' of the 1960s and 1970s came to an abrupt end at the beginning of the 1980s. The second oil shock in 1979 reversed economic conditions, and there was a huge increase in interest rates due to the economic stabilization policies in the developed countries. Developing countries were faced with a combination of higher oil prices, import compression, and a significant decrease in export opportunities due to slower overall global growth. The international debt crisis erupted, and macroeconomic imbalance became characteristic. On the political scene Ronald Reagan and Margaret Thatcher came to power in the USA and the UK respectively, and at the World Bank Anne Krueger became Vice President and Chief Economist, replacing Hollis Chenery. This change was both symbolic and substantive (Kanbur 2003). Economic circumstances in the developing countries and the relations between the North and South changed radically. The crisis hit hard, especially in many African countries. Focus on development strategy and policy shifted to internal domestic policy failure, and achieving macroeconomic balance (externally and internally) became widely perceived as an essential prerequisite for renewed development.

'Rolling back the state' turned into a rallying call in the subsequent structural adjustment efforts, and reliance on market forces, outward orientation, and the role of the private sector, including non-governmental organizations (NGOs), were emphasized by the World Bank and others. In parallel, poverty alleviation slipped out of view in mainstream agendas for economic reform, but remained at the centre of attention in more unorthodox thinking such as the 'adjustment with a human face' approach of UNICEF (Cornia, Jolly, and Stewart 1987). At the same time, bilateral donors and international agencies struggled with how to channel resources to the developing world. Quick-disbursing macroeconomic programme assistance, such as balance of payments support and sector budget support (which were not tied to investment projects, and which could be justified under the headings of stabilization and adjustment), appeared an ideal solution to the dilemma of maintaining the resource flow and the desire to promote policy reform. Financial programme aid and adjustment loans (and eventually debt relief) became fashionable and policy conditionality more widespread. In other words, a rationale, which corresponded well with the orthodox guidelines for good policy summarized by the 'Washington Consensus' (Williamson 1997), had been found for maintaining the aid flow.[8]

Total aid continued to grow steadily in real terms until the early 1990s, but after 1992 total aid flows started to decline in absolute terms until the turn of the millennium. Many reasons account for the fall in aggregate flows after 1992, including first of all the end of the Cold War. The same can be said for the weakening patron–client relationships among the developing countries and the former colonial powers. The traditional support of foreign aid by vocal interest groups in the industrial countries receded. Bilateral and multilateral aid institutions were subjected to criticism, and at times characterized as blunt instruments of commercial interests in the industrial world or as self-interested, inefficient, rent-seeking bureaucracies. Moreover, acute awareness in donor countries of cases of bad governance, corruption, and 'crony capitalism' led to scepticism about the credibility of governments receiving aid.

The potential role of foreign aid in all this attracted attention, and the fear that aid can generate undesirable dependency relationships became clear during the second part of the 1990s and persisted into the twenty-first century. In parallel, the perception that policy conditionality was failing to promote policy reform started to assert itself (see Killick 1995; Mosley, Harrigan, and Toye 1995; Kanbur 2000; and Svensson 2003). This assessment prompted World Bank and independent academic researchers to start digging into the aid–growth relationship using modern panel data analytical techniques and, even more recently, attempts to develop randomized programme evaluation also appeared on the scene (see Duflo 2004).[9]

Finally, when reviewing the role and impact of foreign aid, it should be kept in mind that the world economy has seen major changes in international

---

[8] See Rodrik (2006) for a critical up-to-date review.
[9] I will not pursue the set of issues related to this approach to aid impact evaluation here. See Bigsten, Gunning, and Tarp (2006); and Thorbecke (2007) for elaboration.

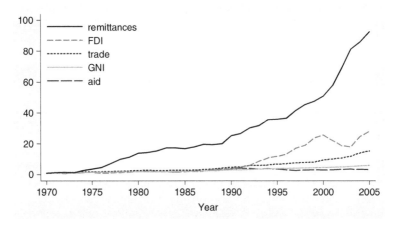

Figure 2.3 Macroeconomic indicators in aid-receiving countries

Notes: All variables are expressed as an index equal to one in 1970 and constructed from series of constant 2000 prices in US$. FDI is constructed from net FDI inflows and trade is based on the sum of exports and imports.

Source: World Bank (2007).

relations that go far beyond changes in foreign aid. Figure 2.3 shows how global trade as well as ODA, GNI, remittance, and FDI flows to aid-receiving countries evolved from 1970 onwards. This figure reflects only the relative changes in flows, not their relative magnitudes,[10] but it is evident that global trade has been growing faster than both GNI and aid flows to poor countries. This is especially so from around the mid-1980s, and the importance of FDI started changing very considerably in the early 1990s. However, the most impressive change is that of remittance flows. Lastly, aid funds from private foundations have also increased very significantly in recent years (not shown). In sum, globalization has modified the context in which foreign aid is implemented. This suggests, on the one hand, that a broader and more refined awareness of the implications of coexistence between public and private investment in developing countries would be beneficial. It implies, on the other hand, that aid's role in generating foreign exchange has changed significantly relative to other flows.[11]

[10] FDI accounted for only 2.3 per cent of GDP in low- and middle-income countries in 2003, and 0.6 per cent in 1990. Trade was 41 per cent in 1990, and 60 per cent in 2003.
[11] See Roland-Holst and Tarp (2004) for further discussion.

2.4. Aid allocation

Foreign aid has been justified in public policy pronouncements in widely differing ways, ranging from pure altruism to the shared benefits of economic development in poor countries and political ideology, and the foreign policy and commercial interests of the donor country. Few dispute that humanitarian sentiments have also motivated donors. Action following severe natural calamities, which continue to be endemic in poor countries, is an example. Food and emergency relief remains an important form of aid. Moreover, the data available in Table 2.3 suggest that donors allocate relatively more ODA to the poorest countries. The broader validity of this casual observation is confirmed in cross-country econometric work, a useful overview of the literature being McGillivray (2003). Considerable variation among donors can also be noted.

Emphasis on the needs of poor countries was a particularly prominent characteristic—and the underlying economic rationale—in much of the policy literature on foreign aid in the 1950s and 1960s. Here the focus was on estimating aid requirements in the tradition of the two-gap model (Chenery and Strout 1966). The two-gap model has been subjected to criticism,[12] and in parallel the role of aid has changed to a much more multidimensional set of concerns (Thorbecke 2000). Economic return is by no means the only goal of aid. Nevertheless, growth and economic development in aid-receiving countries have continued as yardsticks for the effectiveness of aid both in their own right and as necessary conditions for the realization of other development aims. It is from this perspective that the discussion in section 2.5 on aid's impact on growth should be seen.

It is not new that selfish motives are critical in bilateral donor decisions, and bilateral donors do indeed behave very differently. Up to about 1990, the Cold War was used as a powerful justification for providing aid to developing countries to stem the spread of communism. Similarly, aid from socialist governments was motivated to promote socialist political and economic systems. Other strategic interests play a role as well: the USA has over the years earmarked very substantial amounts of aid to Egypt and Israel;[13] being a former colony is an important determinant in getting access to French aid; and voting behaviour in the UN can affect aid allocation both bilaterally (Alesina and Dollar 2000) and through the multilateral system (Andersen, Harr, and Tarp 2006). Berthélemy and Tichit (2004) and Berthélemy (2006) offer further valuable insight on how bilateral donors are influenced in aid allocations by their own strategic and commercial interest versus the development motives of aid recipients, and on the fact that not all donors behave in the same way.

---

[12] See Jones (1995); and Easterly (1999).
[13] To this list can be added Iraq and Afghanistan. For example, US aid to Iraq amounted in 2005 to US$3.5 billion.

In sum, the donor community has failed to meet the established international target of contributing 0.7 per cent of national income as ODA. This is the case despite widespread endorsement of the recommendations for a large scaling-up in the context of the Millennium Development Goals (MDGs); see Anderson 2007 and Sachs 2005. As shown in Table 2.1, only the Scandinavian countries and the Netherlands have consistently met this target since the mid-1970s, while the USA contributed around 0.2 per cent of its GNI in 2006.

2.5. The impact of foreign aid

Various approaches have been tried to deal with the challenge of measuring the 'true' impact of aid on development, as reflected for example by growth or progress in social indicators.[14] One is to compare implicit or explicit targets with actual outcomes, and another quite common approach is to rely on before and after comparisons. These lines of analysis suffer from their inherent inability to attribute changes in observed outcomes to foreign aid. In other words, it is not satisfactory in assessing the impact of aid to argue casually that since growth in Africa is far from satisfactory aid 'does not work'. Similarly, the fact that some aid projects have failed does not in any way prove that aid as a whole is a fiasco. Unsuccessful investment projects and public sector activities abound in even the best political, social, and economic circumstances. In fact, most would probably agree that if investments are always successful then investor behaviour is likely to be too risk averse. Development is and will always be a particularly risky business. Any serious analysis must either (i) try to dig deeper in an attempt to uncover whether foreign aid has on average had a positive impact on development in aid-receiving countries or not; or (ii) aim at identifying the mechanisms through which aid impacts on, for example, growth, including the potential positive and negative effects (or returns) associated with foreign aid.

To be able to measure the effect of aid, the researcher must in principle be able to compare the value of a chosen indicator (such as growth or poverty reduction) in two strictly independent situations—with and without aid. To establish the 'true' measure of aid impact, the importance of all other circumstances that have affected a given country over time needs to be properly accounted for.[15] Alternatively, if a group of countries is compared (with and without aid) the analyst needs to account for the impact on the chosen indicator of the other differences that exist among the units of observation, like in a controlled experiment. This is the fundamental evaluation challenge,

---

[14] See Bigsten, Gunning, and Tarp (2006) for further elaboration of this point.
[15] This includes choosing the length of individual time units and an appropriate overall time horizon, which are by no means simple choices.

and there is in social science no way of addressing this problem (that is, the challenge of establishing an appropriate counterfactual) in a broadly acceptable way without making assumptions that are bound to be debatable, in theory and in practice.[16]

In section 2.4, it was pointed out that aid has been given for many reasons that have little to do with socio-economic advancement in aid-receiving countries. This has undoubtedly constrained the impact of aid on growth and development. The targets for aid have also varied considerably from one decade to the next. The same goes for the general political, social, and economic circumstances as discussed in section 2.3, and the modalities and sources of aid have changed as well. As a result, the conditions under which aid has had to operate have changed dramatically from one decade to the next. There is, to be sure, no simple way of accounting properly for all the many varied and complex factors which have played a role in development over the past thirty years—alongside foreign aid amounting to around US$35 per capita per year.

Despite the challenges, a great number of studies have been produced in recent years on the effectiveness of foreign aid. This topic has been a central and recurring theme with which many development economists, subscribing to the different paradigms of development thinking, have grappled, and methodologies have varied. More specifically (i) the impact of aid has been evaluated at the micro- and macroeconomic levels; (ii) cross-country comparisons as well as single-country case studies have been used; and (iii) aid effectiveness research includes broad surveys of a qualitative and interdisciplinary nature as well as more quantitative econometric work.[17] As a point of departure for the remainder of this chapter, it is relevant to stress that there is widespread agreement in the literature that aid has in many cases been highly successful at the microeconomic level. The most rigorous project evaluations are done by the World Bank, and reports from the Independent Evaluation Group of the World Bank are generally encouraging. For the period 1993 to 2002 an average rate of return of 22 per cent has been noted and decent project rates of return have over the years been reported regularly in one survey after the other, including for example Mosley 1987 and Cassen 1994. Overall, a mass of project evidence has been collected. Few dispute that aid interventions have worked in helping improve social outcomes through better health, helping promote develop appropriate technology (such as the green revolution), and so on. Yet, doubts about aid's

---

[16] This does not of course mean that economics ignores the possibility of using both laboratory and field experiments to generate knowledge. Experimental economics is a subdiscipline that has been advancing significantly in recent years.

[17] The reader may wish to consult, for example, Cassen and Associates (1994) for a useful survey with a broader scope than the present study. Other references include World Bank (1998).

overall impact on growth and development linger on, and the question is regularly raised whether all this adds up at the macro level.

It is therefore relevant to turn to how the empirical literature on aid's macro-economic impact on growth has evolved. This choice of focus can be justified on several grounds. First, as an extension of the microeconomic evidence, numerous case studies support—according to the World Bank (1998)—the observation that aid has, at times, been a spectacular success. In establishing causal links, the critical challenge is as noted above to pinpoint a credible counterfactual, and it is never straightforward to generalize from case studies. Another reason for the popularity in the past ten to fifteen years of the cross-country panel data approach is that it makes it possible to move well beyond simplistic aid–growth correlation analysis, where the analysis of causal effects is indeed rather primitive. It should, in fact, come as no surprise to the informed observer that the simple correlation coefficient between growth and aid can easily turn out to be insignificant, or negative. Donors allocate, as already discussed, more aid to poorer countries, which are subject to difficulties and shocks of many kinds, including natural and man-made calamities. When countries have done well for a while, donors tend to transfer less aid, especially when measured as a percentage of GDP, and eventually they will withdraw (as happened in the case of Korea). While such 'graduation' may take a while, simple correlations are likely to show a negative relationship and will definitely not reveal the 'true' impact of aid.

In the modern aid–growth work, the analyst can attempt to control for the impact of a large range of variables, and becomes in this way able to move closer to the ideal of having a reliable counterfactual.[18] The analyst is, at least in principle, capable of addressing issues such as the identification problem inherent in having aid allocated endogenously in the foreign aid system. Second, a focus on growth makes it possible in a wider perspective to draw on both traditional growth theory and new growth models to illustrate how aid can potentially impact through a highly diverse set of channels.[19] Third, macroeconomic studies are required in order to help generalize about the overall impact of aid on growth and economic development. Fourth, the aid–growth literature continues to be highly influential in shaping common perceptions about the significance and impact of foreign aid. Fifth, whether aid helps growth or not is essentially an empirical question.

The quantitative cross-country analyses of the macroeconomic impact of foreign aid on growth, which spans almost four decades, can be classified into three generations (see Hansen and Tarp 2000). Work in the first two generations (where aid's impact on growth via savings and investment was the focus) was

---

[18] The same can be said about the use of randomized programme evaluation, which I do not pursue, as already noted above. For perspective, see Thorbecke (2007).

[19] For a pertinent cautioning set of observations, see Solow (2001).

inspired by the simple Harrod–Domar model and the two-gap Chenery–Strout extension. This framework was, as mentioned in section 2.4, used extensively in the past as the analytical framework of choice for assessing aid impact; but from the early 1990s a third generation of panel-based econometric studies came to dominate the academic and public discourses. This work was motivated in part by the availability of much better (panel) data across a range of countries and in part by insights emerging from new growth theory and the rapidly increasing number of general empirical studies of growth. In addition, the endogeneity of aid and other variables is addressed more consistently than before,[20] and the aid–growth relationship is appropriately perceived as non-linear. The underlying idea behind the Harrod–Domar model was indeed simple. Assume that physical capital is the only factor of production (so investment is the key constraint on growth) and assume as well that all aid is invested. Then it is straightforward to calculate the growth impact of additional aid. If aid corresponds to 6 per cent of the GNP and the capital–output ratio is estimated at 3.0,[21] which is a typical estimate, then aid adds two percentage points a year to the growth rate. The impact of aid is clearly positive, and aid works by helping to fill either a savings or a foreign exchange gap. The latter gap relates to the argument that aid represents foreign currency and as such can facilitate imports of goods and services that may in some cases be critically important in output production over and above aid's impact on relieving the savings constraint. This kind of reasoning has, however, led to wildly over-optimistic expectations about aid's potential impact.[22]

First, it is a tall order to expect both a linear relationship between output and capital and that all aid is invested. Aid is, as discussed in section 2.4, provided for many reasons. For example, food aid in famine situations is not intended as investment. In addition, the share of aid that ends up being invested (rather than consumed) will, in even the very best circumstances, depend on the degree of fungibility of the foreign aid transfer.[23] On the other hand, even if

---

[20] The wider ranging and complex econometric endogeneity problems inherent in relying on time averages for aid and growth, typically used in panel data growth regressions, are laid out in Dalgaard; Hansen, and Tarp (2004). They point out that not only aid but also policy is likely to be endogenous.

[21] Note from Figure 2.1 that the annual median aid to GNI ratio amounted to 6.8 per cent from 1993 to 2002.

[22] Whether this discredits the two-gap model as argued by Easterly (1999), or whether it can serve a useful purpose as an admittedly simple analytical framework, if applied with due care, remains in my view to be established. In any case, the fact is that this model continues to be widely used in practice, and, whether one believes the two-gap model should be discarded altogether or not, the notion that aid may contribute to growth via investment and capital accumulation remains relevant.

[23] Fungibility arises when the recipient can reallocate its own resources to other ends when aid is provided. There is limited and conflicting evidence on the degree of fungibility of foreign aid; see, for example, Feyzioglu, Swaroop, and Zhu (1998). A more balanced and critical assessment can be found in McGillivray and Morrissey (2004).

aid adds to domestic savings and investment on less than a one-to-one basis, aid does continue to have a positive impact on growth in the traditional line of thinking—as long as total savings and investment go up.[24]

A second line of critique of the Harrod–Domar and two-gap approach has been the argument that growth is less related to physical capital investment (including aid) than often assumed (Easterly 2001). If the key driver of the productive impact of aid is related more to incentives and relative prices and more generally to the policy environment then it becomes important to consider potentially distortionary effects of aid on incentives and economic policies in the aid-receiving system and vice versa. An example is 'Dutch disease', and domestic demand and resource allocation may be twisted in undesirable directions following a large aid inflow, especially if macroeconomic management is weak. One concrete example is that aid donors often pay much higher wages than equally important and, in many cases, more important national institutions.[25]

Third, a large and growing literature on the political economy of aid, with roots back to Bauer (1971)—see, for example, Svensson (2000) and Kanbur (2003); Gunning (2005);—has argued that if aid allows a recipient government (local elites) to pursue behaviour that is in any way anti-developmental then the potential positive impact of aid can be undermined. There are many such examples available in practice ranging from outright misuse of aid by corrupt governments to more subtle issues such as the potential negative impact of aid on domestic taxation (Adam and O'Connell 1999).

The third generation debate about aid's impact on growth is rooted in the above kinds of observations as well as in Mosley's (1987) micro–macro paradox. He suggested that while aid seems to be effective at the microeconomic level,[26] identifying any positive impact of aid at the macroeconomic level is harder, or even impossible. In fact, the micro–macro paradox seemed self-evident to many at the time it was formulated where the general atmosphere was one of aid fatigue and lack of belief in a positive impact of aid on growth. Another explanation, sometimes referred to as the 'Iron Law of Econometrics', in the

[24] This observation goes back to Papanek (1972, 1973) and inspired Hansen and Tarp (2000), who reviewed 131 cross country regressions produced over three decades. They challenged the widespread perception among academic researchers and aid practitioners that there is no significant macroeconomic links associated with foreign aid as stated by, for example, Michalopoulos and Sukhatme (1989); and White (1992). A re-examination of the then existing literature revealed that (i) aid increases savings, although not by as much as the aid inflow; (ii) aid increases investment; and (iii) aid has on average a positive effect on the growth rate whenever growth is driven by capital accumulation. Hansen and Tarp therefore suggested that the micro–macro paradox identified by Mosley (1987), to which I shall return below, is non-existent even in the context of the traditional aid-growth literature.

[25] See Rajan and Subramanian (2005) for a contribution on this.

[26] Dalgaard and Hansen (2005) also discuss the micro-economic evidence on positive ex-post rates of return of World Bank aid projects, referred to above. Median returns range between 10 per cent and 30 per cent for the period 1996–2001.

terminology of Hausman (2001), received less attention.[27] It must never be overlooked that once we try to explain a 'dirty' dependent variable with noisy data and weak proxies it should come as no surprise that the result is biased towards zero, or in this case even towards the negative given the aid allocation behaviour of donors. What Mosley and many after him have struggled with is how to control for the wildly changing circumstances under which aid has been implemented. We can (and should) look to history and try to treat it as a controlled experiment, but we are at the end of the day limited by the extent to which our proxies capture the massive changes in circumstances under which aid is implemented over time and across countries.

Boone (1994) managed to stir up the aid–growth debate again in the early-to-mid-1990s. His work was cited in *The Economist* on 10 December 1994 under the colourful heading 'Down the Rathole', and Boone did indeed suggest that aid does not create, nor correlate with, those underlying factors which cause growth. Boone did not, however, occupy centre stage for long. His underlying theoretical model was qualified by Obstfelt (1999). Moreover, Boone treated the aid–growth relationship as linear and, as is the case with many other aid papers, did not account convincingly for the potential endogeneity of aid.[28] Finally, and much more importantly, a highly influential idea spread, in part due to effective backing by the World Bank. This is the idea that while aid has, on average, no impact on growth, aid may still work in some countries or time periods. Burnside and Dollar (1997, 2000) pursued this and argued that 'aid has a positive impact on growth in developing countries with good fiscal, monetary and trade policies', and they added that in 'the presence of poor policies, aid has no positive effect on growth'. In other words, aid works, but only in countries with 'good policy'. They based this conclusion on an aid–policy interaction term, introduced to capture the non-linearity between aid and growth which emerged as statistically significant in their panel data analysis. In sum, Burnside and Dollar provided an attractive and very elegant solution to the micro–macro paradox with clear-cut and easy to interpret policy implications. They are, in addition, very much in line with orthodox development thinking.

Burnside and Dollar, and more recently Collier and Dollar (2001, 2002), have used the foregoing framework as a basis for suggesting that aid should be directed to 'good policy' countries to improve aid's impact on poverty alleviation. The index meant to capture 'good policy' has gradually been expanded from the Burnside–Dollar focus on budget surplus, inflation, and openness to

---

[27] Hausman (2001: 58) notes: 'At MIT I have called this "The Iron Law of Econometrics"—the magnitude of the estimate is usually lower than expected. It is also called "attenuation" in the statistical literature'. In what follows I will use the technical term, 'attenuation bias'.

[28] In Boone's (1994) aid–growth regressions, he did not instrument for aid, but he did include country fixed effects.

the World Bank's Country Policy and Institutional Assessment (CPIA) index[29] (for a related critique of the CPIA see sections 4.2 and 4.3 in Machiko Nissanke's chapter in this volume). The argument for allocating aid selectively is also, at least partly, justified with reference to the finding that the amount of aid countries receive has no impact on the quality of their macroeconomic policies, a finding that also appeared to emerge from Bank-funded research (Devarajan, Dollar, and Holmgren 2001).[30] While the Bank's Monterrey document (World Bank 2002) toned down these recommendations, and the World Bank (2005) strikes a very different line of argument in its interpretation of the policy reform process during the 1990s, the basic thrust in much of the international aid debate remains that macroeconomic performance evaluation and policy criteria should play a key role in aid allocation.

There is, however, an academic dilemma around this issue: (i) Hansen and Tarp (2001) found that the Burnside–Dollar result is far from robust. In fact, it appeared at the time that diminishing returns where aid squared is introduced into the analysis to capture non-linear effects between aid and growth was the empirical specification with most support in the data. In contrast, the data did not support the Burnside–Dollar aid–policy interaction term;[31] (ii) Dalgaard and Hansen (2001) showed the same with the Burnside and Dollar data set, once it had been made available to researchers outside the World Bank, performing a general-to-specific test; (iii) Easterly, Levine, and Roodman (2004) found the Burnside–Dollar aid–policy story to be fragile in the face of an expansion of the data set in years and countries;[32] and finally (iv) Roodman (2004) offered a comparative assessment of the large number of stories on the relationship between how much foreign aid a country receives and how it grows, which the contemporary econometric literature has generated. He

[29] The CPIA index assesses the quality of a country's present policy and institutional framework in twenty different dimensions, assessed by World Bank experts on a scale from one to six. Each item has a 5 per cent weight in the overall rating. The items are grouped into four categories: 'economic management', 'structural policies', 'policies for social inclusion/ equity', and 'public-sector management and institutions'.

[30] This volume was reviewed by Tarp (2001).

[31] The turning-point at which increased aid will start having a negative impact on growth was originally estimated around 25–40 per cent. This is, as is clear from Figure 2.1, very far above the typical aid country, and Hansen and Tarp (2000) warned that the empirical identification of the turning-point should in any case be interpreted with great care. The diminishing returns' thesis was not put forward as a definitive statement about how aid impacts, or what would happen if aid was increased, more as a way of characterizing the data and putting the fragility of the Burnside–Dollar policy story into perspective. When trying to capture non-linearities in the aid–growth relation it is advisable to test all respectable alternative economically and statistically meaningful specifications before conclusions are drawn. In sum, the diminishing returns story should not be interpreted as an argument against more aid per se.

[32] Easterly (2008) seems to suggest that he and his co-authors have been the main critics of the Burnside–Dollar study. I encourage the reader to carry out the Google Scholar searches to which he refers in his nn. 15 and 16 and to review his reference list in this light.

originally concluded that the aid–policy link (identified by Burnside–Dollar) proves the weakest, while the aid–tropics link (identified by Dalgaard, Hansen, and Tarp 2004) is most robust. Roodman subsequently modified his study to focus purely on the issue of fragility.

Dalgaard, Hansen, and Tarp (2004) argue that aid and policy both depend on the average rate of growth even though they are predetermined in the original system. They therefore take account of this in their empirical testing, which also controls for the potential endogeneity of institutions. In their attempt at assessing the importance of structural characteristics on aid effectiveness they add the fraction of land in tropical areas as a proxy for climate related variables. This variable and its interaction with aid outperform both the 'good policy' and 'the diminishing returns' model. In concluding, Dalgaard, Hansen, and Tarp (2004) make the point that it does appear from the data as if aid has been far less effective in tropical areas over the last thirty years. They also stress that it is hard to believe that aid should, inherently, be less potent in the tropics. The real explanation for the aid–tropics link is, in their assessment, likely to lie elsewhere; and they call for further research to help disentangle the channels through which aid matters for productivity and efficiency. Their result also highlights that while there is merit in more sophisticated versions of arguments for selectivity, macroeconomic allocation rules depend critically on understanding the complex links in particular country circumstances between aid, growth, and development objectives such as poverty reduction. What this (and the many other studies listed in, for example, Clemens, Radelet, and Bhavnani 2004) adds up to can be summarized as follows:

- It is highly likely that 'aid pays a growth price' as growth regularly gives way to other concerns as the most important criterion for aid.[33] Yet, that aid has a positive impact on per capita growth is supported by a significant body of empirical aid–growth studies.[34] At the same time, aid is by no means a panacea for growth and poverty reduction, and the aid–growth link remains contentious.[35]

---

[33] Food aid in famine situations geared toward increased consumption is a specific case in point, as is, more generally, aid for consumption that is not investment targeted.

[34] See the literature already cited and note that Dalgaard and Hansen (2005) estimate that the aggregate real rate of return on foreign-aid-financed investments is in the range of 20–25 per cent. Rajan and Subramanian (2008) are more critical, and their approach to the use of external instruments in cross-section analysis is interesting. Yet, it should be kept in mind that their instrumentation strategy implies that they provide an estimate of the impact of aid driven by non-developmental objectives. It cannot be concluded that the impact of 'real developmental aid' is the same (i.e., nil). Arguably, regressions that rely on pooled aid may underestimate the true impact of 'developmentally motivated aid'.

[35] See, for example, the revised version of Roodman (2004) and Roodman (2007).

- The way in which data are dealt with to address the complex issue of identifying the impact of aid on growth is critically important for the conclusions drawn. Methodological choices matter.
- The impact of aid on growth is not the same across aid recipients. There are differences in aid efficiency from country to country (see Mavrotas and Nunnenkamp 2007); and it remains unclear what drives these differences. In particular, the importance of 'deep' structural characteristics in affecting how aid impacts on growth is not yet fully understood.

Furthermore, using 'good policy' (in the form of the CPIA index) as a basis for allocating aid selectively is questionable. There are at least three reasons:

(1) An attraction of the original Burnside–Dollar index was its simplicity. It was controversial but easy to interpret. It is much harder to derive clear-cut policy advice based on any positive interaction between aid and the CPIA. The CPIA is a composite index of sixteen different variables grouped into four categories (see Table 4.1 in Chapter 4 of this volume). In spite of the descriptive value of the CPIA index, which I do not question, it is from an analytical point of view far from easy to decipher what drives aid efficiency when indicators of 'economic management', 'structural policies', 'social policies', and 'public sector management and institutions' are aggregated into one measure. In addition, trade-offs between the elements of the index are bound to arise in practice. For example, placing greater emphasis on budget balance (an element in 'economic management') may well be in conflict with improving health care, education, and so on, belonging to the component 'building human resources' which forms part of 'policies for social inclusion/ equity'. Improved budget balance may also lead to a lower 'pro-poor expenditure index' shown to be poverty reducing by Mosley, Hudson, and Verschoor (2004).

(2) The changes in the CPIA index may be caused by the growth performance, in which case the CPIA should not be used as an exogenous variable.[36] Moreover, Mauro (1995) highlights that using expert evaluations may be problematic. The argument is that evaluators are likely to conclude that a particular set of institutions is good if the country in question is growing rapidly.

(3) The use of 'good policy' may lead us to punish countries with unfavourable conditions instead of helping them. There is a very high probability that a country with a low CPIA is in the tropical region. If the

---

[36] Similar concerns are alluded to by Cornia (2005) when he points out that it is far from clear what can be concluded based on negative correlation between 'bad governance/corruption' and 'slow/negative growth in GDP per capita'. It may, in Cornia's formulation, be that other unobserved variables are at work, such as 'high illiteracy and low land productivity that simultaneously reduce growth and the salaries of civil servants, who therefore asks bribes whenever possible'.

variation in aid effectiveness across countries is not policy induced, but rather a result of poor initial conditions, a different approach to allocating aid has to be established. At the same time, every effort has of course to be made to help put in place improved policy, which helps growth and poverty reduction.

In sum, it is advisable to be alert about what is in fact unknown. This implies, for example, that more attention should be paid in future research on foreign aid and development to different modalities of aid (such as project versus programme assistance) and their design and application in different types of aid-receiving countries.

2.6. Discussion of the current aid and development debate

Has foreign aid been a success or failure in promoting development? Based on some of the contributions to the foreign aid literature over the past decade, including, for example, the works of Boone, Burnside and Dollar, Sachs, and Easterly, it might appear that 'The answer, my friend, is blowin' in the wind'.[37] Boone (2006) has recently reiterated that 'the history of large aid flows is, to date, a major failure', while Burnside and Dollar (2000) found that aid promotes growth, but only when policy is 'good'.

Nevertheless, Sachs (2005) and the UN Millennium Project (2005) argue emphatically that aid has worked and should be 'scaled up'. Sachs has played a key role as special adviser to the UN Secretary General on the MDGs, and he makes a concerted effort to reinstate many of the traditional arguments within development economics for believing aid works in helping poor countries break out of poverty traps. He refers to investments attuned to local needs and uses a vocabulary, which is phrased along gap-filling lines of thinking. He also dismisses corruption and domestic policy failure as the fundamental 'cause' of Africa's problems, and argues instead that the causal links originate in poverty and the lack of growth. Sachs furthermore provides 'ten dramatic examples that prove the naysayers wrong' (Sachs 2005: 259). These examples, which are referred to as 'clear aid triumphs', range from aid's contribution to the Green Revolution of Asia to the eradication of smallpox and polio and on to the mobile phone revolution in Bangladesh. They demonstrate, in Sachs' words, some common themes (ibid. 265). 'First and foremost, scaling up is possible when it is backed by appropriate and widely applicable technology, organizational leadership, and appropriate financing'; and he goes on to state that in 'the case of the Millennium Development Goals, the promising technologies exist, but have not been scaled up'.

---

[37] Song by Bob Dylan. For the full text, see <http://www.bobdylan.com/#/songs/blowin-wind>.

Cornia (2005) pointedly notes that Sachs deserves a lot of credit for his 'passionate advocacy'. Moreover, Sachs does manage to call attention to at least some of the ways in which aid has helped poor people in the past. His suggestion that much more can and should be done deserves in my assessment attention together with his menu of initiatives.[38] At the same time, as argued by Cornia, it is problematic that so much of the present development debate is being cast in terms of increases in aid flows for the achievement of the MDGs. This is, to quote Cornia, 'reductionist'. In addition, even if it is accepted that aid works, and works well, it is unlikely that the MDGs can be reached if aid is increased to 0.7 per cent of donor GNI as argued by Sachs. The return will not, even in the best circumstances, be big enough. I am afraid that mobilizing such optimistic expectations may in the final analysis lead in a few years to frustration and an undesired backlash.

Easterly has over the years authored an impressive number of books and papers, a few of which are listed in the references. He is a sharp and articulate critic of foreign aid, and his contributions to the academic and broader policy literature are influential. In two recent studies (2005, 2006), Easterly attacks, head on, the UN Millennium Project and the work of Sachs. Easterly refers to the 'white man's burden' and ponders 'Why the West's efforts to aid the rest have done so much ill and so little good'. Easterly deserves a lot of credit for demonstrating in his many writings that much went wrong with aid in the past, and he is spot on when he argues that a lot of individual initiative has been stifled under the burden of dogmatic and centralized planning practices and bureaucratic incompetence in the past decades. I believe that human initiative and appropriate incentives are correctly identified by Easterly as two critically important elements in making development happen. Much can, and should, be gained in thinking about development and the appropriate role of foreign aid in the future from taking this to heart.

Sen (2006) has, in a similar vein, noted that there is much in Easterly's book that offers 'a line of analysis that could serve as the basis for a reasoned critique of the formulaic thinking and policy triumphalism of some of the literature on economic development'; and Cornia (2005) argues that Easterly is right on target in arguing that 'poverty, mortality and so on are in fact much more sensitive to macroeconomic, financial and technological changes (or their lack thereof) than to the aggregate volume of aid flows'. At the same time, both Sen and Cornia raise a series of critical points. They range from what Cornia calls the 'demonization of world "planning"' to Sen stating that 'Perhaps the weakest link in Easterly's reasoning is his almost complete neglect of the distinctions between different types of economic problems'. In any case, my experience and reading of the existing analytical evidence does not suggest that

---

[38] The UN Millennium Project (2005) goes on to recommend no fewer than 449 interventions to end poverty.

aid has on balance been as ineffective as Easterly seems to suggest. Finally, I do sense that Easterly's sarcastic style, and his rejection of any type of 'planning' and coordination, gets in the way of much needed dialogue.[39]

Summing up, Easterly and Sachs have done a commendable job in energizing the current debate about foreign aid. But, looking ahead, it is in my assessment important that their respective conflicting approaches do not end up confining a constructive and forward-looking search for how best design and implement aid in the future (see also Chapter 13 of this volume on the ' "big push" versus absorptive capacity' debate). Against this background, I would summarize the existing situation of the current aid and development debate by highlighting that there does seem to be consensus about at least the following three points:

(1) Much has been learnt from both successes and failures about development and development policy over the past fifty years, and lots of disagreement remains as well. On many questions our profession is still searching for appropriate answers.

(2) The more than one billion people in the world who are living in extreme poverty should not be left to themselves. Birdsall, Rodrik, and Subramanian (2005) state 'developed countries should not abandon the poor to their plight'; Easterly (2005) notes 'aid can still do much for the poor'; and even Boone (2006) argues that 'the aid successes with which we are all familiar... are important'. Much of the controversy in the academic and policy debate is about aid's performance in the past. The need and relevance of such action in the future is (ignoring the 'pure' ideologists) not disputed,[40] but whether such action is justified by political, economic, or moral considerations varies.

(3) There are many examples where aid has worked at the micro level to the benefit of developing countries and their populations. It is also true that aid is far from flawless. There are many cases where aid has not worked to help the poor, as suggested by Sachs (2006). Whether all this adds up to a positive average impact on growth at the macro level is contentious.

2.7. Conclusion

Controversy is rampant in the debate about aid, growth, and development. This is not particularly surprising. Even a cursory look at history shows that development over the past thirty to fifty years has been a complex and variegated process. There have been interrelated changes in resource accumulation,

---

[39] It is certainly amusing to read about 'Bono, Sachs, the Dalai Lama, and the Pope' at Easterly (2001: 126), but Easterly (2006) creates, as I see it, too many caricatures.

[40] To illustrate, I fully acknowledge the key incentive and agency problems associated with aid transfers, such as those uncovered by Svensson (2000, 2005), and, on this basis, he does not conclude that aid is without potential impact on the development process.

population growth, growth in knowledge, and improvements in production technology, all operating in an environment characterized by frequent and dramatic transformations in politics and institutions.[41] Social science has to rely on interpretations of history in trying to come to grips with these processes, and the analyst must be aware of the dangers of over-simplification. Single-cause theories have not fared well in development economics. This reflects that simple policy recommendations are often inappropriate in a complex world, and this is so whether such recommendations have emanated from the planning tradition of the 1960s and 1970s or from the free-market thinking of the 1980s.

I have tried to highlight in this chapter that one cannot conclude that aid has been a failure just because growth, in, for example, Africa, has been less than desired, or because projects have failed. It is exceedingly easy to arrive at a negative association between aid and growth, but such correlations do not provide a definitive causal answer. There is no logical inconsistency in development terms between little growth and aid inflows of the size experienced in the past. Aid allocation matters for the analysis; and complex development problems and issues are looming in the background. Major changes have taken place in the global economy and affected the environment in which aid is implemented, and targets for aid have been changing from one decade to the next. Simple correlation analysis or storytelling cannot, and should not, be allowed to settle the causality debate on their own. I also recognize, as should be clear from this chapter, that cross-country econometric studies are associated with critical methodological choices. Coming up with the 'true' aid–growth relationship is far from easy, and aid is of much too limited size to turn the wheels of history. Yet, this does not make it justified to reject aid as a useful instrument in the fight against poverty. If we are agreed that aid works at least somewhere and sometimes, then aid must be outright harmful elsewhere for the average impact to be nil. I can follow that some aid has not done all that much good, and this is a shame. Yet, there is a significant difference between doing little good and doing outright harm. I fail to see that the empirical evidence adds up to a suggestion that a lot of ill has actually been done across an important sample of countries. Similarly, it is one thing to call attention to problems that should definitely be addressed, it is quite another to dismiss foreign aid as harmful. My overall conclusion is that nuanced and subtle assessments are advisable with the empirical evidence in hand at present.

Burnside and Dollar added welcome analytical nuance to Boone, as have others. But the Burnside–Dollar solution to the micro–macro paradox has been countered in the literature and shown to be highly delicate. Methodological choices do matter, and a substantial part of the modern aid–growth

---

[41] See Tarp (2000), and here especially the summary and synthesis authored with Sherman Robinson.

literature does suggest that aid has a positive impact on per capita growth. No excessive claims about parameter sizes and total aid impact should be made on this basis. Yet, this should not overshadow the positive results at hand. In this context I am puzzled that critics such as Easterly so often ignore these and instead use cross-country work as a basis for questioning foreign aid.[42] Attenuation suggests that with noisy data, a 'dirty' dependent variable, and weak proxies results will be biased towards zero. Given this, the challenge is to clarify whether the data still have anything meaningful to say.[43]

Turning to the debate about the allocation of aid, there is merit in more sophisticated versions of arguments for selectivity. For example, it makes little sense to do structural adjustment lending when the macro-policy environment is 'bad' and there is little possibility for policy reform. However, based on the empirical work on aid effectiveness during the past decade, I am convinced that macro criteria cannot and should not stand alone in evaluating the effectiveness of most development assistance and determining its allocation. 'Good policy' can be dangerously misleading as the fundamental criterion for aid allocation, and simplistic macro rules-of-thumb may reinforce the adversity of those living under substandard governance. It is a regrettable fact that many of the world's poorest people live in conditions of substandard national, regional, and/or local governance and lack any tenable means of changing these institutions. It would be gravely ironic for aid agencies to compound the misfortunes of these people with discriminatory aid allocation.

Overall, it is justified to argue for increased aid, but expectations about its impact on growth should be kept at reasonable levels. This is where the many claims of Sachs and the Millennium Project can at times cause concern. It would be unfortunate if unrealistic expectations about aid impact are built up much along the lines of what happened back in the 1950s and 1960s, in the early stages of aid. At the same time, asserting that (i) aid has a positive impact; (ii) should be 'scaled up'; and (iii) that its impact does not appear to be conditional on 'good policy', is not in any way in contradiction with suggesting that future aid should be carefully redesigned. In this we should draw on the many insights offered by aid critiques; but it must not be overlooked that much is indeed already happening on the foreign aid scene. Major shifts have taken place in aid modalities over the past fifteen years as noted by Adam (2005). He also argues that the general rise of a culture of transparency and accountability is more than superficial, and goes on to point out that the March 2005 Paris Declaration

[42] See Tarp (2006), published about two years before Easterly (2008), for comparison.
[43] One can also note that the conventional wisdom at the end of the 1980s tended to overemphasize or misinterpret studies which had found a negative or insignificant relationship; see Hansen and Tarp (2000).

of Aid Effectiveness is an attempt to codify some of the best practice developments observed in a number of countries.[44]

Trying, in summary, to identify three sets of core, but unresolved, issues and indicate where further research is needed, they include:[45]

(1) Foreign aid is associated with development successes and failures, and the fundamental analytical problem in assessing its impact is that nobody has, to date, identified the underlying development model. We are therefore necessarily working with reduced form models, which are bound to be debatable. In parallel, existing data suggest that foreign aid is far from equally effective everywhere. The necessary and sufficient conditions for aid to have a positive contribution on the development process remain controversial. In other words, how better to come to grips with what actually 'drives' existing differences in the impact of foreign aid remains a challenge. This is so, for example, in relation to potential interaction with economic policy but the same goes for deeper structural characteristics, which play a key role.

(2) We do not at present have the necessary complete and generalized understanding of the complex links in particular country circumstances between aid, growth, and development objectives such as poverty reduction to justify selectivity as the basic approach in aid allocation. This does not mean that old-fashioned conditionality should be brought back but that a better understanding of the intricacies of the donor–recipient relationship in theory and in practice (including topics such as ownership and associated concepts) would be valuable. Key elements include addressing issues such as (i) how best to channel resources to the poor when national governments are not capable of taking on (and/or are not willing to take on) this task; (ii) how to ensure that aid delivered directly to national governments does not undermine local accountability; and (iii) establishing the appropriate balance between aid going to the government vis-à-vis individuals and others in the private sector. Accordingly, how best to strengthen incentives in support of genuine domestic policy leadership (including the commitment to the learning-by-doing of development policy) is a challenge. The same goes for the fundamental task of furthering accountability and transparency vis-à-vis local populations.

(3) In the present drive to scale up aid, it is critically important to avoid making the past mistake of promising too much; that is, of contributing to the misconception that aid can on its own turn history. Based on history, aid has much to offer, but managing expectations is far from easy. Making sure that promises made are actually kept is demanding. There are many unresolved issues here, including how best to design incentives in aid agencies to meet

---

[44] For the text of this forum, see <http://www.oecd.org/dataoecd/11/41/34428351.pdf>. See also Adam and Gunning (2002) and Adam et al. (2004).

[45] See Bourguignon and Sundberg (2007) for their suggestions on how to 'open the black box'.

this challenge alongside topics such as the role of independent evaluation, of coordination among multiple donors, and of the need to sharpen the incentives for recipients to maximize 'reform effort', which are all alluded to by Adam (2005).

In conclusion, I would stress, first, that it would be gravely ironic if we let disagreement about overall development strategy and the macroeconomic impact of aid get in the way of pursuing practical and useful aid-funded activities in poor countries. There is much to criticize in foreign aid, but possibilities for constructive and forward-looking action should be kept in mind throughout. There are, in my experience, lots of examples in practice. These deserve to be uncovered more precisely and implemented effectively for the benefit of those in need.

References

Adam, C. S. (2005) 'Comments on the Paper, "Absorption Capacity and Disbursements Constraints" by Jakob Svensson'. EUDN discussion paper. <http://www.afd.fr/jahia/webdav/site/myjahiasite/users/administrateur/public/eudn2005/Svensson_Adam.pdf>.

——and S. O'Connell (1999) 'Aid, Taxation and Development in Sub-Saharan Africa'. *Economics and Politics*, 11: 225–54.

——and J. W. Gunning (2002) 'Redesigning the Aid Contract: Donors' Use of Performance Indicators in Uganda'. *World Development*, 30: 2045–56.

——G. Chambas, P. Guillaumont, et al. (2004) 'Performance-based Conditionality: A European Perspective'. *World Development*, 33: 1059–70.

Alesina, A., and D. Dollar (2000) 'Who Gives Aid to Whom and Why?' *Journal of Economic Growth*, 5: 33–63.

Anderson, E. (2007) 'Aid Allocation and the MDGs'. Overseas Development Institute Briefing Paper 19. <http://www.odi.org.uk/resources/odi-publications/briefing-papers/19-aid-allocation-mdgs.pdf>.

Andersen, T. B., T. Harr, and F. Tarp (2006) 'On US Politics and IMF Lending'. *European Economic Review*, 50: 1843–62.

Arndt, C., S. Jones, and F. Tarp (2006) 'Aid and Development: The Mozambican Case'. University of Copenhagen Department of Economics Discussion Paper 06-13. Copenhagen: Københavns Universitet.

Bauer, P. (1971) *Dissent on Development*. Cambridge, Mass.: Harvard University Press.

Berthélemy, J. C. (2006) 'Bilateral Donors' Interest vs Recipients' Development Motives in Aid Allocation: Do All Donors Behave the Same?' *Review of Development Economics*, 10: 179–94.

——and A. Tichit (2004) 'Bilateral Donors' Aid Allocation Decisions: A Three-dimensional Panel Analysis'. *International Review of Economics and Finance*, 13: 253–74.

Bigsten, A., J. W. Gunning, and F. Tarp (2006) 'The Effectiveness of Foreign Aid: Overview and an Evaluation Proposal'. Mimeo. Report prepared for Sida.

Birdsall, N., D. Rodrik, and A. Subramanian (2005) 'How to Help Poor Countries'. *Foreign Affairs*, 84: 136.

Boone, P. (1994) 'The Impact of Foreign Aid on Savings and Growth'. London School of Economics CEP Working Paper 677. London: LSE.

——(2006) 'Effective Intervention, Making Aid Work'. Centre for Economic Performance Centre Piece, Winter 2005–6. London: LSE. <http://cep.lse.ac.uk/centrepiece/default.asp>.

Bourguignon, F., and M. Sundberg (2007) 'Aid Effectiveness: Opening the Black Box'. *American Economic Review*, 97: 316–21.

Burnside, C., and D. Dollar (1997) 'Aid, Policies, and Growth'. World Bank Policy Research Department Working Paper 1777. Washington, DC: World Bank.

———(2000) 'Aid, Policies, and Growth'. *American Economic Review*, 90: 847–68.

Cassen, R. (1994) *Does Aid Work?* 2nd edn. Oxford: Clarendon Press.

——and Associates (1994) *Does Aid Work?* Oxford: Clarendon Press.

Chenery, H. B., and A. M. Strout (1966) 'Foreign Assistance and Economic Development'. *American Economic Review*, 56: 679–733.

Clemens, M., S. Radelet, and R. Bhavnani (2004) 'Counting Chickens When They Hatch: The Short-term Effect of Aid on Growth'. Center for Global Development Working Paper 44. Washington, DC: CGD.

Collier, P., and D. Dollar (2001) 'Can the World Cut Poverty in Half? How Policy Reform and Effective Aid Can Meet the International Development Goals'. *World Development*, 29: 1787–802.

———(2002) 'Aid Allocation and Poverty Reduction'. *European Economic Review*, 46: 1475–500.

Commission for Africa (2005) *Our Common Interest: Report of the Commission for Africa.* <http://www.commissionforafrica.org/english/report/introduction.html>.

Cornia, G. A. (2005) 'Comments o[n] the Paper, "How to Assess the Need For Aid? The Answer: Don't Ask" by William Easterly'. <http://www.afd.fr/jahia/webdav/users/administrateur/public/eudn2005/Easterly_Cornia.pdf>.

——R. Jolly, and F. Stewart (1987) *Adjustment with a Human Face: Protecting the Vulnerable and Promoting Growth.* Oxford: Clarendon Press.

Dalgaard, C.-J., and H. Hansen (2001) 'On Aid, Growth and Good Policies'. *Journal of Development Studies*, 37: 17–41.

———(2005) 'The Return to Foreign Aid'. University of Copenhagen Institute of Economics Discussion Paper 05-04. Copenhagen: Københavns Universitet.

———and F. Tarp (2004) 'On the Empirics of Foreign Aid and Growth'. *Economic Journal*, 114: F191–F216.

Devarajan, S., D. Dollar, and T. Holmgren (eds) (2001) *Aid and Reform in Africa: Lessons from Ten Case Studies.* Oxford: Oxford University Press for the World Bank.

Dichter, T. (2005) 'Time to Stop Fooling Ourselves about Foreign Aid: A Practitioner's View'. Foreign Policy Briefing 86. Washington, DC: Cato Institute.

Duflo, E. (2004) 'Evaluating the Impact of Development Aid Programs: The Role of Randomized Evaluation'. Paper presented at the 2nd AFD-EUDN Conference Paris, 25 Nov.

Easterly, W. (1999) 'The Ghost of Financing Gap: Testing the Growth Model Used in the International Financial Institutions'. *Journal of Development Economics*, 60: 423–38.

——(2001) *The Elusive Quest for Growth.* Cambridge, Mass.: MIT Press.

——(2003) 'Can Foreign Aid Buy Growth?' *Journal of Economic Perspectives*, 17: 23–48.

——(2005) 'Reliving the 50s: The Big Push, Poverty Traps, and Take-offs in Economic Development'. Center for Global Development Working Paper 65. Washington, DC: CGD.

——(2006) *The White Man's Burden: Why the West's Efforts to Aid the Rest Have Done So Much Ill and So Little Good*. New York: Penguin Press.

——(2008) 'Can the West Save Africa?' National Bureau of Economic Research Working Paper 14363. Cambridge, Mass.: NBER.

——R. Levine, and D. Roodman (2004) 'New Data, New Doubts: A Comment on Burnside and Dollar's "Aid, Polices and Growth" [2000]'. *American Economic Review*, 94: 774–80.

The Economist (1994) 'Down the Rathole; Many Argue that Foreign Aid is a Waste of Money: They May be Right' (10 Dec.): 2.

Feyzioglu, T., V. Swaroop, and M. Zhu (1998) 'A Panel Data Analysis of the Fungibility of Foreign Aid'. *World Bank Economic Review*, 12: 29–58.

Gunning, J. W. (2005) 'Why Give Aid?' <http://www.eudnet.net/Download/AfD-EU-DN04_Gunning-revised.pdf>.

Hansen, H., and F. Tarp (2000) 'Aid Effectiveness Disputed'. *Journal of International Development*, 12: 375–98.

——————(2001) 'Aid and Growth Regressions'. *Journal of Development Economics*, 64: 547–70.

Hausman, J. (2001) 'Mismeasured Variables in Econometric Analysis: Problems from the Right and Problems from the Left'. *Journal of Economic Perspectives*, 15: 57–67.

Jones, C. I. (1995) 'Time Series Tests of Endogenous Growth Models'. *Quarterly Journal of Economics*, 110: 495–525.

Kanbur, R. (2000) 'Aid, Conditionality and Debt in Africa'. In F. Tarp (ed.), *Foreign Aid and Development: Lessons Learnt and Directions for the Future*. London and New York: Routledge.

——(2003) 'The Economics of International Aid'. Prepared for Serge Christophe-Kolm and Jean Mercier-Ythier (eds), *The Economics of Giving, Reciprocity and Altruism*. Amsterdam: North-Holland (2006).

Killick, T. (1995) 'Conditionality and the Adjustment–Development Connection'. *Pakistan Journal of Applied Economics*, 11: 17–36.

McGillivray, M. (2003) 'Modelling Foreign Aid Allocation: Issues, Approaches and Results'. *Journal of Economic Development*, 28: 171–88.

——and O. Morrissey (2004) 'Fiscal Effects of Aid'. In T. Addison and A. Roe (eds), *Fiscal Policy for Development: Poverty, Reconstruction and Growth*. Basingstoke: Palgrave Macmillan: 72–96.

Mauro, P. (1995) 'Corruption and Growth'. *Quarterly Journal of Economics*, 110: 681–712.

Mavrotas, G., and P. Nunnenkamp (2007) 'Foreign Aid Heterogeneity: Issues and Agenda'. *Review of World Economics*, 143: 585–95.

Meier, G. M. (1964) *Leading Issues in Economic Development*, 1st edn. Oxford: Oxford University Press.

——(1995) *Leading Issues in Economic Development*, 6th edn. Oxford: Oxford University Press.

——and J. E. Rauch (2000) *Leading Issues in Economic Development*, 7th edn. Oxford: Oxford University Press.

Michalopoulos, C., and V. Sukhatme (1989) 'The Impact of Development Assistance: A Review of the Quantitative Evidence'. In A. O. Krueger (ed.), *Aid and Development*. Baltimore, Md.: Johns Hopkins University Press.

Mosley, P. (1987) *Overseas Aid: Its Defence and Reform*. Brighton: Wheatsheaf Press.

——J. Harrigan, and J. Toye (1995) *Aid and Power: The World Bank and Policy Based Lending*, 2nd edn. London and New York: Routledge.

——J. Hudson, and A. Verschoor (2004) 'Aid and Poverty Reduction and the "New Conditionality"'. *Economic Journal*, 114: 217–43.

Obstfelt, M. (1999) 'Foreign Resource Inflows, Saving and Growth'. In K. Schmidt-Hebbel and L. Servén (eds), *The Economics of Savings and Growth*. Cambridge: Cambridge University Press.

OECD (2008) OECD.Stat. <http://stats.oecd.org/wbos/Index.aspx?DataSetCode=ODA_RECIPIENT_REGION>.

Papanek, G. F. (1972) 'The Effect of Aid and Other Resource Transfers on Savings and Growth in Less Developed Countries'. *Economic Journal*, 82: 934–50.

——(1973) 'Aid, Foreign Private Investment, Savings, and Growth in Less Developed Countries'. *Journal of Political Economy*, 81: 120–30.

Rajan, R. G., and A. Subramanian (2005) 'What Undermines Aid's Impact on Growth?' National Bureau of Economic Research Working Paper 11657. Cambridge, Mass.: NBER.

————(2007) 'Aid and Growth: What Does the Cross-country Evidence Really Show?' International Monetary Fund Working Paper WP/05/127. Washington, DC: IMF. <http://www.imf.org/external/pubs/ft/wp/2005/wp05127.pdf>.

Rodrik, D. (2006) 'Goodbye Washington Consensus, Hello Washington Confusion?' *Journal of Economic Literature*, 44: 973–87.

Roland-Holst, D., and F. Tarp (2004) 'New Perspectives on Aid Effectiveness'. In B. Tungodden, N. Stern, and I. Kolstad (eds), *Toward Pro-Poor Policies: Aid, Institutions and Globalization*. Oxford, New York, and Washington, DC: Oxford University Press/World Bank.

Roodman, D. (2004) 'The Anarchy of Numbers: Aid, Development, and Cross-country Empirics'. Center for Global Development Working Paper 32 (rev. May 2007). Washington, DC: CGD. <http://www.cgdev.org/content/publications/detail/2745>.

——(2007) 'Macro Aid Effectiveness Research: A Guide for the Perplexed'. Center for Global Development Working Paper 135. Washington, DC: CGD.

Rosenstein-Rodan, P. N. (1943) 'Problems of Industrialization of Eastern and South-Eastern Europe'. *Economic Journal*, 53: 202–11.

Sachs, J. D. (2005) *The End of Poverty: Economic Possibilities for Our Time*. New York: Penguin Press.

——(2006) 'Why Aid Does Work'. *BBC News*. <http://news.bbc.co.uk/1/hi/sci/tech/4210122.stm>.

Sen, A. (2006) 'The Man Without a Plan'. *Foreign Affairs*, 85: 171.

Solow, R. (2001) 'Applying Growth Theory Across Countries'. *World Bank Economic Review*, 15: 283–8.

Svensson, J. (2000) 'Foreign Aid and Rent-Seeking'. *Journal of International Economics*, 51: 437–61.

——(2003) 'Why Conditional Aid Doesn't Work and What Can Be Done About It?' *Journal of Development Economics*, 70: 381–402.

——(2005) 'Absorption Capacity and Disbursement Constraints'. European Development Research Network Conference Paper. <http://www.eudnet.net/Download/Svensson.pdf>.

Tarp (ed.) (2000) *Foreign Aid and Development: Lessons Learnt and Directions for the Future.* Routledge Studies in Development Economics 17. London: Routledge.

——(2001) 'Aid and Reform in Africa'. *Journal of African Economies*, 10: 341–53.

——(2006) 'Aid and Development'. *Swedish Economic Policy Review*, 13: 9–61.

Thorbecke, E. (2000) 'The Evolution of the Development Doctrine and the Role of Foreign Aid, 1950–2000'. *Foreign Aid and Development: Lessons Learnt and Directions for the Future.* London and New York: Routledge.

——(2007) 'The Evolution of the Development Doctrine, 1950–2005'. In G. Mavrotas and A. Shorrocks (eds), *Advancing Development: Core Themes in Global Economics.* Basingstoke: Palgrave Macmillan for UNU-WIDER.

UN Millennium Project Report (2005) *Investing in Development: A Practical Plan to Achieve the Millennium Development Goals.* New York: United Nations.

White, H. (1992) 'What Do We Know about Aid's Macroeconomic Impact? An Overview of the Aid Effectiveness Debate'. *Journal of International Development*, 4: 121–37.

Williamson, J. (1997) 'The Washington Consensus Revisited'. In L. Emmerij (ed.), *Economic and Social Development into the XXI Century.* Washington, DC: Inter-American Development Bank.

World Bank (1998) *Assessing Aid: What Works, What Doesn't, and Why.* Oxford, New York, and Washington, DC: Oxford University Press/World Bank.

——(2002) *A Case for Aid: Building a Consensus for Development Assistance.* Washington, DC: World Bank.

——(2005) *Economic Growth in the 1990s: Learning From a Decade of Reform.* Washington, DC: World Bank.

——(2007) *World Development Indicators 2007.* <http://web.worldbank.org/WBSITE/ EXTERNAL/DATASTATISTICS/0,,contentMDK:21298138~pagePK:64133150~piPK:641 33175~theSitePK:239419,00.html>.

World Economic Forum (2005) 'Global Leaders Call for Big Push on Aid to Africa at World Economic Forum Meeting in Davos'. Press release <http://www.csrwire.com/press>.

Part II

Enhancing Aid Effectiveness

3

Towards the Enhanced Effectiveness of Foreign Aid

Gustav Ranis

Until the Great Recession struck, one could notice a revival of interest in foreign aid in recent years. In the wake of the 2002 Monterrey Consensus, donors had been promising large increases, even doubling the volume they are willing to commit. Yet at the same time general scepticism about the past record of aid effectiveness has reached all-time highs. How do we reconcile this apparent paradox and what can we do to about it?

That increased interest in aid on the part of the major donors can undoubtedly be laid in large part at the doorstep of a US post-9/11 push, supported by Gordon Brown's enthusiasm for African development and by the Millennium Development Goals campaign of Kofi Annan, Jeffrey Sachs, and Bono. Although terrorists have generally been identified as educated and middle class, there is nevertheless a general agreement that countries in poverty, à la Afghanistan, Sudan, and Somalia, are more likely to provide a supportive environment. In any case, the US National Security Strategy Memorandum of 2002 was quite explicit in calling for a 50 per cent increase in aid while simultaneously admitting that 'development aid has often served to prop up failed policies'. Even the hoary Organisation for Economic Co-operation and Development (OECD) aid target of 0.7 per cent of gross national product (GNP), while not endorsed by the USA, had been dusted off. And, while actual allocations had been currently falling behind executive branch promises all around, the net result was still likely to amount to a substantial increase in rich countries' willingness to jack up resources for foreign assistance—and this at a time of severe budgetary constraints in most donor countries.

During the same period, we have witnessed a plethora of studies fundamentally questioning the effectiveness of aid in achieving the professed objectives of achieving growth and poverty alleviation in the third world. The 1980s and 1990s era of 'structural adjustment' lending, aid accompanied by conditions enshrining the so-called Washington Consensus of reforms, has by now generally been declared a failure, not only by academic critics but also by the major donors themselves. On the quantitative side of the ledger, aid has often caused a reduction in domestic taxes and private savings. Especially in sub-Saharan Africa where aid has been large, 13 per cent of gross domestic product (GDP) on average, it seems to have 'crowded out', instead of 'crowding in' private investment. On the qualitative side, the inflow of aid has frequently been associated with the appearance of the so-called 'Dutch disease'; that is, causing an undue strengthening of the exchange rate via an increase in spending on non-tradables and a decline in exportables, especially of the non-traditional, labour-intensive variety. But an even more damaging problem relates to an extended and more virulent strain of the 'Dutch disease', namely that aid may take the pressure off reforms—rather than inducing them—while enhancing a scramble for rents, high levels of corruption, and a reduction in domestic checks and balances (Auty and Mikesell 1998; and Sachs and Warner 2001; examples such as Nigeria and Venezuela abound; see also Richard M. Auty in this volume (Chapter 14) for a discussion on aid as a form of rent).

Burnside and Dollar (2000) have famously tried to dispel the overall gloom by claiming that aid still works in the presence of good domestic policies and, later, in response to critics, added the need for appropriate institutions to be in place (Burnside and Dollar 2004). But the attacks have continued to be relentless, led by Easterly (2006), but finding their most devastating crescendo in the exhaustive review of much of the cross-country econometrics literature by the International Monetary Fund's (IMF) Rajan and Subramanian (2005), concluding that aid has had a negligible and at times even negative impact on development. Among the several reasons usually given for such poor performance is the multiplicity of donors, each with their own axe to grind, the lack of nuanced country information at their disposal, the continued politicization of most aid programmes, and, most critically, the absence of more than skin-deep real ownership on the part of recipients.

There are, of course, still staunch defenders of aid, beyond such self-interested groups as aid administrators, non-governmental organizations (NGOs), and exporters. For example, Steve Radelet (2006) and others at the Center for Global Development, a Washington think-tank, have suggested that if we decompose aid and exempt from consideration both its humanitarian and long-term components, we can still find a positive impact on growth. And, of course, there is Jeffrey Sachs (2008) who argues fervently that aid can and should be usefully tripled, essentially by spending large amounts on health, education, and the like in pursuit of the Millennium Development Goals. Even Easterly, probably aid's severest critic, has no problem in still finding some merit at the micro or project level—for example, building schoolhouses or financing deworming programmes.

So, the basic question comes down to this: has bitter experience taught us that foreign aid—addressed to the recipient country as a whole and using fast-disbursing policy-based loans as an instrument—cannot work and that do-nors should be satisfied with doing lots of specific identifiable little 'good things'. That conclusion would, of course, fly in the face of a controversy presumably settled many decades ago to the effect that it makes little sense to build a better schoolhouse if educational policies inside that house continue to be misguided, or for aid to support preventive health if the recipient's budgetary allocations freed up its own resources for a shift to military hardware. It should, moreover, not be forgotten that non-project policy-based lending has on occasion proven to be a useful instrument at the macro or country level. In the 1960s and 1970s, that list would include South Korea, Taiwan, Chile, Costa Rica, and Botswana; more recently, one can cite Poland, Ireland, and Slovakia. The reasons for not finding more such exceptions probably have more to do with the advent of diminishing returns to the ritual dance of the aid process, described below, than with the intrinsic demerits of the country programme aid instrument.

To its credit, the Bush administration seemed to have recognized the need to continue to view the country as 'the project' when, in 2002, it announced the creation of the Millennium Challenge Account (MCA), intended to provide more generous assistance, but only to countries which have passed sixteen threshold objective 'good behaviour' criteria. The concept which 'offers governments the opportunity . . . to undertake transformational change by designing their own reform and development programmes' has considerable merit, but the proof of that particular pudding is still in its implementation. Unfortunately, we have already witnessed a substantial number of country 'exceptions', that is, aid to strategic friends which do not necessarily 'govern justly, invest in their people and foster economic freedom'. Shifting the Agency for International Development deeper into the Department of State under a new director of foreign assistance—while also providing 'guidance' to the MCA—was hardly the way to depoliticize foreign assistance. Obama has been too otherwise engaged to focus on aid thus far.

Other efforts have been made, including those by the international financial institutions, to rescue country-wide programming efforts from the 'structural adjustment' era debacle. High on that list is the 'poverty reduction support programme' initiative of the World Bank—with its customary mirror image at the IMF—intended to correct earlier shortcomings by enhancing the ownership dimension of country programmes. But the effort to repair some of the damage by shifting to the poverty reduction support programme system, supposedly enhancing local voices and cutting the customary sixty conditions in half, has not really made much difference. The IMF and the World Bank have issued large, detailed manuals instructing recipients how to ask and what to ask for. At a 2001 Kampala meeting, fifteen African countries agreed that the poverty reduction support programmes were simply structural adjustment loans wear-ing somewhat different clothing.

Unfortunately, fundamental defects in how the foreign aid business is trans-acted have remained. It takes a willingness to act 'out of the box' if the fundamental problem is to be addressed. Admittedly, foreign aid at the macro or country level has generally continued to follow a deteriorating and self-destructive pattern. Donors, acting individually or in a World Bank-chaired consultative group setting, usually consult with recipients, determine their resource needs, and formulate reform programmes plus aid-level-related conditions precedent set to trigger, usually tranched, fund releases. A ritual dance then ensues: early on donors insist that a large number of conditions be strictly adhered to, but recipients also know that later the need to commit and disburse will overcome all else; a judgement is then rendered that enough conditions have been 'more or less' met so that disbursement can follow, if on occasion after some delay. Success can then be declared, and next year's instalment of the ritual dance can commence. Both parties clearly have an incentive to continue to fashion such relatively superficial agreements; and, what is worse, resources which were intended to ease the pain of adjustment accompanying stipulated policy change have the very opposite effect by taking the pressure off. The result is increasing levels of cynicism and fatigue concerning the entire process as the years go by. Donor personnel recognition and promotion continue to be tied to commitments and disbursements, not results; and recipients enjoy the pursuit of additional rents and the relaxation of fiscal discipline made possible by the inflows.

Is there a way out of the paradox? In my view, fast disbursing, policy-based loans remain the chosen instrument for donors to help achieve meaningful reforms in the third world. But what is required is a basic change in how the instrument is deployed, that is, via the opening of a new assistance window. While 'business as usual' country programmes will inevitably continue—donors will always have their domestic pressures and their pet projects—the new procedure would insist on donors acting more like bankers, that is, sitting back and encouraging would-be borrowers to approach only if and when they are ready with their own, internally generated, reform initiative, complete with self-conditionality. Donors, acting with one voice—either that of the consultative group or a United Nations Development Programme (UNDP) roundtable—would, of course, not be expected to sign on the dotted line, but the entire relationship would have shifted rather fundamentally.

There could well result long fallow periods in any given developing country case, but commitments, once made, would also be dependable and sensitive to the recipient's political as well as economic constraints. Donors would have to be ready to provide aid ballooning over periods long enough to be consistent with the adjustment requirements occasioned by the reforms. Given that the profession does not have anything close to agreement on what constitutes an ideal generalizable development model, traditional donor paternalism makes little sense. Each country case will require a nuanced interpretation of what two or three policy actions are both desirable and feasible over the next few years in order to remove some binding constraints or bottlenecks—not an extensive

Washington Consensus checklist. Passivity must become the watchword for donors.

It is generally agreed that the last time foreign aid worked exceedingly well across the board was during the Marshall Plan days following the Second World War. Conditions were admittedly unusually favourable: one donor (the USA), high recipient human capability and ownership, plus peer review. The current situation is admittedly more difficult but not beyond repair. The March 2005 Paris Declaration on Aid Effectiveness made some sensible recommendations on 'ownership' but insisted that change needs to come from within the developing world rather than emphasizing the need for a complementary change in the posture of donors. As long as some 'business as usual' bilateral country programmes can continue, the 'one voice' (consultative group) manning the new window should not be impossible. The provision of real scope for local initiative in assessing both the political and economic constraints which need to be tackled can be assumed to bring out local talent which already exists but is commonly underestimated and not 'in the loop'. On the other hand, when a recipient does feel it is still not quite ready to prepare a home-grown-reform-cum-self-conditionality package it can be encouraged to seek technical assistance. But it is important that such advice be divorced from the usual lending agencies and instead be lodged in third party, self-destructing teams, preferably financed by foundations or NGOs. Peer reviews, on a regional basis, would also be helpful but are not essential at the outset. In this fashion the above-described ritual dance would be replaced by occasional serious bargaining, vetting both the economic and political dimensions of any reform package. Donors would have to commit themselves to respond and supply the new windows with sufficient resources to make aid ballooning over a multi-year period feasible. They would also have to commit themselves to restoring the credibility of the exercise by discontinuing support in the case of non-compliance with an agreed-on, if now reasonably short, self-conditionality list.

The obstacles to this proposed new way of doing business should not be underestimated. Donors may be most reluctant to reduce supporting 'their thing' and speak with one voice; the feeding and promotion of aid agency personnel, accustomed to a rewards culture tied to commitments and disbursements, will continue to be an obstacle. And donor country parliaments, as well as the international financial institutions, will have to be willing to give the new window a real chance. Certainly the new process could be counted on to disarm those on the left who claim that foreign aid is too neo-colonial and those on the right who view it as a bottomless pit.

Recipients, for their part, may cynically wonder whether the new window is really more than just another donor fad and worry about those implied fallow periods. But, when all is said and done, the only reliable way to stop a corrosive ritual dance is to change the music.

References

Auty, R. M., and Raymond Mikesell (1998) *Sustainable Development in Mineral Economies*. Oxford: Clarendon Press.

Burnside, C., and D. Dollar (2000) 'Aid, Policies, and Growth'. *American Economic Review*, 90: 847–68.

——————(2004) 'Aid, Policies, and Growth: Reply'. *American Economic Review*, 94: 781–4.

Easterly, W. (2006) *The White Man's Burden: Why the West's Efforts to Aid the Rest Have Done So Much Ill and So Little Good*. New York: Penguin Press.

Radelet, S. (2006) 'A Primer on Foreign Aid'. Center for Global Development Working Paper 92. Washington, DC: CGD.

Rajan, R. G., and A. Subramanian (2005) 'Aid and Growth: What Does the Cross-country Evidence Really Show?' International Monetary Fund Working Paper 05/127. Washington, DC: IMF.

Sachs, J. D. (2008) *Common Wealth: Economics For a Crowded Planet*. New York: Penguin Press.

——and A. Warner (2001) 'The Curse of Natural Resources'. *European Economic Review*, 45: 827–38.

United States Government (2002) *The National Security Strategy of the United States of America*. <http://www.whitehouse.gov/nsc/nss.pdf>.

4

Reconstructing the Aid Effectiveness Debate

Machiko Nissanke

4.1. Introduction[1]

In the early 1980s, there was a radical change in aid delivery structure from project aid towards policy-based programme aid. Structural adjustment programmes (SAPs) had become a favoured conduit for both multilateral and bilateral aid, with strict policy conditionalities instituted. Policy conditionality was justified on the grounds that donors should actively influence the policy and conduct of recipient countries through aid leverage. *Ex ante* conditionality, whereby foreign aid and budget supports were delivered conditional on the promises of implementation of stabilization-cum-structural reforms, had become a dominant feature in the donor–recipient relationships. As Kanbur (2005) notes, conditionality itself is nothing more than the rules and procedures according to which a donor transfers resources to a recipient. What is debated, however, is the *nature* of conditionality, in particular that of policy conditionality, which has been practised to date in one form or another.

By the mid-1990s, however, despite adding an array of political and economic conditionalities, the donor community had to face the uneasy reality: *ex ante* policy conditionality was not effective in tying the recipient governments to the reform agenda of donors (see, for example, Killick 1996, 1997; Collier 1998; Collier and Dollar 2004). This sparked off a new round in the aid effectiveness

[1] The author is grateful to Alf Morton Jerve, Yasutami Shimomura, the project team at the Japan Bank for International Co-operation JBIC, and other participants in the workshops organized by the JBIC, for stimulating discussions and suggestions on evaluating aid effectiveness of project aid to infrastructure development. Their inputs helped to sharpen the analysis summarized in sect. 4.4.2 of this chapter. The author is particularly grateful to Yasutami Shimomura for his insights into drawing policy implications from our comparative analysis. The author is also grateful to the anonymous referees for their detailed comments, additional references, and helpful suggestions. Naturally, the author takes full responsibility for any remaining errors.

debate against the background of declining public support for foreign aid in donor countries (World Bank 1998). The poor record of compliance and enforcement of policy conditionality was recognized in various evaluation reports on the World Bank's adjustment loans (World Bank 2005c).[2]

Thus, the efficacy of policy conditionality has been a central question in the aid effectiveness debate over the last decade or so. In the debate, *ex ante* policy conditionality has been examined largely from a narrow perspective of the 'moral hazard' problem; that is, the problem arising from granting foreign aid without a firm commitment on the part of recipient countries to reform programmes. Assessed from this perspective, it has been argued that policy conditionality was faulted on incorrect rationales given to adjustment lending, since an effective mechanism to deal with the moral hazard problem was absent. Collier (1998) argues, for example, that none of the three rationales for programme lending—namely the use of aid as an incentive for reform, financing the 'cost of adjustment', and 'defensive lending' to service external debt—is soundly based. Similarly, Easterly (2003) explains the failure of *ex ante* conditionality in terms of incentive systems affecting donor behaviour. He suggests that despite a continuous breach of policy conditionality by recipient governments, donor agencies have kept 'moving money' and 'pushing loans' under the constant pressure of improving their own performance indicators, assessed in terms of aid disbursements.

In recognition of the difficulty of overcoming the moral hazard problem *ex ante*, it has been proposed that the aid allocation rule should be overhauled, so that aid is allocated on an *ex post* policy performance basis. Thus, while *ex ante* conditionality is seen as 'incentives-based' aid allocation on promises for policy change, *ex post* conditionality is claimed to be 'selectivity-based' on retrospective assessments of performance. That is, instead of using conditionality to induce policy change, it is suggested that aid should be used to target financial flows on those governments that have already established good policy environments (World Bank 1998). Creating star performers by engineering aid allocation, Collier (1998) further argues, would induce non-reforming governments to change their policies through the pressures of emulation, and would result in enhanced overall aid effectiveness. It has been argued that by adopting an *ex post* selectivity approach donors can affect growth and poverty reduction more effectively through their allocation of aid and debt relief.

Further, the aid effectiveness debate has been conducted in parallel with the search for lasting debt relief measures to deal with the severe debt overhang conditions found in the heavily indebted poor countries (HIPCs). The donor community launched the HIPC Initiative in 1996 and three years later enhanced its scope and depth, as a real and durable exit option from the

---

[2] See Alesina and Dollar (2000); Burnside and Dollar (2000), and Dollar and Svensson (2000) for a summary of empirical findings.

protracted debt crisis for HIPCs.[3] Under the HIPC Initiative, the process conditionality is instituted as part of formulating the poverty-reduction strategy papers (PRSPs), which is supposed to be a recipient-driven process.[4] The debt sustainability analysis has been routinely integrated into the PRSP process and the HIPC debt relief negotiations. Finally, the comprehensive development framework, introduced in 1999 in place of structural adjustment programmes, emphasizes the importance of ownership and partnership in aid relationships. It has been heralded as a new aid architecture, where a selectivity based aid allocation is used as *ex post* policy conditionality and the debt sustainability analysis is integrated into the 'performance-based' aid allocation process.

The principal objectives of this chapter are (i) to assess the analytical and empirical basis of the selectivity-based, Country Policy and Institutional Assessment (CPIA)-centred aid allocation currently in operation and the associated debt sustainability analysis embedded therein;[5] and (ii) to present the case for fundamentally reconstructing the aid effectiveness debate by offering alternative perspectives and approaches. Towards these objectives, the chapter is structured as follows. Section 4.2 first presents the analytical basis of the CPIA-based selectivity approach and then discusses the CPIA-centred aid allocation mechanism adopted by the International Development Association (IDA) facility at the World Bank. Section 4.3 critically evaluates the CPIA rating system and empirical evidence presented for the selectivity-based, CPIA-centred aid allocation mechanism and debt-sustainability framework. In section 4.4, alternative approaches to evaluating aid effectiveness are proposed in the form of (i) the need to institute incentive-compatible state contingent aid and debt contracts to address the vulnerability of low-income countries to external shocks stemming from their dependence on commodity export earnings; and (ii) the need to adopt a distinctively institutional approach to examining the role of aid in economic development, wherein development management is seen as more *process* oriented, rather than *output* oriented. This chapter focuses more on the second approach. Hence, after briefly discussing how state-contingent aid and debt contracts could address the difficulty in overcoming the aid dependence and debt sustainability of low-income countries in the face of external shocks (section 4.4.1), it proceeds to discuss the institutional approach in more details (section 4.4.2). In particular, using

---

[3] See Addison, Hansen, and Tarp (2004) for a critical evaluation of the HIPC Initiative—in particular, chaps 3, 4, 5, and 12.

[4] Mosley, et al. (2004) propose a new conditionality to tie aid specifically to poverty reduction in the form of the pro-poor expenditure PPE index in the PRSP process.

[5] CPIA stands for Country Policy and Institutional Assessment. It is a scoring matrix used by the World Bank to assess country policy and institutions of developing countries for aid allocation. See sects. 4.2 and 4.3.1 below for more details on how the CPIA is constructed and used. See also Gibson et al. (2005) and Haut (2007: chap. 2) for similarly critical discussions on this question and related topics.

the case studies of aid-financed infrastructure development projects, it illustrates how this approach could be used for examining aid effectiveness in a broader context of institutional development of recipient countries. Section 4.5 offers concluding remarks, where I emphasize the need to shift the aid effectiveness debate away from the conventional perspectives of viewing aid as leverage for donor-inspired policy and institutional reforms, where *ex ante* or *ex post* policy conditionality prevails and 'marketing' institutional models deemed appropriate by donors becomes a dominant feature of aid relationships.

4.2. The CPIA-based selectivity approach to aid allocation as *ex post* policy conditionality[6]

4.2.1. Analytical rationales for the selectivity approach to aid allocation

Donor–recipient aid relationships are usually examined in the principal–agent theoretical model wherein recipients are agents implementing the conditions desired by donors; that is, the principals (Killick 1996, 1997). Conditionality is then the means of using leverage accorded by 'aid giving' to promote donor objectives. As such, it can be administered in a cooperative manner between the principals and the agents (Killick 1996). However, in reality, there are conflicts and congruence between the objectives and interests of donors and recipients. In particular, it is often assumed that donors have altruistic preferences (for example, caring about the voiceless poor), whereas recipient governments are typically constrained in pursuing such objectives by domestic political economy considerations. Furthermore, it is admitted that in aid relations characterized by asymmetric powers, conditions are more likely to be drafted and imposed by donors and accepted, often unwillingly, by recipients.[7] As a consequence, it is this *coercive* nature of policy conditionality which has largely shaped donor–recipient relationships over the recent decades. This can be best illustrated in the 'languages' used to analyse the multiple roles of policy conditionality in the aid relationships. For example, Collier and Gunning (1996) classify the objectives of policy conditionality into four categories:

(i) paternalism, where donors believe they know what is best for the recipient;
(ii) bribery, when donors persuade recipients to implement reforms that are otherwise not undertaken;

---

[6] Sects. 4.2 and 4.3 draw in a large part on the analysis and discussion presented in Nissanke (2008).

[7] White and Morrissey (1997) suggest that (i) it should not be assumed that recipients are necessarily unwilling to reform; (ii) where recipients are willing, conditionality can be counterproductive; and (iii) if recipients are unwilling, donors can only exert leverage, since the threat to withhold aid is credible only when donors are actually ready to cut aid. See the text below for further discussion on this issue.

(iii) restraints, when donors place conditions to prevent the recipient from policy reversal on reforms;

(iv) signalling to the private sector and other donors that the reform programme is sincere.

From a similar perspective, the World Bank (2005c) discusses rationales for conditionality in terms of:

(i) compensation by the donor to the recipient government for adopting the policies preferred by the former, when each party has different beliefs on the appropriateness of the policy;

(ii) restraint/counterbalance device for the government in the face of domestic opposition to policy reforms; and

(iii) signalling of commitments to reforms to potential private investors.

Using the principal–agent framework, Killick (1996, 1997) explains the inherent tension engendered by policy conditionality in aid relationships in terms of: the asymmetrical burden of risks between donors and recipient governments; the high short-term economic and political costs associated with reform measures compared with slowly emerging benefits; and the high monitoring and enforcement costs. In particular, he notes that the involuntary nature of policy conditionality undermines the legitimacy of reforms. Thus, when reform measures are not home-grown, recipient governments try to evade commitments and regress when the opportunity arises, as they are supposed to bear political risks and adjustment costs. Yet, the incentive structures to monitor and enforce aid contracts are weak when the donor agencies are prone to a 'pro-lending' ethos, and hence donor commitment to enforce conditionality and sanctions is not seen as credible. Killick concludes that '(ex ante) conditionality does not meet its promise of greater aid effectiveness . . . A further cost is that conditionality distorts the nature of the discourse between the donors and developing country governments' (1997: 493). He suggests that a new model of donor–recipient relationships should be based on 'selectivity' along with other principles such as ownership, support, and dialogue.

In evaluating the efficacy of conditionality when donor and recipient preferences for policy reform and aid vary, White and Morrissey (1997) also show that *ex ante* conditionality tends to create conflicts between donors and recipients even when recipient governments are sincere about economic reforms. They conclude that conditionality is neither an effective mechanism to induce reform on unwilling governments nor an appropriate mechanism for genuine reformers. They suggest that the switch to *ex post* conditionality could reduce such conflicts, if it is solely based on performance measures that are truly independent of external shocks or unavoidable implementation problems that are beyond the control of recipient governments.

Consequently, the new aid architecture, as emerging today from the aid effectiveness debate, has adopted the *selectivity* rule as a guiding principle for aid allocation. However, it is well-known that the analytical and empirical basis for the selectivity approach rests almost entirely on cross-country regression results of the growth–aid relationship, such as the study by Burnside and Dollar (1997 and 2000). They draw a very strong policy conclusion from the significant positive coefficient on the policy–aid interaction term in their cross-country regressions. According to these authors, while aid generally does not have any significant effect on the rate of economic growth or investment, the growth-enhancing effect of aid can be found only in a *good policy* environment.[8] These empirical studies have been severely challenged on technical grounds. For example, Easterly, Levine, and Roodman (2003) argue that the regression results obtained by Burnside and Dollar are not robust as they are extremely sensitive to how the included key variables such as aid, policy, and growth are defined and measured. Dalgaard and Hansen (2001) question the theoretical underpinning of the Burnside–Dollar study as well as the sensitivity of their econometric results to the data samples. Guillaumont and Chauvet (2001) argue that aid is most effective when it is available to countries disadvantaged by large external shocks and climatic conditions. Their cross-country pooled regressions show that the external environment factor rather than the policy environment is a determining factor in improving aid effectiveness.

Hansen and Tarp (2000, 2001) further challenge the validity of the empirical analysis by Burnside and Dollar, comparing their results with a large number of past and current empirical studies on the aid–growth relationships. They conclude that the difference between the results obtained by Burnside and Dollar and others stems mostly from the model specification and other technical issues.[9] Hence, they caution strongly against basing aid allocation rules on the single-cause explanations. Wangwe (2003), assessing the three criteria adopted by Burnside and Dollar for defining good policies, that is, budget surplus, inflation, and openness, concludes that they are too narrow.

In recognition that the policy-performance indicators used in the original Burnside–Dollar study are too limited, the World Bank subsequently presented

---

[8] They also found that aid is subject to diminishing marginal returns. While Lensink and White (2001) agree on the existence of such an aid-Laffer curve, they suggest that this is due to the limited absorption capacity of recipient countries in using aid productively, and that the threshold level above which aid starts having a negative effect on growth in the Laffer curve is about 50 per cent of the aid/GDP ratio, much higher than the level suggested by Collier and Dollar (2001, 2002).

[9] See also Hudson (2004) and Morrissey (2004) for discussions on econometric issues arising from the differences in model specification, sample size, and estimation methods adopted in these studies.

a more comprehensive matrix—the Country Policy and Institutional Assessment—for assessing and ranking countries according to their institutional and policy environment for long-term growth and poverty reduction. Using the CPIA as a screening device, further studies by Collier and Dollar (2001, 2002, 2004) reiterate the earlier claims by Burnside and Dollar that aid and policy can interact in such a positive manner for economic growth that 'aid enhances the growth effect of policy and good policy increases the growth effect of aid' (Collier and Dollar 2001: 1788).

Acknowledging that aid is used by donors for objectives other than accelerating economic growth, Collier and Dollar (2001, 2002) extend their analysis to arrive at a poverty-efficient allocation of aid as a benchmark for assessing the performance of actual allocation in terms of achieving the poverty reduction objective.[10] On the basis of similar cross-country regressions, they advocate that aid should be given to countries with 'good' policy while allowing for the differences in the incidence of poverty to arrive at a poverty-efficient allocation as close as possible within the aid-policy configuration. The technical basis of their cross-country regression results on the aid–growth-policy trajectory remains rather fragile and unconvincing as the basic thrust of their econometric exercises is the same as the original Burnside–Dollar study. Further, the use of the CPIA index can be objected to on several technical grounds, including its endogeneity to the growth process, as discussed below.[11]

Despite these criticisms, the selectivity rule had a strong appeal for the donor community as an effective instrument to overcome the moral hazard problems in dealing with recipient governments. In particular, their poverty-efficient aid allocation proposal has indeed become influential in the policy debate on the feasibility of achieving the Millennium Development Goals (MDGs), where poverty reduction is singled out as the most important objective of giving aid and publicized as such in order to mobilize public support for securing aid budgets in donor countries.[12] On the basis of their simulation analysis, it is claimed that the MDG target in poverty reduction is more likely to be met by a combination of more efficient aid allocation, policy reform, and more generous aid. Their estimates proclaim, for example, that the proposed poverty-efficient aid allocation would reduce the number of poor people by an extra 18 million

---

[10] A poverty-efficient allocation of aid is defined as one in which the marginal cost of poverty reduction is equalized across recipient countries. Collier and Dollar (2004) discuss aid-allocation rules for achieving other donor objectives such as a *security-efficient* allocation.

[11] Dalgaard et al (2004) suggest using instruments such as 'the fraction of land in tropics' for the CPIA index for the regression analysis so that the endogeneity problem of the CPIA index is dealt with. See also Tarp (Chap. 2 in this volume) and the discussion below for further critical issues on the construction of the CPIA index.

[12] Their proposal was, for example, used as a guide in US aid allocation of the Millennium Challenge Account (Collier and Dollar 2004).

per year compared with what can be achieved by poverty reduction under the allocation practiced hitherto.

4.2.2. The CPIA-based aid allocation system

These optimistic predictions have provided the donor community with a basis of adopting the CPIA-based allocation for IDA loan disbursement and HIPC debt relief as its performance-based allocation system (PBA) at the World Bank since 2002 (IDA-13, IDA-14, IDA-15) (IDA 2004, 2007). The PBA now uses the CPIA comprising of sixteen criteria grouped in four equally weighted clusters: (i) economic management; (ii) structural policies; (iii) policies for social inclusion and equity; and (iv) public sector management and institutions, as shown in Table 4.1.

In IDA-14, the country performance ratings (CPR) is arrived at by first constructing the composite index, wherein the CPIA is given 80 per cent weight with 20 per cent weight allocated to the portfolio performance ratings (PORT). The latter is derived from the Bank's Annual Review of Portfolio Performance (ARPP) for reflecting the percentage of IDA-funded project at risk in a country. The composite index is further moderated by a governance factor (*GOV*), which is made up of six criteria: five are drawn from Cluster D of the CPIA rating (measuring public sector management and institutions as shown in Table 4.1 and one from the ARPP (World Bank

Table 4.1. 2004 criteria included in CPIA

A. Economic management
   Macroeconomic management
   Fiscal policy
   Debt policy
B. Structural policies
   Trade
   Financial sector
   Business regulatory environment
C. Policies for social inclusion/equity
   Gender equality
   Equity of public resource use
   Building human resources
   Social protection and labour
   Policies and institutions for environmental sustainability
D. Public sector management and institutions
   Property rights and rule-based governance
   Quality of budgetary and financial management
   Efficiency of revenue mobilization
   Quality of public administration
   Transparency, accountability, and corruption in the public sector

Source: World Bank (2005a: box 2, annex 1).

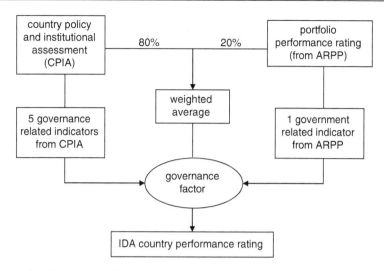

Figure 4.1 IDA country performance rating

Source: IDA (2007a: chart 1).

2005a; IDA 2007a)).[13] Thus, the process of determining CPR is illustrated in the Bank's documentation as Figure 4.1.

The actual formula used to determine CPR in IDA-14 is:

Country performance rating $= (0.8 * \text{CPIA} + 0.2 * \text{PORT}) *(\text{Gov}/3.5)^{1.5}$

The governance rating is divided by 3.5, which is the midpoint of the CPIA scale, and then raised to an exponent of 1.5. This means that for governance scores above 3.5 the rating is increased, while for scores below 3.5 it is decreased. Finally, IDA annual allocation received by each country is determined according to the following formula:

IDA Country allocation per annum = base allocation +
f (Country performance rating$^{2.0}$, Population$^{1.0}$, GNI/capita$^{-0.125}$)

Thus, in IDA-14, IDA country allocation, addition to the base allocation of SDR 1.1 million per annum to all IDA-eligible countries, is a function of CPR as defined above, the population size, and a country's needs reflected in per capita gross national income (GNI).[14] Clearly, these mechanisms and formulas make

---

[13] The CPIA, portfolio performance ratings, and governance factor were publicly disclosed only in 2007.

[14] Only in exceptional circumstances is the performance-based country allocation adjusted in light of countries' access to alternative financial sources or their emergence from conflict or severe natural disaster.

the CPIA the dominant factor in the IDA allocation, while variables such as population (*POP*) and gross national income per capita (*GNIPC*) are merely a moderating factor. This is confirmed by the World Bank, stating that 'there is a modest bias in favour of the IDA eligible countries with a lower GNI per capita' (World Bank 2005a: annex 4). Thus, as Kanbur (2005: 5) notes, 'the performance rating has a much higher weight than the measure of the need' where 'the need' is captured by the income criterion. In short, 'aid productivity' is given precedent over the 'need' in the donor's impact analysis (ibid.: 11). Similar 'rule-based' methods are adopted for allocating highly concessional resources at both the Asian Development Bank and African Development Bank (IDA 2007a).[15]

Furthermore, the debt sustainability analysis (DSA) conducted in parallel within the debt sustainability framework (DSF) is embedded in the current IDA facility, and it is used to determine the outright grant component with an upfront reduction of 20 per cent in overall IDA allocation to a country.[16] To assess debt sustainability, debt burden indicators, calculated in the net present value (NPV) of debt obligations, are compared to indicative thresholds over a twenty-year projection period (IMF-IDA 2004). Based on a few empirical analyses carried out by economists at the World Bank and the International Monetary Fund such as Kraay and Nehru 2004 and IMF-IDA 2004, the DSAs are then conducted regularly to assess the risk of debt distress, judged by indicative debt burden thresholds that are determined by the CPIA rating.

That is, the DSF classifies countries into one of three policy performance categories (strong, medium, and weak) according to the CPIA rating and uses different indicative thresholds for debt burdens for each category as shown in Table 4.2. It is assumed that countries with weak policies and institutions (that is, with a low CPIA rating) would face a repayment problem at the lower level of debt burden than countries with a higher CPIA rating (IMF-IDA 2005).

Finally, countries are classified into three categories—low risk, medium risk, and high risk of having debt distress—depending on actual and estimated debt burden in relation to indicative thresholds. This classification is used annually in the IDA allocation to determine the grant component: countries with high risk would get 100 per cent of aid in grants, those with medium risk would have

---

[15] The formulae adopted by the Asian Development Bank and the African Development Bank give slightly different weights to each variable in arriving at the volume of final allocation. It may be worth noting that the Asian Development Fund gives twice as much weight to the 'needs' variable than that adopted in the IDA allocation, whereas the African Development Fund adjusts the performance rating by the post-conflict enhancement factor (IDA 2007a).

[16] In contrast to the debt sustainability analysis carried out under the HIPC initiative which used backward-looking three-year averages, the new DSF is seen as a forward-looking analysis with its focus on the future path of relevant debt-burden indicators. It has been presented as (i) an analytical tool to assess potential debt-related vulnerabilities; and (ii) an operational tool that helps design a borrowing/leaning path by sovereign borrowers as well as by lending institutions and creditor governments (IMF 2005).

Table 4.2. Debt-burden thresholds under the DSF

	Net present value of debt as percentage of			Debt service as percentage of	
	Exports	Gross domestic product	Revenue	Exports	Revenue
Weak policy (CPIA < 3.25)	100	30	200	15	25
Medium policy 3.25 < CPIA < 3.75	150	40	250	20	30
Strong policy (CPIA > 3.75)	200	50	300	25	35

Source: World Bank and IMF websites.

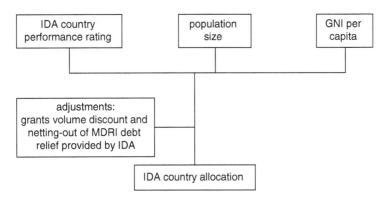

Figure 4.2 IDA country allocation

Source: IDA (2007a).

50 per cent in loans and 50 per cent in grants, and those with low risk would receive IDA 100 per cent in loans. The IDA allocation is also adjusted by netting out the Multilateral Debt Relief Initiative (MDRI). Hence, the overall current system used for IDA country allocation can be illustrated as in Figure 4.2 (IDA 2007). It should be noted that with a 20 per cent upfront reduction applied on the grant component, justified in terms of the need to address the resulting incentive problem, this allocation method actually severely penalizes countries with a lower CPIA rating, which are doomed to be high risks.

The strong bias towards the performance-based allocation noted above has been further intensified in the process of simplification of the formula at the Mid-Term Review of IDA-14 with the stated aim of reducing the volatility for IDA-15 (IDA 2007a, 2007b). After much discussion, the new formula adopted for IDA-15 is:

Country performance rating $= (0.24 * \text{CPIA}_{\text{A-C}} + 0.68 * \text{CPIA}_{\text{D}} + 0.08 * \text{PORT})$
IDA Country allocation $= f$ (Country performance rating$^{5.0}$, Population$^{1.0}$, GNI/capita$^{-0.125}$)

As evident in this new formula, the exponent applied to the CPIA dominant performance rating is raised from the value of 2 to that of 5 for IDA-15, signifying the much increased weight given to the performance rating measured in CPIA compared with the 'needs' variables (IDA 2007b).[17]

4.3. Critical appraisal of the selectivity approach as *ex post* policy conditionality

4.3.1. A critical review of the CPIA

In assessing the selectivity aid allocation rule, based so much on one index, the CPIA, it is critical to examine first how the CPIA itself is constructed, in relation to a more fundamental question as to who defines (and how to define) good policies for country-specific conditions. At the outset, it is important to note that the CPIA is not an *objective* measure of the quality of policies and institutions, but a set of *subjective* scores (1–6 rating scores) by Bank staff, based on questionnaires organized with country teams at the World Bank (World Bank 2005b).

Furthermore, the CPIA is constructed in terms of mixed-score parameters: while some parameters rank policy choices and institutional quality, others reflect outcomes or, more often, both outcomes and policy choices. Hence, the World Bank's assertion that policies and institutional arrangements assessed through the questionnaires can be classified as *input*, which are within the country's control, as opposed to *outcome* (for example, the growth rate), which is influenced by elements beyond the country's control, should be seriously questioned. In reality, such a separation is often fictitious, as is apparent on closer inspection of score guidelines listed under each of the CPIA categories (World Bank 2005d).

Many indicators can be seen as reflecting outcomes influenced by exogenous events. For example, the ability of governments to pursue aggregate demand policy or fiscal policy, consistent with price stability and achieving external and internal balances, is often undermined in the face of large external shocks typically facing fragile low-income countries. The aptitude of governments in providing public goods depends also on their revenue-raising capacity which, in turn, is affected by exogenous events outside their control. Thus, what is assessed is often endogenous to growth, contrary to the claim that the criteria

---

[17] There are a few exceptions that IDA-15 makes in applying the formula for IDA allocation (IDA 2007b).

used in the CPIA are 'in principle independent of growth outcomes' (Collier and Dollar 2004: F255). At the same time, some scores are distinctly related to policy choice variables, as illustrated in rating score under trade policy, which is based mostly (75 per cent) on the 'trade restrictiveness' measured in terms of tariff and non-tariff barriers deployed.

While many of the criteria used are not necessarily controversial in their own terms (for example, those listed under policies for social inclusion/equity), it should also be recognized that the quality of institutions and the implemental capacity for socio-economic policies, evaluated under the CPIA, are often a reflection of structural characteristics of low-income economies. Hence, they should be treated as a manifestation of their stage and level of economic development rather than that of societal subjective preferences or simple choice parameters of recipient governments. These structural characteristics should evolve and change as development proceeds. For example, all three dimensions listed as criteria upon which financial sector policy is assessed (financial stability; the sector's efficiency, depth, and resource mobilization strength; and access to financial services) are a function of the level and stage of economic development. The financial sector develops in tandem with real sector activities as demand and supply for financial services interact dynamically over time (Nissanke and Aryeetey 1998; Nissanke 2004).

Thus, the CPIA-based aid allocation formula cannot be seen as a fair rule, since it gives a common scoring for all countries with the equal weighting of the different factors, irrespective of the level of development and structural characteristics of each country.[18] Indeed, a closer evaluation of the criteria listed in the CPIA reveals that these scores overlap largely with those included in the extended policy conditionality list that the recipient governments had to comply with in return for aid disbursements under the SAPs. The nature of policy conditionality remains largely intact. What has changed is the method of aid allocation mechanisms from *ex ante* conditionality to performance-based *ex post* conditionality. This is not surprising, since the CPIA is based on the premise that 'the broad thrust of World Bank policy advice over the last two decades has been correct' (Collier and Dollar 2004: F246).

While concepts such as ownership and partnership or dialogue are recognized and promoted as an important dimension for success in producing the desired development outcomes through aid delivery, the selectivity rule- and performance-based aid allocation, as practised today, is still an imposition of one particular development model by the donor community on recipient countries as an uniquely appropriate, universal model to be adopted by all countries. From this perspective, the CPIA cannot be treated as truly

---

[18] With reference to his criticism of the CPIA, Kanbur (2005) also remarks that a common scoring for all countries is justified only if we endorse the assumption of 'a common development model for all countries', postulated in a cross-country 'average relationship'.

performance-based parameters measured in terms of choices of policies and institutions leading to desired development outcomes, as claimed. It is instead a matrix contaminated with 'intermediate variables' that measure the extent to which a recipient accepts policy choice parameters seen as desirable by donors (Kanbur 2005).

Consequently, the aid relationships emerging under the 'new aid architecture' are far from ideal for making incentive structures efficient for either donors or recipient governments. Nor are they conducive to forging a genuine partnership between donors and recipients in their common efforts to build local institutions and capabilities to overcome the technical and financial constraints to sustainable development in light of locally prevailing conditions and characteristics; that is, in a country-specific context.

4.3.2. A critical review of empirical evidence used for the selectivity approach

While the empirical studies on aid effectiveness reviewed above had a very strong and direct effect on policymaking and actual aid allocation mechanisms adopted by multilateral and bilateral donors, their analytical weaknesses have subsequently been exposed.[19] Bourguignon and Sundberg (2007) attribute this weakness to the treatment of the complex causality chain linking external aid to final outcomes as the 'black box' in these cross-country regressions, as well as to the heterogeneity of aid motives, and the limitations of the tools of analysis. They argue the need for disentangling the causality chain inside the black box as a first step towards gaining a deeper understanding of the impact of aid on economic development. As shown in Figure 4.3, they identify three types of links in the black box: (i) policies to outcomes (knowledge); (ii) policymakers to policies (governance and institutional capacity); and (iii) donors to policymakers (financial resources, technical assistance, and aid policy conditionality). Such detailed analyses of the causality chain cannot be effectively conducted through simple reduced-form cross-country regressions at the aggregate level, which have been a popular analytical tool in empirical research on aid effectiveness.

Indeed, as discussed in section 4.2.1 above, the empirical basis used to rationalize the current performance-based selectivity approach to aid allocation as *ex post* conditionality is extremely thin. The methodological flaws found in these cross-country regression studies are so fundamentally flawed that the World Bank's flagship publication *Assessing Aid: What Works, What Doesn't, and Why* (1998), based on their empirical regression analyses, is singled out as one of the bank's most problematic research publications in the 'Deaton

---

[19] It is known that CPIA and PBA have been used explicitly in the Dutch aid allocation (see Hout 2007) and in US aid allocation of the Millennium Challenge Account. However, it is to be noted that the CPIA is not used as a driver in aid allocation by all bilateral donors but rather as useful background information.

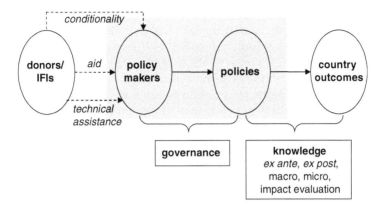

Figure 4.3 The causality chain: inside the black box

Source: Bourguignon and Sundberg (2007: fig. 1).

Report', an influential evaluation report of World Bank research for 1998–2005, conducted by a group of independent academics (Deaton et al. 2006). The Deaton Report refers to the empirical results in the papers by Burnside and Dollar (1997, 2000) as unconvincing at best. It also points out the similar methodological weakness in the subsequent papers by Collier and Dollar (2001, 2002, 2004) which were heavily used to build the Bank's case for aid, resting on the claim that external aid works for economic development, only contingent upon a set of 'good policies'.

Thus, in relation to the cross-country evidence reported in these research papers, the Deaton Report points out many problems that are inherent in trying to use the cross-country evidence to make solid inference about the effectiveness of aid. Warning against the practice of selectively using the empirical evidence to support an advocacy position, the Report assesses that 'much of this line of research appears to have such deep flaws that, at present, the result cannot be regarded as remotely reliable, much as one might want to believe' (World Bank 1998: 53). It criticizes the Bank for its failure 'in the checks and balances within the system that has led to Bank to repeatedly trumpet these early results without recognizing their fragile and tentative nature'. It warns that 'it is very unclear empirically where the line can be drawn, or which policies matter, and in our view, the jury is very much still out on any quantitative assessment of the issue' (ibid.). Indeed, several recent studies such as that of Rajan and Subramanian (2005), which use a similar cross-country regression but with a more-refined and advanced econometric technique, show that the empirical evidence reported in the earlier Bank studies is not robust and cannot be validated.

A similar set of technical problems are also inherent in the empirical studies carried out by Kraay and Nehru (2004) and IMF-IDA (2004) in support of the debt sustainability framework and analysis reviewed in section 4.2. In particular, a critical issue arises as to the way the results of empirical studies on debt distress are actually used in the debt-sustainability analysis, and then in the aid-allocation mechanism. As discussed by Cohen et al. (2008), simulation exercises on debt distress similar to the Kraay and Nehru study show that the likelihood of a debt crisis in low-income countries is indeed triggered by external shocks such as negative price shocks to earnings from exports of primary commodities as much as (if not more than) the governance index developed by Kaufmann, Kraay, and Mastruzzi (2005).[20] These findings shed serious doubts on the central position assigned to the CPIA rating in the debt sustainability analysis and framework reviewed above.[21]

4.4. Alternative approaches to understanding aid effectiveness

4.4.1. The case for contingent facilities as incentive-compatible contracts

The failure of the current framework to assign a more central role to vulnerability to shocks in guiding both the aid allocation and debt sustainability process remains largely unjustified. While the commodity issues were not featured in the early debate on the causes for the debt crisis affecting commodity-dependent low-income countries,[22] there is by now almost unanimous agreement—including at the World Bank and IMF—that vulnerability to external shocks represents a major factor behind the low-income country debt crisis and the renewed accumulation of unsustainable external debt stocks despite the HIPC Initiative. Demonstrating the depth of the commodity crisis in the 1980s, Maizels (1992) convincingly reveals how the beginning of the debt crisis of poor countries in the late 1970s coincided exactly with that of the 'conveniently forgotten' commodity crisis.

Drawing on Maizels' empirical research and Krugman's (1988) classical analysis on debt overhang and forgiveness, it was previously argued that a *state-contingent* debt contract is required as an *ex ante* debt relief mechanism to deal with the debt crises facing commodity-dependent, low-income countries (Nissanke and Ferrarini 2004). This is because the state-contingent schemes could make a distinction between the consequences of a debtor's own efforts and events beyond its control. Such a contract can specify their contractual

---

[20] The governance index developed by Kaufmann, Kraay, and Mastruzzi (2005) is used as a substitute for the CPIA index which was not publicly available till recently. The index covers six dimensions of governance: voice and accountability; political stability and the absence of major violence and terror; government effectiveness; regulatory quality; rule of law; and control of corruption. However, Kaufman (2005) warns of using it mechanically for ranking countries, as margins of error are not trivial and caution is required in interpreting the results.

[21] See Nissanke and Ferrarini (2007) for further critical discussion on the debt sustainability framework incorporated into aid allocation.

[22] See Nissanke and Ferrarini (2004) for detailed discussion.

obligations contingent on the nature of states, and hence deal explicitly and effectively with the uncertainty associated with exogenous shocks and systemic risks that are present in any inter-temporal financial transaction. For example, as Krugman (1988) notes, the trade-off between debt forgiveness and financing in a typical negotiation can be improved by indexing repayment to the 'state of nature', which can be verifiable. I argue that the currently dominant selectivity approach to aid allocation fails to offer incentive-compatible, *state-contingent* aid contracts which would allow an automatic access to contingency financing when recipient countries are hit by adverse unforeseen events. It is critically important to establish genuinely flexible, state-contingent aid and debt contracts in order to align incentives of borrowers/recipients and lenders/donors.

Cohen, Jacquet, and Reisen (2005) also argue that subsidized contingent loans are superior to outright grants in financing productive investment in countries facing high vulnerability to external shocks such as natural resource price volatility. They show that debt and debt cancellations are two complementary instruments which, if properly managed, perform better than either loans or grants taken in isolation. Taking these arguments further, Cohen, et al. (2008) proposes a new contingent facility: the countercyclical loan (CCL). The CCL facility is assigned to transform the grace period of a typical concessional loan into a fixed initial grace period and a floating grace period, which the country can draw upon when a negative shock occurs. More concretely, they propose to reduce the grace period of a typical concessional loan from ten to five years and to keep the remaining grace periods as an asset that the country can draw upon when a negative shock takes place, where the negative shock is defined as an export shock, whereby current exports fall below a moving average of the past five years.

By indexing the contingency facility to the debtor's capacity to pay, rather than to a verifiable state of nature, the CCL may not completely eschew the potential 'incentive' problem. However, it plentifully demonstrates that any technical issues associated with creating an 'efficient' contingent facility can be overcome if a strong political commitment to such a facility exists. Yet, despite advances in the quest for a technically feasible contingency facility, donors have failed so far to show sufficient interest in devising an effective mechanism of protecting vulnerable countries against the negative impacts from external shocks on economic growth and debt sustainability. Insofar as vulnerability to shocks represents a key determinant of debt distress, any DSF that does not effectively translate vulnerability assessments into appropriate policy responses in terms of volume and timing of aid is bound to fail in providing a lasting solution to debt distress of low-income countries.

As discussed above, neither the CPIA-based aid allocation rule nor the CPIA-based debt-sustainability framework currently adopted satisfy the conditions required for making aid really effective and debt truly sustainable, or for improving donor–recipient relationships. The CPIA is not a truly performance-based, outcome-centred assessment. In reality, the selectivity applies at least partly on the basis of the policies implemented that donors deem appropriate. The CPIA-based selection in aid allocation and debt relief is at best an 'eclectic mix' of outcome-based selectivity and policy conditionality. Yet, the present system is seen and promoted as 'programmatic policy-based lending offering a particularly promising way to reconcile the debate between the traditional *ex ante* approach and the aspirations of a results-based approach to conditionality' (World Bank 2005c: 20).

In reality, the current system of aid allocation and debt sustainability framework leaves many critical issues unresolved. First, policy-related selectivity criteria continue to be set by donors. This mechanism would surely undermine the 'ownership' of policies and reform programmes, as recipient governments in the need of foreign aid and debt relief would have strong incentives to opt for policies prescribed by donors rather than alternative policies they might have chosen otherwise. Second, the mechanical 'programmatic' application of the selectivity rule is problematic, since the relationships between the quality of policies and institutions on the one hand, and developmental outcomes on the other, are much more tenuous in a short-term framework than implicitly assumed under the current framework. It often takes considerable lead time for changes in policies and institutions to produce tangible results in development indicators, including poverty indicators. Third, the performance-based system could heavily penalize fragile low-income countries which are more exposed to exogenous shocks, since their performance is more likely to be influenced by many factors beyond the control of governments, such as terms of trade shocks or climate-related conditions.

In fact, in the absence of efficient state-contingent contracts, and without due attention to critical unresolved issues in the performance-based system, the aid relationships that have emerged under the selectivity rule are still predominantly characterized by donors taking a very short-leash approach with intensive monitoring. Aid is disbursed in small tranches with the use of performance indicators as a monitoring device to measure progress. For example, the European Union (EU) adopted performance-based conditionality (at least partially) in twenty-eight budgetary aid programmes in 2001 and introduced a 'variable financing tranche' as a part of financing conventions with African, Caribbean, and Pacific (ACP) countries (Adam et al. 2004). These authors observe that while this mode may have promoted a 'culture of results' it has not succeeded in shifting responsibility for policy formulation to recipient countries (ibid.).

In a more detailed study of Uganda, where foreign aid has financed about a half of government expenditure over the recent decade, Adam and Gunning (2002) argue that the use of sector-specific detailed performance indicators, chosen jointly by the government and the EU, has changed donor–recipient relations with beneficial effect. However, they note several difficulties encountered, not only in deciding on genuine outcome indicators and verifying them but also in dealing with the tension between the monitoring and incentive functions of performance indicators. In the end, the donors had to rely on short-run critical process undertaking, and to lock into micro-management based around a large number of input or process indicators which were discredited under traditional *ex ante* conditionality. This inevitably undermined genuine programme ownership and narrowed the space for effective policy debate. Furthermore, it is clearly acknowledged that the weak and uncertain link between inputs (that is, efforts undertaken by a recipient) and outcome indicators, upon which aid disbursement is based, makes it difficult for incentive structures to work in aid contracts.

There is clearly a critical gap between the rhetoric and the practice under the new aid architecture.[23] The performance-based aid disbursements requiring close monitoring on the part of donors could easily result in a high volatility in aid flows and severe disruptions to the development process in low-income recipient countries, whose aid dependence is overwhelming. Despite the claim that greater ownership and partnership have been achieved under the new aid architecture, donor–recipient relationships are still built on shaky ground, where recipient governments and donors tend to position themselves in an 'aid power game', which could result in an inferior non-cooperative equilibrium.

In this context, certain presumptions incorporated in the principal–agent framework should be critically re-evaluated in its application to the analysis of aid relationships. For example, recipient governments are often assumed to change their behaviour only in order to get more aid in future, as if they do not have a stake in enhancing the welfare of their domestic agents. It is not unusual to start discussions with the assumption that donors are always benevolent, and development-minded, acting on pure altruism, while recipient governments are seen as untrustworthy towards the international agencies as well as predatory towards domestic agents, using redistributional fiscal instruments largely for political and personal gains. This assumption is not only too restrictive for the model to be of general use as an analytical tool, but also not reflective of the reality in which aid relationships should be contextualized: much wider, more complex international political and economic relations.[24] It is true that some recipient governments with politically narrow-based regimes may well behave in a predatory manner towards domestic agents. However, this would not justify the assumption that *all* recipient governments can be characterized by such attributes.

To make aid work for development, it is imperative to depart radically from the use of such a misrepresentative, rather one-sided, analytical framework to model donor–recipient relationships. Indeed, as discussed above, there is an

---

[23] See Gibson et al. (2005) for a similar criticism on the new aid architecture.
[24] See Maizels and Nissanke (1984), among others, for discussion on donors' motivation for giving aid.

urgent need to make aid and debt contract incentives compatible by providing a contingent financing facility to low-income countries which are often susceptible to large exogenous shocks. The recent debate on grants-versus-loans has been triggered by the desire on the part of some donors to eliminate the recurrent problems of debt overhang by providing official development assistance (ODA) in outright grants only.[25] However, as Cohen, Jacquet, and Reisen (2005) note, such a debate becomes somewhat misleading and largely irrelevant if the key issues of maintaining debt sustainability of these low-income countries can be properly addressed.

4.4.2. Aid effectiveness contingent on donor–recipient relationships and their impact on recipient capacity and institutions

As the academic debate on aid effectiveness and conditionality has evolved and unfolded, the need for forging effective partnerships between the donor community and the government and civil society of recipient countries has also increasingly been recognized as one of the conditions for increasing aid effectiveness and the ownership of aid programmes by the recipient countries. Thus, aid effectiveness does also rest critically on the nature of recipient–donor relationships, efficient aid delivery procedures and mechanisms, as well as on the progress of building capacity and institutions conducive to economic development in recipient countries. In fact, the non-compliance of traditional *ex ante* conditionality can be explained by the unfortunate aid relationships developed, in which 'policy' conditionality was dictated by the donor community. Clearly, the issue of aid effectiveness or aid dependence and debt sustainability cannot be effectively analysed and debated without reference to the unequal aid relationships. Equally, the appropriateness of economic policies and political institutions cannot be judged or assessed in isolation from prevailing country-specific conditions. While the blame for the policy failure has been placed too readily on recipient governments and institutions in terms of poor policy environments and their incapacity, the donor community has to take a fair share of the responsibility for the poor relationships that have evolved over the last few decades. As Bourguignon and Sundberg (2007) note, the donor community has imposed policy conditionality with imperfect knowledge of the local environment.

As discussed above, Bourguignon and Sundberg (2007) suggest that to gain a deeper understanding of aid effectiveness it is critical to examine the causality chain linking external aid to final developmental outcomes. As noted above, in standard cross-country regression analyses on aid effectiveness conducted using macro-level economic data, such as those examining the aid–growth

---

[25] See Odedokun (2004); Bulow and Rogoff (2005); Nunnenkamp, Thiele, and Wilfer (2005); and Cohen, Jacquet, and Reisen (2005) for detailed discussion on the grants-versus-loans debate.

relationships, the complex causal links are treated as a 'black box'. These studies also tend to treat aid as a single aggregate, despite the fact that aid is delivered in different modalities and forms of cooperation.

As Bourguignon and Sundberg argue, it is also suggested that opening the 'black box' is critical for understanding aid effectiveness, as discussed in detail in Jerve and Nissanke (2007, 2008). This is because aid effectiveness is indeed the outcome of a *time-bound* causality chain starting with initial conditions and inputs leading to changes in development outcomes in terms of conventional indicators such as GDP growth, poverty rate, income inequality, and human development indicators. However, the approach of this chapter departs from the established line of argument in a rather critical way. The current aid-effectiveness debate tends to be almost singularly dominated by a static and instrumental view of development processes. From this particular perspective, it has been argued that aid becomes effective when the 'right' policies and institutions are in place. It is based on the assumption that there are universally applicable 'right' policies and institutions and donors can condition aid transfer on the existence or adoption of such 'right' factors. Hence, it is argued that aid should be used, through either *ex ante* or *ex post* policy conditionality, as leverage for policy reforms that donors identify as good for development.

In contrast to this currently dominant view, donors should recognize that development is an iterative process where positive ('right') outcomes are the result of the gradual and often unpredictable development of local institutions and sociopolitical configuration. Seen from this alternative perspective, development management becomes more *process* oriented, rather that *output* oriented. It is further suggested that through providing development aid in different forms of cooperation (financial resources, technical advice, and so on), donors could act as an important partner in such processes. Hence, successful development depends on long-term processes of institutional development; and the effectiveness of aid as a contribution to national development processes hinges on its ability to stimulate such processes.

Using a metaphor of the black box, the main differences between the currently dominant approach and the approach of this chapter can be contrasted, in the case of examining aid effectiveness for infrastructure development and service delivery, by taking the example of a road project (Figures 4.4–4.6). As shown in Figure 4.4, most of the previous empirical studies on aid effectiveness for infrastructure development were carried out by extending aid-project evaluation from micro level studies to macro measures, or studying how projects have contributed to improving developing indicators. They involved either (i) *ex ante* policy analysis: analysis of initial inputs and conditions (recipient country's policy, governance, capacity, and so on) that could maximize the impacts; or (ii) *ex post* impact studies: quantitative analysis of the impact of infrastructure projects, measured in such indicators as economic growth and poverty reduction. The main question raised in such conventional studies on

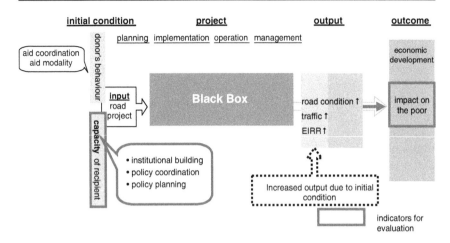

Figure 4.4 Conventional analysis of aid effectiveness to infrastructure development and service delivery

Source: Adapted from Jerve and Nissanke (2007) and JBIC Secretariat.

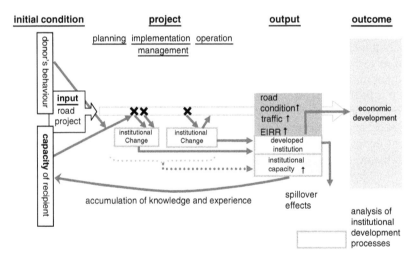

Figure 4.5 Institutional analysis of aid effectiveness to infrastructure development and service delivery

Source: Adapted from Jerve and Nissanke (2007) and JBIC Secretariat.

aid effectiveness is how donors can influence, by using aid as leverage, the quality of policy and institutions to maximize the impacts. Hence, the focus of these studies is the beginning and the end of the causal chain, rather than understanding inside the 'black box'.

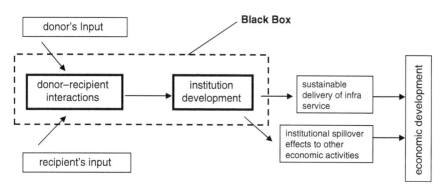

Figure 4.6 Institutional analysis of the black box

Source: Jerve and Nissanke (2007) and JBIC Secretariat.

In contrast, this chapter takes a distinctively institutional approach to examining aid effectiveness in carrying out a comparative analysis of project aid to infrastructure development in Southeast Asia and sub-Saharan Africa. It is conjectured here that what takes place in the black box in terms of institutional changes/transformation and spill-over effects would determine not only the financial and organizational sustainability of infrastructure service delivery and the quality of services as project outcome but also economic development outcomes at large. Beyond just providing grants or concessional loans, project aid in this perspective could be a vehicle that could make a significant contribution towards institutional changes and transformation throughout the project cycles of planning, implementation, operation, and management. It provides a crucial conduit for the transfer and accumulation of knowledge and expertise in the learning-by-doing process for sectoral development. Importantly, beyond sector-specific benefits, the aid-inspired learning process could also have the potential of producing institutional capacity and development of other institutions economy-wide through spillover effects. For this to happen, donors should become involved as a developmental partner and create an environment conducive to mutual learning. This potential process of institutional changes and transformation and spillover effects through project aid is illustrated in Figure 4.5. Thus, project aid can contribute to institutional development at a broader level, and this in turn could affect macro-aid effectiveness. For example, referring to Japanese infrastructure project aid, Arakawa and Wakabayashi (2006) emphasize that the experiences at the project level have led not only to capacity-building of the sector aid supported but also the establishment of comprehensive country systems at the national level.

Figure 4.6 further illustrates how inside the 'black box', aid can be instrumental in stimulating institutional development that could be an important channel for new ideas, exchanges of experiences, and the gradual building of competence and capacity in organizations critical for sustainable infrastructure services in the case of project aid, but more generally for economic development. Such potential beneficial effects of aid on the development process are critically contingent upon the nature of the donor–recipient relationships. If the relationship is characterized by mutual trust and confidence, development aid would be a conduit for the close interactions of numerous stakeholders, which can evolve over time into dynamic institutions, adaptable to changing local conditions with flexibility and resilience.

The synthesis of the case studies on aid effectiveness for infrastructure development in eight countries of Southeast Asia and sub-Saharan Africa has led to several useful observations regarding the sustainability of economic infrastructure service where donors participated through project aid (Jerve and Nissanke 2008). The following three points can be highlighted in relation to the aid-effectiveness debate addressed in this chapter.

First, long-term commitment by local stakeholders on the recipient side is vital for the sustainability of infrastructure services. This should manifest itself in political will by leaders and successive governments to commit to sustainable quality infrastructure services within home-grown long-term development plans and visions. Leaders' strong political commitment would ensure a high priority in fund allocation over the medium and long term to sectors and regions where a specific donor-assisted infrastructure project is placed. In particular, the predictability of sufficient and stable fund allocation over a long-term horizon is crucial for sustainable operation and maintenance of infrastructural services. For this to happen, large infrastructure projects should be placed in the context of national development plans that include sectoral or regional master plans.

Second, donors' long-term commitment should be forthcoming, not only to a financed project but also to recipients' development vision and master plans, as a support for robust allegiance on the part of recipients to capacity-building and institutional development for ensuring sustainability of infrastructure services. In particular, high priority and long-time commitment on both sides work as a 'hidden or implicit guarantee' for the predictability of multi-year aid pledges and budget allocation to a project and sector development. Naturally, the predictability of sufficient and stable fund allocation is crucial for sustainable operation and maintenance of infrastructure services. But, importantly, this provides project management with a longer time horizon and could induce more readily positive institutional changes at all levels, that is, at project, sector, and national levels. Further, in the case of project aid, mutual trust can be nurtured through close face-to-face cooperation, knowledge transfer, and learning-by-doing on the ground between those participating in an infrastructure project, both donors and recipients, to achieve the common goals of sustainable delivery of infrastructure services. Such an opportunity of mutual learning involving both private and public sectors is less likely to be present in other aid-delivery modalities such as budget support.

Third, the driving force for achieving the development mission should come from recipients' endeavours in utilizing and strengthening their own institutions, both formal and informal. In this sense, the presence of initial capacity among local institutions embedded in the social–political system of recipient countries is useful. However, it is suggested thàt if strong commitments by both donors and recipients to development are present as discussed above, donors could stimulate the 'endogenously driven' process of development of local institutions and capacity. Here again it is important to emphasize that donors should try to identify and nurture aspects of strength found in local endogenously developing institutions, and their advice should build on their strengths. It is not at all helpful if donors try to introduce or impose their 'model' institutions on recipients by pointing to a long list of weaknesses or deficiencies in local institutions and systems.

Policy implications arising from these findings and approaches to aid effectiveness are clearly quite different from those originating from the conventional perspectives of viewing aid as leverage for donor-inspired policy and institutional reforms, where *ex ante* or *ex post* policy conditionality prevails and 'marketing' institutional models deemed appropriate by donors is a dominant feature of aid relationships.

4.5. Concluding remarks

Under the SAPs, policy reforms were in many cases forced upon recipient countries as stringent conditions in return for debt relief and foreign aid. Recipient governments often found it impossible to implement these policies in their domestic political economy context, as they were certain to generate a sharp configuration of winners and losers. Plus the timeframe for implementation was often unrealistic. These reform packages were sometimes so contentious that donor governments themselves would have found them hard to implement or to sell to their own domestic constituencies. Thus, donor–recipient relationships have been severely impaired by the two-decade-long experience with *ex ante* policy conditionality whereby a series of restrictive policy conditionalities were imposed as a universally applicable basis for reforms.

The weaknesses associated with the past practice of policy conditionality have been debated and the new emerging aid architecture is supposed to address these issues. In the process, the need for forging effective donor–recipient partnerships has been widely accepted as one of the key conditions for increasing aid effectiveness and the ownership of aid programmes by the recipient countries. Yet, the conventional way of debating the effectiveness and enforcement problems of policy conditionality has so far been inhibiting, for it has hardly departed from the assumption that policy reforms recommended by donors are generally appropriate for dealing with economic problems facing developing economies. Indeed, the principal–agent framework widely used in the aid effectiveness debate is flawed as it is built on the assumption that donors are the principals while recipient governments are merely the agents of donors. However, the true ownership of aid would require donors to become agents of developing countries.[26]

It is not surprising to observe, therefore, that in many low-income countries it has not been easy to work towards a new aid relationship based on a genuine partnership and ownership of policy reforms. Instead of providing aid for enhancing recipients' efforts in building an institutional foundation with the necessary technical capacity for developing their own home-grown strategies and policies, donors continue to police whether recipient governments adopt and adhere to economic policies and institutional governance structures recommended by donors.

Yet, unless an uncompromised 'policy space' is accorded to recipient countries in setting their own development agenda and policy strategy, the real ownership of economic reform programmes cannot be in the hands of recipient countries. The lack of sense of ownership and partnership could propagate and promote 'cheating' behaviour on the part of the agent-recipients. Rather than impose monolithic models, there should be a room for open discussions and debate on different development models. In this context, Morrissey (2004) emphasizes the importance of allowing a process of *policy learning* and *policy experimentation* and leaving the *policy choices* to recipient governments for the sake of establishing ownership as well as encouraging partnership. Donors should play the role of 'second fiddle' in this policymaking process, providing technical assistance and information services. There should also be policy space for *institutional innovations*. In this context, Rodrik argues that 'effective institutional outcomes do not map into unique institutional designs' and that

there is no unique, non-context specific way of achieving desirable institutional outcomes. Since what works will depend on local constraints and opportunities, we should bear in mind that institutional prescriptions should be contingent on the prevailing characteristics of the local economy and that institutional design has to be context-specific. (Rodrik 2004: 9)

What is urgently required is mutual respect so that the two parties can fully and truly engage in learning from each others' development experiences, taking into account their different historical and cultural backgrounds. Recipient governments are increasingly required to be accountable to the donor community. This by itself may not pose a problem, but significant pressures from donors on important policy matters could place recipient governments in

---

[26] The author is grateful to one of referees for drawing attention to this critical weakness of the analytical framework applied to the aid effectiveness debate.

conflict with their responsibility towards their own citizens. Such situations can easily undermine the democratic credentials of recipient governments. It is high time to depart from unproductive aid relationships and to work towards cultivating mutual trust and respect, conducive to producing positive global public goods, sustainable economic development, and enduring political stability in recipient countries.

On reflection, it can be said that the aid effectiveness debate conducted mainly at the aggregate macro-relationships level may not shed real light on how to make foreign aid effective for economic growth and poverty reduction. Remarking that aid is given for many different purposes and in many different forms, Hansen and Tarp (2000, 2001) suggest that the unresolved issue in assessing aid effectiveness is not whether aid works, but how and whether we can make the different kinds of aid instruments at hand work better in varying country circumstances. Assessed from these critical perspectives, the CPIA-based *selectivity* rule is certainly not an ideal base to conduct meaningful policy dialogue between donors and recipients. The allocation process is a mechanical application of the index which is a mix of ranked policy and institutional parameters as well as outcomes. Indeed, in the prevailing economic analysis of the *ex post* conditionality game, there is little discussion on how to build and develop information endowments based on confidence and mutual trust in donor–recipient relationships. Yet, in game theory, sufficient and continuous information flows between the parties is accepted as one of the critical conditions for reaching a superior cooperative equilibrium (with an efficient mechanism for conflict resolution).

Further, it is also well known that in inter-temporal resource transactions a coherent *incentive-compatible* aid–debt contract is necessary to ensure an alignment of the incentive structures governing aid relationships. Hence, the absence of an unconditional contingent financing facility available upon verification of large exogenous shocks to recipient countries should be seen as one of binding constraints for improving aid relationships.

Finally, it should be recognized that while aid is treated as a single entity in most cross-country regression studies on aid-related macroeconomic relationships, aid is delivered in a host of different forms. Hence, it is somewhat misleading to conduct a debate at a general level, such as whether aid should be given in grants or loans.

In this context, this chapter has discussed aid effectiveness as applied to project aid provided to infrastructure development. In contrast to the prevailing dominant perspective of using aid as leverage for donor-inspired policy and institutional reforms, this chapter has presented a distinctively institutional approach wherein aid effectiveness is assessed in its role in stimulating long-term processes of institutional development in recipient countries. From this perspective, a strong case is advanced for the need to reconstitute the aid-effectiveness debate. Aid can contribute to economic development only through establishing and nurturing productive donor–recipient relationships based on true partnerships and ownership as outlined in this chapter. Such relationships would encourage and stimulate the process of policy learning and experimentation as well as institutional experimentation and innovation. Performance assessments could then be made in an environment conducive to nurturing mutual trust and respect on the basis of transparent and free flows of information between donors and recipients. Further, recognizing that the recipients' own institutions could be strengthened or transformed as a part of development processes, aid should be provided even to countries with weak institutional conditions in terms of their capacity for policy formation, implementation, or governance which may initially fail to meet the standards set by donors. Hence, the intellectual hegemony used to justify the CPIA-based aid allocation mechanism currently adopted by many multilateral and bilateral donors is challenged.

References

Adam, C. S., and J. W. Gunning (2002) 'Redesigning in the Aid Contract: Donor's Use of Performance Indicators in Uganda'. *World Development*, 30: 2045–56.

——G. Chambas, P. Guillamont, et al. (2004) 'Performance-based Conditionality: A European Perspective'. *World Development*, 32: 1059–70.

Addison, T., H. Hansen, and F. Tarp (2004) *Debt Relief for Poor Countries*. Basingstoke: Palgrave Macmillan for UNU-WIDER.

Alesina, A., and D. Dollar (2000) 'Who Gives Aid to Whom and Why?' *Journal of Economic Growth*, 5: 33–63.

Arakawa H., and J. Wakabayashi (2006) 'Budget Support and Aid Effectiveness: Experience in East Asia'. *JBIC Review*, 14. Tokyo: Japan Bank for International Co-operation.

Bourguignon, F., and M. Sundberg (2007) 'Aid Effectiveness: Opening the Black Box'. *American Economic Review*, 97: 316–21.

Bulow, J., and K. S. Rogoff (2005) 'Grants versus Loans for Development Banks'. Paper presented at the American Economic Association Meeting, 7 Jan., Philadelphia.

Burnside, C., and D. Dollar (1997) 'Aid, Policies, and Growth'. World Bank Policy Research Department Working Paper 1777. Washington, DC: World Bank.

————(2000) 'Aid, Policies, and Growth'. *American Economic Review*, 90: 847–68.

Cohen, D., P. Jacquet, and H. Reisen (2005) 'Beyond Grants versus Loans: How to Use ODA and Debt for Development'. Paper presented at the AFD-EUDN International Conference, 13–15 Dec., Paris.

——H. Djoufelkit-Cottenet, P. Jacquet, and C. Valadier (2008) 'Lending to the Poorest Countries: A New Counter-cyclical Debt Instrument'. OECD Development Centre Working Paper 269. Paris: OECD.

Collier, P. (1998) 'Aid and Economic Development in Africa'. Mimeo. Oxford: University of Oxford Centre for the Study of African Economies.

——and D. Dollar (2001) 'Can the World Cut Poverty in Half? How Policy Reform and Effective Aid Can Meet the International Development Goals'. *World Development*, 29: 1787–802.

——(2002) 'Aid Allocation and Poverty Reduction'. *European Economic Review*, 46: 1475–500.

——(2004) 'Development Effectiveness: What Have We Learnt?' *Economic Journal*, 114: F244–F271.

——and J. W. Gunning (1996) 'Rethinking Donor Conditionality'. Mimeo. Oxford: University of Oxford Centre for the Study of African Economies.

Dalgaard, C.-J., and H. Hansen (2001) 'On Aid, Growth and Good Policies'. *Journal of Development Studies*, 37: 17–41.

——and F. Tarp (2004) 'On the Empirics of Foreign Aid and Growth'. *Economic Journal*, 114: F191–F216.

Deaton, A., et al. (2006) 'An Evaluation of World Bank's Research, 1998–2005'. Final report. Washington, DC: World Bank. <http://siteresources.worldbank.org/DEC/Resources/84797-1109362238001/726454-1164121166494/RESEARCH-EVALUATION-2006-Main-Report.pdf>.

Dollar, D., and J. Svensson (2000) 'What Explains the Success or Failure of Structural Adjustment Programmes?' *Economic Journal*, 110: 894–917.

Easterly, W. (2003) 'Can Foreign Aid Buy Growth?' *Journal of Economic Perspectives*, 17: 23–48.

——R. Levine, and D. Roodman (2003) 'New Data, New Doubts: Revisiting "Aid, Policies and Growth" ' Center for Global Development Working Paper 26. Washington, DC: CGD.

Gibson, C. G., K. Andersson, E. Ostrom, and S. Shivakumar (2005) *The Samaritan's Dilemma: The Political Economy of Development Aid*. Oxford: Oxford University Press.

Guillaumont, P., and L. Chauvet (2001) 'Aid and Performance: A Reassessment'. *Journal of Development Studies*, 37: 66–87.

Hansen, H., and F. Tarp (2000) 'Aid Effectiveness Disputed'. *Journal of International Development*, 12: 375–98.

——(2001) 'Aid and Growth Regressions'. *Journal of Development Economics*, 64: 547–70.

Hout, W. (2007) *The Politics of Aid Selectivity: Good Governance Criteria in World Bank, US and Dutch Development Assistance*. London: Routledge.

Hudson, J. (2004) 'Introduction: Aid and Development'. *Economic Journal*, 114: F185–F90.

IDA (International Development Association) (2004) 'Debt Sustainability and Financing Terms in IDA-14'. IDA-14 Background Paper. Washington, DC: IDA.

——(2005) 'Additions to IDA Resources: Fourteenth Replenishment. Final Report'. Washington, DC: IDA-World Bank.

——(2007a) 'IDA's Performance-based Allocation System: Options for Simplifying the Formula and Reducing Volatility'. International Development Association, Resource Mobilization (FRM) Washington, DC: IDA-World Bank.

——(2007b) 'IDA's Performance-based Allocation System for IDA 15, Annex 1'. Washington, DC: IDA-World Bank.

IMF (International Monetary Fund) (2004) 'Debt Sustainability in Low-income Countries: Proposal for an Operational Framework and Policy Implications'. Washington, DC: IDA-World Bank.

——(2005) 'Operational Framework for Debt Sustainability Assessments in Low-income Countries: Further Considerations'. Washington, DC: IDA-World Bank.

Jerve, A.M., and M. Nissanke (2007) 'Aid Effectiveness to Infrastructure: A Comparative Study of East Asia and sub-Saharan Africa: Framework Paper'. Tokyo: Japan Bank for International Co-operation.

————(2008) 'Aid Effectiveness to Infrastructure: Looking into the Black Box: A Comparative Study of East Asia and Sub-Saharan Africa'. Tokyo: Japan Bank for International Co-operation.

Kanbur, R. (2005) 'Reforming the Formula: A Modest Proposal for Introducing Development Outcomes in IDA Allocation Procedures'. Paper presented at the AFD-EUDN conference, 25–7 Nov., Paris.

Kaufmann, D. (2005) '10 Myths about Governance and Corruption'. *Finance and Development*, 42: 41–3.

——A. Kraay, and M. Mastruzzi (2005) 'Governance Matters IV: Governance Indicators for 1996–2004'. World Bank Policy Research Working Paper 3237. Washington, DC: World Bank.

Killick, T. (1996) 'Principals and Agents and the Limitations of BWI Conditionality'. *World Economy*, 19: 211–29.

——(1997) 'Principals, Agents and the Failings of Conditionality'. *Journal of International Development*, 9: 483–95.

Kraay, A., and V. Nehru (2004) 'When is External Debt Sustainable?' World Bank Policy Research Department Working Paper 3200. Washington, DC: World Bank.

Krugman, P. (1988) 'Financing vs Forgiving a Debt Overhang'. *Journal of Development Economics*, 29: 253–68.

Lensink, R., and H. White (2001) 'Are There Negative Returns to Aid?'. *Journal of Development Studies*, 37: 42–65.

Maizels, A. (1992) *Commodities in Crisis*. Oxford: Clarendon Press for UNU-WIDER.

——and M. Nissanke (1984) 'Motivations for Aid to Developing Countries'. *World Development*, 12: 879–900.

Morrissey, O. (2004) 'Conditionality and Aid Effectiveness Re-evaluated'. *World Economy*, 27: 153–71.

Mosley, P., J. Hudson, and A. Verschoor (2004) 'Aid, Poverty Reduction and the "New Conditionality"'. *Economic Journal*, 114: 217–43.

Nissanke, M. (2004) 'Donors' Support for Microcredit as Social Enterprise: A Critical Reappraisal'. In M. Odedokun (ed.), *External Finance for Private Sector Development: Appraisals and Issues*. Basingstoke: Palgrave Macmillan for UNU-WIDER.

——(2008) 'Donor–Recipient Relationships in the Aid Effectiveness Debate'. In A. M. Jerve, Y. Shimomura, and A. S. Hansen (eds), *Aid Relationships in Asia: Exploring Ownership in Japanese and Nordic Aid*. Basingstoke: Palgrave Macmillan.

——and E. Aryeetey (1998) *Financial Integration and Development in sub-Saharan Africa*. London and New York: Routledge.

——and B. Ferrarini (2004) 'Debt Dynamics and Contingency Financing Theoretical Reappraisal of the HIPC Initiative'. In T. Addison, H. Hansen and F. Tarp (eds), *Debt Relief in Poor Countries*. Basingstoke: Palgrave Macmillan for UNU-WIDER.

————(2007) 'Assessing the Aid Allocation and Debt Sustainability Framework: Working Towards Incentive Compatible Aid Contracts'. WIDER Research Paper 2007/33. Helsinki: UNU-WIDER.

Nunnenkamp, P., R. Thiele, and T. Wilfer (2005) 'Grants Versus Loans: Much Ado About (Almost) Nothing'. Kiel Economic Policy Paper 4. Kiel: Kiel Institute for the World Economy.

Odedokun, M. (ed.) (2004) *External Finance for Private Sector Development: Appraisals and Issues*. Basingstoke: Palgrave Macmillan for UNU-WIDER.

Rajan, R. G., and A. Subramanian (2005) 'Aid and Growth: What Does the Cross-country Evidence Really Show?' National Bureau of Economic Research Working Paper 11513. Cambridge, Mass.: NBER.

Rodrik, D. (2004) 'Getting Institutions Right'. CESIfo DICE Report 2/2004. Munich: Ifo Institute for Economic Research.

Wangwe, S. (2003) 'Foreign Aid and Development in Sub-Saharan Africa'. In E. Aryeetey, J. Court, M. Nissanke, and B. Weder (eds), *Asia and Africa in the Global Economy*. Tokyo: UNU Press.

White, H., and O. Morrissey (1997) 'Conditionality When Donor and Recipient Preferences Vary'. *Journal of International Development*, 9: 497–505.

World Bank (1998) *Assessing Aid: What Works, What Doesn't, and Why*. Oxford, New York, and Washington, DC: Oxford University Press/World Bank.

——(2005a) *IDA 14 Replenishment: Final Report to the Board of Governors*. Washington, DC: World Bank.

——(2005b) 'Managing the Risk of Exogenous Shocks in Low-income Countries'. World Bank Background Paper. Washington, DC: World Bank.

——(2005c) 'The Theory and Practice of Conditionality: A Literature Review'. Background Paper 5 for Review of World Bank Conditionality, Washington, DC: World Bank.

——(2005d) *Country Policy and Institutional Assessments: 2004 Assessment Questionnaire*. Washington, DC: World Bank.

5

The Implications of Horizontal Inequality for Aid

Graham Brown, Frances Stewart, and Arnim Langer

5.1. Introduction

This chapter examines the implications of horizontal inequalities—inequalities between culturally defined (ethnic, religious, racial, or regional identity) groups for aid policy in developing countries.[1] Horizontal inequalities (HIs) are important because they affect individual well-being, economic efficiency, and social stability, while in some circumstances they can lead to serious violent conflict, thereby undermining most development efforts (Stewart 2002; Langer 2005; Mancini and Langer 2008; Østby 2008).

As Cohen (1995) noted over a decade ago, much academic and donor research has been undertaken linking aid with development, and development with ethnicity, but rarely have the three factors been drawn together. This is all the more a matter for concern as

> the formally technical and neutral character of decision-making processes and alternative criteria at the international institutional level carry important, often unforeseen, consequences for ethnic conflict...[if more were known it might] enable foreign aid donors to become more aware of relationships between the resources and advice they provide and inter-ethnic relationships in the countries in which they intervene. (Esman and Herring 1995, quot. Cohen 1995: 3)

In this chapter, we examine how aid policy affects horizontal inequalities; how the impact can often be adverse if HI considerations are not taken into account, and how aid might be redirected to contribute to the reduction of such inequality. The chapter is organized as follows. Section 5.2 introduces the concept of

---

[1] We are grateful to the participants at the UNU-WIDER Development Conference on Aid, 'Aid: Principles, Policies, and Performance', held on 16–17 June 2006 in Helsinki, for helpful comments on a previous draft of this chapter.

HIs and explains why they matter for aid. Section 5.3 explores how policies that do not take horizontal inequalities into direct consideration may affect HIs and may inadvertently exacerbate such inequalities. Section 5.4 discusses how aid policy might be used to reduce HIs. Section 5.5 concludes.

5.2. Horizontal inequalities: what they are and why they matter for aid

Horizontal inequalities are conceived of as multidimensional, with economic, social, and political dimensions. Each dimension encompasses a number of elements. For example, economic inequalities include a variety of assets (financial, natural resources, human, and social capital) as well as opportunities for their use (especially employment) and the current resources that flow from these assets (that is, income); social HIs include access to a variety of services (education, health services, housing) and also outcomes in the form of human indicators (for example, life expectancy, literacy, and infant and maternal mortality); while political HIs consist in the group distribution of political opportunities including who controls the presidency, the cabinet, parliamentary assemblies, the army, the police, and regional and local government. Each of these lists includes both inputs and outputs (for example, assets and incomes; health services and health outcomes), while some dimensions of HIs influence other dimensions (for example, political power affects the economic and social dimensions). This extensive approach is deliberate because (i) many of the elements are not only inputs but also contribute directly to individual well-being; and (ii) inputs are generally easier to affect directly through policy than outcomes. While the broad dimensions are relevant in any context, the actual elements that matter will vary according to the economy and society; for example, land is less important in industrialized countries than in many developing countries.

Horizontal inequalities are important because they affect well-being directly and because they affect other objectives instrumentally. People's well-being is affected not only by their individual circumstances, but also by how well their group is doing. This is partly because membership of the group is an aspect of a person's identity and hence the group's situation is felt as part of an individual's situation; and partly because relative impoverishment of the group increases perceptions of members that they are likely to be trapped permanently in a poor position, or, if they have managed to do better than many in the group, that they are likely to fall back into poverty. Hence the well-being of Muslims in Western Europe, Catholics in Northern Ireland, Hutus in Rwanda, Afro-Americans in the USA, black people in apartheid South Africa, to take just a few of many examples, is (was) deeply affected by the relative impoverishment of the group—over and above the position of the individual themselves. Psychologists have shown, for example, that Afro-Americans suffer from many psychological ills due to the position of their group, or 'Being Black and Feeling Blue' as Brown and Williams put it (Broman 1997; Brown and Williams 1999). The direct impact on well-being is not only more powerfully felt but is also a more-important consideration, because horizontal inequalities often persist over generations, showing more persistence, typically, than individuals' ranking within a group (Tilly 1999; Stewart and Langer 2008).

Horizontal inequalities also matter for three instrumental reasons. First, it may not be possible to improve the position of individuals without tackling the position of the group as a whole. For example, programmes to advance credit to poor producers, or to promote universal education, may not be achievable so long as group inequality remains. An example here is extending education to all girls which may be prevented not by a lack of schools or teachers but by parental attitudes to girls' education (USIS and USAID 1992; Hafeez 1993). For sharply divided countries, the poverty reduction targets of aid agencies may be impossible to achieve, or very costly, unless HIs are directly targeted. The position of Vietnamese minorities provides an example (van de Walle and Gunewardena 2001).

Second, correcting such horizontal inequalities should have a positive effect on efficiency. Any situation in which a group is discriminated against is likely to be less efficient than in the absence of discrimination, since talented people in the group discriminated against will be held back, while too many resources, or too high a position, will go to less-talented people in the favoured group. For example, Macours (2004) argues that ethnic diversity in a context of weak property rights enforcement can result in market segmentation and less than optimal land allocation. In Guatemala, informal land contracts are more likely to take place within the same ethnic group. Conversely, most studies show that affirmative action for Afro-Americans in the USA has had a positive impact on efficiency (for example, Badgett and Hartmann 1995).

A third and most critical instrumental reason for trying to moderate HIs is that group inequality can be a source of violent conflict (Stewart 2000; and see Chapter 6 of this volume by Sakiko Fukuda-Parr). Group inequality provides powerful grievances which leaders can use to mobilize people to political protest, by calling on cultural markers (a common history or language or religion) and pointing to group exploitation. This type of mobilization seems especially likely to occur where there is political as well as economic inequality, so that the group leaders are excluded from formal political power while the mass of group members are economically deprived. Examples where group inequalities have been a factor in provoking conflict include Côte d'Ivoire, Rwanda, Northern Ireland, Nepal, Chiapas, the Sudan, to mention just a few (see, for example, Gurr 1993; Gurr and Moore 1997; Stewart 2002; Gates and Murshed 2005; Langer 2005). Sharp horizontal inequalities within countries (and between them) are an important source of grievance and potentially of instability, independently of the extent of vertical inequality. There is econometric cross-country and within-country (as well as case-study) evidence showing that conflict potential is higher where HIs are more severe (Barrows 1976; Mancini and Langer 2008; Østby 2008). It seems that conflict is less likely, however, if economic and political HIs go in opposite directions, when the group that dominates the political system does not also dominate the economic one (for example, Langer 2005; Østby 2008).

From an aid perspective, each of these reasons for taking horizontal inequalities into account should be regarded as highly relevant: efficiency and growth, poverty reduction, and the enhancement of well-being, or freedoms, are generally accepted as key objectives by aid donors. Moreover, political stability is essential for achievement of any of these objectives and is also an imperative in itself—both for the consequences instability has for the suffering of the people concerned and for the potential overspill into regional and international arenas in a way that may threaten strategic interests and the security of the donor nations. Indeed, even in the absence of political instability, severe horizontal inequalities can be a source of international migration; and where the cultural groups in question correspond to cultural divisions internationally and within donor countries, severe HIs in one part of the world, especially if supported with international aid, may become a factor leading to terrorism/instability in the donor countries. An obvious case is the Muslim/Christian division—which shows up in severe HIs in many parts of the world (from Thailand to Nigeria, the Philippines to Israel) and is found within donor countries as well—so that what happens in one part of the world with respect to horizontal inequalities has clear implications elsewhere (Stewart and Langer 2008).

For these reasons the objective of moderating HIs should be an important aspect of aid policy wherever HIs seems to be large. Yet it does not form a significant part of either rhetoric or the operation of aid instruments, as is discussed below. We should emphasize that it is not just a matter that should be of concern in what have been defined as 'fragile' states, that is, countries already identified as being conflict-prone. The need to take HIs into consideration also applies to everyday aid to politically stable countries because the reasons that relate to enhancing well-being and promoting efficiency and poverty reduction, apply just as much to these countries as to fragile states because, if severe HIs are neglected, these countries might fall into a fragile state.

5.3. Impacts of aid on horizontal inequalities

Where HIs are not a consideration in aid distribution it may well exacerbate rather than offset them. There are two reasons for this: first, because the normal considerations governing aid allocation lead to a distribution of resources which worsens HIs; and, second, because in the implementation phase, projects and programmes may be liable to being 'captured' or abused in such a way as to worsen horizontal inequalities. We take these two possibilities in turn.

The normal considerations governing aid primarily concern efficiency and poverty reduction, at both programme and project levels. In both cases, the net impact may be to worsen HIs. For example, structural adjustment programmes at programme level typically favour the tradable sector as against the non-tradable. Often this means a worsening of the internal terms of trade in a way that favours the well-off groups, because these are often concentrated in the tradable sector. Poverty reduction programmes might plausibly be expected to help the worst-off groups. But often this is not the case, as the poor in under-privileged groups are hardest to reach. Project finance can also fall into the same trap, with the most 'efficient' seeming projects being those in the more developed areas; and poverty-directed projects (such as social funds) primarily benefiting the urban poor near the capital.

Ghana's development illustrates these points. The structural adjustment programmes of the 1980s and 1990s involved resuscitating the cocoa and gold sectors and improving their terms of trade, but both are located in the relatively richer parts of the country. As McKay and Aryeetey (2004: 35) point out, 'not surprisingly, the poorest regions in Ghana are those that have little or no produce in the basket of tradables'. Ghana's Programme of Action to Mitigate the Social Consequences of Adjustment (PAMSCAD), introduced in the late 1980s, which was a set of projects intended to help reduce poverty during adjustment, was found to have limited impact on poverty and to be largely focused on the urban areas.[2] And, while Ghana has succeeded in reducing national poverty rates, this has been achieved disproportionately through a reduction in the high levels of poverty in the relatively privileged South, rather than in the poorer North. Indeed, between 1992 and 1999, the poverty rate in the Northern and Upper East regions actually increased while aggregate poverty fell (Table 5.1).

The transmigration programme in Indonesia is another example of how a programme can increase HIs, where these are disregarded. This programme relocated hundreds of thousands of families from overpopulated Java and Bali to the more sparsely populated outer islands, encouraged and financially supported by the World Bank. The programme impacted on indigenous ethnic groups and horizontal inequalities in two ways. First, the deforestation that accompanied the programme's settlement practices displaced smaller, migratory

---

[2] An assessment based on community-level fieldwork concluded that 'the effect PAMSCAD has had on the communities in which the surveys was carried out has been very limited'. It was found that nearly 80 per cent of the funds for PAMSCAD went to the non-poor (redeployed public sector workers above the poverty line) while the vast majority (over 90 per cent) of the poor received no benefit at all (Brydon and Legge 1996: 110).

Table 5.1. Ghana: horizontal inequalities by region (various years)

	Incidence of poverty (percentage)[1]		Incidence of poverty as a ratio to national average		Literacy (percentage literate)[2]		Literacy as a ratio to national average	
	1992	1999	1992	1999	1993	1998	1993	1998
Western	60	27	1.15	0.68	37	54	1.10	1.10
Central	44	48	0.85	1.20	43	55	1.26	1.08
Greater Accra	26	5	0.50	0.13	60	76	1.76	1.49
Volta	57	38	1.10	0.95	46	58	1.35	1.37
Eastern	48	44	0.92	1.10	46	66	1.35	1.29
Ashanti	41	28	0.79	0.70	31	64	0.91	1.25
Brong Ahafo	65	36	1.25	0.90	30	53	0.88	1.04
Northern	63	69	1.21	1.73	8	13	0.24	0.25
Upper West	88	84	1.69	2.10	12	20	0.35	0.39
Upper East	67	88	1.60	2.20	8	20	0.24	0.39
National	52	40	1.00	1.00	34	51	1.00	1.00

Notes:
[1] The poverty line was the same in both years, i.e., GHS 900,000 per adult per year.
[2] Authors' calculations based on data from the 1993 and 1998 Demographic and Health Surveys.
Source: Data drawn from Songsore (2003).

local communities and deprived them of their livelihoods. The World Bank's own assessment of the Transmigration II settlement noted that it had 'a major and probably irreversible impact' on the Kubu ethnic groups (World Bank 1994: 22). Second, the transmigration programme exacerbated rural ethnic inequalities and tension by assigning to the mostly Javanese transmigrants prime land, often in substantially larger family plots than those owned by local residents (see Leith 1998). Figure 5.1 shows the distribution of landholdings among agriculturalists in the outer islands (that is, all of Indonesia except Java and Bali), according to broad region of birth—that is, among those from Java and Bali (the origin of transmigrants) as against the local-born population, based on 1990 census data. It shows how larger landholdings were concentrated on the Java-/Bali-born agriculturalists. Overall, the interpolated median landholding of Java-/Bali-born agriculturalists in the outer islands was 1.17 hectares, some 44 per cent higher than that of local-born agriculturalists, at 0.82 hectares.

One reason for these effects is that the consequences for HIs were simply ignored (or thought justified for perceived benefits). But scholars have suggested that the Indonesian government under Suharto had an ulterior ethno-regional motive for the transmigration programme, which was seen as a way of providing a bedrock of support in the outer reaches for the Javanese-dominated

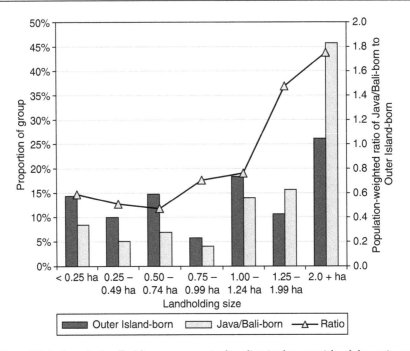

Figure 5.1 Indonesia: landholding among agriculturalists in the outer islands by region of birth, 1990

Notes: 'Agriculturalists' are defined as persons who responded 'agriculture' to question on 'industry of main occupation last week'.

Source: Authors' calculations from 1990 census sample.

and territorially organized armed forced (Tirtosudarmo 1995). In this context, it is unclear whether World Bank officials involved in the design and support of transmigration projects were aware of these motives and whether, if they did know, they had paid any thought to their potential repercussions on ethnicity and the distribution of resources or whether they simply assumed that the expected developmental gains of the project would outweigh any local tensions raised.

The second way in which aid might impact negatively on horizontal inequalities is through poor implementation processes which allow a horizontally 'neutral' programme/project to be skewed in favour of one or more groups. This process in turn could occur in either programme or project aid. Programme aid to support a government that practises exclusionary policies, whether formally or informally, would contribute towards horizontal inequalities. This might happen, for example, in the case of general budget support (GBS) to ethnically biased governments, such as was the case for a long time in Nepal. Despite severe regional and ethnic inequalities, throughout much of the recent period, donor strategy and conditionality in Nepal were mainly linked to macroeconomic and governance reforms, even after the outbreak of the Maoist insurgency that has been strongly linked to HI-based grievances (Gates and Murshed 2005); the World Bank's 1998 country assistance strategy (CAS), for instance, proposed lending triggers almost entirely related to macroeconomic reforms aimed at increasing domestic revenue and reducing domestic borrowing, including the satisfactory implementation of VAT. None of the conditionalities related to inequality in any form. More recent aid strategy documents released after the end of the conflict have recognized these shortcomings and now address the need for inclusive development, including 'equitable education' and improved representativity in the civil service.

In addition to programme aid, project aid might contribute towards the exacerbation of horizontal inequalities if the project is vulnerable to ethnic distortion by individuals or groups involved in its implementation. Thus, for instance, Cohen describes a capacity-building programme for Kenyan civil service officials that was supposed to be blind to ethnicity but was in reality skewed by senior officials in favour of their own ethnic groups during the selection process. Cohen concludes that

aid agency professionals were well aware of the possibilities of ethnic biases in all the capacity building projects they funded. When they felt that ethnic biases were emerging in the capacity building components of technical assistance projects, they went out of their way...to ensure that such biases were reduced or eliminated. They were generally unsuccessful in these efforts. (Cohen 1995: 13)

Other examples are to be found in Rwanda and Burundi. In pre-1994 Rwanda, according to Uvin (2000): 'Development projects and programmes lavishly funded by foreign aid, are one of the prime mechanisms through which the process of exclusion operates.' He supports this conclusion with the example of the Mutara Agricultural and Livestock Development project. 'The result of this project was a great increase in inequality between regions, classes, groups and individuals', much at the expense of Tutsi and Hima pastoralists. 'It was no accident that those who benefited were often from the president's region' (Uvin 2000: 170). In Burundi, aid accounted for 20 per cent of gross domestic product (GDP) from 1988 to 1992—considerably more than the total investment rate of around 16 per cent; hence all the investment in the Fifth Five-year Plan was financed by aid. The plan allocated just 16 per cent of investment funds to rural development, which would mainly benefit the Hutus, and the rest to the Tutsi-dominated urban sector. Moreover, Gaffney estimates that from 1980 to 1985 (when aid accounted for 13 per cent of GDP, or 80 per cent of investment) half the total investment went to Bujumbura and its surrounds, and the province of Bururi, where the (Tutsi) politico-military elite lived, received another 16 per cent (Gaffney 2000). In these cases, it is not being argued that the aid was intentionally distributed to accentuate existing horizontal inequalities, but rather that it did nothing to counter the strong biases within the systems, which in both Rwanda and Burundi had horrifying results. Hence, there is a need for explicit and conscious policies towards HIs in heterogeneous societies.

5.4. Aid policy to correct horizontal inequalities

The first requirement is to accept the need to moderate horizontal inequalities as an important objective of aid policy. For many aid donors today, poverty reduction is the overriding and often the only objective of aid. The correction of HIs could be subsumed under the poverty reduction objective to the extent that sharp HIs may lead to conflict and this will increase poverty. But this is a roundabout, and not always convincing, justification. We suggest that moderating HIs, where they are severe, should be one of the objectives of policy *in itself*, because it leads to a fairer and more-inclusive society. In some cases, adopting this as an objective will involve trade-offs with other objectives (for example, short-run growth and poverty reduction), even though the objectives are likely to be compatible in the longer term because of the connection between HIs and political stability. Or other objectives may still be achieved, but in a more expensive way (for example, reducing poverty in remote parts of the country instead of in the capital city). Choices must then be made. There is no simple or automatic way of deciding what trade-offs are acceptable, but, in general, the more severe the HIs the more importance needs to be given to this objective, while trying to meet the objective in a way that is consistent with helping to meet the other objectives wherever possible—for example, reducing HIs by tackling poverty of deprived groups, not by enriching the elite of deprived groups, or through growth-promoting investments among deprived groups. Consulting governments may not be the best way of determining priorities in this area, since quite often the government itself is instrumental in causing the horizontal inequalities, or has to be convinced of the importance of moderating them.

In this section we explore how aid policy could be used to help reduce horizontal inequalities, once it is accepted that this is an important objective. The modalities of aid obviously vary, and the ways in which consideration of HIs in aid will affect aid policy consequently also vary according to the aid instrument. We discuss four major aid instruments: country distribution of aid; programme aid accompanied by policy dialogue or conditionality, including poverty-reduction strategy papers (PRSPs); public expenditure reviews and poverty-reduction budget support (PRBS); and sectoral and project aid. We will also briefly consider how new approaches to aid, notably a human rights (HR) approach and a social exclusion approach, relate to an HI approach.

5.4.1. Mapping horizontal inequalities

The first step in devising aid policy to correct horizontal inequalities is to gain a thorough understanding of the current status and dynamics of horizontal inequalities in the country. This is not straightforward for several reasons: first, as already mentioned, there is a problem of defining appropriate groups. There are always many ways of categorizing people; for example, it is common to classify according to age and gender, urban and rural. Gender and age are relatively straightforward, urban/rural less so. But assessing and measuring HIs involves classification by ethnic/religious/racial group. Boundary lines may be blurred and the relevant group selection may not be immediately clear. For example, in Ghana, surveys indicate that ethnic, religious, and regional identities are each important to people in different respects.[3] Should one then classify by ethnic group, regional location, or religion? If by ethnic group, should one count the Akan as a single group, even though they encompass many important subgroups, or should one differentiate by subgroup, picking out, for example, the Ashanti, who appear to be a particularly privileged group? If by region, where should one draw the line, and why? In Ghana's case, North/South, or also differentiating east from the rest? Should one assess horizontal inequalities according to region of origin, including people who have migrated to the south as 'northerners', or by region where people currently live; if by religion, should one take 'Christian' and 'Muslim' as the main groups, or differentiate *within* the two major religions? And what should one do about traditional religions? There is no simple answer to these questions. One is looking for group boundaries that people mind about, and on the basis of which discrimination or favouritism occurs. A proper response to the question of how the group boundaries are to be defined would require in-depth investigation of opinions, discrimination, and history. Even this might not throw up simple and agreed distinctions, and it goes well beyond what can be expected from aid agencies on a day-to-day basis.

In such a context, a threefold approach by aid agencies seems most apposite, which would comprise:

(1) An initial in-depth study of the country in question, which would investigate the history, political economy, and sociology of the country and produce suggestions about important group distinctions; this would include drawing on surveys of people's own perceptions of identity distinctions, where available.

(2) A multiple approach, taking a variety of group classifications (ethnic, regional, religious) and seeing if and where the main inequalities emerge. If

---

[3] When people were asked how they saw themselves, religion was the most important consideration in private life (e.g., in relation to marriage), while ethnicity was most important with respect to public decisions about jobs, contracts, etc. (see Langer 2007).

no significant inequalities emerge, then this is a country where HI may not be a concern. Where sharp inequalities emerge in one type of grouping but not another, the grouping showing sharp inequalities is the most relevant from the perspective of reducing HIs. Where identities overlap and similar findings emerge from the different groupings (for example, religion and ethnicity overlap with region, as in Nigeria) then the particular categories used may not matter.

(3) It is important to try and get evidence of the multiple dimensions/ elements of HIs, because for aid-policy purposes one needs to know where the main problem lies—for instance, whether it is a matter of access to education, or poor economic opportunities, or both (see van de Walle and Gunewardena 2001 for an excellent investigation of this issue for minorities in Viet Nam).

A serious problem that will confront the mapping process in many countries is the lack of high-quality socio-economic data broken down by the relevant ethno-cultural categories. Such data are often sparse either because of poor-quality data collection or because such questions are not included in household and census surveys, often because of their political sensitivity: Nigeria is an example where ethnic data is deliberately not collected because of its potential political implications (Okolo 1999). Working together with recipient countries to develop appropriate mapping tools may form an important part of an aid agenda in such countries, but for the initial assessment suggested above, it may be necessary to take some other characteristic as a proxy for ethno-cultural difference to provide an initial picture of the extent and nature of horizontal inequalities. Here we discuss two options: regional data and a linguistic proxy.

In contrast to socio-cultural data, regional data are often more readily available and may thus be seen as a useful for ethno-cultural inequalities. How useful regional inequalities are as proxies for HIs depends on the degree to which identity groups are geographically segregated. In many African countries, for instance, ethnic groups are regionally concentrated so that regional and ethnic identities are virtually coterminous and regional inequality may be a suitable proxy for ethnic inequality. In Ghana, for example, there is a concentration of Muslims and poorer groups, such as the Mole-Dagbon in the North, and in socio-economic terms the biggest cleavage is to be found between the North and the South. In Peru, similarly, place of birth is indicative of group, and Figueroa and Barrón (2005) use this as a proxy for ethnicity in investigating horizontal inequalities. In other cases, where ethnic groups are not or are less-geographically segregated, the use of regional inequalities as a proxy for HIs may lead to erroneous conclusions. In Malaysia, for instance, where geographical segregation of ethnic groups is relatively low, ethnic inequalities have fallen considerably since 1970, but regional inequalities between the country's thirteen states have risen consistently over the same period (Brown 2006). Another word of caution must be voiced relating to the treatment of the national capital region; in many developing countries, GDP is highly concentrated in the capital region, but this region is usually also the site of much greater ethnic heterogeneity than other regions, owing to the migratory pull of the capital. This is likely also to be true of urban centres other than the capital region; for example, of the 306 districts in the 2002 SUSENAS survey in Indonesia, the sixty-seven urban *kota* had an average level of ethnic heterogeneity almost double that of the rural *kabupaten*.[4]

An alternative proxy for ethnicity used in many quantitative studies is a language variable (for example, Easterly and Levine 1997; Alesina, et al. 2002; Collier and Hoeffler 2004),[5] which can sometimes be appropriate. In Indonesia, for instance, ethnicity data were not collected in census and socio-economic surveys under the New Order period, but language was. Comparison of these language statistics at the district level with ethnic data available in the post-New Order period show close correlations, suggesting that language would be an effective proxy for ethnicity in this context (Mancini 2005). Two major problems arise with the use of language as a proxy, however. First, in many other contexts, significant ethno-cultural distance does *not* entail language difference; in the United States, for instance, the vast majority of black and white people alike speak English. Second, in many countries that do manifest linguistic divides there is significant language loss among minority groups, which is often driven by the socio-economic advantage of speaking the 'national' language, usually that of the dominant ethnic group (Crystal 2000). This can thus be problematic for the use of a language proxy for ethnicity, as those who retain their native language are likely to be those with lower levels of education or less social mobility. Thus, comparison of socio-economic performance based on language divisions may, in fact, overestimate the level of horizontal inequality because the higher performing members of a generally disadvantaged minority may be included in the majority group data on the basis of having adopted their language. While these problems render regional and linguistic data inappropriate as proxies for ethno-cultural inequalities in some contexts, their careful use in detailed single-country analysis should provide some important insights into the dynamics of horizontal inequality where ethno-cultural data are unavailable.

---

[4] Using a common measure of ethnic diversity, the Herfindahl concentration index, the urban *kota* score a mean value of 0.480 against a mean score of 0.275 for the rural *kabupaten* (*t*-test stats: $t = 5.6579$, $P > t = 1.000$).

[5] All these studies, as well as many others, make use of the so-called ethnolinguistic fractionalization index, based on the Soviet-produced *Atlas Narodov Mira*. This atlas, however, only compiled groups based on linguistic difference.

5.4.2. Country aid allocation

Like all good-policy–bad-policy distinctions between countries, a difficult issue is whether to allocate more aid to countries with severe inequalities, on the basis that they need more help, or to those with limited inequalities, on the basis that they should be rewarded for inclusive policies. Since HIs generally have deep historic origins, it seems wrong to punish current generations for high horizontal inequalities, and indeed justified to give additional aid to such countries to assist them to overcome the HIs.

Taking horizontal inequalities into account in allocation of aid across countries then suggests that more aid should go to heterogeneous countries than to homogeneous countries, *ceteris paribus* because aid is needed to support the reduction of HIs in heterogeneous countries, but not homogeneous ones. Since there is growing evidence that homogenous countries grow faster for a given investment than heterogeneous ones (for example, Easterly and Levine 1997; Gradstein and Justman 2002), the policy can be seen as helping countries overcome disadvantages arising from heterogeneity. Since uneven regional and cross-group development often has colonial roots (or the saliency of difference and HIs were enlarged as a result of colonial policy), there is additional justification for allocating more aid to such countries, to the extent that aid is some form of compensation for past colonial ills. The policy would be likely to increase the aid allocation of large countries at the expense of small, since large countries in general can be expected to show more heterogeneity than small, offsetting some of the existing bias in aid allocation which favours small countries.

Regressing aid distribution across countries shows, as expected, that aid receipts per capita are strongly and negatively correlated both with national income and country population size (Table 5.2: model 1). Additional variables for ethnic and religious diversity (models 2 and 3, respectively) are also significantly and negatively correlated with the level of aid received, although they only marginally improve the overall fit of the model. Linguistic diversity has no significant relationship (model 4). This suggests that even holding for income and size, aid policy tends to disfavour ethnically and religiously diverse countries.

Aid allocation might also take into account the severity of HIs across heterogeneous countries. This requires some aggregate measure of the severity of HIs for each country, which is not straightforward since there are multiple groups of varying sizes in most countries. For example, it is estimated that there are at least forty-five distinct groups in Nigeria, including only groups that account for 1 per cent or more of the population; and seventy in Indonesia.[6] A review of alternative aggregate measures (Stewart, Brown, and Mancini 2005) suggests

[6] Data derived from the 1999 Demographic Health Survey in Nigeria <http://www.measuredhs.com/pubs/pub_details.cfm?ID=295> and the 1995 Inter-Censal Survey in Indonesia.

Table 5.2. Regression analysis: aid levels and recipient country diversity, 1965–2004

Aid per capita (US$, current (000s))	1	2	3	4
Gross national income per capita (US$, current)	−1.517	−1.611	−1.554	−1.505
	(−5.58)	(−6.02)	(−5.76)	(−5.23)
Population (log)	−18.814	−17.416	−19.392	−16.969
	(−28.42)	(−29.17)	(−28.09)	(−27.04)
Ethnic fractionalization		−23.358		
		(−8.19)		
Religious fractionalization			−23.832	
			(−6.11	
Linguistic fractionalization				−2.474
				(−0.94)
Constant	336.849	325.937	356.213	307.815
	(28.42)	(31.34)	(29.39)	(28.67)
R^2 (with robust standard errors)	0.278	0.277	0.287	0.254
N	4,320	4,280	4,312	4,125

Source: Aid per capita (dependent variable), GNI per capita, and population from World Bank's WDI database and CIA World Factbook; fractionalization data from Alesina et al. (2002).

that a population-weighted coefficient of variation of mean group incomes, termed 'group coefficient of variation', appears to be the best measure from most perspectives (see also Williamson 1965 for an earlier usage of this formula).[7] This measure is very highly correlated with other possible aggregate measures of country HIs, including group Ginis, and group Theils, according to data from Indonesia, South Africa, and the USA, but the measures show very little correlation with individual or household inequality measures, so these cannot be used as a proxy (Stewart, Brown, and Mancini 2005).[8]

It is useful to distinguish two dimensions affecting countries' response to HIs: their capacity and willingness. The extent to which a country has the capacity to deal with horizontal inequalities (the financial, technical, and administrative wherewithal to institute targeted programmes and transfer payments to benefit deprived groups) is likely to be strongly related to broader state capacity, and is

---

[7] Algebraically, where a population with a mean income (years of schooling, etc.) of $\hat{y}$ is split into n groups, each of which comprises proportion p_i of the population ($p_1 + p_2 + \ldots + p_n = 1$) and has group mean income (years of schooling, etc.) of y_i, the formula is given by:

$$GCov = \frac{1}{\hat{y}} \left(\sum_{i=1}^{n} p_i (y_i - \hat{y})^2 \right)^{1/2}$$

[8] As far as within country policy is concerned, there is no need to add up the various group inequalities into a single measure. The simple ratios of achievements of each group on the various dimensions to national averages, or to other major groups in a country, are sufficient. The more complex measures needed for aggregation into a single measure for each country are generally not very meaningful to the population itself, and consequently can lack welfare and political meaning.

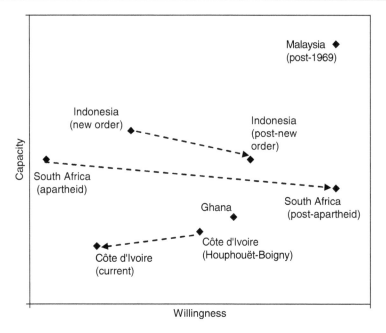

Figure 5.2 Schematic diagram of country context for aid policy

Source: Compiled by authors.

thus likely to be relatively easily factored into existing donor calculations. Countries' willingness to address HIs may vary for a number of reasons. Where the group that is deprived economically is in a politically dominant position—as in Malaysia or South Africa—there is likely to be considerable willingness to tackle HIs. Where the deprived groups are in a political minority, willingness may be less. In some contexts, governments may be generally inclusive, but not aware of the true extent of ethnic or religious disparities within their territory, or they may take the view that generic pro-poor policies would constitute a sufficient response to address HIs. In some cases, governments may be deliberately exclusionary.

Figure 5.2 gives a schematic and oversimplified representation of these two dimensions. Clearly, the HI-related purpose of aid would be to help countries move towards the top-right section of the diagram.[9] Appropriate aid policy

---

[9] It is possible that a positive shift on one axis may be accompanied by a regressive shift on the other. Indonesia is instructive here. Under Suharto's New Order, horizontal inequalities were mainly ignored and indeed effectively banned from public discourse under the so-called 'SARA' regulations that prohibited public discussion of *suku* (ethnicity), *agama* (religion), *ras* (race), and *antar-golongan* (inter-group) relations. Following the transition to democracy in 1998 and the outbreak of a number of conflicts in the archipelago, however, the Indonesian

then depends on where a country is in the willingness/capacity space. (Chapter 7 of this volume has a related discussion on willingness and capacity in the context of aid to fragile states; see section 7.4 and Figure 7.1.)

Where countries are willing to address horizontal inequalities and possess the broad state capacity necessary to introduce such measures, the horizontal inequality-related role of aid may best be accomplished through general budgetary support to support the government's existing efforts. Other countries may have a broadly inclusive attitude but have no explicit policies or monitoring processes and need support on this as well as technical and financial resources; Ghana is perhaps an example here. In this case, policy dialogue is required on the need to translate generally inclusive attitudes into specific policies towards HIs, plus sectoral and project aid directed at correcting them. In the low-capacity cases, technical assistance will then also be needed on data collection, monitoring, and budgeting to help moderate HIs.

Finally, some countries may have severe HIs but the government is doing very little about correcting them and may even be pursuing deliberately exclusionary policies. Côte d'Ivoire has moved increasingly in this direction since the end of the Houphouët-Boigny regime (Langer 2005). This is the most difficult type of case for aid policy. Three approaches are appropriate: first, dialogue and policy conditionality to try and secure a more favourable attitude by the government, although experience suggests this is rarely effective; second, project and sectoral support directed at the deprived groups (an example is Operation Lifeline that supplied food and other basic goods to the south of Sudan in the 1980s); and third, promotion of other objectives which are acceptable to the government and which would also assist the poorer groups: comprehensive education and health services, for example.

PROGRAMME AID ACCOMPANIED BY POLICY DIALOGUE OR CONDITIONALITY, INCLUDING PRSPS

Aid policy in countries unwilling to remedy HIs clearly requires some degree of policy dialogue or conditionality. This may seem somewhat anachronistic, given the increasing replacement of 'conditionality' by an emphasis on 'participatory' approaches to aid which aim to maximize the 'ownership' of development strategies by the recipient country (for example, Kanbur 2000; Morrissey 2004). There is a strong view among many aid donors that aid should be country 'owned' and modalities and PRSPs are intended to help achieve this ownership. However, donors' presence in the PRSP process (sometimes a very large presence, including drafting the papers) and in the discussions over budgets in the poverty-reduction budget support, as well as

government has accepted the need for horizontal restructuring. Yet the transition has arguably also resulted in a considerable reduction in state capacity (Brown, Tajima, and Hadi 2005).

their power to switch financial flows on and off, has meant that in practice 'ownership' is more about appearance and process than reality (Stewart and Wang 2006). Hence, while the detailed conditionalities of the old-style structural adjustment programmes appear to be a thing of the past, the same donors still have a quite 'hard' agenda of policies they wish to promote, including a conventional, Washington consensus model set of policies promoting budgetary balance and pro-market policies at national and international levels, as well as poverty reduction and fulfilment of the Millennium Development Goals (MDGs). In addition, a number of implicit 'soft' conditionalities have entered aid discourse, particularly project aid, through discourses on 'governance' and 'gender mainstreaming' (for example, UNDP 2003; UNESCO 2003).

In this context, introducing HIs into the hard agenda could potentially make a difference. However, if 'ownership' becomes more of a reality, then donors' influence will be much more limited. In this situation, donors can still promote a group-equity agenda through dialogue, but may expect less-direct influence over decisions. In the more-willing cases, the dialogue can be expected to be quite fruitful (although less needed); in the unwilling case, where dialogue with the government is clearly needed, it might fruitfully be extended to other agents, such as local civil society, the media, and so on.

Since the PRSP process is at present the place where much policy dialogue takes place in poor countries, the selection of participants to be inclusive of all significant groups in society is important. To date, however, the selection process appears to have been a bit ad hoc and not to have been systematically inclusive.

While participation is one of the underlying principles of the PRSP approach, there are no specific rules about who to include and how the process should work. Under these circumstances, the participation of minorities or indigenous peoples is either often overlooked or simply regarded as impractical due to their marginalization. (Booth and Curran 2005: 11)

Participation is also limited by language. Analysis of twenty-seven PRSPs showed that in several cases the choice of language limited participation. For example, Cambodia's PRSP was made available in Khmer only in the final version, not in earlier drafts (NGO Forum on Cambodia 2001). In Bolivia some PRSP documents were initially produced only in English (Christian Aid 2001: 13). A Spanish version followed but documents were never translated into local languages (Stewart and Wang 2006).

In any policy dialogue aimed at reducing HIs, the following considerations need to be included.

- That HIs are important and should be monitored.
- Exploration of

- ○ investment, credit, extension policies to help offset regional imbalances;
- ○ education and health policies aimed at ensuring ethnic/religious and regional balance in access;
- ○ policies to outlaw discrimination including fair employment legislation;
- ○ policies to help disadvantaged groups to realize their legal rights (for example, via legal aid);
- ○ policies towards rights to land and natural resources to ensure balance in access and benefits;
- ○ policies towards achieving equality in cultural recognition;
- ○ policies to regulate the media to ensure equal access; and
- ○ policies towards civil society.
- Consideration of affirmative action policies if these do not contribute enough to reducing inequalities.

This is a long list. In practice, assessment of the country situation should reveal where the priorities are. For example, in Ghana, where the largest socio-economic HIs are on a regional basis, it is apparent that the major problem is the economic development of the North and integrating it into the southern economy, so infrastructure investment is a priority and assistance in generating productive opportunities in the North, while many of the other requirements in the list seem to be met.

Analysing the content of PRSPs shows universal inclusion of the 'normal' macro conditions, and almost always social-sector policies. Gender equity enters in a substantial majority of cases, but protection of ethnic minorities is mentioned in just six out of twenty-seven cases. The cases, where ethnic minorities are *not* mentioned include countries which are evidently heterogeneous, such as Azerbaijan, Benin, Burkina Faso, Chad, Guyana, Malawi, Mali, Mauritania, Mozambique, Niger, Rwanda, Tanzania, and Uganda (Stewart and Wang 2005). The 2003 Ghanaian Poverty-Reduction Strategy (GPRS) gave considerable emphasis to regional disparities, while this was absent in the subsequent 2005 version. In 2003, there were few specific policies related to the objective of reducing regional disparities: for example, in the 2003 version virtually all policies were general in nature, while of the list of 52 indicators for monitoring progress only one had a regional dimension. Neither report made any reference to ethnic or religious horizontal inequalities.

The inclusion of horizontal inequalities in policy dialogue thus appears to involve a quite radical addition to the current socio-economic policy dialogue which, as just noted, is primarily focused on securing the adoption of 'good' macro policies, promoting efficient markets, and achieving poverty reduction. Policies towards *political* HIs are an extremely important aspect of generating an inclusive society. Multilateral donors generally claim not to get involved in overtly political aspects. However, the PRSPs do include policies towards public sector governance and management, with budget management, decentralization, public administration reform and anti-corruption measures as sub-elements. HI considerations could potentially play an important role here, including securing ethnic balance within the public sector at all levels as an aspect of governance reform.

Bilateral donors may be involved in discussions and advice on more explicitly political policies, including the extent of democracy and human rights. Incorporating political balance and inclusiveness into the dialogue on these issues implies analysis and discussion of topics such as the nature of the constitution, the extent of federalism and decentralization and the extent and modalities of power sharing. At a general level, this represents an addition to (and departure from) the present governance and politics dialogue. As noted, the former consists of policies to secure greater transparency, accountability, and responsibility, while the latter is focused on promoting multiparty democracy. In fact, the simple multiparty democracy message may be inconsistent with the sort of inclusive government that is required for stability in multiethnic states (Lijphart 1977; Horowitz 1985; Stewart and O'Sullivan 1999; Snyder 2000) while the good governance agenda does not treat issues of political inclusion or exclusion at all.

PUBLIC EXPENDITURE REVIEWS AND POVERTY REDUCTION BUDGET SUPPORT

There are a variety of ways in which donors interact with budgetary allocations. In the 1990s, public expenditure reviews (PERs) were introduced: 'PERs simply refer to the method or procedure used to analyse the level and composition of public expenditure. The main objective is to provide recommendations to governments on the composition and (to some extent) size of public spending'.[10] Incorporating HIs into PERs would involve an assessment of the distribution of the benefits of public expenditure by group, although, as noted earlier, given data problems regional distribution might often have to be used as an initial approximation.

At present, public expenditure reviews do not systematically include any ethnic or regional dimension but, according to Pradhan (1996), involve criteria of efficiency and poverty reduction, aiming to identify whether there is a rationale for public expenditure; and to investigate the impact of alternative expenditure allocations on the poor. While an appropriately modified PER would provide the informational basis for HI-sensitive public expenditure allocation, influence over actual allocation requires some donor role in budgetary decisions. This role is performed by PRSB which was introduced to deal with the weak connection between PRSP and a country's budget

---

[10] See <www1.worldbank.org/education/economicsed/finance/public/perev.htm>.

because 'most PRSPs have a tenuous relation at with the procedures for allocating budgets' (Booth and Curran 2005: 3). From a horizontal inequality perspective, then, an HI-sensitive PER could contribute to an HI-sensitive PRBS. Yet, experience suggests that discussions over exclusion are difficult to conduct in general PRBS: 'The experience of many advisers [for DFID] has been that in comparison with support through projects and through PRBS sector support, *general PRBS has reduced the room for policy dialogue on issues that have always been tricky—such as inequality*' (Payne and Neville 2006: 9; original emphasis).

Yet, others have stated that the 'the longer preparation processes and in-depth engagement with national governments and other partners inherent in new aid mechanisms such as sectoral and general budget support is providing an opportunity for early engagement on sensitive issues such as gender discrimination' (Macdonagh 2005; Payne and Neville 2006: 10). Although it seems that it is easier to get 'sensitive' issues on the agenda with sectoral rather than general budgetary loans, it is important to supplement sectoral and project donor policies with policies towards and discussion about public expenditure as a whole because HIs go beyond particular sectoral allocations and concern the economy (and budget) as a whole.

To plan expenditure so as to reduce horizontal inequalities requires knowledge of the major HIs in a country, the pattern of non-aid government expenditure, and the contribution aid might make—in the light of government public expenditure plans—to offsetting them. A major and difficult issue is to identify what is holding back progress on HIs. In some cases it may be straightforward—for example, lack of education and credit. But, in others, the problem may be low returns on both because of asymmetrical social capital and discrimination (Stewart and Langer 2008). Where the problem seems to be a simple matter of resources, the aid solution is relatively easy. But with more complex issues related to social capital and discrimination, expenditure alone can do little, and one is back to a situation where a policy dialogue is required. PERs and budgetary support thus represent an opportunity to assess the distribution of both current and capital public expenditure from an HI perspective and to discuss desirable shifts in its sectoral composition and ethnic/regional allocation. Hence, together these could be invaluable instruments for promoting public expenditure that will contribute to moderating horizontal inequalities.

SECTORAL AND PROJECT AID

Sectoral aid is currently disbursed as sector-wide approach (SWAP) programmes:

The defining characteristics of a SWAP are that all significant public funding for the sector supports a single sector policy and expenditure programme, under Government leadership, adopting common approaches across the sector, and progressing towards relying on

Government procedures to disburse and account for all public expenditure, however funded. (Foster and Mackintosh-Walker 2001: 1)

To date, SWAPs have been concerned with poverty reduction, but not exclusion or HIs: Booth and Curran conclude (2005: 18) that 'there appears to be little evidence of exclusion being explicitly addressed in SWAPs', and, moreover, '[t]here has been little systematic thinking about tackling exclusion in SWAPs' (ibid.: 19). Indeed, an analysis of education and the SWAP approach concluded that the shift to SWAPs could make it more difficult to focus on concrete actions for gender equality in the short term (Rose and Subrahmaniam 2005). As far as poverty is concerned, however, Foster and Mackintosh-Walker conclude that 'more encouraging than the results achieved is that the joint reviews conducted as part of the SWAP process have generated analysis and debate that has helped to focus on poverty in Ghana and Bangladesh health and Bolivia agriculture' (Foster and Mackintosh-Walker 2001: p. ix).

In principle, SWAPs could be a useful instrument for promoting HIs, since they are more specific than the PRSB, and more comprehensive than projects, offering an opportunity for monitoring HIs in particular sectors and reforming resource allocation and policies in the sector. Introducing horizontal inequality-considerations into the process of sectoral planning could contribute to correcting HIs in the sector concerned, even though balance in economic and social access across groups does not necessarily mean balance in every sector—inevitably some groups will be more specialized in agriculture, some in mining or industry. But group balance *is* needed in the provision of basic social sectors (health, education) and in economic infrastructure, so HI considerations are more directly relevant to SWAPs related to these sectors, rather than industry or trade. In the latter, imbalances should be recorded and reasons for them identified, as there may be issues of fair access or affirmative action which should form part of sectoral policies. While the sectoral analysis of expenditure relates to government and (official) aid expenditures, it is necessary to assess inequalities including all assets and expenditures (private and NGO as well) before expenditure needs can be identified, while projects in particular sectors are included in the general coordinated approach of SWAPs, NGO or private-sector-financed projects are not usually included. Where government policy is favourable to redressing HIs, general budgetary support may be sufficient, plus technical assistance if required. However, in situations where the government is unwilling, projects targeted at particular deprived groups may be the most effective approach. Yet, limitations on a project-only approach must be acknowledged: first, there is the issue of fungibility, which may reduce the net impact of the projects on the deprived group; and, second, projects may correct particular infrastructural deprivations, but can mostly do little about unfavourable economic opportunities. None the less, there is considerable scope for exploring types of project most suitable for correcting HIs in generally hostile environments. Such projects might include education and training, credit schemes, and marketing assistance specifically directed towards particular groups.

HUMAN RIGHTS AND SOCIAL EXCLUSION APPROACHES TO AID

Some aid donors and NGOs have begun to adopt a 'human rights approach' (CIDA, DFID, the DAC, Wateraid), while others are considering putting social exclusion at the centre of their agenda (DFID). Both are highly compatible with the HI approach, though much depends on how they are interpreted in practice. The comprehensive nature of HRs, including social and economic, civil and political, and cultural rights, is consistent with our comprehensive approach to the definition of HRs, which also have socio-economic, political, and cultural dimensions. However, the extent of the consistency depends on the interpretation of an HR approach (by no means clear despite the fact that it is often talked about). Some put prime emphasis on civil and political rights, ignoring economic and social rights which form a critical component of HIs. Moreover, the interpretation of civil and political HRs is usually in terms of various political entitlements—to vote, to free speech, to a free press, freedom to practise religion. These can be realized while leaving major imbalances—political liberties, for example, are consistent with total exclusion of minority groups from government, or from the bureaucracy. The relatively weak political and socio-economic position of Muslims in India, for example, is consistent with broad realization of political HRs.

If an HR approach is to encompass horizontal inequalities, it clearly must include social and economic rights. But, as with political and civil rights, whether this will be sufficient to encompass HIs depends on the interpretation. Economic and social HRs can be interpreted as involving comprehensive access to certain basic services, which can be consistent with high group inequalities, especially in middle-income countries. Others interpret the realization of HRs as including the requirement of balance among groups (for example, Wateraid), in which case the approach would contribute to moderating HIs. The principle of 'progressive realization' (that is, that low-income countries cannot be expected to realize comprehensive economic and social HRs in the short-term) can also leave major imbalances and deprivations. Minority groups may be left to last in the prioritization process. A further issue is how an HR approach is operationalized. Unless the approach becomes embodied in a country's constitution, and then legally enforceable, it means little other than a general aspiration that HRs should be fulfilled. Even then severe inequalities may remain. For example, post-Apartheid South Africa has placed human rights at the centre of its agenda—indeed they are enshrined in the Constitution. Yet, horizontal inequalities remain extremely severe, and, indeed, according to some measures, income HIs actually rose in the first five years after Apartheid was ended (Stewart, Brown, and Mancini 2005). Here the problem is implementation in the context of severe economic constraints.

In general, it seems that promoting HRs is certainly complementary with, and indeed may be regarded as a necessary aspect of, achieving an inclusive society without severe HIs, but it is not generally a sufficient condition.

The adoption of considerations of 'social exclusion' as a principle in aid allocation is also generally consistent with an HI approach. It is still at an early stage, so precise interpretation is not possible. In principle, however, political and economic inclusion is a necessary aspect of an approach devoted to eliminating social exclusion, as it is for an HI approach (Stewart 2004; DFID 2005).

5.5. Conclusions

Addressing HIs should be an important part of development policy in multicultural societies with severe inequalities. This is true whether or not a society appears to be fragile, or has suffered or is suffering conflict. Aid has an important role to play here, especially in countries where it accounts for a large proportion of government resources and thus can be expected to have a considerable influence over patterns of development. To achieve this, in some countries aid donors will have to be prepared to try to influence development objectives in countries which have not themselves chosen to tackle horizontal inequalities. This goes against current rhetoric of participation and ownership, though the practice shows that aid donors still do exert considerable influence over development policy in many areas.

This chapter has argued that for the most part HIs have not formed part of aid policy. Indeed, sometimes aid policies have exacerbated HIs, albeit probably unintentionally, as in the case of structural adjustment in Ghana. Exploration of current aid instruments shows many ways in which aid could contribute towards changing HIs if there were a decision to do so. In general, making the reduction of HIs an objective of aid policy would suggest allocating more aid resources to heterogeneous societies. Cross-country evidence shows that at present the bias is in the opposite direction, with homogeneous countries, at any given income per capita level, getting more aid than heterogeneous. This arises probably from a small country bias in aid distribution. Frequently, in countries with severe HIs, these are entrenched in the political system, and then aid donors' influence is likely to be rather marginal. In such situations, local political change is the real requirement for the correction of horizontal inequalities. All aid donors can do is to put the topic on the agenda, as part of the norms of 'good policy', as well as making a (normally marginal) contribution via their own projects.

Most of the chapter was devoted to exploring how aid might affect social and economic horizontal inequalities. But, in the field of political HIs too, an HI approach would affect donor dialogue on questions of governance and political systems in ways that differ quite sharply with the usual dialogue in this area. Two recent approaches to aid policy—a human rights approach and a social exclusion one—would be consistent with the approach suggested here. To date, neither of these approaches has been interpreted with the precision that is suggested by one focused on horizontal inequalities. Although the chapter has been concerned to analyse how taking HIs seriously would affect aid allocation and conditionality, this does not, of course, mean that all other principles of aid become irrelevant. The objectives of poverty reduction and economic development generally should remain fundamental aspects of aid policy.

References

Alesina, A., et al. (2002) 'Fractionalization'. National Bureau of Economic Research Working Papers. Cambridge, Mass.: NBER.

Badgett, M. V. L., and H. L. Hartmann (1995) 'The Effectiveness of Equal Employment Opportunity Policies'. In M. C. Simms, *Economic Perspectives in Affirmative Action.* Washington, DC: Joint Center for Political and Economic Studies.

Barrows, W. L. (1976) 'Ethnic Diversity and Political Instability in Black Africa'. *Comparative Political Studies,* 9: 139–70.

Booth, D., and Z. Curran (2005) 'Aid Instruments and Exclusion'. Report for the UK Department for International Development. London: Overseas Development Institute.

Broman, C. (1997) 'Race-related Factors and Life Satisfaction among African Americans'. *Journal of Black Psychology,* 23: 36–49.

Brown, G. K. (2006) 'Dimensions of Inequality in Malaysia: Individual, Ethnic, and Regional'. Unpublished MS.

——and D. R. Williams (1999) 'Being Black and Feeling Blue: Mental Health Consequences of Racial Discrimination'. *Race and Society,* 2: 117–31.

——Y. Tajima, and S. Hadi (2005) 'Overcoming Violent Conflict: Peace and Development Analysis in Central Sulawesi'. Jakarta: Conflict Prevention and Recovery Unit, United Nations Development Programme (CPRU-UNDP), Lembaga Ilmu Pengetahuan Indonesia (LIPI), Badan Pusat Perencangan Nasional (BAPPENAS).

Bryden, L., and K. Legge (1996) *Adjusting Society: The World Bank, the IMF and Ghana.* London: Macmillan.

Christian Aid (2001) 'Ignoring the Experts: Poor People's Exclusion from Poverty Reduction Strategies'. *Christian Aid Policy Briefing.* <http://training.itcilo.it/decentwork/staffconf2002/presentations/ref-christianaid-excluding%20the%20poor%20from%20PRSP.pdf>.

Cohen, J. M. (1995) 'Ethnicity, Foreign Aid and Economic Growth in sub-Saharan Africa: The Case of Kenya'. Development Discussion Papers 520. Cambridge, Mass.: Harvard Institute for International Development.

Collier, P., and A. Hoeffler (2004) 'Greed and Grievance in Civil War'. *Oxford Economic Papers*, 56: 563–95.

Crystal, D. (2000) *Language Death*. Cambridge: Cambridge University Press.

DFID (Department for International Development) (2005) 'Reducing Poverty by Tackling Social Exclusion'. DFID Policy Paper. London: DFID.

Easterly, W., and R. Levine (1997) 'Africa's Growth Tragedy: Policies and Ethnic Divisions'. *Quarterly Journal of Economics*, 112: 1203–50.

Esman, M. J., and R. J. Herring (1995) 'The Problem: How Development Assistance Affects Ethnic Conflict'. Paper presented to the Conference on Development Assistance and Ethnic Conflict. Ithaca, NY: Cornell University.

Figueroa, A., and M. Barrón (2005) 'Inequality, Ethnicity and Social Disorder in Peru'. University of Oxford Centre for Research on Inequality, Human Security and Ethnicity Working Papers. Oxford: CRISE.

Foster, M., and S. Mackintosh-Walker (2001) Sector Wide Programmes and Poverty Reduction. Overseas Development Institute Working Paper 157. London: ODI.

Gaffney, P. D. (2000) 'Burundi: The Long Sombre Shadow of Ethnic Instability'. In E. W. Nafziger, F. Stewart, and R. Väyrynen (eds), *War, Hunger, and Displacement: The Origins of Humanitarian Emergencies*. Vol. ii. *Weak States and Vulnerable Economies: Humanitarian Emergencies in Developing Countries*. Oxford: Oxford University Press, 159–85.

Gates, S., and M. S. Murshed (2005) 'Spatial–Horizontal Inequality and the Maoist Insurgency in Nepal'. *Review of Development Economics*, 9: 121–34.

Gradstein, M., and M. Justman (2002) 'Education, Social Cohesion, and Economic Growth'. *American Economic Review*, 92: 1192–204.

Gurr, T. R. (1993) *Minorities at Risk: A Global View of Ethnopolitical Conflicts*. Washington, DC: United States Institute of Peace Press.

——and W. H. Moore (1997) 'Ethnopolitical Rebellion: A Cross-sectional Analysis of the 1980s with Risk Assessments for the 1990s'. *American Journal of Political Science*, 41: 1079–103.

Hafeez, S. (1993) *The Girl Child in Pakistan*. Islamabad: UNICEF.

Horowitz, D. L. (1985) *Ethnic Groups in Conflict*. Berkeley, Calif.: University of California Press.

Kanbur, R. (2000) 'Aid, Conditionality and Debt in Africa'. In F. Tarp (ed.), *Foreign Aid and Development: Lessons Learnt and Directions for the Future*. London: Routledge.

Langer, A. (2005) 'Horizontal Inequalities and Violent Group Mobilisation in Côte d'Ivoire'. *Oxford Development Studies*, 33: 25–45.

Langer, A. (2007) 'The Peaceful Management of Horizontal Inequalities in Ghana'. CRISE Working Paper No. 25. Oxford: Centre for Research on Inequality, Human Security, and Ethnicity, University of Oxford.

Leith, J. (1998) 'Resettlement History, Resources and Resistance in North Halmahera'. In S. Pannell and F. von Benda-Beckmann (eds), *Old World Places, New World Problems: Exploring Issues of Resource Management in Eastern Indonesia*. Canberra: Australian National University Centre for Resource and Environmental Studies, 113–42.

Lijphart, A. (1977) *Democracy in Plural Societies: A Comparative Exploration*. New Haven, Conn.: Yale University Press.

Macdonagh, S. (2005) *Maternal Mortality: Evaluation of DFID Development Assistance: Gender Equality and Women's Empowerment; Phase II Thematic Evaluation*. London: Department for International Development.

McKay, A., and E. Aryeetey (2004) 'Operationalizing Pro-poor Growth: A Country Case Study of Ghana'. Paper presented at the ISSER/World Bank/DfID/USAID International Conference on Shared Growth in Africa, Accra, 21–2 July.

Macours, K. (2004) *Ethnic Divisions, Contract Choice and Search Costs in the Guatemalan Land Rental Market*. Washington, DC: Paul H. Nitze School of Advanced International Studies, Johns Hopkins University.

Mancini, L. (2005) 'Horizontal Inequality and Communal Violence: Evidence from Indonesian Districts'. Centre for Research on Inequality, Human Security and Ethnicity, University of Oxford Working Paper 22. Oxford: CRISE.

——and A. Langer (2008) 'Horizontal Inequality and Communal Violence: Evidence from Indonesian Districts'. In F. Stewart (ed.), *Horizontal Inequalities and Conflict: Understanding Group Violence in Multiethnic Societies*. Basingstoke: Palgrave Macmillan.

Morrissey, O. (2004) 'Conditionality and Aid Effectiveness Re-evaluated'. *World Economy*, 27: 153–71.

NGO Forum on Cambodia (2001) 'Results of Initial Discussions among NGOs/CSOs on the National Poverty Reduction Strategy of Cambodia'. <http://www.imf.org/external/np/prsp/2002/khm/01/122002.pdf>.

Okolo, A. (1999) 'The Nigerian Census: Problems and Prospects'. *American Statistician*, 53: 321–5.

Østby, G. (2008) 'Horizontal Inequalities, Political Environment and Civil Conflict: Evidence from 55 Developing Countries'. In F. Stewart (ed.), *Horizontal Inequalities and Conflict: Understanding Group Violence in Multiethnic Societies*. Basingstoke: Palgrave Macmillan.

Payne, L., and S. Neville (2006) 'Aid Instruments, Social Exclusion and Gender: Background Paper for DFID's International Guidance on Aid Instruments'. London: Social Development Direct.

Pradhan, S. (1996) 'Evaluating Public Spending: A Framework for Public Expenditure Reviews'. World Bank Discussion Paper 323. Washington, DC: World Bank.

Rose, P., and R. Subrahmaniam (2005) *Evaluation of DFID Development Assistance: Gender Equality and Women's Empowerment; Phase II Thematic Evaluation: Education*. London: Department for International Development.

Snyder, J. (2000) *From Voting to Violence*. New York: W. W. Norton.

Songsore, J. (2003) *Regional Development in Ghana: The Theory and the Reality*. Accra: Woeli Publishing Services.

Stewart, F. (2000) 'Crisis Prevention: Tackling Horizontal Inequalities'. *Oxford Development Studies*, 28: 245–62.

——(2002) 'Horizontal Inequalities: A Neglected Dimension of Development'. Queen Elizabeth House Working Paper Series 81. Oxford: CRISE. <http://www3.qeh.ox.ac.uk/pdf/qehwp/qehwps81.pdf>.

——(2004) 'The Relationship Between Horizontal Inequality and Social Exclusion'. *CRISE Newsletter*, Winter.

——and A. Langer (2008) 'Horizontal Inequality and Communal Violence: Evidence from Indonesian Districts'. In F. Stewart (ed.), *Horizontal Inequalities and Conflict: Understanding Group Violence in Multiethnic Societies*. Basingstoke: Palgrave Macmillan.

——and M. O'Sullivan (1999) 'Democracy, Conflict and Development: Three Cases'. In G. Ranis, S.-C. Hu, and Y.-P. Chu, *The Political Economy of Comparative Development into the 21st Century: Essays in Memory of John C. H. Fei*. Cheltenham: Edward Elgar.

——and M. Wang (2006) 'Do PRSPs Empower Poor Countries and Disempower the World Bank, or is it the Other Way Round?'. In G. Ranis, J. R. Vreeland, and S. Kosack (eds), *Globalization and the Nation State*. London: Routledge.

——G. Brown, and L. Mancini (2005) 'Why Horizontal Inequality? Issues of Application and Measurement'. University of Oxford Centre for Research on Inequality, Human Security and Ethnicity Working Papers 19. Oxford: CRISE.

Tilly, C. (1999) *Durable Inequality*. Berkeley, Calif.: University of California Press.

Tirtosudarmo, R. (1995) 'The Political Demography of National Integration and its Policy Implications for a Sustainable Development in Indonesia'. *Indonesian Quarterly*, 23: 369–83.

UNDP (2003) *Transforming the Mainstream: Gender in UNDP*. New York: United Nations Development Programme.

UNESCO (2003) UNESCO's Gender Mainstreaming Implementation Framework for 2002–7. Paris: UNESCO.

USIS and USAID (1992) 'Educating the Girl Child: A Seminar'. Islamabad: United States Information Service and United States Agency for International Development.

Uvin, P. (2000) 'Rwanda: The Social Roots of Genocide'. In E. W. Nafziger, F. Stewart, and R. Väyrynen (eds), *War, Hunger, and Displacement: The Origins of Humanitarian Emergencies*. Vol. ii. *Weak States and Vulnerable Economies: Humanitarian Emergencies in Developing Countries*. Oxford: Oxford University Press, 159–85.

van de Walle, D., and D. Gunewardena (2001) 'Sources of Ethnic Inequality in Viet Nam'. *Journal of Development Economics*, 65: 177–207.

Williamson, J. G. (1965) 'Regional Inequality and the Process of National Development: A Description of the Patterns'. *Economic Development and Cultural Change*, 13: 1–84.

World Bank (1994) 'Indonesia Transmigration Program: A Review of Five Bank-supported Projects'. Operations Evaluation Study 12988, Washington, DC: World Bank.

Part III

Aid to Fragile and Conflict-affected Countries

6

Conflict Prevention as a Policy Objective of Development Aid

Sakiko Fukuda-Parr[1]

6.1. Introduction

The current consensus objective of development aid in the international community is to reduce poverty in general and to achieve the Millennium Development Goals (MDGs) in particular. But the objectives of aid can be defined in many ways, and have in fact varied over time with shifting priorities within the international community about the ultimate ends of development and the means of advancing these ends. While MDGs define the consensus policy objective of the development community, the dominant analytical framework identifies economic growth as the principal means to achieving them, with particular concern over poor governance—institutions and policies—as major obstacles to accelerating growth.[2]

This chapter argues that more attention should be given to conflict prevention as a policy objective of development aid and explores the implications of doing so for aid programme priorities and the international aid architecture in general. Section 6.2 chapter reviews current trends in violent conflict as an obstacle to achieving the MDGs; it identifies sixty-one worst-performing countries and examines their vulnerability to conflict owing to the presence of the socio-economic correlates of internal war. Section 6.3 reviews how vulnerability can be addressed, focusing on ways that development policies and development aid can raise risks of civil war. Section 6.4 reviews the adjustments that would be made in aid architecture if conflict prevention were incorporated as a policy objective. Section 6.5 concludes.

---

[1] Research support from Rachel Nadelman and Carol Messier is gratefully acknowledged.
[2] This is reflected, for example, in the way that the World Bank's Country Performance Assessment Indicators are constructed. These points will be elaborated in the following sections of the chapter.

6.2. Violent conflict as an obstacle to achieving the MDGs

Review of global data on key MDG indicators on income poverty, hunger, primary education, gender equality, child mortality, and access to water and sanitation shows that the majority of countries least likely to achieve the MDGs are affected by conflict, in most cases with destructive consequences for development.

6.2.1. Violent conflict in the worst performing countries

MDG assessment reports[3] consistently show progress towards achieving the MDGs generally lags behind the ambition of meeting the targets globally by 2015, and is highly uneven among goals and targets, regions and countries. While the global goal of halving income poverty is likely to be met, this is due mostly to the progress in China and the rest of Asia. Progress has been slow across almost all the indicators in most countries of sub-Saharan Africa. Violent conflict is an important factor that affects those countries that are farthest behind and least likely to reach the goals. *Human Development Report* 2003 (UNDP 2003) categorizes countries according to their prospects into four groups:

  (i) Low levels of poverty and adequate progress to achieve MDGs (such as Chile).
 (ii) High levels of poverty and rapid progress, adequate to achieve MDGs (such as China).
(iii) High levels of poverty and slow progress, needing to accelerate progress to achieve the MDGs, but possessing considerable domestic resources to do so (such as Brazil).
(iv) High levels of poverty and slow progress, needing to accelerate progress to achieve the MDGs, and lacking domestic resources to do so (such as Burundi and Papua New Guinea).

Achieving the targets is the greatest challenge for the fourth category of countries for several reasons. They are starting from high levels of poverty (in income but also in other MDG dimensions such as education) and therefore will have to achieve more to attain the targets of reducing the proportions of people in income and human poverty.[4] They are making slow progress now and therefore likely to be straddled with difficult obstacles involving financial,

---

[3] For example, Niger must reduce income poverty by 30.7 percentage points, down from 61.4 per cent; whereas for Bolivia, the target reduction is 7.2 percentage points, down from 14.4 per cent over the same period of time.

[4] For example, Niger must reduce income poverty by 30.7 percentage points, down from 61.4 per cent; whereas for Bolivia, the target reduction is 7.2 percentage points, down from 14.4 per cent over the same period of time.

capacity, technical, institutional, and political factors. Urgent action is needed to accelerate progress in this group of countries, some of which are not only stagnating but have experienced reversals.[5] Some action can be taken by the countries themselves without relying upon external resources. These include policy and institutional reforms to improve efficiency in the delivery of social services or to foster economic growth that benefits poor people (UNDP 2003). But other actions can best be facilitated with external financial and technical resources. This fourth group, therefore, captures the *worst-performing countries* that require *priority* international attention. Using the data and methodology of the 2003 *Human Development Report*,[6] we can identify sixty-one countries in this category (Annex 1).

6.2.2. War undermines development

One of the most striking findings of recent studies on the relationship between civil war and development is the strong statistical association between low levels of gross domestic product (GDP) per capita and the occurrence of conflict (Hegre et al. 2001; Collier and Hoeffler 2002a; Elbadawi and Sambanis 2002; Fearon and Laitin 2003). Rate of growth is also inversely correlated with the occurrence of conflict: twice as high for a country with a growth rate of –6 per cent compared with a country whose growth rate is +6 per cent (Humphreys 2003). These correlations have given rise to a rich debate on their relationship.

There is little controversy that at least one explanation is that low GDP per capita is the consequence of war. The destructive consequences of armed conflict have been well documented and can be traced to immediate impacts on human well-being as well as longer term development.[7] Wars destroy and disrupt physical infrastructure, human capital, government capacity, and services. As GDP shrinks, government revenues also decline, and with resources diverted to war effort, expenditures for productive and social sectors shrink further. Collier (1999) estimates that the cumulative effect of a seven-year war is

[5] In fact, development data on trends of the 1990s show new extremes, where well-performing countries did spectacularly well while the worst performers experienced reversals (UNDP 2003). Poverty increased in several dimensions; twenty-one countries registered a rise in hunger rates, fourteen in child mortality, twelve in primary enrolment and, for the thirty-seven out of sixty-seven where there are data, in income poverty.

[6] See Box 2.4 and Feature 2.1 in UNDP (2003) for basic methodology for assessing countries as 'top' or 'high' priority based on the level of achievement and rate of progress. Here I use the data from United Nations Development Programme (2003) that assess the levels and rate of progress in the following indicators: income poverty, hunger, primary education, gender equality, child mortality, access to water, and access to sanitation. Countries are included if they are priority in at least two indicators, or top priority in one of two indicators for which data are available, and are low-income countries. It is important to note that data are missing in many countries.

[7] The study of these consequences has now grown but was relatively new. See, for example, the 1994 project led by Frances Stewart and Valpy FitzGerald at Queen Elizabeth House, Oxford University, that was one of the first studies, in Stewart et al. (2000).

around 60 per cent of annual GDP. A recent study by Milanovic (2005), which looks at causes of slow growth in the world's poorest countries over the last two decades, identifies war and civil strife as the single most important factor to explain slow growth, accounting for an income loss of about 40 per cent, while poor policies and slow reforms play a minimal role, and democratization, education, and health attainments have no or negligible effects.

Human and economic costs of conflict vary across countries considerably, and in some countries the economy continues to grow, social indicators continue to improve, and poverty continues to decline even as violent armed conflict is waged (Stewart and Fitzgerald 2001; Collier 2003). This has been the case, for example, in Sri Lanka and Uganda for over a decade (Stewart and Fitzgerald 2001), Nepal in the recent insurgency period (World Bank 2006), and in Guatemala in the 1980s and 1990s (Stewart, Huang, and Wang 2001). But, the majority of wars lead to deterioration and increased poverty. A detailed empirical review of eighteen countries by Stewart, Huang, and Wang (2001) finds that per capita income fell in fifteen of them, food production in thirteen, export growth declined in twelve, and that debt increased in all eighteen.

These consequences have immediate impacts on human lives. Income poverty rises as employment opportunities shrink and shift to the informal sector. Nutrition deteriorates with the disruption of food supplies. Diseases spread with population movements. These consequences are reflected in such indicators as higher infant and child mortality rates, poorer nutritional status, and lower education enrolment. These costs are not always spread evenly across the population; some suffer much more than others. Children and women tend to be particularly vulnerable in these situations. These immediate consequences also translate into long-term consequences that can undermine, for example, the human potential of a generation, formal and informal institutions, social capital, and government capacity. The eighteen-country review (Stewart, Huang, and Wang 2001) shows thirteen countries experiencing rising infant mortality and declining caloric intake. The negative consequences of war continue into the long term and undermine the basis for development as they not only erode the stock of human and physical capital but also weaken social capital and institutional capacity in public, private, and community sectors (Stewart and Fitzgerald 2001).

6.2.3. Vulnerability to outbreak of violent conflict: the socio-economic correlates of conflict

Past war not only retards development in the worst-performing countries, but also increases their vulnerability to future outbreaks of conflict. Statistical evidence shows that the single most important factor to predispose countries to conflict is a history of war (Collier and Hoeffler 2002a). The rich and growing literature on the socio-economic causes of civil war in developing countries[8] identifies several other factors: poverty and the low opportunity costs to taking up arms; demographic structure and the youth bulge (Cincotta, Engelman, and Anastasion 2003); migration and environmental pressure (Homer-Dixon 1991); 'horizontal inequalities' and the exclusion of ethnic and other cultural identity groups (see Chapter 5 of this volume; and Stewart 2002); and dependence on mineral resources (Collier and Hoeffler 2002a).

One explanation for why poverty is associated with high risk of civil war is that in situations of economic stagnation and high poverty people have little to lose in waging war. In particular, in periods of economic stagnation there are larger numbers of disaffected youths, especially males, who may be more easily mobilized to join armed rebel groups. Cincotta, Engelman, and Anastasion (2003) study the demographic structures and incidence of war in the 1990s. They find that the outbreak of civil conflict was more than twice as likely in countries in which the youth aged 15 to 25 years comprised more than 40 per cent of the adult population compared with countries with lower proportions. War was also twice as likely in countries with urban population growth rates above 4 per cent than countries with lower rates. At the early stages of the demographic transition, a surge in the adolescent population outpaces job growth. This exacerbates problems of low incomes, low levels of female education, and high levels of unemployment and poverty that can leave young men frustrated with poor life prospects and susceptible to being easily recruited by rebel movements.

Homer-Dixon and the 'Toronto Group' (Homer-Dixon 1991) argue that many wars stem from struggles over resources in the context of environmental deterioration. As population growth puts pressure on the environment, people migrate. Local communities compete with migrant groups for increasingly scarce resources. Stewart and her collaborators at Queen Elizabeth House have made extensive studies of 'horizontal inequalities' or 'inequalities between culturally-defined—ethnic, religious, racial or regional identity—groups' as a source of conflict (Stewart 2002, 2003). Graham Brown, Frances Stewart, and Arnim Langer's contribution to this volume (Chapter 5) argues that individuals mobilize on the basis of group loyalty rather than individual gain. While the literature on conflict indicates evidence of either weak or no relationship between inequality measured as distribution of incomes among individuals (vertical inequality), researchers do find evidence of a relationship between inequality among groups (horizontal inequality) and conflict (Brown 2007). Case studies of many conflicts document how they are deeply rooted in historically entrenched grievances that result from a long history of 'horizontal

---

[8] Excellent reviews of this literature have been published in Humphreys (2003); Humphreys and Varshney (2004); Murshed (2007); and the Human Security Centre (2003).

inequalities'; the exclusion of ethnic/religious groups from economic, political, and social opportunities can escalate into violent attack on the state.

Collier and Hoeffler (2002a) find that a country with more than 25 per cent dependence on primary commodity exports is more than five times more likely to experience conflict than countries with lower dependence on these resources. Resources that are easily transportable, such as diamonds, are particularly susceptible to capture by rebel groups, particularly as this does not require control over large territory. Collier (2003) argues that while the search to gain control of rich mineral resources may not be at the origin of an armed rebellion, it can become an incentive that in itself fuels conflict. And, because rebel armies need a source of financing to continue, it becomes a critical factor in perpetuating the conflict.

This literature on the socio-economic correlates of poverty has generated controversy and disagreement.[9] Much remains to be understood about the causes of civil war. Yet, a decade of rigorous research has produced findings with important policy implications for development strategies and aid priorities. These policy implications have received little attention in the international community, and mis-governance of natural resources is the only identified risk factor around which there has been a policy response. Moreover, much of the debate over these findings has focused on the divergent explanations and controversies while the points of consensus have received little attention. For one thing, they do share in common a strong conclusion that economic and social factors are important aspects of conflict. It is also important to see that the divergent explanations of conflict are not mutually exclusive but complementary (Stewart and Brown 2003) and mutually reinforcing. Moreover, each conflict is unique so that different factors and dynamics operate. It is also widely agreed that state fragility and weak capacity is a common element in all civil wars in developing countries. Poor countries with weak capacity are less able to manage negative dynamics (Fearon and Laitin 2003; Goodhand 2003; Picciotto, Olonisakin, and Clarke 2006). Weak states are less able to protect themselves against insurgency, to deploy political peaceful means to resolve conflict and prevent its onset, or to resolve local disputes when they arise. Weak states are also less able to fulfil their minimum obligations of maintaining security and providing basic social services. Declining social services can lead to a breakdown in the social contract between government and governed (Nafziger and Auvinen 2000). People lose confidence in the state's ability to protect them when threatened by gross violations of human rights by rebel groups, or sometimes by agents of the state itself.

Review of data for sixty-one worst-performing countries with respect to MDGs reveals in almost every country the presence of more than one risk factor.

---

[9] See Murshed (2007) for an excellent summary critique of this literature.

By definition, all of the sixty-one countries have high levels of poverty.[10] Demographic pressures are high in these countries; in twelve of the sixty-one, youth (15 to 29 years) make up more than 40 per cent of the population while in thirty-two others this age group comprises between 35 per cent and 39 per cent of the population.[11] Horizontal inequality is a marked characteristic of many of these countries. In a range of one to ten (ten being the worst rating) in the failed-states index indicator of 'uneven economic development along group lines', all countries with data (fifty-six out of the sixty-one countries) are rated at five or above, and thirty-four are rated at above eight. Most also have a history of group grievance, with fifty scoring above four in the indicator of 'legacy of vengeance-seeking group grievance', and twelve above eight. All score above five in the indicator of 'rise of factionalized elites'. In fact, all but six of the top forty countries in the failed-states index that measures vulnerability to violent internal conflict are in our list of sixty-one worst-performing countries (Fund for Peace 2007).[12]

Another important risk factor is neighbourhood—sharing a border with countries at war puts significant burdens on the development resources of a country especially regarding the inflow of refugees. Tanzania is affected by conflicts in Uganda and Congo; Guinea by Liberia and Sierra Leone, Burkina Faso by Côte d'Ivoire, and Kenya by Somalia. Conflict in neighbouring countries creates economic disruptions that lead to slower growth (Murdoch and Sandler 2002; Collier 2003). Political dynamics also lead to spillover effects as neighbouring countries become involved with the warring parties, illicit activities such as arms and minerals trade spread, and a conflict becomes regional in nature, such as the conflicts in West Africa involving Sierra Leone, Liberia, Côte d'Ivoire, Guinea, and the Great Lakes region involving Congo, Burundi, and Rwanda. Recent studies have found that in 2002 eleven of fifteen conflict cases were, in fact, spillover cases (Seybolt 2002).

Table 6.1 summarizes the risk factors present in the sixty-one worst-performing countries in which MDGs will not be achieved without significant acceleration: forty-three have a history of violent conflict since 1990; another eight border countries that have experienced conflict; and two had experienced protracted war before 1990. Most of these countries score high on indicators of horizontal inequality as a risk factor for civil war, and have a significant youth bulge.

---

[10] Poverty is used here to mean not only income poverty but other dimensions of inadequate capability such as health and education. The sixty-one countries were selected for having both high levels and slow progress in poverty reduction in more than one dimension.

[11] Data based on calculations using United Nations (2007).

[12] See <http://www.fundforpeace.org>.

Table 6.1. Sixty-one worst performing countries requiring priority international assistance to achieve the MDGs by 2015

Conflict affected 1990–2005	Number of countries 43
Neighbourhood (not affected but bordering on countries conflict affected countries) Horizontal inequality: high scores in	8
1. Legacy of vengeance seeking group grievance	50
2. Uneven development along group lines	56
3. Rise of factionalized elites	64
Youth bulge	
4. Over 40%	12
5. 35%–39%	32

Source: Calculated from Table 6.2.

6.3. Addressing vulnerability to conflict

How should this vulnerability to conflict be addressed? An important policy implication of the research on the links between conflict and development is that not all development is good for peace. There are important policy choices that can contribute to conflict prevention in the areas of both development policy and aid policy.

6.3.1. Development can exacerbate or reduce risks of conflict

There is a strongly held belief that development and peace are complementary and necessary conditions for each other.[13] The strong statistical relationship between the level of national per capita GDP and the incidence of civil war supports this view (Collier 2003). This can lead to a conclusion that economic growth is good for peace, even a solution to the problem of spread of civil wars. This may be true in general but it does not mean that all patterns of growth and development have a positive impact on reducing the risks of civil war. Development that exacerbates the socio-economic correlates of conflict worsens the prospects for peace and increases vulnerability. A strategy focussing on conflict-preventing growth and development is one that does not exacerbate the identified risk factors.

Patterns of growth that increase horizontal inequality and entrench exclusion of ethnic or regional groups and their political oppression may increase risks of conflict. If only the elite groups benefit from economic growth,

---

[13] This belief has underpinned the work of the United Nations and has been recently restated. See, for example, United Nations (2005).

expanding education, and other social facilities, and or if historically marginalized ethnic or other identity groups continue to be excluded from the benefits of development, horizontal inequalities will widen. Development could then aggravate the sense of grievance felt by excluded groups who see dynamic growth of jobs, incomes, schooling, and other opportunities benefit others and bypass them. Retrospective analyses often attribute the origins of conflict to past development patterns that were unequal and exclusionary. For example, the Guatemala Peace Accords make provisions for improving opportunities for indigenous people in recognition of socio-economic inequality, entrenched discrimination, and political oppression as a root cause of the thirty-five-year war. For example, the conflict in Nepal is attributed to decades of development that neglected the west and far-western regions and excluded Dalits who were then susceptible to mobilization by the Maoist insurgency (Gates and Murshed 2005; World Bank 2006; Brown 2007; Do and Iyer 2007). The international donor community that finances most of the development budget had been aware of the entrenched group inequalities in the country, but had neglected development in the west and far west; since the escalation of insurgency in 2004, donors have rushed to develop projects in those regions and to initiate projects that benefit excluded groups (Brown 2007; Fukuda-Parr 2007). As Graham Brown, Frances Stewart, and Arnim Langer argue in Chapter 5 of this volume, development aid can have an important impact on horizontal inequalities.

The youth bulge and demographic pressures cannot be addressed to achieve immediate impact but policies are important in accelerating the demographic transition. Girls' education, child nutrition, and other social policies are important determinants of fertility[14] which remains high and has only begun to decline in most countries of sub-Saharan Africa (UNDP 2003; UN 2007). The slow pace of progress in these areas, as reflected in the unlikely prospects for achieving MDGs for education, maternal mortality, child mortality, water, and sanitation reflects inadequate policy effort in these areas (UN 2005).

Expansion of youth employment and household incomes depend not only on the level of economic growth but its pattern.[15] Labour-intensive sectors such as smallholder agriculture and small-scale manufacturing have greater potential to generate employment. Recent reviews of poverty-reduction strategy paper (PRSP) processes have found that none of the PRSPs in Africa addresses employment (Nkurunziza 2008) nor has policies to ensure that growth is pro-poor (UNDP 2003; Fukuda-Parr 2007).

The risks associated with natural resources have received considerable policy attention at global levels. Global initiatives have been introduced to manage

---

[14] There is a well-established literature on the socio-economic determinants of fertility and policies that influence the demographic transition.

[15] There is a well-established literature on pro-poor growth. See, for example, UNDP (1996).

trade in natural resources that finance rebels, such as the Kimberley Diamond Certification Process to restrict trade in 'blood diamonds'. Other initiatives aim to restrict private corporate collusion with rebel groups such as the USA–UK voluntary principles on security and human rights and the OECD convention on combating bribery of foreign public officials in international business transactions (USAID 2004).

Finally, the risks associated with state fragility are affected by a broad set of governance issues. Less is known about the nature of state fragility, policies for strengthening governance, and conflict prevention. Much of the policy work on governance has been directed to improving economic efficiency and relatively little has been written in the development literature about governance for conflict prevention. One clear issue is the capacity of states to meet citizen expectations to deliver on their essential roles in areas such as food security, education, and access to justice. When the state is unable to deliver on these expectations, it will lose legitimacy (Nafziger and Auvinen 2000). Citizens can be more easily mobilized by insurgencies when they lose hope of the state defending their interests and rights.

6.3.2. Development aid and conflict risks

An important recent study finds that the volume of aid does not increase the risk of civil war, though the capture of aid resources may provide an incentive to rebel groups (Collier and Hoeffler 2002b). However, development aid can influence risk factors through two other channels: first, as an input to shaping government policy; and, second, as a factor in domestic politics that empowers or disempowers parties in conflict and that acts as an incentive or disincentive to violence. What matters in these contexts is not the volume of aid but its programme content; how, what, and who are supported has an impact on the structural conditions and the political dynamics in the country.

Development aid donors have significant influence in shaping government policy, particularly in the countries that are the focus of this chapter which are highly aid dependent. Official development aid (ODA) as a percentage of gross national income in 2005 averaged 13 per cent for these countries in contrast to 1.3 per cent for all aid recipients and 9.9 for the least-developed countries.[16] More significantly, it ranges from 1 per cent in Somalia, Côte d'Ivoire, and Uzbekistan to a high of 70 per cent in the Solomon Islands, 58 per cent in São Tomé, 54 per cent in Liberia, 46 per cent in Burundi, and 36 per cent in Eritrea. In most low-income countries, development aid finances almost all the capital budget.

---

[16] OECD-DAC data <http://www.oecd.org.dataoecd/52/12/1893167.xls>.

Since external resources finance almost all of the capital expenditures in the budgets of many of these low-income countries, they have a direct influence on the allocation of public expenditures and the conflict-prevention agenda described above. Lack of state capacity in delivering basic social services is a critical weakness that undermines the legitimacy of the state. As debates in the OECD have already recognized, aid can support a development agenda that reduces rather than increases conflict risks (OECD 2004). It can support better management of environmental decline and mitigate horizontal inequality and exclusion. Aid resources and policy advice can help develop institutions of the judiciary, the media, and civil society organizations that promote equity and justice. One critical policy area is the allocation of public expenditures and its impact on horizontal inequalities, an issue that has been analysed by several studies and reviewed by Brown and Stewart (Stewart 2005; Brown 2006; Brown, Stewart, and Langer 2010). As they point out, the current practice of donors in public expenditure reviews focuses on efficiency and poverty reduction, and does not include an assessment of the distributional consequences along group divisions. Drawing on studies of country experience, they note that it is not easy for donors to raise these issues with governments and within the aid community generally, but that public expenditure reviews and budgetary support present an important opportunity to correct horizontal inequalities through budget shifts across sectors and regions.

The second channel through which aid raises or reduces risks of conflict is through its influence on the political dynamics of the receiving country. Sometimes donors intentionally support one side rather than another. But, even when they do not do so, by virtue of the fact that it brings sizeable resources and international endorsement, aid cannot avoid having political impact, empowering some actors and disempowering others, and providing incentives or disincentives to violence (OECD 2004).

6.3.3. Aid can unintentionally exacerbate conflict

Uvin (1998) provides a particularly detailed analysis of donor actions in Rwanda prior to 1994 when the country's development performance was considered very positively by the donor community. Much as donors were fully aware of the political tensions in the country and were promoting political change towards democratization, their actions had 'unintended' consequences for conflict. This and other studies of conflicts from Afghanistan to Sierra Leone have argued persuasively that both development aid and humanitarian relief aid during, before, and after violent conflict, represent financial resources and influence that can reinforce tensions and repressive behaviour (Uvin 1998, 1999; Anderson 1999). In pre-conflict situations where social and political tensions are high, aid resources can worsen disparities between parties to a potential conflict. During periods of violence, these effects are even starker;

humanitarian assistance to provide food, shelter, and health services in conflict zones can worsen tensions between groups and risks strengthening the leadership of warring factions.

6.3.4. Aid can also be used intentionally for peace

In situations of rising tensions, aid can be applied deliberately to shift the dynamics in favour of reducing tension. It can act as an incentive to influence the behaviour of repressive regimes, to help strengthen pro-peace actors' capacities, to change relations between conflicting actors, or to alter the socio-economic environment in which conflict and peace dynamics take place. It can strengthen the capacity of national actors through such measures as human rights training of the military and police.

6.3.5. Aid can be used as a disincentive against violence

Donors can threaten to cut off their funds as a disincentive. Donors can withdraw in protest against government policies or actions that are repressive or corrupt and wilfully neglect peoples' needs. Recent examples include protests against corruption and lack of transparency and accountability in governance as in Kenya, protests against a range of human rights violations and poor economic management in Zimbabwe, and protests against curtailment of democratic institutions in Nepal. The effectiveness of these measures is uncertain. One study commissioned by the OECD concludes that conditionality rarely works (Uvin 1999). Donor coordination is clearly important for these incentives for peace and disincentives for violence to take effect, but is often lacking. Much more systematic analysis is needed of the impact of aid conditionality and aid withdrawal. No comprehensive study has been carried out that looks at the impact of aid withdrawal on its intended purpose, but also at the broader impact on the population and longer term development of the country.

Withdrawing aid is a diplomatic statement of protest and sends a strong, powerful message to the government in power. Donor agencies may be under pressure from their own publics who see support to regimes that engage in human rights violations, corruption, and repression as condoning those actions. Using aid as an incentive or disincentive may be useful in obtaining one-shot changes but not necessarily as a means of effecting longer term change. However, withdrawing aid also incurs an opportunity cost for building a longer-term safeguard for peace. Aid contributes to preventing state collapse in situations where no state is the worst of all possibilities for human well-being. But, little aid goes to countries with weak states because of the logic of aiding good performers to ensure that aid has most impact.

Donors all too often withdraw in situations of rising political tensions or when governments engage in increasingly unacceptable behaviour. While the socio-economic consequences are not as heavy as comprehensive sanctions, there is none the less a large opportunity cost to development. While humanitarian assistance only mitigates the immediate human suffering, aid can make a difference to maintaining socio-economic policies that protect human development.

6.3.6. Aid for development during conflict

While war is inevitably destructive, some countries do better at keeping economic activities going, sustaining government revenues and protecting social expenditures, and thus mitigating negative consequences on both the economy and human survival (Stewart 2003). For example, Indonesia, Nicaragua, Uganda, and Sri Lanka have experienced significant conflict yet have continued to make progress on key social and economic indicators. One explanation for this outcome is that the impact of violence is geographically contained, such as in Uganda and Indonesia, so national averages mask the declines in regions affected by conflict. But, another explanation is that government policies that continue to provide services for people make a huge difference, as in the case of Nicaragua and Sri Lanka (Stewart and FitzGerald 2000). Thus it makes a difference that national governments do not abandon their developmental role, and that international donors do not resort to humanitarian relief efforts exclusively. In the recent case of Nepal, income poverty continued to decline owing to increase in remittances (World Bank 2006). Social indicators also improved even though government services closed down (World Bank 2006; Fukuda-Parr 2007).

6.4. Reconceptualizing policy objectives of aid

6.4.1. Poverty reduction, economic growth, and good governance as consensus objectives

The objectives that are emphasized in aid policies depend on how the ultimate ends of development are defined as well as on an assessment of the key obstacles to achieving them. Individual donor governments may see the ultimate ends of their aid programmes in a variety of ways, often motivated by foreign policy concerns as well as the particular way in which they define important objectives of development in the recipient country. Alongside such bilateral concerns, however, development aid is also motivated by the global agenda of the international community as a whole that help to define the ultimate ends of development for donor programmes. The 2000 Millennium Declaration (UN 2000), adopted at a historic General Assembly, the largest ever gathering of heads of state and government, articulated a strong commitment to development aid as an instrument for achieving global objectives of development, environmental sustainability, peace, security, and human rights. In this context, a strong consensus has emerged on poverty reduction as the main purpose of development aid.[17] This has been formalized with the adoption of the MDGs which define concrete, quantitative, and time-bound targets which now guide multilateral and bilateral donor programmes and frame key international development debates, such as in the G8 summits and the ongoing consultations of the OECD's Development Assistance Committee (DAC).

While the ending of poverty in the context of the Millennium Declaration is the consensus end of development, there is also a consensus, or a dominant, view on the means to achieve these ends. This focuses on economic growth as the principal means to poverty reduction, and on governance, especially macroeconomic policies and institutions, as central issues in accelerating growth. While good governance is not as explicit as poverty reduction and MDG objectives, this view is implicit in the policy priorities and analysis deployed in global development debates such as the UN Millennium Project's business plan for achieving the MDGs or the World Bank's *Global Monitoring Report* (2007).[18] It is reflected in the Monterrey Consensus (UN 2002) adopted at the UN Conference on Financing for Development held at Monterrey in 2003 as an understanding between donors and developing countries as a basis for partnership. Under this consensus, donors commit to increasing aid financing when developing countries demonstrate commitment to strengthen their institutional and policy environment including addressing issues such as corruption (UNDP 2003). It draws on policy research literature on constraints to growth and on aid effectiveness. A particularly influential study that set the stage for this policy was the World Bank study *Assessing Aid: What Works, What Doesn't, and Why* (1998) that argues that aid is only effective in contributing to economic growth when countries have sound macroeconomic policies and institutions. Other studies also built a case for aid allocation priorities to favour countries with good policies and institutions (Burnside and Dollar 2000; Collier and Dollar 2004; Mosley, Hudson, and Verschoor 2004).

Current debates and research on aid effectiveness question the robustness of some of these studies, as discussed by Machiko Nissanke in Chapter 4 of this volume. But for now these studies have set the framework in which aid effectiveness is evaluated according to the criterion of contribution to economic growth. This framework motivates the policy-oriented academic literature that has grown over the last several years, such as the papers presented at the 2006 UNU-WIDER conference as well as the highly publicized studies that come to

---

[17] As argued elsewhere (Fukuda-Parr 2005), this focus on poverty is relatively new; in the 1970s and 1980s, there was greater emphasis on economic growth.
[18] These reports address issues such as gender equality and fragile states, within the growth framework.

divergent conclusions, ranging from *Assessing Aid* (World Bank 1998) to *White Man's Burden* (Easterly 2006) to *The End of Poverty* (Sachs 2005). This line of thinking has important implications for aid priorities in the allocation of resources to countries and to types of activities. Resource-allocation policy will be to 'reward the good performer' and favour those countries with able leadership and administrative strengths, and those activities are oriented to economic governance institutions such as efforts to address corruption, as well as macroeconomic policy management. They will leave out countries that have weak state capacity. Adjusting any one of the elements of the paradigm and defining the ends and means of development differently would lead to different aid priorities.

There are arguably many important development objectives, depending on how we define the ultimate end of development and on how we identify the critical means to achieving those ends.[19] While economic growth is an important means to poverty reduction, it is not necessarily the only one. The World Bank's 2000–1 *World Development Report* looks at the lack of political voice or disempowerment, lack of security, and lack of opportunities that result from institutionalized discrimination as causes of poverty. There are several more direct mechanisms than economic growth for addressing the problems in poor peoples' lives. It is also well established that while growth has a positive impact on poverty reduction, the links are not automatic (UNDP 1997). There is a wide range of potential policy objectives for aid; this chapter is concerned with only one of them, preventing civil war and other forms of violent conflict.

6.4.2. Conflict prevention as a global objective in the development agenda

Conflict prevention is an important policy objective of development aid because it is a major obstacle to reducing poverty for reasons that have already been explained. But, conflict prevention is also an important end in itself for the international community, and particularly for the global development agenda and global development actors. Peace and security constitute one of the central global objectives for the twenty-first century set out in the 2000 Millennium Declaration, along with development, democracy, and human rights. Security is an essential dimension of human well-being that is fundamentally and universally important for people.

There is nothing new in the idea that security is an important global objective. What is new is that security and conflict prevention should be part of

---

[19] If we adopt the capability and human development perspective, the ultimate purpose of development extends far beyond poverty reduction and achieving the MDGs. It would encompass many capabilities that are universally valued, including those that are captured in the MDGs, such as being knowledgeable and healthy, as well as those that are not, such as enjoying political freedom and participation, freedom of identity, and being secure.

development agenda, rather than peace and political stability agenda. For the last half-century, issues of security and development have been carefully separated institutionally and conceptually in both global institutions and academia. Within the UN system, while political units pursued the peace agenda, economic and social units pursued the development agenda. Even academic research was separated in a similar fashion, with political scientists and international relations scholars studying issues of peace and war while economists and social scientists study development. It is only since the emergence of civil war in poor countries in the last decade that development agencies have engaged with problems of violent conflict and their consequences for development, and with poverty as a possible cause of conflict. It is only natural that the security agenda would not currently be part of development agenda, nor seen to be a policy objective of development aid. Defining conflict prevention as a policy objective in development aid would be a departure from this historical trend and a break with the legacy of the cold war.

The reason conflict prevention should be an important policy objective of development aid is because of the causal linkages between development, conflict, and aid described in the previous section of this chapter, and the fact that the problems of this nexus loom large on a global scale. As the *Human Security Report* 2005 (Human Security Centre 2005) shows, the global patterns of war have dramatically shifted; while the world has become more secure overall, with a decline in violent conflicts and civilian deaths over the last few decades, there has been an increase in conflict in sub-Saharan Africa. And, as the report notes succinctly,

the combination of pervasive poverty, declining GDP per capita, poor infrastructure, weak administration, external intervention and an abundance of cheap weapons, plus the effects of a major decline in per capita foreign assistance for much of the 1990s, mean that armed conflicts in these countries are difficult to avoid, contain or end. (Human Security Centre 2005: 4)

Recognizing security as a policy objective with intrinsic value from the development perspectives demands new work on understanding the importance of security and freedom from violence as a part of human well-being and how this relates to other dimensions of well-being, poverty, and development. Some work is already under way. The concept of human security has emphasized the importance of security in human well-being while recent work on poverty has increasingly recognized the relevance of security as part of poverty and development challenges.[20] For example, *World Development Report 2000/01: Attacking Poverty* identifies security together with opportunity and

---

[20] See, for example, the work of Moser on violence and poverty (Moser 2006).

empowerment to be the three pillars of the global poverty agenda (World Bank 2000).

6.4.3. Aid effectiveness

The literature and policy debates about 'aid effectiveness' today are largely defined in terms of effectiveness in contributing to economic growth. If conflict prevention is both an end in itself but also a means to achieving the MDGs, aid can be as much an investment in conflict prevention as in economic growth. Its effectiveness should be judged not only against the economic benchmark but against contribution to building democratic governance. Aid to Tanzania in the 1980s was declared an unmitigated disaster by the World Bank study that pointed out that millions spent in building roads were washed away by poor government policies that did not provide for maintenance (World Bank 1998). But, that aid may have been important in establishing the lead that Tanzania now has in educational attainment among low-income countries, and in the country's progress towards democratization as well as social and political stability that the country enjoys.

By standard efficiency criteria, aid for Tanzanian roads may have had low returns in the presence of weak macroeconomic policy and administrative capacity. But, even badly maintained roads may have been better than no roads, particularly if they helped keep communications open to the hinterland and government responsive to the needs of otherwise neglected populations. Tanzania has been less successful than its neighbours by measures of GDP growth, but more successful by measures of social indicators. It is a poor country that enjoys more social peace and stronger democratic governance than its neighbours. If the foregone benefits of having prevented conflict in Tanzania were taken into account, the returns to aid might be considered to be highly positive. Much more needs to be learned about the effectiveness of aid in preventing conflict; methodology for such analysis needs to be developed.

6.4.4. Resource allocation priorities

The Monterrey consensus builds an approach to aid allocation around the logic of 'rewarding the good performer', with performance centred around policies that would be effective for growth and poverty reduction. This logic marginalizes the worst-performing countries that are being considered here; countries most vulnerable to conflict and with most entrenched poverty, countries most in need of international support. As Picciotto, Olonisakin, and Clarke (2006) argue, the logic of rewarding the good performer assumes that existing policies cannot be changed by donor engagement, that aid cannot be used to minimize the effect of poor policies, and that governance and policy, as defined by the Bank's country policy and institutional assessments (CPIA) measure, determine aid effectiveness. They advocate a case-by-case assessment of possibilities for change in policy and governance that could instead serve as a basis for aid allocations. At the same time they acknowledge that aid to fragile states will always be full of risk. They propose a 'venture capital model' of aid allocation. This study reviews the experience of aid in fragile states and shows that only 58 per cent of the projects succeeded, but that average returns were high.

The donor community has become increasingly concerned with the needs of the countries with weak governance, now termed 'fragile states', an ill-defined category (Cammack et al. 2006). It is often defined as those countries that lack the capacity and/or will to put in place effective policies for development and poverty reduction, or those that are vulnerable not only to violent conflict but also to terrorism, organized crime, epidemic diseases, natural disaster, and environmental degradation. For want of a more precise concept and definition, international debates use the criterion of World Bank's CPIA[21] that incorporates policy for economic management, structural policies, social inclusion and poverty reduction, and public sector management and institutions (see Chapter 2 of this volume). Fragile states now encompass thirty-five countries based on the CPIA classification. All of these countries, with the exception of two, are included among the sixty-one worst performing countries being reviewed in this chapter.

What has been the actual allocation of resources to countries with weak institutions and policies? Recent analyses find evidence of disproportionately low allocations. The 2006 OECD monitoring of aid flows to fragile states shows post-Monterrey increase in aid flows has been smaller for fragile states compared with non-fragile states (OECD 2006). The 2007 OECD monitoring report finds a small group of countries that are marginalized: eight countries receiving low aid flows relative to need and capacity, and/or highly volatile aid flows and international engagement (OECD 2007). A recent analysis by the UK's Department for International Development (DFID) on the pre-Monterrey consensus period (1996–2001) shows a decline of flows to poorly performing states (bottom two quintiles of the World Bank's country performance index (CPI)) in contrast to increases in flows to the well-performing countries (top two quintiles of the index) (DFID 2004). The poor-performance countries received only 14 per cent of bilateral aid whereas the good performers received two-thirds of all aid. Moreover, poor performers receive less aid that would be expected on the basis of need. Other studies find that these countries are not only under-aided but that aid flows are twice as volatile. Among these countries, post-conflict countries receive large volumes of aid; others tend to be under-aided, especially when they are very large or very small, have a small number of donors, but also are very poor and very poorly governed (Levin and Dollar 2005; McGillivray

---

[21] OECD (2007); World Bank (2007).

2006). Jones, Riddell, and Kotoglou (2005) find that aid allocation to the less-well-performing countries are not being reduced but some countries are under-aided or end up as 'aid orphans'. They explain that donors are motivated by concerns of state failure and its political consequences, and argue that the form of engagement is as important as the level of aid in engaging with these countries.

6.4.5. Donor policy approaches to fragile states and to conflict prevention

Donor debate about the development–conflict nexus has been evolving for over a decade. The March 2007 DAC High-Level Meeting adopted 'Principles for Good International Engagement in Fragile States' (OECD 2007). These principles include:

- Take context as the starting-point (differentiate countries recovering from conflict or political crisis from those facing declining governance and from those with collapsed state capacity).
- Move from reaction (to conflict) to prevention.
- Focus on state-building as the central objective.
- Align with local priorities.
- Recognize the political–security–development nexus.
- Promote coherence between donor government agencies.
- Agree on practical coordination mechanisms.
- Do no harm.

All these principles, with the exception of the second, do not differ substantially from the basic principles for more effective aid through improved coherence and more country-specific approaches that the donor community has been promoting over the last several years, contained in the Paris Declaration (OECD 2005). The second principle reflects the 2001 DAC Guidelines on Conflict Prevention (OECD 2001). In that sense, a new policy initiative has not yet been developed. The earlier 2001 DAC guidelines *Helping to Prevent Conflict* advocated 'ensuring peace through security and development', with an emphasis on building accountable systems of security, strengthening public-sector management overall, and 'engaging long term and putting a conflict prevention "lens" to policies in all areas from development to trade to investment'. They also emphasize conflict prevention as a central issue in poverty reduction.

In practice, post-conflict reconstruction and aid-practice issues tend to dominate policy debates and agenda, and neither reducing risks that are part of development patterns nor conflict prevention generally figures large. Despite an increasing focus on fragile states, a consensus policy framework is still in the making. Perhaps this is because the interest and concerns of various bilateral donors over the issues of states which are fragile have quite varied origins (Cammack et al. 2006). Some donors are concerned with poor development and poverty reduction performance in countries where government is unwilling to pursue that agenda; some are concerned with terrorism and global threats; some with human security and peace-building; and others with the functional relationship between poverty and conflict.[22] There is considerable ambiguity in the concept of fragile states that captures overlapping sets of countries but that responds to several concerns and criteria for inclusion. Thus, for now, there is no coherent international agenda for conflict prevention as a policy objective of development aid that focuses on addressing diverse risk factors for different countries.

6.5. Conclusions

This study has argued that more attention should be given to conflict prevention—along with other objectives, including poverty reduction—as a policy objective of development aid, and has explored the implications of doing so for aid programme priorities and the international aid architecture in general. Violent conflict is a major obstacle to achieving the MDGs because the countries that face the greatest challenges are characterized by conflict risk factors. These are also countries in greatest need of assistance from the international community.

The study has identified sixty-one worst-performing countries where development and poverty reduction will need to be sharply accelerated if they are to achieve the MDGs by 2015 (see Table 6.2). The majority of the countries are affected by civil war, either in the recent past or as a reality in a neighbouring country that has spillover effects in the subregion. While there is high risk of recurrence of conflict, other risk factors are present in the socio-economic structures of these countries, notably: horizontal inequalities and group exclusion, the youth bulge in their demographies, dependence on natural resources, and their weak management as well as weak state capacity overall. Preventing conflict is important not only as a means to the accelerated achievement of MDGs but also because as an end in itself security is both an important global agenda as well as an important aspect of human well-being.

Not all development and poverty reduction contribute to conflict prevention; in fact, some patterns of development might contribute to raising risks. For example, development that reduces poverty among the privileged ethnic

---

[22] Picciotto, Olonisakin, and Clarke (2006) point out this category is inconsistently used by different donors. For example, DFID focuses on state capacity and willingness, UNDP focuses on a wide range of economic, social, and political characteristics and the World Bank's approach originated with the initiative on low-income countries under stress based on poor country performance indicators attributable to a variety of causes.

Table 6.2. Worst-performing countries regarding their process to achieving the MDGs (category 4)

Country	Lower performance indicators	Conflict affected		Failed state index			ODA p.c. 2005	2005 ODA/ GNI	Primary exports as percentage of GDP
				(1)	(2)	(3)			
Afghanistan	income hunger	Yes	1990–2005	9.6	8.0	8.0	110.57	38.55	
Angola	income child mortality	Yes	1990–2004	8.5	8.0	9.0	27.72	1.73	2
Bangladesh	hunger sanitation	Yes	1990–2	5.8	8.9	9.0	9.31	2.1	11
Benin	child mortality sanitation			5.1	3.8	7.3	41.36	8.2	9
Burkina Faso	hunger education gender child mortality			5.9	7.7	8.8	49.85	12.78	
Burundi	income hunger education child mortality	Yes	1991–2 1994–2005	9.1	7.8	8.8	48.34	46.79	13
Cambodia	hunger child mortality	Yes	1990–8	6.5	7.5	7.2	38.22	10.39	1
Cameroon	income gender child mortality water	Yes	1996	6.8	7.9	8.7	25.35	2.5	14
Central African Republic	income hunger education child mortality sanitation	Yes	2001–2	7.7	8.0	8.5	23.59	6.97	6
Chad	income hunger child mortality sanitation	Yes	1997–2005	9.0	9.5	9.0	38.96	8.55	
Comoros	income	Yes	1997				42.05	6.64	
Congo	income hunger gender child mortality	Yes	1993–4 1997–9 2002				362.21	36.82	
Congo, Dem. Rep. of the	income hunger education child mortality sanitation	Yes	1996–2001	9.5	9.6	9.0	31.76	27.54	
Côte d'Ivoire	income child mortality sanitation	Yes	2002–4	7.6	9.8	8.0	6.56	0.78	
Djibouti	income child mortality	Yes	1991–4 1999				99.49	10.09	
Dominican Republic	hunger sanitation			7.0	7.4	8.0	8.66	0.29	
Eritrea	education child mortality gender sanitation	Yes	1997–2000 2003	7.2	7.5	6.0	80.72	36.32	

(continued)

Table 6.2. Continued

Country	Lower performance indicators	Conflict affected		Failed state index			ODA p.c. 2005	2005 ODA/GNI	Primary exports as percentage of GDP
				(1)	(2)	(3)			
Ethiopia	gender child mortality water sanitation	Yes	1990–2005	7.6	8.9	8.5	27.19	17.39	
Gambia	income hunger education child mortality			5.0	5.8	7.0	38.26	13.06	
Guinea	water sanitation	Yes	2000–2	7.2	9.0	8.0	19.37	6.89	
Guinea-Bissau	income child mortality	Yes	1998–9	4.9	6.5	9.3	49.76	27.33	
Haiti	income child mortality water sanitation	Yes	2004	5.0	9.6	8.3	60.37	12.13	
Honduras	Hunger gender sanitation	Yes	1990–2005	2.1	6.4	9.0	94.56	8.2	13
India	Hunger education gender child mortality	Yes	1990–6	2.8	5.7	7.5	1.58	0.22	3
Iraq			2003–5	8.3	8.8	8.7	773.34		
Kenya	Income hunger child mortality			7.1	7.6	8.0	22.43	4.27	14
Kyrgyzstan	Income			6.6	7.9	8.0	52.03	11.37	10
Lao People's Dem. Rep.	Gender child mortality	Yes	1990	5.9	8.9	5.9	49.95	11.17	
Lesotho	Hunger child mortality	Yes	1998				38.45	3.84	
Liberia	Income child mortality	Yes	1990–5 2000–3	2.1	8.8	8.6	72.01	54.12	
Madagascar	Income hunger child mortality water sanitation						49.93	18.75	12
Malawi	Gender child mortality			6.0	6.7	8.8	44.67	28.37	
Mali	Income hunger education Gender child mortality Water	Yes	1990 1994	4.2	3.5	6.8	51.14	14.08	21
Mauritania	Income child mortality water			5.9	7.9	7.0	62.01	10.43	

Moldova	Income child mortality	Yes	1992	4.7	6.8	7.5	45.55	5.85	23
Mongolia	Income hunger			1.0	5.0	5.7	83.08	11.57	44
Mozambique	Education gender child mortality sanitation			2.0	5.5	7.1	64.98	20.78	23
Myanmar	Child mortality	Yes	1990–2005	8.8	8.0	9.0	2.86		
Nepal	Hunger sanitation	Yes	1996–2005	4.8	9.0	9.2	15.77	5.81	
Niger	Income hunger education gender child mortality water	Yes	1992 1994 1996–7	4.3	6.0	7.2	36.92	15.17	
Nigeria	Income child mortality water sanitation	Yes	2004	5.9	9.0	9.0	48.94	7.41	
Pakistan	Income child mortality	Yes	1990 1995–6	9.3	9.1	8.9	10.7	1.54	
Papua New Guinea	Income child mortality water sanitation	Yes	1990 1992–6	2.6	6.7	9.0	45.19	6.64	3
Rwanda	Income hunger	Yes	1990–4 1997–2002	7.0	8.9	7.2	63.72	27.39	
Sao Tome and Principe	Education						199.38	58.56	
Senegal	Income hunger child mortality	Yes	1990–3 1995 1997–2001 2003	4.3	3.5	6.8	59.11	8.44	11
Sierra Leone	Income hunger gender child mortality	Yes	1991–2000	7.9	7.7	8.7	62.1	29.58	
Solomon Islands	Income						413.0	70.51	
Somalia	Hunger child mortality	Yes	1995–6 2001–2	8.1	9.8		28.72		
Sudan	Child mortality sanitation	Yes	1990–2005	9.7	9.1	9.2	50.47	7.1	17
Swaziland	Income hunger child mortality						40.73	1.67	
Tajikistan	Income child mortality	Yes	1992–6 1998	6.6	8.7	7.4	37.08	10.79	
Tanzania	Income hunger education gender child mortality			6.8	5.2	7.0	39.27	12.48	10
Togo	Income gender child mortality water sanitation			5.8	7.8	7.5	14.1	4.0	11
Turkmenistan	Income child mortality			4.2	8.0	7.2	5.85		

(continued)

145

Table 6.2. Continued

Country	Lower performance indicators	Conflict affected		Failed state index			ODA p.c. 2005	2005 ODA/ GNI	Primary exports as percentage of GDP
				(1)	(2)	(3)			
Uganda	Child mortality water	Yes	1990–1 1994–2005	9.2	7.9	8.4	41.57	14.02	8
Uzbekistan	Income child mortality	Yes	2000 2004	5.8	9.1	8.1	6.48	1.27	
Vanuatu	Income child mortality						188.0	11.98	
Yemen	Hunger child mortality sanitation	Yes	1994	6.7	9.4	9.0	16.02	2.61	41
Zambia	Income hunger child mortality			5.2	5.2	7.3	80.98	14.21	22
Zimbabwe	Income hunger child mortality sanitation			8.9	8.5	9.2	28.26	11.55	39

Notes: Column (1) = legancy of vengeance-seeking group grievances. Column (2) = rise of factionlized elites. Column (3) = uneven development along group lines.
Source: UNPP (2005); OECD/DAC online database; Fund for Peace (2007).

groups or regions but neglects historically marginalized groups or regions might fuel social and political tensions. Development in natural resource exploitation that is not accompanied by measures to manage its distribution might easily be captured by rebel groups and fuel and intensify war.

Similarly, not all development aid contributes to conflict prevention; in fact, some patterns of aid can exacerbate the potential for war. Aid is too powerful an instrument to be politically neutral. Defining conflict prevention as one of the policy objectives of aid would have far-reaching implications. New criteria for aid effectiveness would need to be devised. Development priorities would also need to shift and be reconsidered. Most importantly, analysis of the root causes of historic conflict and social and political tensions would need to be carried out as an essential information base for development and aid programming and the socio-economic correlates of violent conflict addressed as a priority.

References

Anderson, M. (1999) *Do No Harm: How Aid Can Support Peace—or War*. Boulder, Colo.: Lynne Rienner.

Brown, G. (2006) 'Inequality, Ethnic Diversity and Conflict: Implications for a Human Rights Poverty Reduction Strategy'. Paper prepared for the Office of the United Nations High Commissioner for Human Rights. Geneva: OHCHR.

—— (2007) 'Social Exclusion, Horizontal Inequalities and Conflict in Nepal: Issues and Evidence'. Paper prepared for the Office of the United Nations High Commissioner for Human Rights. Geneva: OHCHR.

—— F. Stewart, and A. Langer (2010) 'The Implications of Horizontal Inequality for Aid'. In G. Mavrotas (ed.), *Foreign Aid for Development: Issues, Challenges, and the New Agenda*. Oxford: Oxford University Press (Chap. 5 of the present volume).

Burnside, C., and D. Dollar (2000) 'Aid, Policies, and Growth'. *American Economic Review*, 90: 847–68.

Cammack, D., D. McLeod, A. Rocha Menocal, and K. Christiansen (2006) 'Donors and the "Fragile States" Agenda: A Survey of Current Thinking and Practice'. <JICA/ODI <http://www.odi.org.uk/resources/download/1317.pdf>.

Cincotta, R., R. Engelman, and D. Anastasion (2003) *The Security Demographic: Population and Civil Conflict after the Cold War*. Washington, DC: Population Action International.

Collier, P. (1999) 'On the Economic Consequences of Civil War'. *Oxford Economic Papers* 51: 168–83.

—— (2003) *Breaking the Conflict Trap: Civil War and Development Policy*. Oxford, New York, and Washington, DC: Oxford University Press/World Bank.

—— and D. Dollar (2004) 'Development Effectiveness: What Have We Learnt?' *Economic Journal*, 114: F244–F261.

—— and A. Hoeffler (2002a) 'Greed and Grievance in Civil Wars'. Centre for the Study of African Economies Working Paper 2002–01. Oxford: Centre for the Study of African Economies.

Collier, P., and A. Hoeffler (2002b) 'Aid, Policy and Peace: Reducing the Risks of Civil Conflict'. *Defence and Peace Economics*, 13: 435–50.

Department for International Development (2004) *Why We Need to Work More Effectively in Fragile States*. London: DFID.

Do, Q.-T., and L. Iyer (2007) 'Poverty, Social Divisions and Conflict in Nepal'. World Bank Policy Research Department Working Paper 4228. Washington, DC: World Bank.

Easterly, W. (2006) *The White Man's Burden: Why the West's Efforts to Aid the Rest Have Done So Much Ill and So Little Good*. New York: Penguin Press.

Elbadawi, I., and N. Sambanis (2002) 'How Much Civil War Will We See? Explaining the Prevalence of Civil War'. *Journal of Conflict Resolution*, 46: 307–34.

Fearon, J. D., and D. D. Laitin (2003) 'Ethnicity, Insurgency and Civil War'. *American Political Science Review*, 97: 75–90.

Fukuda-Parr, S. (2005) 'Millennium Development Goals: Why They Matter'. *Global Governance* 10: 395–402.

—— (2007) 'Human Rights and National Poverty Reduction Strategies: Conceptual Framework for Human Rights Analysis of Poverty Reduction Strategies and Reviews of Guatemala, Liberia and Nepal'. University of Connecticut Working Papers in Economic Rights. Storrs, Conn.: University of Connecticut Human Rights Institute.

Fund for Peace (2007) *Failed State Index 2006* <http://www.fundforpeace.org/web/index. php?option=com_content&task=view&id=104&Itemid=148>.

Gates, S., and M. S. Murshed (2005) 'Spatial-horizontal Inequality and the Maoist Insurgency in Nepal'. *Review of Development Economics*, 9: 121–34.

Goodhand, J. (2003) 'Enduring Disorder and Persistent Poverty: A Review of the Linkages between War and Chronic Poverty'. *World Development*, 31: 629–46.

Hegre, H., T. Ellingsen, S. Gates, and N. P. Gleditsch (2001) 'Toward a Democratic Civil Peace? Democracy, Political Change and Civil War, 1816–1992'. *American Political Science Review*, 95: 33–48.

Homer-Dixon, T. F. (1991) 'On the Threshold: Environmental Changes as Causes of Acute Conflict'. *International Security*, 19: 5–40.

Human Security Centre (2003) 'Mapping and Explaining Civil War: What to Do about Contested Datasets and Findings?' Paper prepared for the Oslo Workshop, 18–19 Aug.

—— (2005) *Human Security Report, 2005*. Vancouver: University of British Columbia.

Humphreys, M. (2003) *Economics and Violent Conflict*. Cambridge, Mass.: Harvard University. <http://www.preventconflict.org/portal/economics/Essay.pdf>.

—— and A. Varshney (2004) 'Violent Conflict and the Millennium Development Goals: Diagnosis and Recommendations'. Center on Globalization and Sustainable Development Working Paper 19. New York: Columbia University. CGSD.

Jones, S., R. Ridell, and K. Kotoglou (2005) 'Aid Allocation Criteria: Managing for Development Results and Difficult Partnerships'. Document for the OECD-DAC Senior Level forum on Development Effectiveness in Fragile States. DCD 2005/4.

Levin, V., and D. Dollar (2005) 'The Forgotten States: Aid Volumes in Difficult Partnership Countries (1992–2002)'. Summary paper prepared for the OECD-DAC Learning and Advisory Process on Difficult Partnerships, 6 Jan., Paris.

McGillivray, M. (2006) 'Aid Allocation and Fragile States'. WIDER Discussion Paper 2006/01. Helsinki: UNU-WIDER.

Milanovic, B. (2005) 'Why Did the Poorest Countries Fail to Catch Up?' Carnegie Paper 62. Washington, DC: Carnegie Endowment.

Moser, C. (2006) 'Reducing Urban Violence in Developing Countries'. Policy Brief 2006–01. Washington, DC: Brookings Institution.

Mosley, P., J. Hudson, and A. Verschoor (2004) 'Aid, Poverty Reduction and the New Conditionality'. *Economic Journal*, 114: F217–F243.

Murdoch, J., and T. Sandler (2002) 'Economic Growth, Civil Wars and Spatial Spillovers'. *Journal of Conflict Resolution*, 46: 91–110.

Murshed, S. M. (2007) 'The Conflict–Growth Nexus and the Poverty of Nations'. United Nations Department of Economic and Social Affairs Working Paper 43 (ST/ESA/2007/DWP/43). Washington, DC: DESA.

Nafziger, E. W., and J. Auvinen (2000) 'The Economic Causes of Humanitarian Emergencies'. In E. W. Nafziger, F. Stewart, and R. Väyrynen (eds), *War, Hunger, and Displacement: The Origins of Humanitarian Emergencies*, Vol. i. *War and Displacement in Developing Countries*. Oxford: Oxford University Press for UNU-WIDER.

Nkurunziza, J. (2008) 'Generating Rural Employment in Africa'. In K. S. Jomo and A. Ocampo (eds), *Towards Full and Decement Employment*. London: Zed Books.

Nissanke, M. (2010) 'Reconstructing the Aid Effectiveness Debate'. In G. Mavrotas (ed.), *Foreign Aid for Development: Issues, Challenges, and the New Agenda*. Oxford: Oxford University Press (Chap. 4 of the present volume).

OECD (2001) *The DAC Guidelines: Helping Prevent Violent Conflict*. Paris: OECD.

—— (2004) 'The Security and Development Nexus: Challenges for Aid'. Paper presented at the DAC High-Level Meeting, 15–16 April, OECD, Paris.

—— (2005) *2006 Development Co-operation Report*, OECD Document DCD/DAC(2006)36/REV1. Paris: OECD.

—— (2006) 'Principles for Good International Engagement in Fragile States and Situations'. Paris: OECD. <http://www.oecd.org/dataoecd/61/45/38368714.pdf >.

—— (2007) 'Paris Declaration on Aid Effectiveness: Ownership, Harmonization, Alignment, Results and Mutual Accountability'. Paper presented at the High-Level Forum, 28 Feb.–2 Mar., OECD, Paris.

OECD-DAC (2007) 'Statistical Annex of the 2006 Development Co-operation Report'. <http://www.oecd.org/document/9/0,3343,en_2649_34447_1893129_1_1_1_1,00.html>.

—— (2009) 'Statistical Annex of the 2009 Development Co-operation Report' <http://www.oecd.org/document/9/0,3343,en_2649_34447_1893129_1_1_1_1,00.html>.

Picciotto, R., F. Olonisakin, and M. Clarke (2006) 'Global Development and Security: Towards a Policy Agenda'. *Global Development Studies*, 3. Stockholm: Swedish Ministry of Foreign Affairs.

Sachs, J. D. (2005) *The End of Poverty: Economic Possibilities for Our Time*. New York: Penguin Press.

Seybolt, T. B. (2002) 'Transational Conflict Contagion: Alternative Theories of the Spread of War'. Paper presented at the annual meeting of American Political Science Association, 28 Aug., Boston.

Stewart, F. (2002) 'Horizontal Inequalities: A Neglected Dimension of Development'. WIDER Annual Lecture 5, Helsinki: UNU-WIDER.

Stewart, F. (2003) 'Conflict and the Millennium Development Goals'. *Journal of Human Development*, 4: 325–51.

—— (2005) 'Policies towards Horizontal Inequalities in Post-conflict Reconstruction'. University of Oxford Centre for Research on Inequality, Human Security and Ethnicity Working Paper 7. Oxford: CRISE.

—— and G. Brown (2003) *The Economics of War: Causes and Consequences*. University of Oxford Centre for Research on Inequality, Human Security and Ethnicity Working Papers. Oxford: CRISE.

—— and V. FitzGerald (2001) 'The Costs of War in Poor Countries: Conclusions and Policy Recommendations'. In F. Stewart and V. FitzGerald (eds), *War and Underdevelopment*, Vol. i. *The Economic and Social Consequences of Conflict: Economic and Social Consequences of Conflict*. Queen Elizabeth House Series in Development Studies. Oxford: Oxford University Press.

—— ——, et al. (2000) *War and Underdevelopment*, Vol. ii. *Country Experiences: Country Experiences*. Queen Elizabeth House Series in Development Studies. Oxford: Oxford University Press.

—— C. Huang, and M. Wang (2001) 'Internal Wars: An Empirical Overview of the Economic and Social Consequences'. In F. Stewart and V. FitzGerald (eds), *War and Underdevelopment*, Vol. ii. *Country Experiences: Country Experiences*. Queen Elizabeth House Series in Development Studies. Oxford: Oxford University Press.

UN Millennium Project (2005) 'Investing in Development: A Practical Plan to Achieve the Millennium Development Goals'. London: Earthscan.

UNDP (United Nations Development Programme) (1996) *Human Development Report 1996: Economic Growth for Human Development*. New York: Oxford University Press.

—— (1997) *Human Devepment Report 1997: Poverty and Human Development*. New York: Oxford University Press.

—— (2003) *Human Development Report 2003: A Compact to End Human Poverty*. New York: Oxford University Press.

United Nations (2000) 'Millennium Declaration'. UN document A RES 55/12. New York: United Nations. <http://www.un.org/Depts/dhl/resguide/r55.htm>.

—— (2002) 'Outcome of the International Conference on Financing for Development, Monterrey Consensus'. UN document A/57/344. New York: United Nations.

—— (2005) 'In Larger Freedom: Towards Development, Security and Human Rights for All'. Report of the Secretary General, UN document A/59/2005. New York: United Nations.

—— (2007) 'World Population Prospects: The 2006 Revision and World Urbanization Prospects'. UN Population Division. New York: United Nations.

UNPP (2005) 'World Population Prospects 2005 Revision'. <http://www.esa.un.org/unpp>.

USAID (2004) *Minerals and Conflict: A Toolkit for Intervention*. Office of Conflict Management and Mitigation. Washington, DC: USAID.

Uvin, P. (1998) *Aiding Violence: The Development Enterprise in Rwanda*. West Hartford, Conn.: Kumarian Press.

—— (1999) 'The Influence of Aid in Situations of Violent Conflict: A Synthesis and a Commentary on the Lessons Learned from Case Studies on the Limits and Scope for the

Use of Development Incentives and Disincentives for Influencing Conflict Situations'. Paris: DAC Informal Task Force on Conflict, Peace and Development Co-operation.

World Bank (1998) *Assessing Aid: What Works, What Doesn't, and Why*. Oxford, New York, and Washington, DC: Oxford University Press/World Bank.

—— (2000) *World Development Report 2000/01: Attacking Poverty*. New York: Oxford University Press for the World Bank.

—— (2005) 'Toward a Conflict-sensitive Poverty Reduction Strategy: Lessons from a Retrospective Analysis'. World Bank Report 32586. Washington, DC: World Bank.

—— (2006) 'Resilience Amidst Conflict: An Assessment of Poverty in Nepal, 1995–96 and 2003–04'. World Bank Report 34834-NP. <http://www-wds.worldbank.org/external/default/WDSContentServer/WDSP/IB/2006/07/13/000090341_20060713084841/Rendered/PDF/348340NP.pdf>.

—— (2007) 'Global Monitoring Report: Confronting the Challenges of Gender Equality and Fragile States'. Washington, DC: World Bank.

7

Aid to Fragile States: Do Donors Help or Hinder?

Stephen Browne

When countries give foreign economic aid, they have many motivations: humanitarian impulses, strategic concerns, interest group politics, and simple bureaucratic inertia. We compared the amount of foreign aid countries receive per capita with the [failed-states] index rankings and found that the countries at greatest risk of collapse often get paltry amounts of aid. The exceptions appear to be countries that have been the recipients of large-scale international military intervention.

'Give and Take', *Foreign Policy* (July–Aug. 2005)

Although Australia has been a generous donor to East Timor, the Australian government is reaping over $1 million per day from oil and gas in a disputed area of the Timor Sea that is twice as close to East Timor as it is to Australia. Australia has received nearly ten times as much revenue from Timor Sea oil and gas than it has provided in aid to East Timor since 1999 . . . Australia has access to two-thirds of the known oil and gas deposits in the Timor Sea, even though a maritime boundary set according to international law could deliver most, if not all, of these resources to East Timor.

'Two Years on . . . What Future for an Independent East Timor?', Oxfam Executive Summary (Fitzroy: Oxfam, 2004a)

7.1. Introduction

Strong powers used to fear each other. Now their concerns emanate from states that are fragile and which threaten global stability. These states are still numerous; by most definitions, at least one-third of all developing countries. And they harbour up to 1.5 billion people, almost a quarter of the world. Fragile states are of universal concern because they are the source of many of the most challenging global problems. Many are chronically prone to conflict—with more than a dozen civil wars raging at any one time. Some are major exporters of narcotic drugs (Afghanistan, Burma, Colombia). Some are developing nuclear weapons and exporting the capability to develop them (North Korea, Pakistan). Some are incubators of violence and terrorism, such as Afghanistan under the Taliban regime, and Somalia today. In the zones of death, people are displaced, property is destroyed, and natural resources are plundered. Weak states are also host to traffickers of people and to the still-widespread practice of slave-labour. People quit failing states under the threat of persecution or economic deprivation and seek asylum or refugee status elsewhere.

Fragile states are also stalked by the silent crises of peacetime. People still starve to death in them—as in some of the West African countries in 2005—and epidemic diseases can grow and spread alarmingly. The HIV/AIDS pandemic is the most obvious example, with 40 million carriers of the virus worldwide and 5 million additional infections every year. The much older disease of malaria—until recently the cause of even higher mortality rates in Africa than HIV/AIDS—has been almost completely eradicated in many tropical countries, but continues to afflict countries which have not applied the resources to sustain national campaigns. And polio, a disease spread by poor sanitation, but which can be controlled through universal immunization with a vaccine discovered fifty years ago, is still endemic in six countries (Afghanistan, Egypt, India, Niger, Nigeria, Pakistan). In 2005, it was carried across borders to several others, including Indonesia and Yemen.

Richer countries have more reasons than ever to address this new world disorder. But, the record has been uneven, to say the least. The world power has helped to create a failed state, for a variety of self-interested motives, contributing to even greater global insecurity. The aid supposed to support Iraqi reconstruction has been mired in distortions designed to maximize the benefits for US companies.[1] Elsewhere, donors have been inconstant partners. Many of the most fragile countries receive little assistance. Just as with all developing countries, donors have many criteria for allocating, or not allocating, aid. But, even if need were the main incentive, trying to compensate for failure poses dilemmas. It is in the failing states where the intended beneficiaries of aid—the poor and marginalized—are worst off and who most urgently need to be reached. But, under the prevailing orthodoxy, donors are inclined to withhold aid from governments with weak policy and governance records. Aiding fragile states carries high stakes. Aid driven by motives other than

---

[1] For example, Krugman (2006). Electric power could have been restored much faster if existing plants had been rebuilt by the original European contractors. Instead, US companies started building new ones. Indeed, the cost of destroying and then attempting to rebuild the state of Iraq—recently estimated at US$2 trillion [sic]—is so monumental as to make arguments about the value of aid rather spurious.

need can be destructive. But, the right aid applied in the right manner can transform the prospects of millions of people.

This chapter examines state failure as an aid concern—and the failings of aid in the face of fragility. It first looks at poor development performance as a criterion for state failure. It then examines the anatomy of failed states and enquires about some common causes. Finally it asks how donor engagement could address the twin challenges of state failure—lack of political will and incapacity.

7.2. Failing development performance

The notion of development laggards is not new. In 1971, the UN identified a category of twenty-five least-developed countries (LDCs) defined by three sets of criteria: low income levels (less than gross national income (GNI) per head of US$775); a low human assets index (a composite of nutrition, health, education, and adult literacy); and high economic vulnerability (volatility of agricultural production and trade, small economic size, and proneness to natural disasters). Least-developed status was consistent with the traditional orthodoxy of aid entitlement. It was equated with a priority for aid, as compensation for what was construed as inherent disadvantage. Within the overall target of 0.7 per cent of gross national product (GNP) for aid from the OECD countries, a target of 0.15 per cent to 0.20 per cent was established for the LDCs, although it was never respected (OECD aid for the LDCs actually fell by 20 per cent in real terms during the 1990s, which is much more than the overall aid decline). The few graduates from this dismal club include the well-governed Botswana, Cape Verde, and the Maldives. Otherwise, the overall numbers of the LDCs have grown steadily and there are now forty-nine, seeming to vitiate the criteria of natural disadvantage. Most LDCS would be unambiguously included among the poorest performers.

For many years, countries were compared using data of GNP growth and levels of income per head. From 1990, the UN Development Programme broadened the income criterion and began analysing development performance by ranking countries according to a human development index (HDI).[2] The rankings immediately enlivened the development debate, especially because they were published at a time when many bilateral donors were reviewing their

---

[2] The HDI is a composite index which purports to measure average achievement along three dimensions of 'human development': longevity, knowledge, and standard of living. For these it uses proxies: life expectancy for longevity; a combination of adult literacy and gross combined enrolment rates for knowledge; and a normalized calculation of GDP per head for standard of living. The HDI is measured from 0 to 1; a level below 0.5 is determined to be 'low human development'.

criteria for beneficiary selection.[3] Development results, and especially human development outcomes, provide an objective basis for determining individual country performance, and therefore, for defining development failure.

The most comprehensive and widely acknowledged set of indicators for developing-country performance-tracking is the Millennium Development Goals (MDGs). The MDGs are based on the seven international development goals originally drawn up by the OECD in 1996, which were derived from a selection of targets defined by the global development conferences convened by the UN during the 1990s. There is nothing really new about these goals. A version of these OECD goals was incorporated into the Millennium Declaration which emerged from the Millennium Summit of world leaders called by the UN in September 2000.[4] Following the Summit, an eighth goal, containing mainly the obligations of the developed countries was added (UNDP 2003b).[5]

MDG non-achievement (discussed in detail in Chapter 6 of this volume) confirms the predominance of sub-Saharan Africa as the region of greatest concern. Overall, up to one-third of all developing countries are, by different measures, falling short of sustainable development progress.

7.3. Fragility factors: maturity, government size, leadership, conflict

What are the origins of fragility? And what are the conditions and circumstances which cause states to become and remain fragile? In this section we review several of the factors which help to explain why some developing countries are weaker and more poorly governed than others, starting with history.

7.3.1. *Maturity*

Some independent states have existed for many centuries; several millennia in the case of China. But, most developing countries have led an independent existence for only a few decades, since the post-war end of colonialism. The so-called transition countries emerged (or re-emerged) when the Soviet Union splintered in 1991. Some states—such as Timor-Leste (2002)—are even newer

---

[3] UNDP was actually expelled from Oman because of an observation in a Human Development Report comparing the country unfavourably with Costa Rica.

[4] The term 'Millennium Development Goal' was first used in a country progress report on Tanzania, developed by the author in Feb. 2001.

[5] Even though it was an obvious quid pro quo for monitoring developing country performance, the idea of goal 8 was strongly opposed by some of the donors at first. One of the most vocal opponents was the UK Secretary of State at the time, although subsequently the British government became more supportive.

than that, and some are still emerging—Kosovo. Some states in the modern era have, in a sense, already come and gone: Somalia lasted for barely thirty years as a unified territory and is trying again to reconstitute itself. Longevity confers confidence and identity, and while it does not guarantee capability, it is true to say that most of today's fragile states are among the newest. The experience of the post-war states has been highly variegated, however. Inevitably, the degree of colonial penetration was a major factor in these experiences, particularly in Asia and Africa, from where most of the post-war states emerged[6] (in Latin America, decolonization had been much earlier). In Asia, colonial rule was broad and shallow. There were not the resources to maintain a large presence, and given the strength of culture and religion, local elites were empowered as much as they were co-opted. Mostly, states emerged strongly from the colonial presence, but statehood was under assault from cold war rivalry in Indochina and the Korean peninsula, and by the contestation by minorities in several countries. The two states which were not formally colonized, Nepal and Thailand, were both under authoritative regimes, but adjusted very differently to the new era.

In Africa, states in many cases had been the original creation of colonial powers, with national boundaries clumsily etched across ethnic lines. Some were thus inherently artificial and the deeper colonial presence attempted to foster new (Western) traditions of education, religion, and culture. Moreover, statehood was superimposed on the powers of local chiefdoms, whose authority had been determined in traditional ways, including heredity. Statehood was not underlined by 'nationhood' in the single-people sense and was an inherently unfamiliar concept. It tended to be identified with, and driven by, one strong man,[7] often a pioneer of the independence movement. Some of these states became what have been described as 'neo-patrimonial'. They depend on personalized exchanges, clientelism, and politics by patronage. There is a strong executive (the male head of state), a weak judiciary and parliament, and a corrupt and ineffective civil service (Bratton and van de Walle 1997).

7.3.2. Big government

These executives were strong because much was expected of the state at independence. Worldwide, the growth of government had followed from the conduct of and recovery from two world wars. In the developing world, it was natural for the new governments to grasp the levers of political, social, and commercial control. There was a patriotic attachment to big government and a prevailing sentiment of state nationalism.

---

[6] See discussion in Pinkney (2003).
[7] In our table of fragile states, only two—Bangladesh and Liberia—are headed by women.

In most of the newer states civil society was weak, or lacking altogether. There were no organized social groups or political parties which states were required to accommodate and adjust to. The authoritarian governments which most often emerged in the newer states were thus 'filling a vacuum that would have been filled in Europe by political parties, pressure groups, and a variety of autonomous bodies' (Pinkney 2003).[8] In most developing countries, the emergence of civil society, which helped to dilute the monopolization of political power by the state, was to come much later. The newly independent states also assumed wide-reaching economic powers made fashionable by the successful examples of state intervention in the West epitomized by the Marshall Plan, the emerging welfare systems, and Keynesian-style demand management. The Soviet Union also provided a central planning model for many countries. Newly independent states took responsibility for building infrastructure, developing infant industries, directing agricultural production, and playing a large part in the allocation of resources, including through the administering of prices and subsidies and the control of labour, foreign exchange and financial markets (World Bank 1997).

These extensive powers of the state were used to very different effect. In some countries (including the East Asian tigers: Korea, Taiwan, Hong Kong, Singapore), government built an efficient and well co-ordinated planning system, while also investing in human resources through the social sectors. The private sector also thrived and was provided with incentives to develop. But, in many other countries, state-led development turned out very differently. Public sectors became bloated and were run inefficiently, and the monopolistic powers of governments—often with political power overlapping with commercial and economic interest—left very little space for independent private enterprise and initiative to flourish. The 'dirigiste dogma' (Lal 1983) was driven as much by form as by function. Big government seemed the natural accompaniment of development and alternative means of public goods and service provision were never explored.

An acid test of state effectiveness was the use of resources. Some developing countries used the commodity price booms of the early 1950s, and indeed in 2006 and 2007, as a basis to expand state activities, but never adjusted to the ensuing decline in revenues. The oil price shocks of the 1970s were a proving ground. Some oil exporters, such as Malaysia, built productively on their windfall while others, such as Nigeria and Angola, used it wastefully. For many oil

[8] Pinkney (2003). See also IDS (2005): 'Many countries in the South today have formal institutions of representation, accountability and administration built on models transferred from OECD countries, but they often work very differently. They lack legitimacy and effectiveness because they were not forged through a political process of state/society negotiation, and are not supported by socio-economic structures that encourage organization around broader, common interests. In particular, organization around ethnic identity rather than economic interests can be problematic because the former is less likely to provide a basis for compromise, and for identifying positive sum outcomes.'

importers, the shocks were disastrous. Many were driven to a level of indebtedness from which they have never recovered. But not all. In some, like South Korea, the government built economic strength through a deliberate policy of diversification.

7.3.3. Leadership

Leadership qualities have also played a critical part in determining development capacity, particularly in younger, institutionally immature states, where the character of the ruling elite, and particularly the head of government, can exert a major influence. Even in the absence of democratic institutions, enlightened and committed leadership can be instrumental in guiding countries onto paths of solid progress. But ill-motivated leadership will have the opposite result. Strong leaders can, for good or ill, create or influence policies and lay down norms of procedure and execution. Their personality and example is a further guiding factor. In many developing states, strong leaders often emerged from within the most disciplined and cohesive institution—the armed forces—which then served to buttress the leader's position. The manner in which they have led, however, has then depended on their personalities and their patterns of co-opting support within the elite: in the best case, by soliciting individuals on the basis of merit; in the worst case, through family and crony relationships. The record of generals has mostly been egregious. From Argentina to Burma, from Liberia to Zaire, development has suffered the depredations of military men.

Damaging leadership has not been confined to military dictators; civilian leaders have also presided over self-interested kleptocracies. But there have also been some shining exceptions. Seretse Khama, the first President of Botswana, inherited an impoverished state from British tutelage in 1966. For the next 14 years, until his death in office in 1980, Botswana had one of the fastest growing economies in the world, turning revenues from beef, copper, and diamonds into investments in infrastructure, education, and health. President Khama used his authority to foster democracy and promote the rule of law, helping to set the country on a course of steady progress, which has been followed by his three successors (Quett Masire in 1980, Festus Mogae in 1998, and Seretse Khama—son of the first President—in 2008).[9]

In pre-modern states, Weber (1946) emphasizes the significance of charisma and tradition in the vesting of authority. Charisma is the factor that precipitates the emergence of an individual leader, but tradition begets continuity and can reinforce dynastic tendencies, handing succession down the generations. It can

---

[9] Botswana today has one of the highest levels of per capita income in Africa. But its success has not been entirely unalloyed: it suffers from chronic inequality, a very high rate of HIV/AIDS incidence, and one of the lowest life expectancies in the world.

also perpetuate authoritarian rule. The nature of leadership, and of its perpetuation, can take a very different hold over the fortunes of new states. Contrast the divergent fortunes of the two halves of the culturally homogeneous Korean society, led down different paths by strong but very differently motivated authoritarian regimes. One half has joined the OECD club of rich democracies as a full-fledged industrial power, while the other is a quintessential failed state and one of the single greatest threats to global security. Some states that have benefited from strong and developmentally effective leadership have never been democracies (Uganda, Vietnam). But most have become more democratic and clearly choice provides a better guarantee of good leadership. With very few exceptions, poorly led crisis states have remained undemocratic, and fragility and weakness are perpetuated where leaders are resistant to more democracy.

7.3.4. Conflict

Within the developing world, those states which have made the least progress and have remained mired in low-income and high-poverty levels have been the most prone to conflict, while those which have done relatively better have reduced the risks of conflict and insecurity (see also Chapter 6 of this volume). Here the statistical correlations are quite solid—there is a close empirical relationship between civil war and low income. Poverty increases the likelihood of civil war and war is a prime cause of poverty. Conflict vulnerability is also chronic: within five years, half of all countries securing peace slip back into conflict (Collier 2003).

Over the last four decades, following completion of the main independence wave, there was a substantial increase in the number of civil wars. The 1990s saw a subsequent reduction. But, while wars have been contained in Angola, Guatemala, Liberia, Mozambique, Peru, and Sierra Leone, some long-standing conflicts have continued to fester (for example, in Burma, Colombia, Indonesia, Papua New Guinea, Somalia, Sri Lanka, Sudan, and Uganda) and some new conflicts have started or been rekindled (Afghanistan, Côte d'Ivoire, Haiti, and Nepal).[10] Civil war incurs huge costs and has been described as development in reverse. The human cost through loss of life is compounded by injury and permanent disability. There are also the psychosocial consequences associated with the destruction of livelihoods and the concern for survival. Economies are undermined, not just at the local level, but through the diversion of resources into expanded military budgets, at the expense of social development. Unfortunately, the impact of civil conflicts is rarely confined within one country. Fragility is exacerbated by conflict in a contiguous state. Civil wars in recent

---

[10] During the 1990s an estimated 6 million people were killed in violent conflict, most of them poor and civilian. Some 40 million people were internally displaced or became refugees, 80 per cent of them women and children.

years in Afghanistan, Angola, Burma, Colombia, Congo (Democratic Republic), Liberia, Rwanda, Somalia, and Iraq, have all burst their borders, adding to refugee burdens and destabilizing their neighbours.

7.4. Aiding fragility

For the OECD's Development Assistance Committee (DAC) fragile states constitute 'difficult partnerships', a term coined to connote countries

where development objectives play little role compared with prolongation of power, with the result that partner governments do not have credible commitment to effective policies and their implementation.... corruption and political repression, among other characteristics, are commonly associated with such regimes. (OECD-DAC 2001)

In 2002, the World Bank identified a category of low-income countries 'under stress' (LICUS) which pose liabilities for its lending portfolio. They include the delinquent debtors and the least-bankable clients. Among bilaterals, the UK's Department for International Development (DFID) has defined a target group called Poverty Reduction in Difficult Environments (PRIDE). DFID talks about 'difficult environments' where the state is 'unwilling or unable to harness domestic and international resources for poverty reduction'. The US Agency for International Development (USAID) refers to 'failing, failed and recovering states' and stresses concerns of conflict and security (USAID 2005). As these definitions imply, there are two dimensions of state fragility which donors seek to address: lack of political *will* and weak development *capacity*. State failure may reflect the unwillingness of a government to commit itself to policies of inclusion and human welfare, and to ensuring that available resources are utilized for productive purposes. Will may be bound up with political legitimacy. Where a regime is undemocratic and unrepresentative, its leadership is less likely to pursue a development agenda. Capacity determines effectiveness: in administration and service delivery, in the maintenance of order and security and in economic and resource management. Both *will* and *capacity* are important for effectiveness in the utilization of aid and for the quality of the relationship between recipients and donors.

Figure 7.1 attempts to plot the two dimensions of fragility for several failing states.[11] Bolivia and Uzbekistan are shown as relatively more capacitated states (with stronger institutions and human resources). Sierra Leone is shown as relatively less capacitated, but more willing in its post-conflict phase. Several states, such as North Korea, are shown as lacking both capacity and will. The arrows indicate (often changing) trends towards or away from greater stability.

---

[11] Figure 7.1 is inspired in part by the analysis in the USAID paper (2005) on 'Service Delivery in Fragile States'.

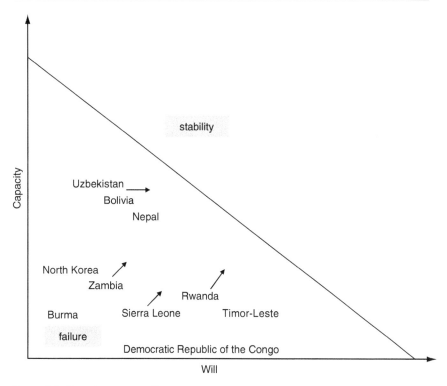

Figure 7.1 Capacity versus will

(Chapter 5 of this volume has a related discussion on willingness and capacity in relation to addressing horizontal inequalities—see section 5.4.2 and Figure 5.2.)

The role of donors is to help countries to move from the fragility to the stability zone, by influencing political will and supporting development capacity. But, there are no simple formulae linking aid and fragility and the record of aid has been ambiguous. The examples of Burma, Rwanda, and Zambia—three quintessentially fragile states embroiled in different kinds of development crisis—are illustrative of this ambiguity.

The circumstances of every fragile state is unique. However, the two-dimensional (capacity/will) challenge of overcoming fragility and backwardness applies to all: how much are they willing to change and how much are they able to improve? The most egregious regimes are the unwilling, those whose leaderships have impoverished their countries and are resisting change, whatever the reasons: dogma, greed, military paranoia, but invariably a determination to hold on to power whatever the development cost. In other fragile states, the leadership may be more amenable, but capacity is limited. Such would be the case in Liberia, Rwanda, Sierra Leone, and other countries emerging from conflict, or Mali, Nicaragua, Niger, Zambia, and others seeking to compensate for poor management and the adversities of HIV/AIDS, natural disaster, or global economic conditions. We shall look respectively at these challenges for donors.

7.5. Aid and will: engagement and consistency

There is an extensive literature on the limited effectiveness of donor conditionality.[12] Some of these arguments apply *a fortiori* to fragile states that are not in open conflict, but where the leadership is more entrenched and plays an unchallengeable role in steering the direction of the country. Since the record of conditional aid shows that it has limited impact in countries where the leadership is at least developmentally inclined and open to examining policy alternatives, aid with strings is even less likely to lead to beneficial change in the circumstances of fragile states. However, *political engagement* by donors can stimulate change if certain conditions are met.

First, engagement can help to connect cynical regimes with global values. While it may be premature to talk of universal convergence, those values are becoming increasingly centred on more open democracy and market principles. This growing consensus can play a helpful framing role in advocating for political and economic change. Advocacy is being driven by demonstration, in a world in which globalization has sharpened the sense of inter-state competition and when development performances are compared more overtly than before. For example, reform in India has been goaded in part by a desire to catch up with the growth and income levels of China. South Korea has set its sights on Japan. Brazil, Malaysia, Nigeria, South Africa, Thailand, and others aspire to middle-income status. All these countries have been finding their own way to the democratic free-market road.

Demonstration effects have become extremely powerful for at least two reasons. One is the spread of global information and media via new information technologies, which allow people in one country to learn about and compare life in almost every other. The second is the rise of the global civil society movement, which has helped to connect people within and between countries and act as an alternative voice to governments.[13] In the West we now take technologically facilitated networking for granted, but connected civil society has become a redoubtable force for change. In the late 1980s and early

[12] A sample includes Killick (1997); Kanbur (2000); Buira (2003); Hall and de la Motte (2004); Uvin (2004), and Browne (2006).
[13] This phenomenon has been appropriately described by the *New York Times* as the second global superpower.

1990s, it helped turn Eastern Europe from autocracy and accelerated the demise of the Soviet Union by piercing the barriers to information exchange. It has raised the aspirations of people in the developing world by making millions more aware of how much better their lives could be.

Connectedness is specifically denied in the more abject examples of state failure such as Burma and North Korea, where governments have permitted very limited internet access and placed drastic restrictions on the media. As in the states of the Soviet Union before the break-up, isolation is taking a heavy toll. If these barriers cannot be broken down, then the role of donors should be to encourage more engagement, and not reinforce a country's isolation. The process needs to start with this same cynical leadership.

Engagement—through dialogue and demonstration—should then be the conduit of value change. Minds cannot be altered from behind unbroken walls, but they can see through the cracks. In the northern parts of both Burma and North Korea it is—almost ironically—China which is encouraging a furtive encroachment of capitalism via the development of free enterprise enclaves. These small bridgeheads could become significant forces for change, and could precede a wider opening of these societies.

In the second place, solidarity and consistency are important. The impact of US and European sanctions on Burma is already diluted by the breaches in their own foreign investment ban. But, more importantly, the country's immediate neighbours are willing to engage. To be effective, Burma's partners should—at least with respect to influencing political will—speak with a single voice. Similar arguments apply to Zimbabwe. The political (if not the economic) impact of US and European sanctions is undermined by close and generally uncritical relations which the country enjoys with South Africa and China. On Cuba, the world is similarly divided—the US and Canada cannot agree on relations with the regime (even to the extent of the US threatening to impose sanctions on Canadian and European companies which continue to do business with Havana). The chinks must be mended, not only between the rich states, but among all the partners of fragile states.

An OECD consensus around fragile states has often proved elusive. But, aid from the rich West is losing its influence anyway. Trade and economic relations within developing regions are growing in importance, and non-DAC donors, such as India, China, and Brazil have entered the stage. India looms large on the strategic horizons of its neighbours, including the fragile states of Burma and Nepal. China has long been a significant donor to recipient countries in Asia and in Africa (where it has built a sports stadium in virtually every country).[14] Through aid, it actively supports weak states such as North Korea, Burma, Laos, and Zimbabwe. Like India, China's aid is strongly influenced by commercial

---

[14] Except the few that recognize Taiwan. Chinese aid can therefore be seen as a means of buying loyalty.

interest, currently driven by the need to secure supplies of energy and raw materials to fuel its voracious expansion. The desire for influence leads to aid, and vice versa. Since 2005, China has succeeded in preventing Sudan from a harsher censure by the UN Security Council over Darfur, and it is an important counterweight to Western donor interest as a member of the 'Group of 77' developing countries.

In some circumstances, regional organizations could play a role in influencing states. For Burma, the Association of Southeast Asian Nations (ASEAN), to which it belongs (along with Thailand, Malaysia, Singapore, and others), could help the international community to forge a common position on a desirable political roadmap for the country. An opportunity has already been provided by the agreement by Burma not to take up chairmanship of ASEAN in 2006, in order to save the grouping from an embarrassing boycott by Western countries. A similar position with respect to Zimbabwe has been threatened by an African sub-regional grouping (the South Africa Development Community (SADC) to which South Africa and Zimbabwe both belong) or by the African Union, which plays a more political role in the continent.

Third, donors need to stay engaged with the people of fragile states. Their humanitarian needs should be met even though they are exacerbated by the actions of misguided leadership. Humanitarian engagement is important for several reasons. One is obviously altruistic. Others are more political. Aid connects people in need with the international community and is a foundation for building longer-term goodwill beyond periods of crisis. Humanitarian aid has its own beneficial demonstration effect from the sacks of 'USAID' wheat and UNHCR tenting to the selfless toil of the camp doctors. Humanitarian aid, if sensitively applied, can make an example of bad government.

In sum (i) engagement is better than isolation, particularly where fragile states are already seeking to isolate themselves; (ii) engagement should be consistently applied and based on collective action, preferably backed by the authority of a regional grouping and by globally acknowledged norms of international comportment; (iii) donor engagement should take full cognizance of, and attempt to compensate for, the humanitarian plight of the populations in fragile states who are the victims of wrong-headed policies which are driving them to impoverishment.

7.6. Aid and capacity

The record of aid in building sustainable capacity has been a very mixed one, even where leadership is committed. The record is unfortunately no better in the building or reconstruction of fragile states, where failure comes at much higher costs, but where the dividends of success can be enormous. This section reviews the impact of aid on capacity in three different scenarios: during what may be described as 'pre-conflict' periods; during conflict; and during periods of reconstruction and state-building (which are quite often post-conflict).

7.6.1. 'Pre-conflict'

Somalia in the mid-1980s was a country at peace, and Mogadishu was one of the safest capitals in Africa. But all was not well. A despotic president ruled with total intolerance of dissent as well as indifference to the process of development. The country was one of the most generously aided in the world but the donors were having a negligible impact on either the policies of the regime or the capacities of the country. Supply-driven aid carried the donors' trademarks and the landscape was littered with some of the starkest relics of aid failure: broken tractors, silted pumps, fuel-less turbines, vacant schools, darkened hospitals, and crumbling new roads to nowhere. Typical of 'capacity-building' was a large bilateral programme at the National University of Somalia, worth much more than the total national education budget. The main beneficiaries were the expatriate professors from the donor country who enjoyed lucrative six-monthly tours of duty in the capital.

Somalia began to implode in the late 1980s as the president sought with mounting desperation to hold onto power, favouring his own and discriminating against unfriendly clans. A country in which so much hope had once been vested as an example of unique ethnic, cultural, linguistic, and religious uniformity, splintered into domains of warlordism and remains divided today.[15] In 1960, the international community had successfully reunited Somalia under a UN mandate but subsequent donor interests were dominated by cold-war competition. First, the Russians sought to bring the country into their sphere and then, quite abruptly, the Western camp, as allegiances switched in 1977. When the country began to fall apart, the Western donors departed except for the hardiest humanitarian agencies. Unluckily for Somalia, the cold war was ending and most of the remaining strategic interest in the country evaporated. Italy—the former colonial power—decided to back one of the warlords attempting to form a new government, but he was virulently opposed by other factions and civil war raged openly from 1991. The international community returned to Somalia in 1993 but in different guise.

Through complicity in or oblivion to state collapse, Rwanda has also taught us that aid can do harm in the wrong circumstances, with deadly results. The nexus between aid and conflict is extremely delicate and deserves much closer and more subtle consideration than it has received in the past (Andersen 1999). To the sounds of stable doors closing, there has been considerable donor introspection on Rwanda, Somalia, Bosnia, Angola, and the many other war-

---

[15] The territory includes two self-proclaimed mini-states in the north: Somaliland and Puntland.

torn states. It has led to the development of increasingly sophisticated meth-odologies for analysing conflict-proneness,[16] as well as whole new 'crisis' departments. This new-found conflict sensitivity among donors is only to be welcomed. As with much that is good about donor intention, however, it is important that it is followed in practice.

7.6.2. During conflict

Attempts by the international community to stop civil wars have had mixed success. An analysis by Dobbins et al. (2005) finds that of seven UN-led peacekeeping operations since 1989, all had been partially or wholly success-ful.[17] Where the USA led the missions, or was heavily involved, there were successes in Bosnia and Kosovo, but failures in Somalia and Haiti (Dobbins et al. 2003).

Somalia was a watershed, for troops were sent in for the first time under a Chapter VII UN Charter mandate to try to quell a civil conflict through force, without a government invitation. The intervention was, as we know, spectacu-larly unsuccessful. Soldiers under UN command were killed, prompting the US to send troops to join them. But, when the US lost eighteen of its own men,[18] they began to withdraw. By 1995, there were no UN troops in Somalia, but civil conflict, albeit at a more subdued level, still simmered.

Rwanda was another failure when, in April 1994, the UN did not deploy peace-enforcing troops, which by all accounts could have stopped the slaughter of 800,000 civilians. Unquestionably, failure in Somalia was a factor in dissuad-ing intervention in Rwanda, although the two situations and the anticipated results would have been very different. Again, since 2004, a UN mandate has not been forged in time to quell genocide in Darfur (Sudan).

Whatever the outcomes of these peace-enforcing initiatives, an important threshold was crossed in the 1990s. For the first time since the beginning of the post-war independence movement, sovereignty is being subordinated to the notion of wider responsibility. As the UN High-level Panel on Threats, Chal-lenges, and Change puts it, 'successive humanitarian disasters . . . have concen-trated attention not on the immunities of sovereign governments but their responsibilities, both to their own people and to the wider international com-munity' (UN 2004).

The Panel—which comprised eminent persons from both north (seven) and south (nine)—went on to provide the rationale for engagement, 'while

---

[16] See, for instance, DFID (2002); World Bank (2005); UNDP (2003a); GTZ (2001); and the Netherlands Ministry of Foreign Affairs (2005).

[17] A study by Dobbins et al. (2005) notes that the eighth mission to Congo 1960–4 had been a failure.

[18] In an operation which was the subject of the 2001 film, *Black Hawk Down*.

sovereign governments have the primary responsibility to protect their own citizens from such catastrophes, when they are unable or unwilling to do so that responsibility should be taken up by the wider international community'. In effect, the right to intervene under Chapter VII is reinterpreted as responsibility to protect:

We endorse the emerging norm that there is a collective international responsibility to protect, exercisable by the Security Council authorizing military intervention as a last resort, in the event of genocide and other large scale killing, ethnic cleansing or serious violations of international humanitarian law which sovereign Governments have proved powerless or unwilling to prevent.

The report provides a clear mandate for intervention in Sudan.

In spite of mixed outcomes, international engagement is morally correct where regimes have lost control. There is also an important economic rationale. While enforcing and keeping the peace can be expensive, the prospect of reducing the catastrophic costs from civil conflict can easily be justified. By way of illustration, an economic study has attempted a cost–benefit analysis of peacekeeping initiatives (Collier and Hoeffler 2004). It yields an impressively positive ratio. Based on the record of recent civil wars, it finds that US$4.8 billion spent on peacekeeping could yield almost US$400 billion in benefits.

7.6.3. Reconstruction and state-building

After conflict, and in all other circumstances where states are attempting a fresh start, the role of development assistance can and should be of primary importance in building sustainable new capacity. As conflicts are resolved, as wills turn, and as persistent non-performance finds fewer excuses, there is a keener edge to the realization that rich countries hold some of the keys to the prosperity of the recipients. More-of-the-same aid will perpetuate failure because it has for so long pursued the wrong objectives. A recent verdict by Francis Fukuyama (2004) on the role of gap-filling is less than sanguine: 'the international community is not simply limited in the amount of capacity it can build; it is actually complicit in the destruction of institutional capacity in many developing countries.' And, speaking of the public sector in fragile states, he goes on the say that the 'deterioration in capacity has happened precisely during a period of accelerating external aid flows'. The correlation may not be robust, but the fact is that donors' efforts in capacity development have failed to arrest failure. A more-recent critique of aid's failures in state-building can be found in Ghani and Lockhart (2008).

The author's own conclusions from a study of aid and capacity development in six major aid recipients, two of them on the 'fragile' list (Bangladesh and Uganda), are also sceptical about the sustainability of the results of past aid:

The outputs of aid projects have abounded and these are manifestations of development. But they are also in part a substitute for it, to the extent that technical cooperation has not resulted in the building of sustainable capacities to enable countries to manage their own development independently. The word sustainable is important. Inappropriate technical cooperation, far from building sustainability, may undermine it. (Browne 2002: 7)

But, if it is not to be more of the same, then more of what? Analysis suggests that there are several ways in which aid could be better applied to the reconstruction of fragile states.

TREAT EVERY CASE AS UNIQUE: 'KNOW THY SUBJECT'

No two fragile states are similar. They are not similar in current profile, and there are always unique sets of causes of fragility. We should therefore beware of standard typologies, as well as the kind of standardized solutions which have undermined aid effectiveness in the past. Donors have an uncomfortable tendency to consider some fragile states as ailing patients amenable to standard types of treatment, whether humanitarian, reconstructive, or developmental. There are some common manifestations of fragility, however, and these can be used to determine appropriate types of donor engagement. As mentioned earlier, they include: institutional maturity; nature of leadership; size and role of state; and proneness to conflict. The proclivity for standardization is related to a poverty of learning which must also be addressed. Donor and development agencies are notorious re-inventers of wheels. There are many thousands of development practitioners who would have worked in or on any one of the recipient countries, fragile states included. There is a vast and rich experience to draw on, but it is rarely captured, codified, and shared even within individual agencies, let alone between them.[19] Because this knowledge is not tapped, standardized clean-slate solutions are often applied to states in crisis by donor staff who actually have very limited experience of the countries in question and who fail to discover and build on the experience of others.

UNDERSTAND WHAT STATE CAPACITY MEANS

The challenge in fragile states is the reconstitution of basic state functions of three general kinds: political and institutional; economic and social; security. All are important and they are interconnected. Table 7.1 outlines some of the main challenges which need to be addressed in these three spheres, implying that any aid effort should be both broad based and finely tuned.

An understanding of the different dimensions of state capacity is also vital, but there has been a tendency in the past for donors to concentrate on state size as of primordial importance. It is true that oversized public sectors, in concentrating too many resources and powers to themselves and using them

---

[19] The UN system is certainly one of the worst offenders.

Table 7.1. Fragile states by different definitions

Country[1]	LDCs[2]	Low and falling HDI	MDG under-performer[3]	LIPPS[4]	Corruption perception index (out of 145) (2004)	Conflict-prone[5]
Afghanistan	✓				n/a	✓
Angola	✓		✓		133	✓
Bangladesh	✓			✓	145	
Benin	✓		✓		77	
Bhutan	✓				n/a	
Burkina Faso	✓		✓	✓	n/a	
Burma (Myanmar)	✓				142	✓
Burundi	✓	✓	✓		n/a	✓
Cambodia	✓				n/a	
Cameroon					129	
Central African Republic	✓	✓	✓	✓	n/a	✓
Chad	✓	✓	✓	✓	142	
Congo, Dem.	✓	✓	✓	✓	133	✓
Congo, Rep.			✓		114	✓
Equatorial Guinea	✓				n/a	
Eritrea	✓				102	✓
Ethiopia	✓		✓	✓	114	✓
Gabon					74	
Gambia	✓			✓	90	
Guinea	✓		✓	✓	n/a	
Guinea-Bissau	✓			✓	n/a	
Haiti	✓		✓	✓	145	✓
Indonesia		✓		✓	133	✓
Côte d'Ivoire		✓		✓	133	✓
Kenya			(✓)	✓	129	
Korea, North		(✓)	(✓)		n/a	
Laos	✓			✓	n/a	
Lesotho	✓		✓		n/a	
Liberia	✓		✓		n/a	✓
Madagascar	✓		✓	✓	82	
Malawi	✓				90	
Mali	✓		✓	✓	77	

(continued)

Table 7.1. Continued

Country[1]	LDCs[2]	Low and falling HDI	MDG under-performer[3]	LIPPS[4]	Corruption perception index (out of 145) (2004)	Conflict-prone[5]
Mauritania	✓		✓	✓	n/a	
Mongolia			✓		85	
Mozambique	✓		✓		90	✓
Nepal	✓			✓	90	✓
Niger	✓		✓	✓	122	
Nigeria			✓	✓	144	✓
Pakistan				✓	129	✓
Papua New Guinea					102	✓
Rwanda	✓		✓	✓	n/a	✓
Senegal	✓			✓	85	
Sierra Leone	✓		✓		114	✓
Somalia	✓				n/a	✓
Sudan	✓		✓		122	✓
Tanzania	✓		✓	✓	90	
Timor-Leste	✓	✓	✓		n/a	✓
Togo	✓		✓	✓	n/a	
Uganda	✓			✓	102	✓
Yemen	✓		✓	✓	112	
Zambia	✓	✓	✓	✓	102	
Zimbabwe		✓	✓	✓	114	
Totals	**52 40**	**9**	**32**	**28**		**25**

Notes:
[1] Excluding the smallest states and the transition countries.
[2] Excluding: Cape Verde, Comoros, Djibouti, Kiribati, Maldives, Samoa, São Tomé and Principe, Solomon Islands, Tuvalu, Vanuatu.
[3] Countries listed as 'top priority' for attainment of two or more MDGs (Source: UNDP 2003a).
[4] Low-income poorly performing states, defined by Center for Global Development, Washington, DC.
[5] Open civil or international armed conflict since 1990. See also Annex on Episodes of State Failure.

Source: See text.

inefficiently, have been a detriment to development progress. But, the alternative is not simply the dogmatic pursuit of small government and the wholesale reduction of state capacity. There are activities of governments that may be better in private hands, but there are important functions of government that also need strengthening. The planning and formulation of national policies; the promulgation and enforcement of laws;,the guaranteeing of basic social services—these are just a few of the indisputably essential state functions. Fukuyama makes the useful distinction between the scope of state activity— some of which could be reduced—and the strength of state power—which often needs strengthening (Fukuyama 2004).

As part of the Washington paradigms, many Western donors have been overzealous in their advocacy of privatization in developing countries (reduction in state scope). But, there has been inadequate attention to the development of adequate checks and safeguards under public auspices (state strength) to ensure that privatization results in better and more affordable services and that public good (for example, universal service) is not sacrificed to private gain (von Weizsacker, Young, and Finger 2005).

BUILD UP, NOT DOWN

One of the more serious illusions in donor approaches to capacity development is the notion of gap-filling. The build-down fallacy is based on the assumption that there are 'levels' of capacity that can be prescribed in advance, that the gaps between these levels and present levels can be determined, and aid provided as the filler. All too often gap-filling approaches lead to the artificial grafting of 'capacity solutions' onto unwilling institutional hosts. Where these solutions amount to a significant diversion for these institutions, long-term capacity may actually be undermined. In reconstructing fragile states especially, building up, rather than down is all the more imperative. Donors need to take cognizance of the capacity that exists, whether in the public, private, or civil sectors. Where governments are weak, or where they barely exist as in the first stages of rebuilding after conflict, humanitarian assistance through multilateral organizations and through international NGOs provides for populations directly. But, as stability is restored, appropriate local partners—within or outside the state sector—should be brought in and their capacity to administer services gradually built up.[20]

---

[20] The transition is often difficult. In the course of major humanitarian interventions, many well-resourced international NGOs are present and are inclined to stay on as long as possible, leading to their subsequent expulsion by governments: e.g., Rwanda in 1995, Indonesia—post-Tsunami Aceh—in 2005.

ESCHEW LENDING AND TOP–DOWN PRESCRIPTIONS

Africa has provided many unsuitable cases for the standard Bretton Woods lending treatment, whereby countries in difficulty are given loans well beyond any realistic prospect of repayment in return for some forcible advice on reforming their economies. In many cases, this advice has led to the shrinking of the state sector and the cutting of vital public services like health and education, already circumscribed by the necessity to repay the mounting costs of lending. When the author lived in Somalia in the mid-1980s, the same prescriptions were being paid for and the scramble was already on to find donor grants to pay off the International Monetary Fund (IMF) and World Bank. In Haiti, in the early 1990s, new aid was contingent on new grants to pay World Bank and IMF arrears. This 'rob Peter to pay Paul' merry-go-round has continued for over two decades, in fact about as long as structural adjustment itself. The momentum is maintained because even where multilateral debt is cancelled through new gifts of aid, the lending process repeats itself. The July 2005 G8 meeting in Scotland, like almost every other before it, began with the familiar hand-wringing on indebtedness and ended with another 'path-breaking' declaration on debt cancellation. But, among the big bucks, the small penny hasn't dropped—many countries, and most of the fragile ones, were never suitable clients for the Washington consensus. The results are eloquent-enough evidence. In fact, the World Bank has begun to provide more grant assistance—an average of around 20 per cent—out of its international development association (IDA) programmes for the poorer countries. Donors, outside and within the multilateral system, should provide only grants to fragile states and they should also retreat from imposing their agendas. Rather, as part of ground–up capacity development, they should allow consensus to build around national strategies.

CHOOSE AN INTERMEDIARY

Donors do harm by bringing their own agendas to their support for weak states, and one of the hardest principles to try to enforce is one of donor disinterest. Iraq is an extreme case. Over Rwanda, donors have also manifested their strong individual interests, and there is baggage of different shape and bulk associated with many other fragile states. Many of these interests relate to the old colonial ties of European countries (mainly UK, France, Portugal, Belgium, Italy, and the Netherlands) and Russia. In circumstances of chronic administrative weakness and high insecurity, donor engagement with fragile states needs to be mediated, preferably through multilateral means, until the governments concerned can gain the strength and confidence to play the mediation role themselves. The UN, OECD, or a suitable regional grouping can play such a role—even a bilateral—but not an organization with a significant financial stake or other special interest in a country. Smart mediation is not just about managing the aid but managing the transition process cohesively across the whole range of state capacity: political and institutional; economic and social; security.[21]

The UN can claim some success in concerting the management of recovery processes following serious conflict. The UN Transitional Authority for Cambodia (UNTAC) was set up following the signing of the Paris Agreements in October 1991. With support of different donors, it organized elections, maintained security, helped re-establish the civil administration, rebuilt some infrastructure and repatriated and resettled refugees and displaced people. In Timor-Leste, the UN established another Transitional Authority following 1999 elections to lead the country to independence (May 2002). UNTAET administered the territory, exercised legislative and executive authority and helped build capacity towards self-government. It was succeeded after independence by the UN Mission of Support in East Timor (UNMISET), which continued to provide assistance to core administrative structures of the new country.[22] After conflict, the UN also assisted in the establishment of an interim administration in Afghanistan in 2001, led by Afghans, to lead the country to elections and rebuild capacity. The organization of these arrangements could be further improved.[23] For post-conflict states, the UN Secretary-General has accepted the proposal of the High-Level Panel for the establishment of an intergovernmental peace-building commission. It would seek to improve UN planning and coordination in the immediate recovery phase, help to ensure predictable financing, encourage donors to share information about their programmes, monitor progress, and, importantly, 'extend the period of political attention to post-conflict recovery' (UN 2005). These arrangements are possible and necessary where governments are chronically weak or virtually non-existent, and where even country representation is unclear. In other circumstances, local administrations should be supported. They should be assisted at an early stage of rehabilitation to develop comprehensive strategies that lay down a clear itinerary, setting out tasks and timing, and identifying resources and responsibilities. A monitoring mechanism is also needed, and there have been proposals for 'transitional results matrixes' to track progress.

---

[21] A very early model for such an arrangement was the Organisation for European Economic Co-operation, later the OECD itself, established by the recipients of Marshall Aid in 1948.

[22] Following a one-year extension until 2006 to complete the handover to the new government, the mission was renamed UNOTIL. However, the outbreaks of conflict in 2006 would seem to indicate that the UN phased out its military presence too soon.

[23] These institutional arrangements are normally headed by a 'Special Representative of the Secretary General', the experience and qualities of whom are usually critical to the success of the enterprise. Unfortunately, the process of appointment is rather subjective. Knowledge of the country—even the region—and prior experience are often not considered in the selection and in some cases no briefing at all is provided, apart from casual encounters with relevant desk officers.

COORDINATE AID

This principle is all of a piece with the preceding one. If assisted rehabilitation is to succeed, then donors need to subsume their individual programmes for a country within a coordinated framework. This could mean the adoption by individual donors of specific parts of an agreed recovery programme, or the contribution of un-earmarked resources into a central pool. Donors have been agonizing for many years about coordination and harmonization and some progress is being made.[24] There are agreements by a growing number of bilateral agencies to untie their assistance and mingle it more flexibly with that of others. But, to be effective, aid needs to move a radical step beyond the adaptation of individual practices by donors to each other. In each instance, there should be complete alignment with the frameworks and management capacities of recipients. However, the principle of country alignment needs to be reaffirmed, especially in the context of recovery and rehabilitation.

SUSTAIN THE SUPPORT

Being to a significant degree supply-driven, aid is subject to the vagaries of donor circumstances and preferences. Individual recipients are often subject to ebbs and flows. For recovering fragile states, sustained capacity development cannot be realized without an assurance of resources over the long term, and donors need to sign up to multi-year engagements. To encourage sustained support, aid planning needs to become more open-ended. Even while broad objectives need to be defined to permit the monitoring of progress, planning should not be narrowly tied down—project-style—to fixed costs within strict time boundaries. Indeed, traditional project approaches should be avoided entirely. Facilitating the renewal of capacity is fundamentally an unpredictable, even idiosyncratic, trial-and-error process, especially in the more hazardous contexts of fragile states.

BE COHERENT

Donors give with one hand and take with the other. Surprisingly, the necessity to view donor engagement in terms of the totality of economic and other interactions with recipients has virtually eluded the analysis of aid effectiveness until very recently. Yet, the impact of bilateral trade terms, investment patterns, migratory flows, and other factors can have consequences which outweigh, and often directly detract from, the potential benefits of aid.

An interesting attempt to gauge the comparative impacts on developing countries of a range of donor policies has been undertaken by the Center for

---

[24] The OECD facilitated Paris Declaration of 2005 aims for greater donor harmonization alignment, and management aid for results with a set of monitorable actions and indicators.

Global Development since 2003. A 'commitment to development index' is calculated for the twenty-one richest donor countries, ranked according to their policies on aid (relative amount, destination, aid tying, project density), trade (import tariffs and domestic agricultural subsidies), investment (incentives to invest in south), technology (share of research and development in GDP), security (contributions to peacekeeping), environment (levels of pollution emissions, commitment to multilateral agreements) and migration (net immigration flows from the South).[25] There have been other attempts to determine in global terms the total resource flows between donors and recipients. For example, World Bank sources reveal that in 2003 there was a net reverse financial flow—from south to north—of over US$200 billion. Aid and other private capital inflows were dwarfed by loan repayments and purchases of foreign exchange (World Bank 2004, quoted in ActionAid 2005)

Fragility is exacerbated by these uneven terms. Any comprehensive solution to the challenges facing fragile states must take into account not only the non-aid inflows of resources, but also the outflows and the financial and other impediments for which the same donor countries are responsible. This must be done, not globally, but on an individual country basis. Balance sheets should be drawn up, calculating with respect to each major donor the total financial value of the bilateral relationship. The trade/aid nexus alone is important. The rich countries collect in tariffs on the imports of some of the poorest much larger sums than they provide in aid to the same countries. The subsidies provided to rich country farmers distort global markets against the interests of lower-cost producers in the poorer countries.[26] Manifestly, donor engagement with fragile states cannot just be about aid. It has to encompass the totality of bilateral economic and other relationships.

7.7. Conclusion

How donors meet the challenges of fragile and failing states provides the acid test for aid. While most aid has been a vehicle for donors to build relationships with individual developing countries, the predicament of the fragile states presents two outstanding justifications for activism. One is obviously humanitarian, since development failure has continued to impoverish the lives of many hundreds of millions of people. The other is self-interest, given the dangers posed by the fragile states to global security

---

[25] See Carnegie Foundation (2005).

[26] One of the most glaring examples is provided by the USA cotton subsidies, which amounted to US$4.5 billion in 2004. Oxfam has calculated that the economies of the West African countries Benin, Burkina Faso, and Mali lose between 1 and 2 per cent of their GDP as a direct result of these subsidies (Oxfam 2005). The total annual cost to developing countries of rich farmer subsidies has been calculated at US$20 million.

and health. The donor record is patchy to say the least. And, the closer you come, the worse it looks. Donors bear some responsibility for not being there, but that is not the worst accusation. Donors also appeared at the wrong times with the wrong attitudes. Working within their own scripted agendas, they succeeded in sometimes unpicking and undermining development progress.

Now, being there in the right frame is the urgent order of the day. Failure demands constructive engagement, in some cases to save people from their leaders, and in all cases to save failing states from circumstances they cannot control. These adversities are in some cases natural, such as isolation and drought. But mostly they are man-made, whether triggered by internal demagogy, HIV/AIDS and strife, or resulting from conditions which the rich countries themselves can control and ameliorate. Aiding the fragile states means more and better forms of engagement. It also means lifting some of the impediments to progress.

References

ActionAid (2005) *Real Aid: An Agenda for Making Aid Work*. Johannesburg: ActionAid.

Andersen, M. (1999) *Do No Harm: How Aid Can Support Peace or War*. Boulder, Colo.: Lynne Rienner.

Bratton, M., and N. van de Walle (1997) *Democratic Experiments in Africa: Regime Transitions in Comparative Perspective*. Cambridge: Cambridge University Press.

Browne, S. (2002) 'Introduction: Rethinking Capacity Development for Today's Challenges'. In S. Browne (ed.), *Developing Capacity through Technical Cooperation: Country Experiences*. London: Earthscan.

——(2006) *Aid and Influence: Do Donors Help or Hinder?* London: Earthscan.

Buira, A. (2003) 'An Analysis of IMF Conditionality'. In A. Buira (ed.), *Challenges to the World Bank and IMF*. London: Anthem Press.

Carnegie Foundation (2005) *Foreign Policy*. Sept.–Oct. Washington, DC: Carnegie Foundation for International Peace.

Collier, P. (2003) *Breaking the Conflict Trap: Civil War and Development Policy*. New York: Oxford University Press for the World Bank.

——and A. Hoeffler (2004) 'The Challenge of Reducing the Global Incidence of Civil War'. *Copenhagen Consensus Challenge Paper*. Oxford: Oxford University Press.

DFID (Department for International Development) (2002) *Conducting Conflict Assessments: Guidance Notes*. London: DFID. <http://www.dfid.gov.uk/Documents/publications/conflictassessment guidance.pdf>.

Dobbins, J., S. G. Jones, K. Crane, et al. (2005) *The UN's Role in Nation-building: From the Congo to Iraq*. Santa Monica, Calif.: Rand Corporation.

——J. G. McGinn, K. Crane, et al. (2003) *America's Role in Nation-building: From Germany to Iraq*. Santa Monica, Calif.: Rand Corporation.

The Economist (2005) 'How to Save Myanmar' (23 July).

Fukuyama, F. (2004) *State-building: Governance and World Order in the 21st Century*. Ithaca, NY: Cornell University Press.

Ghani, A. and C. Lockhart (2008) *Fixing Failed States*. Oxford: Oxford University Press.

GTZ (Deutsche Geschellschaft für Technische Zusammenarbeit) (2001) 'Konfliktanalyse für die Projektplanung und -steuerung' [Conflict Analysis for Project Planning and Management]. <http://www2.gtz.de/dokumente/bib/04-5230.pdf>.

Hall, D., and R. de la Motte (2004) 'Dogmatic Development: Privatization and Conditionalities in Six Countries'. Public Services International Research Unit Report for War on Want. London: PSIRU. <http://www.psiru.org/reports/2004-02-U-condits.pdf>.

IDS (Institute of Development Studies) (2005) *Signposts to More Effective States: Responding to Governance Challenges in Developing Countries*. Centre for the Future State, Institute of Development Studies. Brighton: IDS.

Kanbur, R. (2000) 'Aid, Conditionality and Debt in Africa'. In F. Tarp (ed.), *Foreign Aid and Development*. London: Routledge.

Killick, T. (1997) 'Donors as Paper Tigers: Why Aid with Strings Attached Won't Work'. London: ODI. <http://www.id21.org>.

Krugman, P. (2006) 'As Bechtel Goes'. *International Herald Tribune*, 4 Nov.

Lal, D. (1983) *The Poverty of 'Development Economics'*. Cambridge, Mass.: MIT Press.

Netherlands Ministry of Foreign Affairs (2005) 'Stability Assessment Framework: Designing Integrated Responses for Security, Governance and Development. Prepared by the Clingendael Institute. <http://www.clingendael.nl/publications/2005/20050200_cru_paper_stability.pdf>.

OECD-DAC (2001) *Poor Performers: Basic Approaches for Supporting Development in 'Difficult Partnerships'*. Paris: OECD-DAC.

OECD-DAC (2005) *Survey on Harmonization and Alignment*. Paris: OECD-DAC.

Oxfam (2004a) 'Two Years on … What Future for an Independent East Timor?' Oxfam Executive Summary. Fitzroy: Oxfam. <http://www.oxfam.org.au/campaigns/submissions/easttimortwoyearson-excsum.pdf>.

——(2004b) 'Undervaluing Teachers: IMF Policies Squeeze Zambia's Education System'. Global Campaign for Education Policy Briefing. Oxford: Oxfam. <https://www.oxfam.org.uk/resources/policy/education/downloads/gce_zambia_imf.pdf>.

——(2005) 'Cultivating Poverty: The Impact of US Cotton Subsidies on Africa'. *Oxfam Briefing Note*, 30. Oxford: Oxfam.

Pinkney, R. (2003) *Democracy in the Third World*. Boulder Colo.: Lynne Rienner.

UNDP (United Nations Development Programme) (2003a) 'Conflict-related Development Analysis'. New York: United Nations Development Programme. <http://www.undp.org/cpr/whats_new/CDA_combined.pdf>.

——(2003b) *Human Development Report, 2003*. New York: Oxford University Press.

United Nations (2004) 'A More Secure World: Our Shared Responsibility'. Report of the Secretary-General's High-Level Panel on Threats, Challenges and Change. New York: United Nations.

——(2005) 'In Larger Freedom: Towards Development Security and Human Rights for All'. Report of the Secretary-General, UN Document A/59/2005, New York: United Nations.

USAID (2005) 'Service Delivery in Fragile States: An Issues Paper'. Washington, DC: United States Agency for International Development.

USAID (2001) 'Difficult Choices in the New Post-Conflict Agenda: The International Community in Rwanda after the Genocide'. *Third World Quarterly*, 22: 177–89.

——(2004) *Human Rights and Development*, Kumarian Press: Bloomfield.

von Weizsacker, E., O. R. Young, and M. Finger (eds) (2005) *Limits to Privatization: How to Avoid too much of a Good Thing*. London: Earthscan.

Weber, M. (1946) *From Max Weber*, trans. and ed. H. H. Gerth and C. Wright Mills. New York: Galaxy.

World Bank (1997) *World Development Report: The State in a Changing World*. New York: Oxford University Press.

——(2004) *Global Development Finance*. Washington, DC: World Bank.

——(2005) *Conflict Analysis Framework*. <http://web.worldbank.org/WBSITE/EXTERNAL/TOPICS/EXTSOCIALDEVELOPMENT/EXTCPR/0,,contentMDK:20486708~menuPK:1260893~pagePK:148956~piPK:216618~theSitePK:407740,00.html>.

8

Foreign Aid and Economic Development in Post-war Lebanon

Ghassan Dibeh

8.1. Introduction

Lebanon experienced a civil war that lasted for more than fifteen years, from 1975 to 1990. The duration and severity of the war led to the devastation of the country's physical, human, and social capital. The damages inflicted by war included: lost output estimated at US$24 billion in 1986; a reduction of gross domestic product (GDP) per capita of around 67 per cent; the death of around 131,000 people; and the emigration of 500,000 citizens—illustrating the huge challenges faced in the immediate post-war period of economic reconstruction (Dibeh 2005).

Foreign aid was an important element of the post-war reconstruction process. The ambitious reconstruction programmes implemented in the post-1992 period relied on substantial amounts of aid. However, the challenges of Lebanon's reconstruction were daunting, spanning the often conflicting needs of reconstruction, fiscal management, and financial stability. The early promises of vast amounts of aid, mainly from Arab sources after the signing of the Taif Peace Accords in Saudi Arabia in 1989, did not materialize as the first post-war governments had hoped.

In 1992, the Lebanese government, led by late Prime Minister Hariri, decided to follow a two-pronged approach to reconstruction: utilization of foreign aid for financing reconstruction projects and reliance on internal funding for deficit-financing and exchange rate stabilization. Lebanon's main source of internal funding was a well-developed commercial banking system which helped Lebanon circumvent financing problems that usually face governments in post-conflict societies with underdeveloped financial systems.[1] In the

---

[1] The importance of the role of the banking system in providing funds for reconstruction and the private sector in post-conflict societies is discussed in Addison et al. (2001).

immediate post-war period the banking system was able to attract capital inflows from foreign sources and from the large pool of Lebanese immigrants whose remittances have traditionally supplied the country with a large share of its foreign currency needs. This post-war open economy approach allowed Lebanon to resolve the financing difficulties stemming from the country's lack of national savings and adequate foreign aid (Gressani and Page 1999).

However, deficit financing in the post-war period, financed mainly by the commercial banks, led to an explosion of public debt and a steady rise in the debt-to-GDP ratio. These debt dynamics increasingly threatened the post-war stabilization programme that used the exchange rate as a nominal anchor, and consequently the stability of the banking system which held the majority of government debt. The main consequence of such unsustainable policies was a shift, starting in 1998, in foreign aid utilization from reconstruction needs to stabilization purposes. This shift culminated in the pre-emptive 'bailout' by the Paris II international donors in November 2002. After the war, in July 2006, two international donor conferences were held: the Stockholm donor meeting in August 2006, and the Paris III conference in January 2007.

This complexity of the Lebanese experience in relying on aid both for reconstruction and development projects and for fiscal balance and financial stability, coupled with internal funding mechanisms, makes Lebanon an important case study of the relationship between aid and post-war development priorities. As is well-known, foreign aid and post-war reconstruction have been closely linked since the implementation of the Marshall plan for Europe in the post-Second World War period. In more recent times, foreign assistance has been instrumental in providing the necessary resources for post-war reconstruction in many war-torn countries, including Iraq, Afghanistan, Bosnia, Kosovo, and the West African states. In many instances, foreign aid has been the only source of funds for reconstruction—for example, in Sierra Leone (Grant 2005). The role of foreign aid in financing infrastructure in particular in post-conflict societies has been discussed in Anand (2005). The fiscal and macroeconomic impact of foreign aid is also important in the Lebanese case as increasingly aid was used for debt relief and the maintenance of financial stability. In this respect, McGillivray and Morrissey (2004) have argued that aid may provide a disincentive for fiscal reforms. Heller et al. (2006) argue that a fiscal anchor is needed in situations of growing public debt and surge in aid. Aiyar, Berg, and Hussain (2008) discuss the policy response of aid receiving countries using different combinations of absorption and spending and the corresponding macroeconomic implications.

This chapter is structured as follows. Section 8.2 delineates the different types and phases of foreign aid in Lebanon. Section 8.3 studies the reconstruction phase in 1992–7. Section 8.4 discusses macroeconomic developments during the post-war era up to the Paris II conference in November 2002 and its subsequent fiscal and economic effects. Section 8.5 reviews the Paris III conference held in January 2007 and the new agreements between Lebanon and the International Monetary Fund (IMF). Section 8.6 concludes.

8.2. Forms of foreign aid in post-war Lebanon

After more than eighteen years since the end of the civil war, Lebanon is still heavily dependent on foreign assistance. During the reconstruction phase, Lebanon failed to develop a 'self-sustaining order'—a prerequisite for the success of post-war reconstruction (Coyne 2005). Reliance on foreign aid has surpassed the typical life-cycle of aid in post-war reconstruction programmes which is usually a few years (Kang and Meernik 2004). This continuing dependence has been caused by the dual nature of aid to Lebanon: aid for reconstruction, and aid for debt relief and financial stability purposes.

Foreign aid in post-war Lebanon passed through two phases with distinct features. In the first phase, lasting from 1992 to 1997, aid totalling US$4.0 billion was channelled towards providing resources for the reconstruction projects planned in the various post-war reconstruction programmes (Helbling 1999). Foreign aid contributed to the massive infrastructure rebuilding in areas such as electricity, water, and telephone and road networks. The results of this reconstruction phase were mixed with many targets for reconstruction missed.

The second phase, which spans the period from 1998 to the present, witnessed a qualitative shift in foreign aid utilization from the demands of reconstruction towards reducing financial vulnerabilities. Aid targeted towards reconstruction dwindled from 1998 onwards while aid in the form of foreign exchange reserve deposits with the central bank and grants and soft loans for debt relief and fiscal support increased. Intermittent foreign currency deposits by foreign governments with the central bank came at crucial times when the Lebanese currency was under severe devaluation pressures resulting from economic and political developments. This type of foreign aid came mainly from countries within the region, such as Saudi Arabia. In November 2002, at the Paris II conference, Lebanon received around US$2.4 billion in soft loans for debt restructuring in a pre-emptive bailout as Lebanon faced an impending financial crisis.

This new phase of foreign aid enabled the government to achieve financial stability. The international reserves of the central bank were augmented and it was able to intervene in the foreign exchange market to defend the currency. Foreign aid also provided debt relief and fiscal support and increased confidence in the government's ability to continue borrowing funds from local commercial banks and foreign investors. Schimmelpfennig and Gardner (2008) have shown that this imputed confidence was one of the reasons for financial stability despite the inherent vulnerability of Lebanese finances. This led some foreign investors to consider Lebanon as a 'moral hazard trade'. This moral hazard trade, however, has allowed Lebanon to avoid fiscal reforms, increased the country's dependence on foreign aid and debt, and, in 2007, resulted in an agreement with the IMF that may pave the way for future Fund conditionality.

8.3. Foreign aid for reconstruction

Lebanon, through the Council of Development and Reconstruction (CDR), the government agency established in 1981 amidst the civil war, vigorously implemented an infrastructure reconstruction programme in the post-1992 period. The emphasis on infrastructure development was a reflection of the severe damage and destruction that the country's physical infrastructure had suffered during the long civil war, either through direct destruction or because of years of neglect and lack of maintenance. Given the circumstances, the emphasis on infrastructure was highly justified (Anand 2005). The main reconstruction projects were planned in what was called the Horizon 2000 plan. Public investments totalling US$17.7 billion were to be allocated to physical infrastructure, social infrastructure, and public services. As of December 1997, foreign financing of the reconstruction programme totalled US$4.0 billion, with US$3.5 billion in loans and US$0.5 billion in grants. The loans component consisted of soft loans and commercial loans with export guarantees (Wetter 1999). Table 8.1 shows that during this period foreign aid formed a significant share of total public capital expenditures.

After this period, the amounts of foreign loans and grants dwindled. The reconstruction phase of the post-war period was nearing its end. By the end of 2004, the total amount of foreign financing, including all types of loans and grants, was around US$5.8 billion. The temporal allocation shows that during 1992–7 around 70 per cent of foreign financing was allocated compared to only 30 per cent during 1998–2004. The source of funding for reconstruction was overwhelmingly from international institutions, Arab Gulf countries and institutions, France, and Italy.

The planned public expenditures targets were not met although the reconstruction programme was successful in revamping the main physical infrastructure including electricity, road and telecommunication networks, and basic services. The failure was partly due to the shortfall in foreign funding

Table 8.1. Foreign loans, grants, and public investments as a share of GDP, 1992–7

	1992	1993	1994	1995	1996	1997
Grants/GDP (percentage)	0.0	1.5	3.3	0.4	0.3	0.3
Foreign loans/GDP (percentage)	−1.1	2.6	7.8	4.9	4.2	3.5
Public capital expenditure/GDP (percentage)	1.5	3.4	9.3	9.4	8.5	8.6

Source: Helbling (1999).

Table 8.2. Planned and realized public investments in various sectors (US$ million) 1992–2004

Type of investment	Horizon 2000 (1993–7)	Achieved (1992–7)	Percentage	Achieved (1992–2004)	Percentage of Horizon 2000
Physical	3,200	2,206	69	3,431	107
Social	1,930	553	29	970	50
Public services	980	615	63	1,856	190
Productive and others	1,236	778	63	1,145	93

Source: Calculations by author from Wetter (1999); and CDR (2005).

(compared to the levels expected at the end of hostilities) and partly because of the lack of absorptive capacity. Post-war reconstruction plans were delayed, and, during 1992–7, only around 60 per cent of the planned projects were realized or were in the process of being completed. It was not until the end of 2004 that the 1992–7 plans for the physical and productive sectors (including airport and ports) were realized. However, it was the social sector that was most severely affected by the unrealized plans; only 50 per cent of the planned expenditures in this sector for the period 1992–7 were achieved by the end of 2004. Moreover, allocation of funds between the different sectors for the reconstruction programme was, in many respects, far from what was envisaged in the Horizon 2000, which had proposed a balanced disbursement of resources. As Table 8.2 shows, actual allocation of expenditures during the period 1992–2004 was skewed against the social sector.

8.4. The macroeconomic road to the Paris II 'bailout'

Post-war reconstruction in Lebanon went hand in hand with monetary stabilization efforts that followed the long inflationary period from 1984 to 1992. At the onset of the reconstruction period in 1992 the budget deficit was 15 per cent of GDP and inflation reached 120 per cent. Disinflationary policy used the nominal exchange rate as an anchor in a typical exchange rate-based stabilization (ERBS) programme. This policy was successful in bringing inflation— which had averaged 110 per cent annually during 1986–92 (BdL 1993)— down to around 10 per cent by 1995. However, Lebanon's fiscal policy was expansionary because of the demands of reconstruction, state-building (especially the army and security apparatus), and social expenditures.

The expansionary fiscal policy, coupled with supply-side tax reforms in 1993, led to a growth of the country's public debt to unprecedented levels. The combination of massive public expenditures and low taxes resulted in persistent budget deficits and exploding debt dynamics. By 2006, Lebanon had one of the highest debt-to-GDP ratios in the world (Schimmelpfennig and Gardner 2008). Table 8.3 summarizes budget deficits and public debt growth in the post-war period up till 2002.

This post-war macroeconomic policy mix led to a sharp increase in nominal and real interest rates (Table 8.4). Urnéchlian, Eken, and Helbling (1999) show that the average annualized excess returns on short-term T-bills in the mid-1990s were around 16 per cent. The ERBS programme had a negative impact on the real economy. The ERBS policy, in conjunction with persistent deficits and

Table 8.3. Public debt and deficits in post-war Lebanon, 1993–2002

Year	Deficit/GDP (percentage)	Debt/GDP (percentage)
1993	9.01	34.4
1994	19.3	43.5
1995	15.6	51.3
1996	18.2	79.9
1997	23.6	96.6
1998	14.1	105.4
1999	14.4	120.0
2000	23.6	141.0
2001	16.9	170.0
2002	16.5	181.0

Source: Dibeh 2005 for the years 1992–2000; calculations by author from Audi Bank 2005 for 2001–2.

Table 8.4. GDP, inflation rates, and real interest rates in post-war Lebanon

Year	Real GDP growth, (percentage)	Inflation rate, (percentage)	Real interest rates, (percentage)
1992	4.5	131.0	−105.4
1993	7.0	24.7	13.3
1994	8.0	8.0	1.9
1995	6.5	10.6	4.1
1996	4.0	8.9	7.6
1997	3.5	7.7	6.4
1998	3.0	1.6	9.83
1999	4.0	1.5	9.38
2000	2.0	−0.9	11.78
2001	1.4	2.9	8.0
2002	1.0	4.2	6.6

Source: UNCDB (nd) for GDP growth; Eken and Helbling (1999) for inflation rates, 1992–7; Audi Bank 2005 for inflation rates, 1998–2002; author calculations for real interest rates (real interest rate = 3 months T-bill rate minus inflation).

growing public debt, triggered a growth cycle that put an end to a short-lived post-war reconstruction boom that lasted till 1997 (Dibeh 2008).

Macroeconomic and stabilization policies, coupled with aid in its post-1997 form, also played a role in the deindustrialization process that occurred during the post-war period. The ERBS policy and the insatiable need for foreign inflows to finance the chronic budget deficits through the banking system have maintained real interest rates at high levels throughout the post-war period. In addition, there was a significant real exchange rate appreciation up till the year 2002. Furthermore, commercial credit to the private sector stagnated and was crowded out by the commercial banks' supply of credit to the public sector. This worked to skew Lebanese development towards a rentier-based economy with 'Dutch disease' effects.[2] In Lebanon, the process of deindustrialization in the post-war period was significant and probably unparalleled in an economy undergoing post-war reconstruction, when the average annual growth rate for industry from 1993 to 2003 was -0.4 per cent and for manufacturing -1.8 per cent (World Bank database).

Starting in 1997, the Lebanese governments became aware of the unsustainability of this post-war macroeconomic policy. The growing public debt and impending economic slowdown were tackled through the convening of a potential donors conference, Friends of Lebanon, in Washington in December 1997. The government proposed projects valued at US$5 billion to be financed over five years through grants and soft loans. Pledges of around US$1 billion were made for 1998. This 'foreign leap' by the country in late 1997 was to become the main policy response of successive Hariri governments in the face of economic challenges and crises.[3] Foreign aid via donor conferences and direct deposits with the central bank were to become the standard governmental procedure for resolving macroeconomic imbalances. The direct deposits with the central bank of Lebanon can be classified as aid neither absorbed nor spent in the classification of Aiyar, Berg, and Hussain (2008) which leads to building up international reserves with no expansionary impact on aggregate demand or the exchange rate. Deposits with the central bank occurred at many crucial junctures: in 1997 (US$700 million by Kuwait and Saudi Arabia), in 2001 (US$1 billion by Saudi Arabia), and in 2006 (US$1 billion by Saudi Arabia and US$500 million by Kuwait). During the first two periods, the central bank was losing reserves and the currency came under severe market pressure. The third period coincided with the July 2006 war between Israel and Lebanon. The

---

[2] The possible role of foreign aid in engendering 'Dutch disease' effects has been discussed in many studies (Vos 1998; Bulir and Timothy 2002; Aiyar, Berg, and Hussain 2008).

[3] Except in the 1998–2000 period when an anti-Hariri government was in power. The government devised a reform plan that articulated necessary reform measures, but the programme was never implemented.

deposits served to prop up foreign exchange reserves, calm the currency markets, and restore confidence in the Lebanese currency.

After the Israeli withdrawal from south Lebanon in May 2000, the government with the assistance of the UNDP prepared another US$5 billion plan. Hoping for foreign aid to finance the plan, the government appealed to the international community for help in the reconstruction of the southern regions. But, owing to mounting political pressure on the Lebanese government from the USA and the West to send the army to the south, foreign aid was not forthcoming even from seemingly sympathetic Arab countries. As a result, the US Congress blocked a US$35 million aid package to Lebanon in 2001 and the Arab Gulf countries allocated only around US$100 million in loans and grants. By 2001, the economy was showing signs of a severe strain and a financial crisis was widely forecasted. The internal financing schemes for post-war reconstruction as well as the fiscal and monetary policies of the successive post-war governments were taking their toll on the economy. Up to this point, the political economy in Lebanon with regard to debt financing had been able to prevent currency and financial crises. The state/commercial banks nexus provided political-economic support for financial stability. The IMF recognized that Lebanon, through balance sheet interconnections between commercial banks and government, was able to sustain the high levels of government deficits and the spiralling public debt without a collapse of the currency, as had been predicted by many observers, including the IMF itself (IMF 2004). However, this state of affairs could not be sustained beyond 2002. Continuing pressure on the Lebanese government by both the local commercial banks that would bear the brunt of any government default or currency collapse and by the IMF was becoming too great. In December 2001, the IMF consultation team called on Lebanon to devalue its currency. This was met with widespread objections from both government circles and the commercial banking sector. As a consequence of such adverse economic and political developments, the government embarked on preparations for a form of preemptive bailout through foreign aid. The Paris I meeting was held in February 2001 with the participation of potential international donors. This preparatory meeting led one year later to the convening of the Paris II conference held in November 2002.

The conference was a landmark in the post-war period, attended by many countries and multilateral institutions such as the World Bank and the IMF. The official goal for convening the Paris II conference was to seek international support for the Lebanese reform programme that included a reduction in debt to GDP ratios, budgetary restraint, and better growth prospects in the medium run (MoF 2003). Even though the government paper presented at the meeting was titled 'Beyond Reconstruction and Recovery Towards Sustainable Growth: A Request for International Support', the government's immediate aim was to prevent an imminent fiscal and financial crisis. Lebanon asked for

Table 8.5. Foreign loans secured in Paris II meetings

Country/agency	Amount (million)	Conditions
Saudi Arabia	$700	15 years, 5-year grace period, 5 % interest
Kuwait	$300	same
UAE	$300	same
Qatar	$200	same
Malaysia	$300	same
Oman	$52	same
France	$500	15 years, 3-year grace period, 5% interest
EU	$12.25	grant
Arab Monetary Fund	$15	Medium-term loan

Source: Ministry of Finance (2003).

concessionary loans and grants that would help to pay off a part of its debt, to extend debt maturities, and to reduce the interest rate on public debt in addition to favourably changing the structure of interest rates in the economy as a whole. International lenders were forthcoming with concessionary loans, as can be seen in Table 8.5 which shows the amounts disbursed by the various countries and institutions.

In addition to the international donors at Paris II, powerful internal financial players in Lebanon contributed to the rescue package. The central bank pledged US$4.2 billion, and the commercial banks, whose role in financing public debt up to that point has provided them with windfall profits, also pledged to subscribe to US$3.6 billion worth of two-year T-bills at zero per cent interest. The package received by the Lebanese government totalled US$10.1 billion. Such an inflow of funds into Lebanon and into the state treasury provided the country with opportunities for economic growth and macroeconomic adjustment unprecedented in its post-war economic history.

There were many positive effects of the foreign concessionary loans and the matching subscription by the central and commercial banks of Lebanon (Table 8.6 and Figure 8.1): (i) public debt growth decelerated; (ii) the cost of government borrowing both in Lebanese pounds (LBP) and dollar-denominated debt instruments was significantly reduced; (iii), and more importantly from a macroeconomic perspective, market interest rates on both LBP and dollar-denominated commercial loans went down; (iv) the foreign exchange reserves of the Bank of Lebanon increased; and (v) the balance of payments improved significantly. Given this positive impact, the Paris II conference helped Lebanon avert a financial crisis and laid the foundations for economic recovery.

Despite these positive effects of the Paris II conference on government finances and on money markets, there was no lasting impact on one of the most worrying trends in Lebanon's post-war economy: the growing debt to GDP ratio. Table 8.7 shows the difference between the projected and actual

Table 8.6. Interest rates, reserves, and balance of payments: before and after Paris II

	Debt			Market interest rate		Banque de Liban reserves	Balance of payments
Cost of borrowing	Livre libanaise (LBP)-denominated	$-denominated	Livre libanaise (LBP)	US$	US$ bn	US$ bn
(percentage)	(percentage)	(percentage)	(percentage)	(percentage)		
Before Paris II 11.97	13.82	9.21	16.10	9.62	3.5	0.3
After Paris II 8.36	9.23	7.39	10.48	7.89	10.4	3.3

Source: Ministry of Finance (2003); and Banque de Liban database.

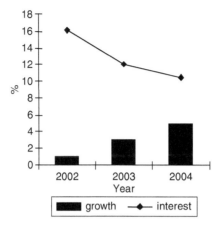

Figure 8.1 Economic growth and interest rates in post-Paris II period
Source: MOF (2003).

debt-to-GDP ratios in the post-Paris II period. More importantly, in the 2002–5 post-Paris II period the Lebanese governments failed to implement the promised structural reforms such as administrative reform, fiscal restraint, and privatization that were proposed in Lebanon's paper to the conference.

8.5. The Paris III conference: enter the IMF

The failure of the successive Lebanese governments in the post-Paris II meetings to implement the promised reforms can be attributed to internal political developments and divisions during this period, and to the disincentives for reform caused by the relatively easy availability of foreign aid for stabilization purposes (see also Chapter 14 of this volume by Richard M. Auty for a discussion on the impact of aid on government incentives). Adverse political developments intensified after 2005. The assassination in February 2005 of the Prime Minister, Rafic Hariri, led to massive protests, resulting in the withdrawal of

Table 8.7. Projected and actual debt-to-GDP ratios (percentage)

	2003	2004	2005	2006	2007
Projected	136	126	114	104	92
Actual	169	167	178	177	171

Source: Ministry of Finance (2003) for projected; and Ministry of Finance (2008) for actual.

Syrian troops in April 2005 (present in the country since 1976). New elections were held in May and June 2005, bringing an anti-Syrian majority into parliament and government.

In July 2006, a war broke out between Israel and Lebanon which intensified the political divisions within the country. The economic losses of the war and the loss of confidence signalled a new impending financial collapse. This pushed the government to call for the holding of another international donors' conference to engineer a further international rescue package for Lebanon. The Paris III conference was held in Paris in January 2007, and raised around US$7.6 billion of pledges in soft loans and grants in support of the Lebanese economic and fiscal reform programmes. The new reform programme, prepared for the Paris III conference, promised significant economic and structural reforms including privatization, tax increases, labour law reform, and reforms to the social security system. In addition, the five-year programme projected a reduction in the debt to GDP ratio to 130 per cent by the end of the programme.

The conference can be seen as a sequel to the Paris II conference. However, Paris III introduced a role for the IMF in monitoring the promised reforms. Although within Lebanon the president of the republic and the pro-Syrian political parties were held responsible for the failure of the Paris II conference, the international community—including the IMF and the United States—has implicitly blamed the whole political system in Lebanon for the non-implementation of the reforms. In early 2006, the United States insisted that Lebanon undergo supervision by the IMF for any funds disbursed at future donors meetings. During the Paris III meetings many countries made it clear to the IMF that they would like it to play an active part in monitoring the Lebanese government's reform programme.

In April 2007, the IMF and Lebanon signed a US$77 million loan agreement under the Emergency Post-Conflict Assistance Programme (EPCA). Under the EPCA, the IMF formally monitors the implementation of the reform plan. Although the dispersal of funds by donors are not preconditioned on IMF approval, many countries are expected to observe the IMF view of Lebanon's progress (the Fund has already issued several reports on Lebanon's fiscal developments and the reform process since Paris III (IMF 2008)). This new donor behaviour may partially solve the disincentive problem that was engendered by previous lenient foreign aid and internal financing of the government deficit. Moreover, the IMF and Lebanon are expected to sign a larger loan agreement under an IMF-Lebanon stand-by arrangement. Such an arrangement would impose IMF conditionality on Lebanon. This development, if realized, can be seen as the culmination of the dependency of Lebanon on foreign aid for stabilization purposes.

8.6. Conclusions

This chapter has argued that foreign aid in post-war Lebanon passed through two phases with distinct features that have had far-reaching implications for economic development. In the first phase, lasting from 1992 to 1997, aid was mainly channelled towards providing resources for post-war reconstruction projects. The second phase, from 1998 to the present, witnessed a qualitative shift in foreign aid towards debt relief and financial stability. This helped Lebanon to avert financial and currency crises at many critical junctures during this period. In addition, it provided the confidence necessary for the government to continue borrowing funds from local commercial banks and foreign investors.

Many lessons from Lebanon's unique experience can be drawn for developing countries and post-conflict societies. First, Lebanon's experience shows that macroeconomic policies and outcomes are crucial for post-war reconstruction and economic development. Macroeconomic imbalances can push governments to sideline reconstruction programmes. In Lebanon, the priority of the reconstruction programme was downgraded after 1997 because of the mounting macroeconomic pressures. The government shifted its priorities from reconstruction towards stabilization despite the country's lag (compared with other post-war economies) in terms of reconstruction success indicators such as economic growth, GDP per capita, and capital accumulation. Lebanon's experience shows that the macroeconomic policy mix must be given special attention in post-war situations where the objectives of reconstruction and stabilization may conflict. In Lebanon, exchange rate pegging coupled with persistent government deficits led to fiscal dominance that threatened the currency peg. The choice of the successive Lebanese governments to continue the exchange rate peg, supported by foreign aid, diverted funds from reconstruction toward stabilization.

Second, in post-war periods reconstruction plans must be commensurate with foreign aid expectations and absorptive capacity. Over-ambitious plans, such as Horizon 2000, risk being unfulfilled and desired balances between different infrastructure priorities may be sacrificed.

Third, although the availability of domestic sources of financing is desirable, Lebanon's overreliance on the banking sector for deficit financing shows how this can lead to explosive debt dynamics with dire consequences for macroeconomic stability. Governments in post-conflict situations should rely on taxation for resource mobilization. In Lebanon, this was sidelined by the supply-side tax reforms in 1993 at great cost to the reconstruction programme. Tax-based resource mobilization for reconstruction reduces the need for domestic and external borrowing in post-war economies.

Fourth, the oversupply of foreign aid can have a negative impact on the propensity of governments to implement fiscal reforms. These disincentives had a significant impact in the Lebanese case due to successive aid flows aimed at averting financial instability. The donors' long-standing willingness to bail Lebanon out gave Lebanese commercial banks and foreign investors the confidence to continue financing the chronic government deficits, despite the lack of any form of fiscal anchor that would have stopped the explosive public debt dynamics of the post-war period.

References

Addison, T., A. Geda, P. Le Billon, and S. M. Murshed (2001) 'Finance in Conflict and Reconstruction'. *Journal of International Development*, 13: 951–64.

Aiyar, S., A. Berg, and M. Hussain (2008) 'The Macroeconomic Management of Increased Aid: Policy Lessons from Recent Experience'. WIDER Research Paper 2008/79. Helsinki: UNU-WIDER.

Anand, P. B. (2005) 'Getting Infrastructure Priorities Right in Post-conflict Reconstruction'. WIDER Research Paper 2005/42. Helsinki: UNU-WIDER.

Audi Bank (2005) *Country and Market Update 2005*. Beirut: Audi Bank.

Banque du Liban (1993) *The Bank of Lebanon Yearly Report: 1993*. Beirut: Banque du Liban.

Bulir, A., and L. Timothy (2002) 'Aid and Fiscal Management'. IMF Working Paper 02/112. Washington, DC: International Monetary Fund.

Council for Development and Reconstruction (2005) *Progress Report: July 2005*. Beirut: CDR. <http://www.cdr.gov.lb/2005/english/openi.htm>.

Coyne, C. T. (2005) 'After War: Understanding Post-war Reconstruction'. Global Prosperity Initiative Working Paper 40, Fairfax, Va.: Mercatus Center, George Mason University.

Dibeh, G. (2005) 'The Political Economy of Post-war Reconstruction in Lebanon'. WIDER Research Paper 2005/44. Helsinki: UNU-WIDER.

——(2008) 'The Business Cycle in Postwar Lebanon'. *Journal of International Development*, 20: 145–60.

Eken, S., and T. Helbling (1999) 'Back to the Future: Post-war Reconstruction and Stabilization in Lebanon'. International Monetary Fund Occasional Paper 176. Washington, DC: IMF.

Grant, J. A. (2005) 'Diamonds, Foreign Aid, and the Uncertain Prospects for Post-conflict Reconstruction in Sierra Leone'. WIDER Research Paper 2005/49. Helsinki: UNU-WIDER.

Gressani, D., and J. Page (1999) 'Reconstruction in Lebanon: Challenges for Macroeconomic Management'. MENA Working Paper Series 16. Washington, DC: World Bank.

Helbling, T. (1999) 'Post-war Reconstruction, Public Finances and Fiscal Sustainability'. In S. Eken and T. Helbling (eds), 'Back to the Future: Post-war Reconstruction and Stabilization in Lebanon'. International Monetary Fund Occasional Paper 176. Washington, DC: IMF.

Heller, P. S., M. Katz, X. Debrun, et al. (2006) *Making Fiscal Space Happen: Managing Fiscal Policy in a World of Scaled-up Aid*. WIDER Paper 2006/125. Helsinki: UNU-WIDER.

IMF (International Monetary Fund) (2004) *Debt-related Vulnerabilities and Financial Crises: An Application of the Balance Sheet Approach to Emerging Market Countries.* Washington, DC: International Monetary Fund. <http://www.imf.org/external/np/pdr/bal/2004/eng/070104.pdf>.

——(2008) 'Lebanon Report on Performance Under the Progam Supported by Emergency Post-Conflict Assistance, 3 April 2008'. Washington, DC: IMF.

Kang, S., and J. Meernik (2004) 'Determinants of Post-conflict Economic Assistance'. *Journal of Peace Research*, 41: 149–66.

McGillivray, M., and O. Morrissey (2004) 'Fiscal Effects of Aid'. In T. Addison and A. Roe (eds), *Fiscal Policy for Development: Poverty, Reconstruction and Growth.* New York: Palgrave Macmillan for UNU-WIDER.

Ministry of Finance (2003) 'One Year Progress After Paris II'. Special Report. Beirut: Ministry of Finance.

——(2008) 'Debt and Debt Markets: A Quarterly Bulletin of the Ministry of Finance'. Issue No.5, Quarter II. Beirut: Ministry of Finance.

Schimmelpfennig, A., and E. H. Gardner (2008) 'Lebanon: Weathering the Perfect Storms'. International Monetary Fund Working Paper 08/17. Washington, DC: IMF.

Urnéchlian, T., S. Eken, and T. Helbling (1999) 'Dynamics of Interest Rate Movements: An Empirical Study'. In S. Eken and T. Helbling (eds), 'Back to the Future: Post-war Reconstruction and Stabilization in Lebanon'. International Monetary Fund Occasional Paper 176. Washington, DC: IMF.

Vos, R. (1998) 'Aid Flows and "Dutch Disease" in a General Equilibrium Framework for Pakistan'. *Journal of Policy Modeling*, 20: 77–109.

UNCDB (n.d.) United Nations Common Database. <http://data.un.org/>.

Wetter, J. (1999) 'Public Investment Planning and Progress'. In S. Eken and T. Helbling (eds), 'Back to the Future: Post-war Reconstruction and Stabilization in Lebanon'. International Monetary Fund Occasional Paper 176. Washington, DC: IMF.

Part IV

Aid Modalities

9

Can New Aid Modalities Handle Politics?

Arjan de Haan and Max Everest-Phillips

9.1. Introduction

This chapter looks at a range of recent developments in the ways in which aid is provided, or 'aid modalities'.[1] In particular, we consider whether donor approaches around budget support, poverty-reduction strategy papers (PRSPs), and direct transfers to the poor are compatible with a political understanding of policy processes in partner or recipient countries, an understanding that is typically not captured in quantitative analyses of aid effectiveness. The theme is given increased urgency with recent calls for, and commitment to, increasing financial flows, scaling-up of aid (Monterrey consensus, Gleneagles, the 2005 Millennium Development Goal (MDG) project, the Millennium Challenge Corporation), and for increased donor coordination and the 'Paris Agenda' to enhance aid effectiveness. The question we raise is whether these commitments sharpen what we believe to be a potential dilemma between increased aid and the political processes and changes that inevitably accompany this.

The chapter is structured as follows. Section 9.2 discusses the nature of the partnership enshrined in the Monterrey consensus and some questions around the realization of this consensus, particularly the debate whether scaling-up is possible or desirable. Section 9.3 discusses budget support and PRSP approaches, and the lessons learnt around increasing aid and the political processes that accompany this. Section 9.4 focuses on assistance directly targeted to the poor as one way of increasing aid flows to the poorest countries, and asks how this way of providing assistance may impact politics. Section 9.5 looks at

---

[1] The opinions expressed are those of the authors and do not necessarily express the views of DFID. We thank anonymous referees and the WIDER editor for useful comments and contributions.

old and new approaches to the role of aid in economic growth, a major subject of debate during the 2006 WIDER Aid Conference, and discusses the need to strengthen an understanding of the politics of growth. Section 9.6 then focuses on the increasingly important work on governance and institutions, and questions whether the current institutions or governance paradigm brings sufficient political context to aid delivery. Section 9.7 discusses the relationship between domestic revenue generation and foreign aid, and how this is understood in donor literature. The concluding section draws out the implications of these concerns for new aid delivery, and discusses the potential role of socio-political analysis in new aid modalities, and ways in which a better understanding of political context and changes can inform the post-Monterrey consensus.

9.2. Monterrey: the political partnership?

Following the period of structural adjustment that largely ignored questions of governance and micro- and macro-institutions, the 1990s increasingly identified governance as crucial to development outcomes. Aid modalities sought governance with 'quick-fix technical solutions', but experience showed reforms implemented without respect for local conditions proved disastrous. As governance became central to development activity, the list of allegedly necessary reforms grew rapidly across all its dimensions, from 'rule of law' to 'capacity-building'. But, after the initial euphoria of the collapse of the Cold War and its client dictatorships in the developing world, it became apparent that these supply-driven generic governance solutions were not working. This dissatisfaction with the proliferation of technocratic solutions shifted the debate away from the early 1990s' ideas of good governance to a more focused and realistic '*good enough* governance' (the term coined by Merilee Grindle 2004) that tried to target fewer but more prioritized and feasible interventions. To match demand, a new mantra developed, context specificity, addressing local needs. Legitimacy of reforms and their general principles (such as the macroeconomic principles of the Washington consensus) required adaptation to the local political and social context. Soon it became apparent that reform feasibility required a better understanding of local politics. The few universal principles that did emerge from the 1990s showed 'political will' and 'political context' needed to be understood much better—for example, legal reforms, while actively encouraged by the teams of highly paid lawyers and consultants, should not be seen as 'solutions' without understanding whether new laws were really needed or would be implemented, rather than reformist governments and activist judges applying existing laws to changing contexts (Kaufmann 2003).

So by the beginning of the new millennium the international community had arrived at a broad agreement; not only did governance matter, but the problems underlying the technocratic challenges in governance were inherently political. The Monterrey consensus in 2002 consolidated politics at the heart of development, and thus also potentially at the centre of its meaning of governance—both domestic and international politics were integral to the governance problem and also to its solution. The Monterrey final report cautioned that

governments must build within their countries—both developed and developing—the public support necessary to translate their collective vision into action. That would require political leadership in the developing countries to overcome the many difficulties in undertaking institutional and policy reform, and in the developed countries to develop engagement and solidarity with the developing countries in their efforts to reduce poverty.[2]

It warned that 'to translate the draft Consensus into action will involve a process of arriving at politically acceptable decisions at the national and international levels. There is a need for strong political will'. The consensus admitted that non-developmental considerations still strongly influenced aid allocation models: 'ODA resources have not always been targeted at the poorer countries but have often been driven by geopolitical considerations'.[3]

The consensus declared that 'the international community has created the political space for unprecedented dialogue among all relevant stakeholders on financing for development'. But

implementation will require major national and international efforts, and . . . substantial technical efforts should be accompanied by a strong and persistent political will . . . Political will and leadership—in both the developed and the developing countries—will be key factors determining its ultimate success.

It asked, 'Who will provide the political leadership for listening to new ideas and changing institutions?' It noted the importance of strengthening coherence between United Nations, the Bretton Woods institutions, and the World Trade Organization, as well as the regional financial institutions, and argued for placing development at the centre of the global political agenda, which has since been reaffirmed by the G8, at the Accra High-Level Forum in September 2008, and at the Doha review of Monterrey in November 2008. The president of the General Assembly of the UN at the time, Dr Seung-Soo Han, declared at Monterrey, 'Something must be done to galvanize the global political will for an accelerated drive to meet the Millennium Declaration targets'. Only the Managing Director of the International Monetary Fund (IMF), Horst Köhler, added a note of caution to the focus on politics, observing that, 'slow progress in the

---

[2] Report of the International Conference on Financing for Development, Monterrey, Mexico, 18–22 March 2002. <http://www.un.org/esa/ffd/monterrey/MonterreyConsensus.pdf>. Quotes in the rest of this section are taken from this Monterrey report.

[3] The then head of the World Bank, James Wolfensohn, declared that 'too much money has been squandered in the past by decisions determined by politics instead of development'. Alesina and Dollar (2000) analyse the political and historical motives behind aid patterns.

reforms needed to fight poverty often reflects lack of institutional capacity rather than lack of political will'. So Monterrey and the 'Paris Consensus' created a 'Faustian' bargain between rich and poor. The developed world would give more money in return for political elites in poor countries delivering the better politics and governance essential for delivering the MDGs. Now these vested interests in the developing world would have to adjust not just the governance structures, but also apparently the political processes of their countries if they want to benefit from surging aid flows and debt relief.

The rest of this chapter focuses primarily on the whether and how this new aid modality can incorporate such politics. However, from the outset it is important to highlight the genuine doubts about whether such increases in aid will and should materialize (de Haan 2009). First, the consensus needs to be seen against the background of the renewed emphasis particularly by USAID—returning from a decade of holiday from history, and criticizing a 'European consensus'—to ensure that aid is aligned with donor country foreign interest (Natsios 2006). Second, while there has indeed been a significant reversal since 2000 of the downward aid trend of the 1990s, the commitment of 0.7 per cent of gross national income (GNI) is, of course, no different from the consensus since 1969 drafted under the Pearson Committee. It is important to note that these commitments have had little sustained impact on total aid flows (except for short periods, in particular countries, but indeed the fluctuations in aid flows have been highlighted as a major concern). Recent changes, including in the Scandinavian countries, also suggest that the trends are not always more favourable for the 'like-minded' donors, and that they can reflect rather different interpretations of priorities for the development agenda, and follow shifts in national politics (and, of course, most recently the impacts of the global financial crisis).

The commitment for increasing aid is made in the face of clearly documented doubts about 'the capacity for absorption of aid' (as well as increased scrutiny of the 'outcomes' of aid). Well-known and often populist concerns about the failure of aid have recently been given a loud voice by Easterly (2006), who suspects that the increased commitments to aid will be subject to a dominance of 'planners' (including those who think they can plan a market, as opposed to 'searchers') and failure to learn from past mistakes. Easterly's book is a direct critique of the Millennium Project, the Commission for Africa, and Sachs (2005), probably the best-known proponent of increasing aid. Sachs has been a fervent supporter of increased aid to Kenya or Ethiopia, for example, and during a presentation at the UK Department for International Development (DFID) in 2005 strongly opposed ideas that increased aid should be subject to improvement in governance, arguing (as he does in his book) that it is impossible to run a health system on current per capita health allocations such as those in Kenya.

The fact that this debate is very much alive is further illustrated in the 2005 *IDS Bulletin*, 'Increased Aid: Minimizing Problems, Maximizing Gains'. Very diverse views are illustrated, for example, by Howard White, on the one hand, who concludes there is a serious shortfall in aid disbursements, and Tony Killick, on the other hand, who argues additional aid will divert attention from the quality and effectiveness of aid (as in Easterly, disagreements regarding conclusions and reliability of quantitative analysis feature strongly). Views differ around questions of absorptive capacity, possibilities for governance reform, likelihood that aid will be delivered in co-ordinated manner, donors' 'unhelpful habits', and issues around aid dependency (Manor 2005).

Hence, the nature of the new political partnership, the Paris Declaration, and technical views regarding its feasibility, remain hotly contested. The point here is that doubts about the desirability of increasing aid exist, not to prove one or the other side in the debate right or wrong. The push for increased aid is occurring in the face of well-documented doubts around the desirability of additional aid (possibly suffering from the 'confirmation bias' identified by Easterly (2006: 48)), and against very clear evidence that new aid modalities engage only in a very limited way with local politics. Later in the chapter we come back to how work on 'governance' has changed alongside the emergence of the new consensus; next we look at how a number of aid modalities incorporate notions of the political nature of development.

9.3. Budget support, sector-wide approaches, and PRSPs

During the late 1990s, two forces came together, leading, at least temporarily, to quite radical changes in the way aid was delivered: the pressure for debt relief and the critique, notably within the World Bank, around aid effectiveness. The concept of Poverty Reduction Strategy Papers (PRSP)—which combined increased debt relief with a focus on ensuring the additional money did focus on poverty reduction while putting recipient governments in the 'driving seat' of development—was the clearest outcome of these changes, and central to the international public debate, but was preceded by related changes in aid modalities.

Both sector-wide approaches and budget support arose out of concerns around uncoordinated donor programmes, and lack of sustained impacts. Sector-wide approaches have been defined as an aid modality, in which all significant funding for the sector supports a single sector policy, under government leadership, adopting common approaches across the sector, and relying on government procedures. The modality emerged as a response to three issues (Foster 2000: 7–8). First, donors found that conditionality, in general, did not work, and sector approaches became a way of providing support against government commitment and track record in providing services for poverty reduction. Second, the emergence of sector approaches was an attempt to focus support on creating a sound policy environment. Rather than donors directly funding services, sector-approach funding is geared towards changes in policies and institutions. A third set of issues revolves around public expenditure frameworks and management: a key problem to which sector approaches were thought to help provide a solution was fragmentation in the budgeting process, with much spending being outside the government budget, and reliance on donor rather than government financial management.

While budget support modalities follow many of the ideas of sector-wide approaches, but are applied to cross-sectoral frameworks and typically in the context of fiscal reforms or adjustment, the PRSP approach incorporated strong civil society critique, linked debt relief to a strengthened poverty focus, and emphasized (recipient) country ownership and in-country consultative processes. As indicated, two forces brought about this new approach. First, the PRSP came about partly as a result of the successful pressure from non-governmental organizations (NGOs) on the international financial institutions (IFIs), particularly through Jubilee 2000, and helped by the changes in European governments in the late 1990s. This broad movement argued for increasing debt relief, particularly but not only by the IFIs. It increased pressure to make this debt relief pro-poor, and to address the negative consequences of structural adjustment. The international financial crisis in East Asia also increased the pressure on the IFIs to review their policies, and their effects on poverty. Second, the changes happened against the background of an intensive debate about the effectiveness of aid. The World Bank in 1998 produced the influential *Assessing Aid* report, which emphasized the need for good economic management as precondition for aid to be effective. The report also acknowledged problems with traditional lending conditionalities, the need for (recipient) government ownership, and problems of fungibility. Changes at the IMF included a response to the critique of the inflexibility in its macroeconomic and fiscal options, of the way conditionality had evolved over time, and the need for better prioritization of policy measures, and division of labour between international institutions.

The PRSP approach has been based on the following (interrelated) principles: an emphasis on country ownership and partnership between donors and recipients; formulation of a PRSP through broad national-level participation; a result-oriented approach including establishing a link between debt relief and impact on poverty (comprehensive and long term). The empirical material generated by reviewing the experience leaves little doubt that at least the debate has brought in a much stronger focus on poverty reduction. It was acknowledged that time pressure greatly influenced early experiences, that the design of the approach had focused too much on the strategy *paper* (and hence it became common to refer to PRS), and reviews indicated much diversity of country experiences (IMF and World Bank 2005).

What do we know about modes of aid delivery through poverty reduction strategies? Debt relief has delivered large amounts of additional aid, yet the lessons from PRSPs are mixed, although there is little doubt that spending has had a more 'pro-poor' direction. The IMF appears to have pulled out from discussions on PRSPs. Is this a sign that the modality has become mainstream, or that it is not working for the IMF? Booth's (2005) assessment that the PRSP was still an 'experiment' can be read as an important warning against the aid modalities that have received most attention since the late 1990s. The question of donor alignment and coordination remains very important, though much work has been done by the Development Assistance Committee (DAC), resulting in the Paris Declaration. Much of the literature (internal and independent alike, including reviewing the 'Paris commitments') continues to question whether donors can really leave countries in the driver's seat, or whether they should continue to push them, often in uncoordinated manner producing 'Christmas tree' PRSPs.

The critiques of PRSPs have been manifold, and only some of these are pertinent here. Booth and Lucas' early emphasis on the missing middle of politics in PRSPs seems particularly important (2001), as is Craig and Porter's (2003) assessment of the technocratic nature of PRSPs. Monitoring of progress is very much—and increasingly—outcome focused with little analysis of the why, the causes, and political economy of change. The anti-political nature of PRSPs is confirmed by reports of a neglect of the legislature in the consultations leading up to PRSPs (while civil society often has seen its space increased). In the paper presented at the 2006 WIDER Aid conference, Booth, Grigsby, and Toranzo emphasize that, rather than a *neglect* of political constituencies, PRSP modalities in Latin America are *unrealistic* in their expectations of political constituencies' commitments to the comprehensive plan encapsulated in the PRSPs (instead, they call for a focus on specific actions, to which governments in power can reasonably be expected to commit themselves). A recent World Bank paper also highlights the issue in relation to budget support:

The provision of funds to a partner country's treasury should provide an incentive to strengthen both internal and external accountability. Finance ministries should demand that sector ministries deliver sustainable development results, line ministries have an interest in receiving adequate funds on a regular basis, supreme audit authorities monitor the proper use of public funds, and parliaments can hold governments accountable for delivering on their promises. Ultimately, however, the quality of this process is dominated by *domestic political dynamics* that can either support or block whatever modest contributions may be made by the policy dialogue underpinning budget support. (Koeberle, Stavreski, and Walliser 2006: 21; emphasis added)

Budget support, the successful debt-relief initiatives and PRSPs, and sector-wide approaches have been very significant reactions to concerns about perceived failures of aid modalities, while simultaneously ensuring ways to make sure commitments for increased spending can be delivered (more recently combined with rapidly increasing private aid flows, including through 'vertical initiatives'). A very different response among the development community during the same period has been the focus on cash transfers, which we discuss next.

9.4. Direct assistance to the poor: solving poverty, or the aid delivery problem

This section looks at the role of social protection and cash transfers in donor practices. Since the critique of structural adjustment, the 1997–8 financial crisis, and revived by the Commission for Africa, cash and other forms of direct transfers to the poor have obtained increased significance. What does this imply for the political dynamics of aid relationships? We focus here on social protection, but the argument could be extended to, and would be strengthened by, a consideration of the politics around decisions on social-sector spending, including the global debates on ceilings that some NGOs argue are being imposed by the IFIs.

Direct assistance to the poor became an increasingly important instrument during the period of adjustment. Social funds were one of the key instruments in the 'human face of adjustment' that the World Bank, regional development banks, and supporting bilaterals tried to show from the 1980s onwards, and were one of the fastest growing sectors in the World Bank during the 1990s (Fumo et al. 2000). One of the first social funds was conceived explicitly as a compensating measure for laid-off mine workers in Bolivia. The Program of Action to Mitigate the Social Cost of Adjustment (PAMSCAD) in Ghana had an open objective of reducing social unrest. And the social fund in Thailand after the East Asian crisis was very explicit about social integration as a key element. The basic idea of social funds, which have shown large variety, has been to provide funds for development activities (across sectors) to poor communities. Indeed, over time, the emphasis of social funds on community-driven development, and providing resources directly to poor communities, has been strengthened.

The literature on social funds is voluminous, with excellent studies about the extent to which money reaches the poor (like the World Bank's own 2004 evaluation by Rawlings, Sherburne-Benz, and Van Domelen), and whether funds are demand- or supply-driven. One of the important critiques in this context has been the effect of social funds on 'mainstream' institutions; in many cases, though not all, social-fund agencies operate as semi-autonomous institutions. It has been argued that social funds bypass line ministries. Indeed, in a way they are a response to the failure of the regular government institutions. Thus, they can have a negative impact on these regular institutions; for example, by attracting personnel from line ministries to work in better-paid jobs in social fund agencies. Social funds as an instrument for delivery of assistance to poor communities may thus have been a way of avoiding the task of addressing inefficiency problems in mainstream institutions.

Of late, the instrument of direct assistance to the poor (under the title social protection, or cash transfers; social insurance has received less attention) has been gaining popularity. The Commission for Africa argued for predictable streams to (pre-emptive) national social protection strategies. The International Labour Organization (ILO) has provided estimates around the cost of social protection, trying to convince the international development community that such systems are less expensive than often assumed (see also Barrientos 2007). At the World Bank, Ravallion's (2003) work provided support to arguments about the importance and feasibility of direct transfers, which was reinforced in a recent paper (Ravallion 2008) which emphasized a strengthened social policy response to the food price and financial crises. Interestingly, much of the evidence on these new instruments to reach the poor directly derive from Latin America, where programmes like Programa de Educación, Salud y Alimentación (PROGRESA) in Mexico are explicitly political, and new and more progressive forms of pensions in Brazil are based on a 'new social contract' (Graham 2002).

While such programmes in Latin America are country-led, in Africa donors play an enormously important role in new programmes; for example, in Zambia and Ethiopia. The argument is that while these are important modalities in many countries, particularly those with weak commitment to poverty reduction or weak governance structures, they can also be a means of circumventing a central problem, of increasing aid without acknowledging the political nature of aid delivery. These aid modalities are not neutral. Addressing poverty as a question of social security runs the risk of neglecting structural, and in particular political dimensions or causes of poverty.[4] At the micro level, such transfers impinge on community and power relations.[5] And at the macro level, we can illustrate this point with reference to Orissa (Jayal 1999, quot. de Haan 2004 n. 73), while outside the donor context, the key points seem pertinent to the way new social-protection programmes—particularly in Africa—are conceptualized. In the state of Orissa, where starvation deaths are a perennial occurrence but usually denied by the state government, claims for increased central assistance are made with reference to 'droughts', and are relief-oriented, arguably in a way that denies the structural nature of problems like land alienation,

---

[4] Poverty analysis has played an important role in this emphasis on targeting the poor, leading to the well-established critique of a 'residual' nature of the dominant social policy paradigm (Mkandawire 2004; de Haan 2007).

[5] Gaspart and Platteau (2006) criticize the practice of providing cheap aid money for poor communities, as this leads to corruption and may strengthen or create unequal power relations. Capacity differentials among communities impact disbursement. The requirement of community contributions can favour projects where contributions can be more easily quantified and projects approved (such as school building), but disadvantage poorer communities, and those for whom the opportunity costs of in-kind contributions are too high.

corruption in access to forest resources, and failure of extensive development programmes over years, if not decades.

The key message here is not whether social protection schemes are a good or bad thing. The point in this chapter is that the assessment in the international donor community remains limited to a very narrow and technocratic framework, with too little understanding of the political dynamics in which such policies are inevitably embedded (see also Dani and de Haan 2008), and the way the global debate (for example, on social sector spending) influences these dynamics.

9.5. Economic growth

Promoting economic growth, or more recently pro-poor growth, has been a key objective of aid, and the 2006 WIDER Aid conference had many papers that looked at the conditions under which economic growth can be promoted. The question we address here is whether the multilateral and bilateral development agencies are becoming smarter at understanding the political conditions necessary for achieving the economic growth needed for poverty reduction.

The proliferation of supposedly necessary technocratic reforms for growth and investment in the 1990s were impossibly demanding for many poor countries. At the same time, the policy prescription on the broad governance reforms needed for investment and growth has evidently been incomplete or misleading: growth spurts or sustained economic development have occurred where the institutional environment appeared 'poor' (notably in China since 1978 and, to a lesser extent, in India since 1980). Vice versa, the adoption of the 'right' institutions often fails to generate growth, notably in Latin America, just as structural adjustment failed to generate a 'supply response'. Moreover, substantial intra-national growth differences exist that cannot be explained by broad generalizations about institutional factors. There are significant examples of rapid growth and investment in some sectors within countries that are otherwise regarded as having poor growth and investment climates (Haber, Razo, and Maurer 2003). Growth differs widely by locality within countries, with local governance factors often explaining the marked regional variations in growth performance (for example, across the Indian states of Gujarat, West Bengal, and Tamil Nadu that were at a comparable level of development at the time of independence (Sinha 2005);[6] and across China (World Bank 2006a).

---

[6] Gujarat has consistently attracted a higher share of investment, West Bengal failed to capitalize on its initial conditions, and Tamil Nadu has a fluctuating performance (investment per capita in Gujarat was two and half times the all-India average by 1994, while in Tamil Nadu such investment stood at 0.85 of all-India levels, and in West Bengal at 0.47). Local politics in Gujarat developed 'strategic capacities' that consistently attracted private capital, while in West Bengal and Tamil Nadu local politics have tended (at least until recently) to have the opposite effect.

Successful growth economies have all witnessed the state playing an important but varying role: attracting investment and improving productivity, technology, and competitiveness. Delivering economic and political stability would seem critical, yet research finds instances when increasing political instability has been correlated with an *increase* in investment (Londregan and Poole 1990; Campos and Nugent 2000a, 2000b). So what matters is how political arrangements have underpinned the competence of key institutions: legal systems, regulation and competition, the public sector, and the flexibility of fiscal and monetary policies. Causality, however, is unclear between governance, investment, and growth. Governance may be critical to the investment climate, which in turn may, or may not, lead to growth. But governance will also influence how the investment climate can lead to growth. For example, India and Brazil, with similar rates of investment (21 per cent of gross domestic product (GDP)), grew at rates as different as 5.7 per cent and 2.1 per cent between 1980 and 2004. Even the evidence for institutional reform impacts on growth is surprisingly patchy (Hausmann, Pritchett, and Rodrik 2005; Hausmann, Rodrik, and Valesco 2005; Jones and Olken 2005). Governance reforms supposedly crucial for growth have had no effect on the economic performance of African countries (Sachs et al. 2004). China has enjoyed significantly higher growth rates than India, yet does not perform better along the supposedly critical dimensions of growth/investment climate factors like stability of property rights, corruption, or the rule of law, but rather has other governance capacities that seem to matter.[7] Increasingly the attention is on what really matters: identifying the key binding constraints to growth, 'good enough governance' (Grindle 2004), and better insight on how governments may have used non-market mechanisms to improve economic performance, such as not initially creating secure property rights but reshaping property rights to put assets into productive hands (Khan 2005: 69–80).

Such innovative approaches require a much better understanding of the politics of growth, as is described in a recent briefing paper for DFID by Williams et al. (2007). Political coalitions for growth are shaped by how political parties, government bureaucracy, and the private sector develop and maintain the state's support for longer-term growth objectives, while balancing concerns for other key priorities: equity, human development, and poverty reduction (Alesina and Rodrik 1994; White and Anderson 2001; World Bank 2006b: chapter on political equity). A good grasp of history is needed to appreciate how the construction of the political settlement for growth, the 'sense of national purpose', develops, including modern economic systems developed in parallel with the rise of nation-states and nationalism (Greenfeld 2001). Even

---

[7] For example, for accelerating resource allocation to growth sectors, prioritizing infrastructure for these sectors, and in making credible and attractive terms available to investors bringing in advanced technologies (Qian and Weingast 1997).

central banks, often portrayed as the archetypal technocratic economic structure, have strong political dimensions (Epstein 2006). State legitimacy matters
for economic growth. The most economically successful African states, such as
Botswana, are also the continent's most legitimate, so their political leaders do
not need to maintain political power at the expense of development. This
historical legitimacy in Africa is estimated to be worth over 2 per cent annual
growth (Engelbert 2002).

Thus, while other chapters in this volume have much more to say on economic growth, and the extent to which this can be pro-poor (see, for example,
Chapters 2 and 4), the central point in the context of this chapter is that politics
lies at the heart of economic growth, and is central to the relationship between
aid and growth, just as it has been for budget support and direct transfers to the
poor. While much progress has been made since the 'Washington Consensus',
we believe that—for a range of reasons—aid agencies' understanding of and
ability to address these politics remains limited. In the following sections we
look the role of governance in donor frameworks and discuss whether this
sufficiently captures politics.

9.6. Governance as institutions and as politics

The post-Washington consensus has put institutions at the centre of attention
of aid delivery, as have the new aid modalities of sector-wide approaches and
PRSPs. 'Lack of political will' over the last decade has steadily moved out from
the 'risk assumption' of development into the spotlight as the problem. The
most important development of recent years has been the recognition that
'good governance is about good politics' (DFID 2006: 23). However, we argue
here that work on governance remains, by and large, too technocratic, and
institutional approaches can reinforce this.

Political scientists have found little entry into donor agencies (unlike economists and sociologists/anthropologists; and with the exception of the former
World Bank president, Wolfowitz, as the joke in the World Bank went). Development economists have been overly content with the new institutional economics concept of *institutions* as *rules of the game* structuring transaction costs.
Such an approach sidesteps the challenge of understanding and influencing
how politics delivers development outcomes, which is now recognized to be
essential, for example, in budget support (as the quote from Koeberle, Stavreski,
and Walliser (2006) above shows). It results in shaping the debate around
technical reform to establish a supposedly critical institution like secure property rights, rather than on understanding property rights as a complex and
constantly politically contested concept generating complex political incentives around achieving sustainable reform (Rochefort and Cobb 1994).

Where does this leave donor ambitions for a policy dialogue to shape and influence the domestic political debate, if donors (particularly the World Bank) are not to be accused of interfering in the domestic affairs of partner countries? Broad generalizations about *political will*, *corruption*, or *elite capture*—common in project documentation—add little understanding of the underlying causes and motives of the individuals and groups involved. Current political governance analysis frequently notes 'the lack of incentives' for individuals or groups to change, while few suggestions are on offer for finding and applying the potential and practical levers of change, or for better understanding how behavioural change could be brought about. Political leadership or support is often mentioned, but little evidence is offered as to whether the problem is lack of knowledge, structural disincentives for tackling long-term developmental challenges, or inherent contradictions and vested interests.

Leaders face incentives to use aid for patronage purposes—for example, by subsidizing employment in the public sector and in state-operated enterprises (and even cash transfers to the poor, as we discussed earlier)—to tighten their grip on power. As rents available to those controlling the government increase when aid levels are higher, resources devoted to obtaining political influence increase; and this applies at least as much in social sectors (see Chapter 14 of this volume by Richard M. Auty for a detailed discussion of aid as a form of geopolitical rent). In fact, corruption and aid can be mutually reinforcing (Degnbol-Martinussen and Engberg-Pedersen 2003: 273). By making control of the government a more valuable prize, aid may even increase political instability (Grossman 1992).

Governance indicators have become a key component of aid delivery (also for the Millennium Challenge Corporation). But significant problems remain, inherent in adapting to governance as political process rather than as technocratic fix, and often with superficial generalities, based in theory rather than actual experience. Any political understanding of governance needs to ask how indicators are constructed, what they really measure (for example, rule of law), hidden assumptions (for example, preference in favour of rules associated with liberal-democratic societies), and how they are being used and why. Governance indicators produce assessments on a narrow set of issues and leave out some important governance dimensions (for example, informal political *voice* or influence, inequality).[8] A key test might be: could the current governance evaluations have been able to predict in the 1960s and 1970s that a repressive authoritarian regime in South Korea was the political vehicle for creating an extraordinary successful economic, political, and social transformation in terms

---

[8] To overcome the dangers of such governance determinism, Hyden, Court and Mease (2004) suggest that, in addition to the usual categories of participation, efficiency, accountability, and transparency, the more intriguing categories of fairness and decency be applied. These imply a qualitative approach, suspicious of quantification of econometrics and the stylization of game theory. See Assessing Governance Programme website <http://www.odi.org.uk/wga_governance>.

of speed and impact of growth on poverty reduction?[9] Would existing governance indicators have predicted the similar economic success of China or Vietnam? Governance indicators remain in their infancy, and certainly do not yet provide a way for tracking how the formal and informal methods delivered this transformation. Donors are struggling with the potential dangers of a normative approach to governance, and the use and abuse of governance indicators to justify aid allocations and aid modalities that will doubtless remain much more political.

Forms of political analysis have been introduced in a number of agencies; for example, SIDA's power analysis, World Bank's institutional governance reviews (IGRs); and DFID's drivers of change (now synthesized by the DAC). While much good-quality analysis has resulted, some fundamental questions remain; for example, who does the analysis and from what perspective? To justify political approaches, the term *political economy* is widely used by donors and the World Bank (for example, Keefer 2004). But, this convenient portmanteau term does as much to obscure as to clarify or facilitate a more political approach to economic growth. Often it seems to mean no more than an attempt to recognize that the linkage of politics and power cannot be separated from economic policy or asset distribution. The ambiguity may be useful where it enables economists to start to recognize that markets and incentives are politically constructed. But, as economists attempt to use their theories to explain politics, social scientists (or 'non-economist social scientists') have largely failed to develop alternative analyses to challenge the dominant economics paradigm in universities and development agencies.

So political economy is often used by economists as a neo-determinist assertion that political power and the (economic and other) policies and institutions of states reflect economic structures and the interests of the dominant economic interests. The 'institutions and growth' literature that has blossomed in recent years has empowered economists, using a limited application of the complexity of history, to construct simple models of institutional change. The findings of various influential papers such as those by Acemoglu, Johnson, and Robinson (2001), asserting that the structure of economies and the distribution of economic power within them have a profound effect on the historical development of political power, would hardly surprise Marxists. What is surprising is the degree to which the poor history underlying many of these sweeping assertions goes unchallenged, perhaps because in the post-Cold War intellectual climate determinist approaches are no longer of wider or ideological

---

[9] The World Bank Institute's 'Governance Matters' indicators seek to track political stability (perceptions of the likelihood that the government will be destabilized or overthrown by unconstitutional or violent means) and government effectiveness (the quality of the civil service and the degree of its independence from political pressures), overly normative concepts for analysing long-term development trends.

concern. But, the real challenge, of genuine interdisciplinary understanding of the linkage between the political and economic spheres in development, remains poorly addressed in development agencies. In the World Bank, for instance, institutional and governance reviews have regrettably faded in prominence and have not become obligatory for country programme managers.

The development agencies and IFIs are very good at producing long lists of the *what* (usually what others need to do for reform); the *how* and the *why* partner governments would undertake these things are, usually, rarely addressed. Much political analysis explains past history and current trajectories, but provides very little, if any, real guidance as to how to create the social cohesion and common interests between elites and the population needed to replicate the development success of the East Asian tigers or Botswana and Mauritius. What, one might wonder, is the operational lesson from insights like this:

pro-development policies are comparatively rare in the developing world less because of the moral fibre of politicians (though that surely matters) than because good politicians typically lack the room for manoeuvre needed to make desired reforms. This lack of manoeuvrability is a product of insufficient social cohesion and weak institutions. (Woolcock, Easterly, and Ritzen 2000: 4)

Although it has belatedly been recognized that economies with strong growth usually lack the institutional structures traditionally recommended by the World Bank and others, even the World Bank has concluded that 'what works' matters more than economic theories (World Bank 2006c).

The process of political analysis is also of concern. Local experts may have inside knowledge but at the risk of local bias vis-à-vis donors; whereas external specialists may possess greater objectivity, they may also be less well informed about the informal processes of power. A historical institutionalism approach may overemphasize static fatalism and path dependence; others may focus on forms of new institutional economics or political economy that highlight incentives but without recognizing deeper social forces. Academic consultants may stress theoretical risks and weaknesses, rather than practical policy implications and possible improvements, or commercial consultants may be creating jobs for themselves. The aim and focus of analysis is often ambiguous about how confidential information is used, how inclusive or transparent the process can be, who the audience is, and how the report will be disseminated. Foreign ministries' political analytical processes remain confidential to allow for the necessary freedom to express and internally debate candid views about governments, their policies, and the quirks of their leading personalities. It can be debated whether development agencies will really be able to find a complementary match of skills in political analysis and country level knowledge, and then value and reward them, especially when top management in development agencies and the World Bank are staffed by economists or administrators under short-term expenditure performance measures. Will political analysis be compressed into simplified governance indicators that permit a new generation of over-ambitious claims for aid effectiveness?

Thus, while the donor community agrees that *institutions matter*, a discrepancy remains between an instrumental version of a governance-indicators approach that tends to focus on development as a technical fix, and the political realities of the messy development process (reflected in messy political science debates) in recipient countries and the way the (equally messy) politics of donor agencies interact with these. The next two sections describe some of the challenges that this poses for aid delivery.

9.7. Aid and the politics of the fiscal contract

With respect to strengthening institutions and enhancing accountability, there is perhaps no more intractable problem than the question of taxation and revenue generation. Yet, the development literature and practice have paid relatively little attention to this (with important exceptions; for example, research at the Overseas Development Institute (ODI) in London). Recent studies suggest that the politics are very complex, and contradictory findings regarding the impact of aid have emerged.

Strengthening tax collection (UN Millennium Project 2005: 245) is at the heart of donor expectations from partner governments; but in many low-income countries with a narrow domestic tax base or large informal economy and agricultural sector, significant operational challenges include national tax administrations tempted to focus on a relatively small number of medium and large formal sector businesses, and largely ignore the others, including large and growing urban informal business activities.[10] Tax administration staff may have few incentives to address the problems;[11] politically influential domestic business and major foreign investors obtain generous tax exemptions. The introduction of a VAT in poor countries has failed to compensate for the revenue effects of trade liberalization (Baunsgaard and Keen 2005). Ross (2004) finds that higher taxes relative to government services tend to make states more democratic. WIDER papers on poverty reduction and tax (for example, Di John 2006) and Mick Moore's work on tax and accountability at the Institute of Development Studies (IDS) Centre for the Future State have been influential

---

[10] In Tanzania, with a population of over 35 million people, 286 large taxpayers pay almost 70 per cent of the domestic taxes. Fewer than 1 per cent of the taxpayers pay more than 85 per cent of the direct taxes levied in Peru (Mostajo 2004).

[11] Tax agency staff do not like to be given posts that take them away from working in lucrative positions and require them to make a great deal of effort to raise small amounts of money from very reluctant taxpayers: see research in Ghana tax system at IDS Future States Programme phase 1 on taxation.

in the development community in suggesting that taxation matters for the link between governance and development outcomes.[12] Mahon (2006) suggests a more-complex relationship between the political process and taxation, while Gloppen and Rakner's case studies on sub-Saharan Africa (2002) find reciprocity in the relationship between state and society and accountability mechanisms have not been strengthened to the degree predicted in the literature.

State legitimacy is, in part, constructed by the fiscal social contract—the political process by which a responsive and accountable government delivers services to its population while building quasi-voluntary compliance from its population to pay the taxes needed to fund those services.[13] And, in turn, state legitimacy is itself an important underpinning for enabling the sustainable economic growth on which ending aid dependency will depend (Engelbert 2002; Moore 2004a). The key plank of governance—accountability—has therefore emerged only when governments need to raise revenue, requiring those in authority to bargain with its citizenry (no taxation without representation) (Moore 2004b). To make a significant impact on poverty, reduction aid effectiveness needs to incorporate better the importance of taxation for improving governance.

Conflicting arguments and supporting evidence exist on the effects of scaling-up aid on government political efforts for revenue mobilization. The IMF has argued in contradictory fashion, suggesting in 2003 that scaling-up was a threat to revenue mobilization (Gupta et al. 2004a, 2004b) but suggesting in 2006 that this was less significant a concern:

In some cases, to the extent that a weaker tax effort reduces domestic distortions, it might spur economic activity. In other cases, where weaker revenue collection reflects poor compliance or unnecessary tax exemptions, it would be more likely to breed aid dependency. Furthermore, a weaker tax effort can have an adverse effect on domestic institutions because citizens are less likely to hold the government accountable when they pay lower taxes (Bevan 2005). An argument can be made that reducing tax rates can be an optimal response to permanently higher aid flows, but this argument has less weight for countries that are currently below their potential for raising tax revenues and for which scaled-up aid inflows will be temporary. This latter group of countries must establish a strategy for coping with an inevitable drop in aid flows. (IMF and World Bank 2006)

The IMF also argues that policymakers in developing countries seeking to deliver the MDGs face a problem of inadequate 'fiscal space' in balancing unutilized borrowing capacity, an increase in aid flows, with reducing

---

[12] See <http://www.ids.ac.uk/futurestate/drc-pubs/index.html>; also Brautigam, Fjeldstad, and Moore (2008).

[13] On Africa's fiscal contracts, see, e.g., Hoffman and Gibson 2005 and Schneider 2004. See also Professor Adrian Wood's important suggestion in the *Financial Times* (4 Sept. 2008) that to preserve the state's accountability to citizens not donors aid should be designed to act as a matching fund for tax effort.

unproductive expenditure (IMF and World Bank 2006: sect. 3.9). But, in countries with weak institutional capacity, aid may reduce incentives for institutional reform, locking donor and recipient into a permanent situation of high aid and low governance capacity (Azam, Devarajan, and O'Connell 1999). A case study on Indonesia finds aid a disincentive to expand domestic revenue through a more efficient and effective taxation system (Chowdhury and Suegma 2005). Additional grants, whether from an overall increase in foreign aid or from a conversion of loans into grants, may be completely offset by a reduction in domestic revenues in countries where institutions are weakest. This risk is perceived to be lower in the case of loan financing (Clements et al. 2004).

The temptation from the above might be to promote conditionality on aid flows and the efficient mobilization of domestic revenue. The IMF suggests 15 per cent tax take of GDP as a general indicator of government determination to meet the Monterrey consensus;[14] and some donors (for example, Belgium) may be using this as a governance benchmark for conditionality of aid. Conditionality, however, would not necessarily address the real political issues for partner governments to tackle the practical and political challenges of efficient, effective, and equitable revenue mobilization, and DFID, for example, supports a more nuanced approach to track 'direction of travel' rather than specific targets.

9.8. Politics and aid delivery

Tensions are emerging between corporate objectives and the implications of power and DOC (drivers of change) analysis, which emphasize the prime importance of local political process and incremental change, in the face of pressures on donors to meet short term spending targets, and to be accountable to their own taxpayers.

This quote from the OECD-DAC's Network on Governance 2005 paper sums up a large part of our expectations around the Monterrey consensus—a 'consensus' that has been forged in the face of knowledge that PRSPs are depoliticized documents, that governance is conceptualized in technical not political terms, and new channels for aid like cash transfers are delinked from political projects in which such provisions are inevitable embedded. Are donors in a position to develop the necessary understanding of, for example, likely political winners and losers from proposed reforms in a way which will really enable them to be effective in pushing realistic solutions to existing development challenges in local contexts? Can a political understanding of aid delivery be

---

[14] Adam and Bevan (2004) suggest the tax ratio for post-stabilization countries should be in the order of 15–20 per cent, and IMF (2005) offers a ratio of at least 15 per cent as a reasonable target for most low-income countries.

squared with other donor-country interests, and are ambitions of better political understanding inevitably thwarted by aims to increase aid flows?

To begin to answer these questions, apart from understanding the politics of
development in recipient countries, it is essential to see donors as political
agents. Aid agencies consist of bureaucrats and political leaders, with interests
and incentives in success, claiming success, and controlling the process such
that success seems to be justified by the results. Donors are part of government
bureaucracies and as such are content with their established developing country counterparts (even though political analysis often suggests that informal
power may lie with non-traditional partners). Donor agencies are part of wider
government bureaucracies without the remove from the mainstream civil service usually accorded to foreign ministries: donor agencies struggle to value and
retain detailed country expertise, including language learning, and are preoc-
cupied with 'corporate' issues. Donors like to perceive themselves as the friends
of the poor; but donors are (also) political actors—without adequate political
checks and balances and transparency.

At the domestic level, the Monterrey challenge is to explain how the partnership and the resulting aid instruments interact with domestic politics on two
levels: first the sources, distribution, control, and conflicts over the use of power
in relation to the policies and institutions influencing MDG outcomes; and,
second, the origins and nature of the political demand for delivering the MDGs.
How can development agencies answer in general and in every specific national
context the key question: how is a sense of national purpose first created, then
maintained in the medium/long term, and what can aid modalities do to
influence the process?[15] Scaling-up aid will increase the importance of political
analysis for development, and it matters whether politics is understood to be a
process (institutions), a set of structures (organizations), or a range of policies
amenable to potentially subtle nuances of overt and covert conditionalities.[16]
Political analysis has many different approaches: of the immediate concerns of
the individual—the 'big man', *caudillo* (development agencies do increasingly
recognize leadership as often key to successful reform); the organization or
institutional level on medium-term reform given the right conditions and
with the right incentives; and at the deep structural level of informal institutions, culture, and tradition that may require an inter-generational change
period. Political analysis tracks power and incentives shaped by the institutional environment, and political governance challenges donors' aid effectiveness

---

[15] In Tanzania, for instance, the World Bank recently noted that the lack of critical scrutiny
of budget proposals and budget execution reports by parliament means that there have been
few political incentives to improve the efficiency of public spending (Koeberle, Stavreski, and
Walliser 2006: 131).

[16] For a summary of IMF views on conditionality and how this interacts with domestic
politics, see Mourmouras (2002).

agenda, to ensure that increasing spending is balanced by adequate attention to political and institutional structures.

The challenge is how to experiment according to experience and local realities, not to roll out the *best practice* but to try to find a *good practice that actually works*. This requires:

- disaggregating the broad governance objectives such as secure property rights into their component parts;
- understanding the inherent theoretical and practical challenges posed by the need to shape effective organizations and practices; laws that are actually implemented because they reflect but also help shape individual, group, and organizational behaviour.

Reforms differ in complexity to put into practice. Successful reform depends on a window of opportunity to challenge vested interests, takes time to embed if requiring behavioural and attitudinal change, and is often administratively complex. Analysis is needed to match the development need. This agenda and the concerns it generates imply clear priorities for donors; for example, to focus on key areas around building domestic accountability and voice; to work better with other donors on political analysis to understand informal political spheres; and to recognize that there are as yet no adequate quantitative indicators for much of the political governance agenda. Improving indicators on governance will remain a priority for the foreseeable future, as donors will need to be able to handle the question of attribution of donor efforts to progress, and maintain long-term engagement (and be flexible to grasp political windows of opportunity, and seeing impact while accepting that there will be setbacks). Finally, political accountability extends to donors, not just partner governments: there will be increasing focus on whether donors are really delivering on their promises.

All this represents a major challenge and potential long-term threat for the governance agenda. As yet, little is known about the real formal and informal processes that contribute to success or failure and perhaps even less about asking the right questions about the underlying conditions necessary for delivering the MDGs. Perhaps ironically this is exactly the same context that donor agencies face internally. It is often the informal incentive environment of 'office politics', norms, practices, and culture that shape development agency responses, which are then justified and externally evaluated by the formal rule environment: human resource guidance, knowledge management systems, and specific policy directives. For this reason, Tendler (1975) and Berg (2000) suggest that aid organizations are poor learners because the incentives to spend cut across the flexible, adaptive structures and procedures that would be needed to encourage institutional learning (also Eyben 2005). If development organizations tend to be characterized by internal staff turnover, weak horizontal information flows, and an excessive reliance on blueprint approaches to project design and implementation, handling the issues of development politics may revert increasingly to foreign ministries. Donors do increasingly recognize publicly that poverty reduction is an inherently political agenda which will require the bilaterals and also the IFIs to rethink their skills and capacities and aid modalities, and have clearer ideas about policy conditionality. The question is whether there will be enough consensus to grapple with political judgement of complex development trade-offs.

References

Adam, C. S., and D. L. Bevan (2004) 'Aid and the Supply Side: Public Investment, Export Performance and Dutch Disease in Low Income Countries'. Oxford University Department of Economics Discussion Paper 201.

Acemoglu, D., S. Johnson, and J. Robinson (2001) 'The Colonial Origins of Comparative Development: An Empirical Investigation'. *American Economic Review*, 91: 1369–401.

Alesina, A., and D. Dollar (2000) 'Who Gives Foreign Aid to Whom and Why?' *Journal of Economic Growth*, 5: 33–63.

——and D. Rodrik (1994) 'Distributive Politics and Economic Growth'. *Quarterly Journal of Economics*, 109: 465–90.

Azam, J. P. S. Devarajan, and S. A. O'Connell (1999) 'Aid Dependence Reconsidered'. World Bank Working Paper 99-5. Washington, DC: World Bank.

Barrientos, A. (2007) 'Financing Social Protection'. Manchester University, Brooks World Poverty Institute Working Paper 5. Manchester: BWPI.

Baunsgaard, T., and M. Keen (2005) 'Tax Revenue and (or?) Trade Liberalization'. International Monetary Fund Working Paper 05/112, Washington, DC: IMF.

Berg, E. (2000) 'Why Aren't Aid Organizations Better Learners?' Paper presented at the EGDI seminar 'What do Aid Agencies and their Co-operating Partners Learn from their Experiences'. 24 Aug. <www.egdi.gov.se/pdf/berg.pdf>.

Bevan, D. L. (2005) 'An Analytical Overview of Aid Absorption: Recognizing and Avoiding Macroeconomic Hazards'. Paper presented at the IMF Seminar on Foreign Aid and Macroeconomic Management, 14–15 Mar., Maputo.

Booth, D. (2005) 'Missing Links in the Politics of Development: Learning from the PRSP Experiment'. Overseas Development Institute Working Paper 256. London: ODI.

——A. Grigsby, and C. Toranzo (2006) 'Politics and Poverty Reduction Strategies: Lessons from Latin American HIPCs'. Paper presented at the UNU-WIDER Development Conference on Aid, 'Aid: Principles, Policies, and Performance'. held on 16–17 June 2006 in Helsinki.

——and H. Lucas (2001) 'Initial Review of PRSP Documentation'. Report commissioned by DFID for the Strategic Partnership with Africa. London: ODI.

Brautigam, D., O.-H. Fjeldstad, and M. Moore (2008) *Taxation and State-building in Developing Countries: Capacity and Consent*. Cambridge: Cambridge University Press.

Campos, N. F., and J. B. Nugent (2000a) 'Who is Afraid of Political Instability?' Centre for Economic Policy Research Discussion Paper 2555. London: CEPR.

——and J. B. Nugent (2000b) 'Investment and Instability'. Centre for Economic Policy Research Discussion Paper 2609. London: CEPR.

Chowdhury, A., and I. Suegma (2005) 'Aid and Fiscal Behaviour in Indonesia: The Case of a Lazy Government'. University of Adelaide Centre for International Economic Studies Discussion Paper 0506. Adelaide: CIES.

Clements, B., S. Gupta, A. Pivovarsky, and E. Tiongson (2004) 'Foreign Aid: Grants versus Loans: Why the Proposed Shift of Aid from Loans to Grants Should Be Accompanied by a Strengthening of Institutions in Developing Countries'. *Finance and Development* (Sept.): 46–9. <http://www.imf.org/external/pubs/ft/fandd/2004/09/pdf/clements.pdf>.

Commission for Africa (2005) *Our Common Interest: Report of the Commission for Africa.* Penguin Books: London.

Craig, D., and D. Porter (2003) 'Poverty Reduction Strategy Papers: A New Convergence'. *World Development*, 31: 53–69.

Dani, A., and A. de Haan (2008), *Inclusive States: Social Policy and Structural Inequalities.* Washington, DC: World Bank.

de Haan, A. (2004) 'Disparities within India's Poorest Region: Why Do the Same Institutions Work Differently in Different Places'. Background paper for World Development Report 2006. <http://siteresources.worldbank.org/INTWDR 2006/Resources/477383-1118673432908/Disparities_within_Indias_Poorest_Regions _Why_Do-the_Same_Institutions_Work_Differently_in_Different_Places.pdf>.

——A. (2007) *Reclaiming Social Policy: Globalization, Social Exclusion and New Poverty Strategies.* Basingstoke: Palgrave Macmillan.

——(2009) *How the Aid Industry Works. An Introduction to International Development.* West Hartford, Conn.: Kumarian Press.

Degnbol-Martinussen, J., and P. Engberg-Pedersen (2003) *Aid: Understanding International Development Co-operation.* London: Zed Books.

DFID (Department for International Development) (2006) 'Making Governance Work for Poor People'. Department for International Development White Paper 23. London: DFID.

Di John, J. (2006) 'The Political Economy of Taxation and Tax Reform in Developing Countries'. WIDER Research Paper 2006/74. Helsinki: UNU-WIDER.

Easterly, W. (2006) *The White Man's Burden: Why the West's Efforts to Aid the Rest Have Done So Much Ill and So Little Good.* New York: Penguin Press.

Engelbert, P. (2002) *State Legitimacy and Development in Africa.* Boulder, Colo.: Lynne Rienner.

Epstein, G. (2006) 'Central Banks as Agents of Economic Development'. WIDER Research Paper 2006/54. Helsinki: UNU-WIDER.

Eyben, R. (2005) 'Donors' Learning Difficulties: Results, Relationships and Responsibilities'. *IDS Bulletin*, 36: 98–107.

Foster, M. (2000) 'New Approaches to Development Co-operation: What Can We Learn from Experiences with Implementing Sector-wide Approaches'. Overseas Development Institute Working Paper 140. London: ODI.

Fumo, C., A. de Haan, J. Holland, and N. Kanji (2000) 'Social Fund: An Effective Way to Support Local Action for Poverty Reduction?' Department for International Development Working Paper 5. London: Social Development Department, DFID.

Gaspart, F., and J.-P. Platteau (2006) 'The Perverse Effect of Cheap Aid Money'. Paper presented at the UNU-WIDER Development Conference on Aid, 'Aid: Principles, Policies, and Performance' held on 16–17 June 2006 in Helsinki.

Gloppen, S., and L. Rakner (2002) 'Accountability through Tax Reform: Reflections from Sub-Saharan Africa'. *IDS Bulletin*, 33: 30–40.

Graham, C. (2002) 'Crafting Sustainable Social Contracts in Latin America: Political Economy, Public Attitudes, and Social Policy'. Center on Social and Economic Dynamics Working Paper Series 29. Washington, DC: Brookings Institution.

Greenfeld, L. (2001) *The Spirit of Capitalism: Nationalism and Economic Growth*. Cambridge, Mass.: Harvard University Press.

Grindle, M. (2004) 'Good Enough Governance: Poverty Reduction and Reform in Developing Countries'. *Governance*, 17: 525–48.

Grossman, H. I. (1992) 'Foreign Aid and Insurrection'. *Defense Economics*, 3: 275–88.

Gupta, S., B. Clements, E. Baldacci, and C. Mulas-Granados (2004a) 'Fiscal Policy, Expenditure Composition, and Growth in Low-Income Countries'. In S. Gupta, B. Clements and G. Inchauste (eds), *Helping Countries Develop: The Role of Fiscal Policy*. Washington, DC: IMF.

————A. Pivovarsky, and E. R. Tiongson (2004b) 'Foreign Aid and Revenue Response: Does the Composition of Aid Matter?' In S. Gupta, B. Clements and G. Inchauste (eds), *Helping Countries Develop: The Role of Fiscal Policy*. Washington, DC: IMF.

Haber, S., A. Razo, and N. Maurer (2003) *The Politics of Property Rights: Political Instability, Credible Commitments, and Economic Growth in Mexico, 1876–1929*. New York: Cambridge University Press.

Hausmann, R., D. Rodrik, and A. Velasco (2005) 'Growth Diagnostics'. Cambridge, Mass.: Harvard University. <http://ksghome.harvard.edu/~drodrik/papers.html>.

——L. Pritchett, and D. Rodrik (2005) 'Growth Accelerations'. *Journal of Economic Growth*, 10: 303–29.

Hoffman, B. D., and C. C. Gibson (2005) 'Fiscal Governance and Public Services: Evidence from Tanzania and Zambia'. Mimeo. University of California, San Diego, Department of Political Science.

Hyden, G., J. Court, and K. Mease (2004) *Making Sense of Governance: Empirical Evidence from Sixteen Developing Countries*. Boulder, Colo.: Lynne Rienner.

IDS Bulletin (2005) 'Increased Aid: Minimizing Problems, Maximising Gains'. *IDS Bulletin*, 36: 2.

IMF (International Monetary Fund) (2005) 'Monetary and Fiscal Policy Design Issues in Low-income Countries'. <http://www.imf.org/external/np/pp/eng/2005/080805m.pdf>.

——and World Bank (2005) 'PRS Review: Balancing Accountabilities and Scaling Up Results'. Washington, DC: World Bank. <http://siteresources.worldbank.org/INTPRS1/Resources/PRSP-Review/2005_Review_Final.pdf>.

————(2006) 'Fiscal Policy for Growth and Development: Interim Report'. Prepared for the Development Committee meeting, 23 Apr., Document DC2006-0003. Washington, DC: IMF. <http://siteresources.worldbank.org/DEVCOMMINT/Documentation/20890698/DC2006-0003(E)-FiscalPolicy.pdf>.

Jayal, N. G. (1999) *Democracy and the State: Welfare, Secularism and Development in Contemporary India*. Delhi: Oxford University Press.

Jones, B. F., and B. A. Olken (2005) 'The Anatomy of Start–Stop Growth'. National Bureau of Economic Research Working Paper 11528. Cambridge, Mass.: NBER.

Kaufmann, D. (2003) 'Rethinking Governance: Empirical Lessons Challenge Orthodoxy'. <http://ssrn.com/abstract=386904>.

Keefer, P. (2004) 'A Review of the Political Economy of Governance: From Property Rights to Voice'. World Bank Policy Research Department Working Paper 3315. Washington, DC: World Bank.

Khan, M. (2005) 'The Capitalist Transformation'. In K. S. Jomo and E. S. Reinert (eds), *The Origins of Development Economics: How Schools of Economic Thought Have Addressed Development*. London: Zed Books.

Koeberle, S., Z. Stavreski, and J. Walliser (2006) *Budget Support as More Effective Aid? Recent Experiences and Emerging Lessons*. Washington, DC: World Bank.

Londregan, J. B., and K. T. Poole (1990) 'Poverty, the Coup Trap, and the Seizure of Executive Power'. *World Politics*, 42: 151–83.

Mahon, J. (2006) 'Revenue and Regimes'. Mimeo. Washington, DC: Williams College.

Manor, J. (2005) 'Introduction'. *IDS Bulletin*, 36: 1–7.

Mkandawire, T. (ed.) (2004) *Social Policy in a Development Context*. Basingstoke: Palgrave Macmillan.

Moore, M. (2004a) 'Revenues, State Formation, and the Quality of Governance in Developing Countries'. *International Political Science Review*, 25: 297–319.

——(2004b) 'Taxation and the Political Agenda, North and South'. *Forum for Development Studies*, 31: 7–32.

Mostajo, R. (2004) *Prospects for an Integral Tax Reform with Equity: Toward a Fiscal Covenant for Peru*. Lima: Department for International Development.

Mourmouras, A. (2002) 'IMF Conditionality and Country Ownership of Reforms'. *IMF Research Bulletin*, 3: 1–4.

Natsios, A. S. (2006) 'Five Debates on International Development: The US Perspective'. *Development Policy Review*, 24: 131–9.

OECD-DAC (2005) *Lessons Learned on the Use of Power and Drivers of Change Analyses in Development Co-operation: Final Report*. OECD-DAC Network on Governance (GOVNET). Paris: OECD-DAC.

Qian, Y., and B. R. Weingast (1997) 'Institutions, State Activism, and Economic Development: Comparison of State-Owned and Township-Village Enterprises in China'. In M. Aoki, H.-K. Kim, and M. Okuno-Fujiwara (eds), *The Role of Government in East Asian Economic Development: Comparative Institutional Analysis*. Oxford: Oxford University Press.

Ravallion, M. (2003) 'Targeted Transfers in Poor Countries: Revisiting the Tradeoffs and Policy Options'. World Bank Social Protection Discussion Paper 0314. Washington, DC: World Bank.

——(2008) 'Bailing Out the World's Poorest'. Policy Research Working Paper 4763. Washington, DC: World Bank.

Rawlings, L. B., L. Sherburne-Benz, and J. Van Domelen (2004) *Evaluating Social Funds: A Cross-country Analysis of Community Investments*. Washington, DC: World Bank.

Rochefort, D., and R. Cobb (1994) *The Politics of Problem Definition*. Lawrence, Kan.: University Press of Kansas.

Ross, M. L. (2004) 'Does Taxation Lead to Representation'. *British Journal of Political Science*, 34: 229–50.

Sachs, J. D. (2005) *The End of Poverty: Economic Possibilities for Our Time*. New York: Penguin Press.

—— W. McArthur, G. Schmidt-Traub, et al. (2004) 'Ending Africa's Poverty Trap'. *Brookings Papers on Economic Activity*, 1: 117–240.

Schneider, A. (2004) 'Accountability and Capacity in Developing Country Federalism: Empowered States, Competitive Federalism'. *Forum for Development Studies*, 1: 33–58.

Sinha, A. (2005) *The Regional Roots of Developmental Politics in India: A Divided Leviathan*. Bloomington, Ind.: Indiana University Press.

Tendler, J. (1975) *Inside Foreign Aid*. Baltimore, Md.: Johns Hopkins University Press.

UN Millennium Project (2005) *Investing in Development: A Practical Plan to Achieve the Millennium Goals*. New York: Earthscan.

White, H., and E. Anderson (2001) 'Growth versus Distribution: Does the Pattern of Growth Matter?' *Development Policy Review*, 19: 267–89.

Williams, G., A. Duncan, P. Landell-Mills, and S. Unsworth (2007) 'Politics and Growth'. Report prepared for Department for International Development. Brighton: Policy Practice, DFID.

Woolcock, M., W. Easterly, and J. Ritzen (2000) 'On "Good" Politicians and "Bad" Policies: Social Cohesion, Institutions, and Growth'. World Bank Policy Research Department Working Paper 2448. Washington, DC: World Bank.

World Bank (1998) *Assessing Aid: What Works, What Doesn't, and Why*. Oxford and New York and Washington, DC: Oxford University Press/World Bank.

——(2006a) 'Governance, Investment Climate, and Harmonious Society: Competitiveness Enhancements for 120 Cities in China'. WB-FIAS Report 37759-CN. Washington, DC: World Bank. <http://siteresources.worldbank.org/INTCHINA/Resources/318862-1121421293578/120cities_en.pdf>.

——(2006b) *World Development Report 2006: Equity and Development*. Washington, DC: World Bank. <http://econ.worldbank.org/external/default/main?pagePK=64165259&theSitePK=469372&piPK=64165421&menuPK=64166322&entityID=000112742_20050920110826>.

——(2006c) *World Development Indicators 2006*. <http://web.worldbank.org/WBSITE/EXTERNAL/DATASTATISTICS/0,,contentMDK:20899413~pagePK:64133150~piPK:64133175~theSitePK:239419,00.html>.

10

Monitoring and Evaluation Reform under Changing Aid Modalities

Nathalie Holvoet and Robrecht Renard

10.1. Introduction

The shift towards programme-based approaches to which the international community has committed itself[1] demands considerable behavioural changes, not only of donors but also of recipients. In the era of poverty-reduction strategy papers (PRSPs)[2] and sector-wide approaches (SWAPs), donors are urged to move away from earmarking and micro-managing their contributions. Instead, they are supposed to let recipient governments sit in the driving seat, and settle for arm's-length control and supervision over recipient policies and implementation procedures. In operational terms, this involves a move from donor-managed projects towards budget support and alignment with recipient countries' national systems of planning, budgeting, implementation, monitoring, and evaluation. Donors who heed this advice and contribute to the national budget with minimal earmarking lose the capacity to trace their own euros,

---

[1] The OECD-DAC document (2005a: 37) uses the notion of 'programme-based approaches' to refer to 'a way of engaging in development cooperation based on the principles of co-ordinated support for a locally owned programme of development'. The approach includes four key elements: (i) leadership by the host country or organization; (ii) a single programme budget framework; (iii) donor coordination and harmonization of procedures; and (iv) efforts to increase the use of local procedures over time with regard to programme design and implementation, financial management, monitoring, and evaluation.

[2] The PRSP is a policy document that is produced by the recipient country and replaces similar documents such as the policy framework paper that used to be imposed by the IMF and the World Bank on low-income aid-dependent countries for the purpose of adjustment lending. More fundamentally, it constitutes the linchpin of a new comprehensive aid approach that concentrates on four basic principles: (i) long-term and holistic vision; (ii) country ownership; (iii) results orientation; and (iv) country-led partnership. Nowadays, donors increasingly use the PRSP as the framework for their aid activities, accompanying the shift from projects to sectoral and general budget support.

dollars, and yens to their ultimate impact. This considerably weakens their capacity to account separately for the use of aid to their home constituencies or shareholders. True, joint donor-policy dialogue with the government, together with technical cooperation to strengthen public-sector capacity, may give the donor community some leverage to influence the outcomes, but that is hardly a substitute for hard-nosed accounting for results. Recipient governments are expected to elaborate sound policies; strengthen (results-oriented) institutions for planning and implementation; and take the lead in the identification of weaknesses in policy and institutional apparatus and elaboration of plans for improvement and capacity-building. As far as monitoring and evaluation are concerned, national governments, national statistical institutes, and oversight institutions should become the major source of data and of analysis, both for domestic accountability, and for donors.

This chapter focuses on the consequences of current aid reform on the functions of monitoring and evaluation (M&E). The salient features of the new aid approach—such as the decrease in donor earmarking, the increase in recipient responsibility for implementation, and the imposition by donors of a string of new process conditionalities that constrain the latitude of the recipients in their use of aid monies—all highlight the need for a restyling of M&E tasks at both donor and recipient ends. As explained in section 10.2, national M&E systems need be strengthened in their twin functions of accountability and lesson-learning, and, likewise, the role of donors in M&E needs to be recast. With time, as recipient M&E systems become stronger, their output should also be able to satisfy a major part of the accountability needs of donors, and this should provide a powerful impetus to wind down parallel M&E activities that many donors still keep in place.

Notwithstanding the fact that the new approach to aid has a well-recognized incidence on M&E, section 10.3 argues that M&E issues do not figure highly on the recipients' reform agendas. If attention to the effective elaboration of recipient M&E systems has been meagre, section 10.4 highlights that the donor part of the reform agenda has not been squarely addressed either. In 2003, the World Bank evaluation of its Comprehensive Development Framework (CDF) revealed that M&E was one of the areas where donors have made least progress in harmonizing practices and where consequently the burdens on recipient government are enormous (World Bank 2003a). In the meantime, the situation may have improved slightly, but it remains deficient. Section 10.4 concludes that donors seem caught in a 'chicken and egg' dilemma. Most continue to rely on their own institutional apparatus for monitoring and evaluating their contributions, they harmonize only slowly with other donors, and align even more timidly with the national M&E systems they rightly consider weak. At the same time, however, the adherence of donors to such parallel structures considerably burdens national systems.

International pressure for harmonization and alignment has moved these topics up the agenda: the 2003 Harmonization and Alignment (H&A)

Conference in Rome; the 2002, 2004, and 2007 Roundtables on Managing for Development Results, as well as the 2005 Paris Declaration on Aid Effectiveness and the 2008 Accra Agenda for Action testify to this.[3] With the importance of harmonization and alignment now generally acknowledged, it remains to be seen how donors will apply these principles to the monitoring and evaluation of their aid efforts. Alignment to embryonic, and in many respects dysfunctional, national M&E systems in low-income countries, believing that these will somehow rise to the occasion and live up to the complex demands set by programme-based approaches, may eventually be as counterproductive as by-passing these arrangements and keeping uncoordinated donor systems intact.

A key point argued in this chapter is that several of the weaknesses currently identified with programme-based approaches, such as the low quality of the annual progress reports produced by recipient countries, or the inconclusive reviews of national or sector programme-based approaches may, in fact, be traced back to M&E-related issues.[4] Section 10.5 will highlight how a more comprehensive understanding of M&E theory can contribute to explaining the observed weaknesses as well as offering possible solutions.[5] Moving beyond the false dichotomy between a principled handing over of M&E responsibilities to the recipient country without any comprehensive prior assessment of the capacity of national M&E systems to take on such tasks on the one hand, and a continuation of non-harmonized and non-aligned donor M&E practices on the other hand, section 10.5 proposes a pragmatic twin-track process approach to get out of the present deadlock. Balancing the need to align as much as possible to the recipient's M&E with the need to fill existing M&E gaps and satisfy accountability needs towards citizens both in donor and recipient countries, an approach is suggested that focuses on strengthening both the demand and supply sides of recipient M&E, combined with complementary donor-steered M&E.

10.2. The M&E reform agenda

Compared to traditional projects, programme-based approaches reduce the level of earmarking and intentionally blend donor resources with those of the

[3] See <http://www.oecd.org/dac/effectiveness>.

[4] This is, for example, acknowledged in the IMF-WB 2005 PRSP evaluation study that stresses the need for making M&E a central issue in PRSP as this may lead to more action-oriented PRSP.

[5] This is particularly true if you adopt an expanded definition of M&E. Boyle, Lemaire, and Rist (1999: 4–5) refer in this respect to Rist (1990: 4–5), who notes that 'the development of programme evaluation, both in terms of its methodologies as well as the kinds of questions it could address, has resulted in a clear expansion of what comes under its umbrella.... But the most recent thinking suggests that programme evaluation can encompass the various stages of life-cycles of a programme or policy—from conception through execution through impact'.

recipient. This gives recipients more responsibility, both in priorities setting and in implementation of policies, while donors, through process conditionalities, foster a more credible national planning–budgeting–implementation cycle. Donors no longer believe in the top–down, blueprint planning that was practised with their blessing in the 1960s and 1970s in aid-recipient countries. Instead, they now favour a policy cycle that relies on continuous feedback through the systematic monitoring and evaluating of progress in the field. What donors have in mind is thus a policy cycle whereby diagnosis, priority and strategy selection, resource allocation and budgeting, implementation, and monitoring and evaluation are all logically linked.

Donors have also their own accountability needs in mind. They are aware that the final results that it is hoped will validate their trust in recipient governments can only be gauged through proper evaluation, and that much of the data for this can only be provided by recipients. Also, in circumstances where resources are pooled with those of other donors and with national fiscal receipts prior to spending, attribution of impact becomes a major headache. The identification of a counterfactual (without-intervention) scenario becomes problematic and the attribution of results to one single actor next to impossible. Techniques of rigorous impact evaluation, in particular experimental design and quasi-experimental designs (see Rossi, Freeman, and Lipsey 2004) that are currently regaining popularity (Center for Global Development 2006), are most readily applicable to clearly demarcated interventions. The few evaluations of the impact of new aid modalities (see IDD 2006; Wood et al. 2008) that have been undertaken so far have mainly used a type of 'contribution' analysis (see Mayne 1999).[6] Attributing results to individual donors in common pool approaches, however, is impossible. Elbers, Gunning, and de Hoop (2007: 13) propose to attribute the effects of those interventions to donors in proportion of their contribution made. But, even to be able to draw such conclusions, a well-functioning national M&E system is needed. If such a system is to be useful for the recipient country, it must devote considerable attention to the twin functions of learning lessons (feedback) and accounting for results. That is why M&E must be high on both donors' and recipients' list of priorities.

One of the principles of the new aid approach is to shift attention away from inputs to results (defined in terms of outcomes and impact) and to the link between the two. If resource allocation and planning are to be increasingly dictated by previous results, then one needs information about results and how they derive from, or fail to derive from, inputs. Results-based management (RBM) thus generates a demand for M&E. In order to ensure the reliability of

---

[6] These studies commonly use logic charts setting out a set of hypotheses about how budget support and the Paris Declaration are meant to work, as well as judgemental approaches, 'shadow' controls (see Rossi, Freeman, and Lipsey 2004) and comparable country case studies based on a triangulation of qualitative and quantitative methods.

data and their analysis, M&E services must be sufficiently autonomous from those that are responsible for implementation.

The PRSP which has been embedded in the new aid approach also fosters participation of a broad range of stakeholders at the macro level. The idea is that non-state actors, and in particular those that directly represent beneficiaries and users of public services, can help to ensure accountability of government towards its citizens with the ultimate aim of improving policy effectiveness and impact. They are expected to play key roles in producing 'independent' assessments of the implementation and impact of service delivery and policy processes. Local organizations and other grassroots associations are in principle well placed to channel and represent the voices of the beneficiaries, and to supply information for the M&E system. The implicit assumption is that such civil society actors are sufficiently 'representative' and sufficiently close to the poor to act on their behalf, and that there is sufficient political space for them to act as watchdogs of the government. These non-state actors will exert pressure for better and timely information, and strengthen the demand side of M&E.

While the majority of aid still goes through traditional channels, the absolute and relative importance of 'new' aid modalities from budget support to programme aid in the context of SWAPs would seem to be on the increase.[7] In practice, the reform agenda, including the one around M&E, has been shaped through various international conferences and related documents, such as the 2002 (Washington), 2004 (Marrakech), and 2007 (Hanoi) International Roundtable on Managing for Development Results; the 2003 (Rome), 2005 (Paris), and 2008 (Accra) High-Level Forum on Aid Effectiveness.[8] To sum up, and using the phrasing of the 2005 Paris Declaration, the expectations are that

partner countries endeavour to establish results-oriented reporting and assessment frameworks that monitor progress against key dimensions of the national and sector development strategies and that these frameworks should track a manageable number of indicators for which data are cost-effectively available (indicator 11). (Paris Declaration: 8)

---

[7] It should be noted that the OECD-DAC statistical tables do not provide accurate estimates of the new aid modalities. The problem is not so much with budget support as with programme-based approaches at a lower level, such as for instance common baskets. There are a number of other sources which, however, only provide partial data for particular samples of countries. The Joint Evaluation of Budget Support, for example, includes detailed country-level data on general budget support for seven countries. There is a significant increase of general budget support over the period 2000–4 for all countries included while the importance of GBS strongly differs among countries (ranging from 8 per cent of total ODA in Vietnam to 31 per cent of total ODA in Uganda) (IDD 2006: 21). Comparing results of the 2004 and 2005 SPA Surveys of Budget Support shows an increase of GBS as a proportion of total aid from 25.7 per cent to 27.8 per cent for (the slightly different) sample set of recipients included in both survey rounds (SPA-6 Budget Support Working Group 2006).

[8] See <http://www.oecd.org/dac/effectiveness>.

Additionally, partner countries should 'reinforce participatory approaches by systematically involving a broad range of development partners when formulating and assessing progress in implementing national development strategies' (ibid.: 9). It is expected that donors 'work with partner countries to rely, as far as possible, on partner countries' results-oriented reporting and monitoring frameworks' and that they

harmonize their monitoring and reporting requirements, and, until they can rely more extensively on partner countries' statistical, monitoring and evaluation systems, [work] with partner countries to the maximum extent possible on joint formats for periodic reporting. (ibid.: 8)

From both partners it is expected that they 'work together in a participatory approach to strengthen country capacities and demand for results based management' (ibid.: 8).

The Development Assistance Committee (DAC) has also broken down its detailed guidelines for donors with respect to reporting and monitoring along five guiding principles: relying and building on country systems; co-ordinating reporting and monitoring systems; simplifying reporting and monitoring systems; making information more transparent; and rationalizing review missions (OECD-DAC 2003).

10.3. Limited and unequal progress on the recipient side

If the M&E reform agenda is so crucial for the success and sustainability of the new aid paradigm, what can we learn from the actual practice in recipient countries? The analysis in this section draws on a review of academic literature and practitioners' documents[9] as well the authors' mid-2004 desk study assessing the quality of recipient M&E systems in eleven sub-Saharan Africa countries, complemented by fieldwork in selected countries.[10] In general,

---

[9] See, among others, McGee and Norton (2000); Evans and Ngalwea (2001); Hauge (2001, 2003); Prennushi, Rubio, and Subbarao (2001); Booth and Lucas (2002); Evans and van Diesen (2002); Robb (2002); IMF-IDA (2003); World Bank (2003a, 2003b, 2004, 2005, 2007); IMF (2004); GTZ/BMZ (2004); Lucas, et al. (2004); IMF-World Bank (2005); Bedi et al. (2006).

[10] The desk study assesses the quality of PRSP M&E systems in eleven SSA countries: Burkina Faso, Ethiopia, Ghana, Malawi, Mali, Mauritania, Mozambique, Niger, Tanzania, Uganda, and Zambia. The elaborated assessment framework (in the Appendix) captures issues of policy, methodology, organization, capacity, participation, and quality. See Holvoet and Renard (2005, 2007) for a more detailed discussion of the methodology and findings. We would like to stress that the results of the analysis in this section hold only for low-income recipient countries, and in particular for the eleven SSA countries of our own desk study. While some of the weaknesses (such as the defective linkage among M&E, budgeting, and policy-making) indicated in the analysis also hold for middle- (and even high-) income countries, M&E systems of the latter are in many cases much more advanced. See, for instance, May et al. (2006) for an overview of M&E systems in Chile, Colombia, Mexico, Brazil, and Peru as well as several

what is striking is the relative lack of attention to M&E issues, both in country-produced PRSP documents and in donor documents such as the joint staff assessments (JSAs)[11] made by International Monetary Fund (IMF) and World Bank staff in the early years of the new century.

Surveys and independent reviews generally confirm that progress towards results-orientation, and particularly a reinforced M&E, has been disappointing. The World Bank's 2004 PRSP evaluation study includes the results of a survey among almost 800 stakeholders in ten PRSP countries which reveals that out of thirty-nine questions the one on M&E received the most negative response (World Bank 2004: 66). In fact, to the question 'An effective structure to monitor and evaluate results has been established', 41 per cent of the respondents 'disagreed', or 'disagreed completely', whereas a further 21 per cent answered 'don't know or unsure'. The 2006 and 2008 surveys on the implementation of the Paris Declaration show that only two out of twenty-nine and three of the fifty-four countries surveyed, respectively, had results-oriented frameworks that were deemed adequate (that is, results for indicator 11; see OECD-DAC 2007: 35, 2008: 58–9).

In what follows we structure our discussion of recipient systems along the following headings: policy, institutional, and organizational issues; methodology; participation of non-state actors; and quality and capacity.

10.3.1. Policy, institutional, and organizational issues

Independent reviews[12] underscore that there is a very fragmentary approach towards M&E, and that the focus is overwhelmingly on technical and methodological issues, to the detriment of the overall policy and the institutional and organizational set-up. Of the eleven countries reviewed in Holvoet and Renard 2005, most had some elements of an M&E plan, heavily skewed towards data-collection issues, but hardly any of the countries provided information about the overarching institutional structure or had a comprehensive 'grand design' for its improvement.

One of the weaknesses in the M&E policy and design of recipient countries is the 'conflation' of monitoring and evaluation. The fact that they are often

country studies on the website of the Evaluation Capacity Development group within the Independent Evaluation Group (see <http://www.worldbank.org/ieg/>).

[11] JSAs are prepared by IMF and World Bank staff members and are submitted together with a country's PRSP to the Board of Directors. Initially, the JSAs had both a feedback and a signalling function: it highlighted the strengths and weaknesses of a country's PRSP and how it might be improved while it also indicated whether the PRSP was a sound basis for concessional assistance from the World Bank and the IMF. Since late 2004 the signalling function has been dropped and JSAs have been renamed joint staff advisory notes. For more information on JSAs, see ODI (2004).

[12] See nn. 8 and 9 above.

referred to as twin concepts is fine, but not when the two functions are confused, or one is subsumed within the other. Frequently the impression given is that monitoring somehow also constitutes evaluation. Evaluation, if mentioned as a separate issue at all, seems almost an afterthought. It is of course true that, in iterative planning, monitoring is of the utmost importance, and it may be justified to devote more energy to it than to evaluation, but there remains a persistent need for the latter. One of the consequences of this leaning towards monitoring at the expense of evaluation is that the focus is much more on pure stocktaking of performance ('were the targets met?') than on probing into the underlying reasons for eventual inadequate performance ('why were the targets not met?') or on questioning the relevance and usefulness of some of the targets themselves and/or of specific interventions designed to arrive at them.

Particularly neglected is the role that 'programme theory evaluation' or 'theory-based evaluation' could play in the numerous cases where the causal chain behind an intervention is not made explicit in the strategic and planning documents. To identify the causes for either success or failure, it is helpful to extract the underlying programme theory on the basis of relevant stakeholders' views, and to differentiate between explanatory factors in implementation and in underlying programme theory (on this, see, for example, Kusek and Rist 2004; Rossi, Freeman, and Lipsey 2004). Given that the role of evaluation theory is played down, it comes as no surprise that annual progress and sector progress reports, the most important donor-targeted outputs of national and sector M&E systems, are often analytically weak. Donors may well have some responsibility in this neglect of evaluation. They are generally more concerned with performance management and input monitoring than with higher-order policy-relevant questions.[13]

The neglect of evaluation also implies that there is hardly any attention given to the linkages between monitoring and evaluation. The use of Poverty and Social Impact Analysis (PSIA)[14] is illustrative. While the increasing popularity of PSIA is a sign of interest in evaluation, it is usually conceived outside the national M&E system and mostly performed by donors with limited participation of national stakeholders. Information from national monitoring does not seem to feed into PSIA, neither are there guarantees that information from PSIA feeds into policy-making.

---

[13] This view is strongly endorsed in the 2002 World Bank Annual Report on Evaluation Capacity Development: 'PRSPs and Bank/Fund JSAs often use the term M&E as shorthand for financial tracking and national development indicators. And the recent Bank/Fund review of the PRSP approach also interpreted M&E as being synonymous with monitoring' (World Bank 2002: 20).

[14] A Poverty and Social Impact Analysis (PSIA) refers to the analysis of the distributional impact of policy reforms on the well-being or welfare of different stakeholder groups, with a particular focus on the poor and vulnerable (World Bank 2003c).

Somewhat related to this is the absence of a thorough discussion in national M&E plans of the different functions of M&E, and the possible trade-offs among them. In fact, it is difficult to find indications of how M&E will fulfil both its basic but potentially conflicting functions of accountability and learning and how the related principles of impartiality, independence, and utility will be guaranteed. Institutional arrangements do not seem to reflect the need to keep a balance between such functions and needs. For instance, it is quite difficult to get a clear perception of how independent M&E units, at either national or sector levels, are from senior management and government ministers. Admittedly, learning from M&E findings and integrating results into management and policy call for close linkages between evaluators and policymakers, and by the same token militates against too much independence of M&E. But, on the other hand, sufficient independence of evaluators is crucial for them to perform their accountability function credibly. What is worrisome is that such trade-offs are not addressed. Issues of independence and credibility of M&E are sensitive issues in countries that are in the process of building up a culture of transparency in public affairs. Independent M&E may disclose not only positive news, but also negative findings and in particular unveil politically sensitive information about mismanagement and rent-seeking, not to mention outright corruption, by the political elite (Palumbo 1987); Center for Global Development 2006.

Most of the documents also remain vague about the location of the oversight function in M&E. In eight of the eleven countries included in our desk study there was no well-established, clear structure for coordination, support, oversight, or feedback (Holvoet and Renard 2005). This is in line with the finding from the 2005 and 2007 Comprehensive Development Framework evaluations that the establishment of 'coordinated' M&E systems proves difficult even in countries where there is substantial improvement in sub-components such as statistical data capacity (World Bank 2005, 2007). While this may not be surprising, as control over M&E conveys power over resources and other agencies,[15] the need for coordination and oversight cannot be in doubt.

What is also striking is the lack of clarity about roles and responsibilities of the actors involved in data collection, analysis, and feedback, in particular statistical agencies, line ministries, decentralized levels of government and central ministries responsible for planning and finance (on this see, for example, Bedi et al. 2006). In most countries, sector-monitoring systems existed before the PRSP, and in a lot of cases they have been strengthened in the context of SWAPs. While one could logically conceive these sector systems as important

---

[15] In an earlier case study on national M&E systems in South Asia, Bamberger (1991) noted that because of severe competition among various central ministries over the control of M&E, no institutional arrangement remained in place for longer than three years. The major reason for the constant changes was the fact that the agencies in charge of M&E were perceived as far too powerful and threatening.

pillars of a national coordinated M&E system, obscurity surrounding roles and responsibilities, and the absence of even rudimentary coordination and alignment mechanisms lead to institutional competition and to dysfunction. In fact, one may consider the balance between independence and quality of sector and decentralized programmes and M&E on the one hand, and their degree of integration with the national level on the other, crucial issues for the sustainability of the new aid approach. Results-based management and budgeting require a minimal degree of horizontal and vertical integration. This involves line ministries and decentralized levels that supply central ministries with the necessary information on intermediate and final outcomes, and central ministries that provide line ministries and decentralized levels with realistic projections on future budgets. At the same time, however, too much focus on integration and centralization may put undue stress on sector and decentralized M&E systems if it means that they are forced to emphasize functions of accountability and feedback towards the central level to the detriment of feedback and management at sector and decentralized levels themselves (see also Valadez and Bamberger 1994: 403–42).

10.3.2. Methodology

Methodological issues tend to be addressed, sometimes in considerable detail, in PRSPs, annual progress reports (APRs), and independent reviews. This is particularly the case with targets and indicators. Even more encouragingly, in countries that already produced more than one APR, lists get more refined from progress report to progress report. The new aid approach in general, and PRSP in particular, has led to an upsurge in data collection, especially on poverty, and to a renewed interest in household surveys. The growing attention to qualitative, difficult-to-measure issues has also given a new impetus to methodological approaches seeking to combine qualitative and quantitative methodologies, while participatory techniques are increasingly propagated to make the conclusions more informed by the poor.

There is, however, a caveat. Booth and Lucas (2002) make the important point that there is a strong tendency, in setting indicators and targets, to emphasize the two extremes of the logic chain, inputs and final poverty outcomes, leaving a 'missing middle' in between. This indicates the absence of an underlying programme theory. The fact that different levels of indicators mentioned in PRSP or sector programmes are often not integrated into one causal chain illustrates the same flaw. Programme theory or logic models, with an embedded process and impact theory, are powerful tools in conceptualizing interventions, monitoring, and evaluation. Not surprisingly, if no prior theory can be referred to that makes clear which actions were expected to produce which results and why, it becomes extremely difficult at the time of reporting to make much sense of the findings generated (see also GTZ-BMZ 2004).

10.3.3. Participation of non-state actors

The overall impression from independent reviews (see, for example, McGee and Norton 2000; McGee, Levene, and Hughes 2002; Robb 2002); World Bank 2003b is that in many countries civil society organizations (CSOs) have been involved in participatory poverty assessments at the moment of preparing PRSPs, but much less during subsequent phases of implementation, monitoring, and evaluation. Generally, participation of CSOs is conceived of as instrumental, as a way of gathering data and insights, but within a process that is strongly government controlled. There is not much discussion in PRSPs about the role that CSOs could play as an independent source of supply of M&E, nor about their capacity as actors on the M&E demand side, and this despite the participation rhetoric of the new aid paradigm. This holds even more for other actors outside the executive branch of government, such as parliament, the auditor general's office, universities, independent research institutes, or national evaluation societies. While the importance of an independent general auditor's office is often stressed with respect to financial auditing, the role this office could play in performance auditing goes largely unnoticed. A similar observation can be made with respect to universities and research institutes that can contribute high-quality data collection and analysis. Some limited progress is being made, but, ominously, the authors came across several cases where genuinely independent non-state actors that got invited upon donor suggestion to play a role in M&E paid for it by having their autonomy curtailed by a distrustful government.

10.3.4. Quality and capacity

A good way to test for quality is to assess the annual progress and performance reports shared with donors, arguably the most tangible outputs of the national M&E systems. The quality of APRs, particularly in terms of analytical depth, is one of the issues donors worry about. APRs do manage to fill in some of the gaps in baseline data that existed at the time the PRSP was first produced, and, in some cases, register changes in actual performance with baseline data, but only in exceptional cases is there an analysis of the reasons for non-achievement. While donors seem to have been taken by surprise by the sometimes poor quality of APRs, even a superficial prior diagnosis should have alerted them to the problems that presaged such poor reporting: absence of programme theory, strong focus on monitoring to the detriment of evaluation, vaguely defined overall M&E design, and unclear coordination among different actors of the system. Unpromisingly, current assessments of M&E capacity constraints and remedial action plans, both by recipient countries and donors, overwhelmingly focus on human and financial resources and technical issues, to the detriment of the broader institutional and policy-related issues.

10.4. Limited progress in implementing the donor-reform agenda

The hugely expanded role of recipient M&E systems under the new aid approach, even if insufficiently acknowledged in PRSP documents and the literature, is plain to see to anyone taking a closer look at the literature on new aid modalities. The future role for donors in M&E is, however, less clearly articulated, and some sensitive issues are not being addressed as frankly as their importance would warrant.

Notwithstanding the fact that donors are setting the agenda for many M&E reforms taking place in the public sector of aid-dependent countries, PRSPs and APRs are fairly silent on the precise role donors are supposed to play. Similarly, even if donors probably spend more resources and energy in parallel M&E exercises than the government is able or willing to spend on national M&E, little reference is made to how such donor M&E outputs feed into the national effort.

There is thus an issue of ownership, or rather, lack of ownership, surrounding M&E. Donors clearly see reform in this area as an important corollary to their reduced micro-management of aid resources, and they do not hesitate to impose process conditionalities to this effect, even if sometimes in a haphazard fashion. At the same time, some donors are obviously uncomfortable with abandoning their own parallel M&E activities. Recipient governments on the other hand sometimes lack a serious commitment to reform their M&E systems. They do what is expected of them, reluctantly, but they are seldom proactive, and do not correct for donor biases. For instance, donors' emphasis on monitoring inputs (public finance management (PFM))[16] combined with a focus on monitoring final poverty outcomes in the forms of Millennium Development Goals (MDGs), as well as their general preference for data collection and quality,[17] are all echoed in the particular pace and scope of recipient M&E systems reform.[18]

---

[16] This is evident from the diagnostic 'bombardment' recipients suffered in the area of public finance management and which led to the public expenditure and financial accountability (PEFA) initiative (see on this, SPA-6 Budget Support Working Group 2004).

[17] To assess statistical capacity and engage in capacity-building, several (diagnostic) frameworks exist. Bedi et al. (2006) describe the data-quality assessment framework (DOAF), the general data dissemination system (GDDS), and the statistical capacity-building indicators (SCBI). The World Bank Country Statistical Information Database contains information for 143 developing countries on some of the above-mentioned indicators and frameworks <http://worldbank.org/data/countrydata/aboutcsidb.html and IMF-WB 2005>.

[18] Systems are mostly focusing on inputs and compliance issues and are only gradually moving towards measuring outputs (Wood et al. 2008: 22). In its assessment of the actual state of M&E recipients' systems on the ground, the 2005 CDF evaluation contrasts improvements in sub-components as statistical data capacity with those in developing 'coordinated' monitoring systems (World Bank 2005).

The 2006 and 2008 Paris Declaration Surveys report that harmonization in the context of donor missions was 18 per cent and 21 per cent and for country analytical work 42 per cent and 44 per cent respectively (OECD-DAC 2007: 33–4, 2008: 54–5). Both indicators have an indirect bearing on our topic, as a considerable part of donor missions and analytical work relate to M&E issues. Similarly, donor alignment to country systems for PFM and procurement has only increased somewhat (that is, from 40 per cent and 39 per cent in 2005 to 45 per cent and 43 per cent in 2007 respectively) (OECD-DAC 2008: 20). As far as direct alignment to national M&E systems is concerned, the OECD-DAC harmonization and alignment survey (2005b) reported that by the end of 2004 about 28 per cent of donor project portfolios were monitored and evaluated through recipients' M&E systems (OECD-DAC 2005b). Interestingly, surveys such as the Strategic Partnership with Africa (SPA) Budget Support Surveys and the 2008 Evaluation of the Implementation of the Paris Declaration reveal important differences among individual donors and in donor assessments of different partner countries. Similar differences among donors may be observed when it comes to engagement in new aid modalities (SPA-6 Budget Support Working Group 2006: 43; Wood et al. 2008).

For their accountability needs towards their own constituencies, budget-support donors are increasingly dependent on APRs or comparable reports produced by recipient M&E systems. Donors accept the fact that this exposes them to some risk. It is an act of good donorship on their part to give national systems time to develop, and to base their assessment more on the progress being made than on the objective quality of present monitoring and evaluation outputs. The same budget-support donors are, for obvious reasons, the most influential in setting the process conditionalities for national M&E reform. Even so, after several annual rounds of APRs, the analytical quality often remains low. The 2005 SPA Budget Support Alignment Survey (p. 51), for instance, indicated that 71 per cent of the budget-support donors considered APRs unsatisfactory for their own reporting (accountability) needs.

Clearly, donor and recipient reform agendas are not independent of each other and the donors, as drivers of the reforms, are caught in a 'chicken and egg' dilemma. A low national M&E capacity puts progressive donors that engage in budget support at risk of not being able to satisfy their own accountability needs, and gives more traditional donors an excuse for not embracing the new aid approach. The reluctance of both types of donors to abandon parallel M&E systems is a part of the problem in that it draws policy attention and resources away from the institutional strengthening of recipient systems. So far, no satisfactory solution has been formulated that takes into account the differentiated donor attitudes towards the new approach to aid.

All this raises the question whether harmonization and alignment should be pushed as far in the field of M&E as in other fields. Handing over responsibility for the use of aid resources to the recipient, provided that a number of prior conditions are met and provided that certain process conditionalities are respected, is an approach that is difficult to fault in theory. Handing over the responsibility for providing the data and analysis that justify the use of the same resources to the same recipient is much less evident, and even seems to violate the principle of independence. The question is whether recipient governments have sufficient institutional incentives to establish a transparent, competent, and independent M&E system. The new aid discourse is fairly optimistic in this respect. However, if one accepts that donors and recipient governments do not have identical agendas and interests, and that the pressures for downward accountability are weak and not very effective in many aid-dependent countries and may well remain so for some time to come,[19] donors may have no other option but to take the initiative and organize strong and independent monitoring and evaluation of their aid resources as long as national M&E arrangements are weak.

10.5. Which way forward?

10.5.1. An M&E reform that is too ambitious?

The new approach to aid aims for institutional reforms that will take considerable time to yield visible results. This creates genuine problems for donors whose time horizons, or more precisely, those of their constituents, are much shorter. Confronted with the tension between the harmonization and alignment agenda they have endorsed, and the need to account to their own parliament, public opinion, or executive boards, donor reactions do not always find the right middle ground. The prevalent attitude, widely observed among both traditional and progressive donors, is to stick to parallel donor M&E system while trying to strengthen national systems more (progressive donors) or less (traditional donors) vigorously (see Wood et al. 2008). Curiously, the donor discourse is not very helpful in setting good principles. An extreme attitude, unlikely to materialize in the current climate, but in line with a strict reading of the new aid discourse, would be for donors to become excessively lenient in assessing recipients and to see something that is in fact not there: a decent recipient M&E system in the making, just about to perform the functions of feedback and accountability in an adequate fashion and starting to live up to minimum international standards so as also to fulfil the accountability needs of donors. Donors, in their zeal to be on the side of harmonization and alignment and wanting to 'give recipient M&E a fair try' might then argue that

---

[19] As Booth (2005: 5) points out: 'The easy notion that donors only have to back off from demanding accountability for aid funds in order for domestic accountability to flower in its place is unrealistic and unhistorical.'

they themselves should not be assessed on final results on the ground—which are mainly the responsibility of the recipient anyway—but rather on the basis of their 'organizational effectiveness'. While there is not yet a standardized definition for 'organizational effectiveness', some agencies have made efforts to render the concept more concrete (see, for example, Lehtinen 2002). Suggestions include looking at internal policies, strategies, processes, relations to partners, resource use, and adaptive capability. Taken to its extreme, this would suggest that a 'donor's accountability towards its own constituencies' could be mainly defined in terms of a realization of the 'harmonization and alignment' agenda, in particular to support the recipient country in taking over this accountability task. In such a hypothetical world, donors might of course continue to sponsor multi-country comprehensive impact evaluations such as the one undertaken on general budget support (IDD 2006).

So far, however, there is insufficient evidence to believe that just more harmonization and alignment will produce the sought-after beneficial effects in terms of poverty reduction (see, for example, Bigsten 2006). Until there is better evidence about the underlying explicit and implicit assumptions of the new aid approach, donors are correct to err on the conservative side. So, what sound advice may be provided to help donors steer a course between a radical but naive reading of the new aid discourse whereby they abandon responsibility for M&E and the other extreme of stubbornly sticking to ineffective donor-driven M&E? It is important that donors address the reform agenda squarely, and that they do so in a concerted manner, but they should also accept that in the matter of M&E there can be too much alignment. There are too many failings in national M&E that will not go away by putting the government in charge and by occasional methodological and technical assistance, or by haphazard process conditionalities that fail to address the fundamental weaknesses.

10.5.2. Seeking the middle ground

In what follows, a pragmatic process approach is proposed that seeks a middle position between over-alignment with a recipient's M&E system on the one hand and a multitude of donor-driven parallel systems that ignore the need for institutional strengthening of national systems on the other.

The approach proposed here starts from the basic preoccupation of the new aid approach: that the institutional capacity of low-income recipient countries, and in particular their M&E systems, has been undermined by uncoordinated and parallel donor-imposed rules and arrangements. Reinforcing the recipient 'systems' by working through them—irrespective of their actual state of development—is arguably the best way forward. However, given the present weaknesses on several fronts, including deep-rooted policy and institutional aspects, it is unrealistic and naive to surmise that a combination of spontaneous dynamics from within and appropriate process conditionalities from outside will be enough to generate these improvements within a reasonable timeframe (see also Booth 2005). Donors, in other words, cannot escape their responsibility for closely supervising national data generation and analysis. A dual-track process approach emphasizing the effective building and strengthening of both supply and demand sides of recipient M&E systems through co-ordinated and holistic diagnosis, capacity-building, independent follow-up, and process conditionality, coupled with complementary donor-managed M&E that, instead of duplicating national efforts, strives at bridging existing gaps in the national M&E system, seems the only way forward.

One can imagine complementary M&E that is driven by external actors such as independent evaluation departments or public auditing offices from donor countries, and that excludes those departments within donor agencies, that are too closely involved, from the M&E tasks which would require independent assessment. Complementary M&E should be conceived and implemented so as simultaneously to serve donor and recipient M&E needs and contribute to capacity-building of national M&E demand-side and/or supply-side actors. Stakeholders on the demand or supply sides should be involved to the maximum degree possible.

10.5.3. Focus on the recipient's system: diagnosis and capacity-building

A good starting-point is a diagnosis of the actual state of a recipient's M&E supply and demand. This diagnosis, identifying strengths and weaknesses, should preferably be done by a team consisting of independent M&E experts and representatives of all stakeholders involved, including donors, government, and non-government actors. It serves multiple purposes:

(i) it guides donors in applying the Addis Ababa principle[20] by assessing the degree to which a recipient's M&E system can satisfy their own accountability needs and determine what complementary M&E if any is needed (see track 2);

(ii) it lays the basis for a coherent approach to capacity-building; and

(iii) it forms the basis for realistic targets to strengthen individual M&E demand and supply components, and for periodic independent assessments within a framework of process conditionality.

---

[20] The Addis Ababa principle favours the use of government systems whenever possible. The principle reads as follows: 'all donor assistance should be delivered through government systems unless there are compelling reasons to the contrary; where this is not possible, any alternative mechanisms or safeguards must be time-limited, and develop and build, rather than undermine or bypass, government systems' (SPA 2001: 2).

In order to avoid parallel donor diagnostic 'bombardments', a multiple stake-holder coordinated approach, similar to the Public Expenditure and Financial Accountability (PEFA) initiative,[21] should be favoured. It is worth emphasizing the obvious: a shared diagnosis need not necessarily trigger identical donor responses. The degree to which a recipient's M&E will be considered satisfactory, for instance, will depend not only on its intrinsic quality, but also on the donor's accountability needs, which in turn depend on the accountability approach adopted in different donor country or agency settings (see, for example, Wood et al. 2008). This has implications for the degree and form of complementary M&E different donors will find necessary and appropriate. Different donors need not set identical targets, as long as targets are not contradictory.

The choice of an appropriate diagnostic instrument will be no easy task. At the moment, donors do not really use diagnostic instruments that pass the test. Most still adopt a fairly narrow approach towards M&E, characterized by a focus on the supply side, in particular on technical and methodological issues, and not even the most crucial ones. Existing diagnostic tools and related capacity-building concentrate on input monitoring (PFM)—most donors would not even classify these as being an integral part of the M&E system—and statistical data quality, particularly outcome data related to the MDGs. Recipient-government accountability towards donors has traditionally been defined in terms of input management (Bamberger 1989, 2000; World Bank 2002); Picciotto 2003. Driven by pressures of results-based management[22] and the MDGs, a layer of 'outcome' accountability has been added on top. This focus on the two extremes of the causal chain has certainly not been inspired by evaluation theory, which almost unanimously emphasizes the importance of programme theory and identification of the full causal chain.

Donor diagnostics further tend to neglect policy and institutional M&E issues, and, by playing down the principle of independence, in particular tend to overlook the M&E demand side. Clearly, a more holistic approach towards M&E necessitates a holistic diagnostic instrument. Whereas there are no tailor-made instruments in current use, there are some interesting donor-led and independent assessments and studies that might provide some inspiration for the elaboration of such a diagnostic instrument. Available tools that might feed into the elaboration of a more holistic M&E diagnostic instrument include:

- The diagnostic tool for designing or reviewing a PRS monitoring system elaborated in Bedi et al. (2006).

---

[21] The PEFA programme aims at strengthening recipient and donor ability to (i) diagnose the quality of country public expenditure, procurement, and financial accountability systems; and to (ii) develop a practical sequence of reform and capacity-building actions. See <http://www.pefa.org> for more information.

[22] See White (2002) for a criticism on results-based management.

- The readiness assessment elaborated by Kusek and Rist (2002) and the highly similar ECD diagnostic guide and action framework (see Mackay 1999).
- The checklist used for the diagnosis of PRSP M&E of five French-speaking SSA countries by the order of the Canadian International Development Agency (Lavergne and Alba 2003).
- The checklist used by Booth and Lucas (2002) in their diagnosis of PRSP M&E in twenty-one countries.
- The checklist used for the diagnosis of PRSP M&E in eight SSA countries by ODI's (2003) PRSP Monitoring and Synthesis Project.
- The checklist used by Holvoet and Renard (2005) in their diagnosis of PRSP M&E of eleven SSA countries (see Table 10.1).

Table 10.1. Checklist used by Holvoet and Renard (2005, 2007) in their diagnosis of PRSP M&E in eleven SSA countries

Topics	Questions
I. Policy	
1 The evaluation plan	Is there a comprehensive evaluation plan, indicating what to evaluate, why, how, for whom?
2 M versus E	Are the differences and the relationship between M and E clearly spelled out?
3 Autonomy and impartiality (accountability)	Is the need for autonomy and impartiality explicitly mentioned? Does the M&E plan allow for tough issues to be analysed? Is there an independent budget?
4 Feedback	Is there an explicit and consistent approach to reporting, dissemination, and integration?
5 Alignment planning & budgeting	Is there integration of M&E results in planning and budgeting?
II. Methodology	
6 Selection of indicators	Is it clear what to monitor and evaluate? Is there a list of indicators?
7 Selection criteria	Are the criteria for the selection of indicators clear? And who selects?
8 Priority setting	Is the need to set priorities and limit the number of indicators to be monitored acknowledged?
9 Causality chain	Are different levels of indicators (input–output–outcome–impact) explicitly linked (programme theory)? (vertical logic)
10 Methodologies used	Is it clear how to monitor and evaluate? Are methodologies well identified and mutually integrated?
11 Data collection	Are sources of data collection clearly identified? Are indicators linked to sources of data collection? (horizontal logic)
III. Organization	
12 Coordination and oversight	Is there an appropriate institutional structure for coordination, support, central oversight, and feedback? With different stakeholders?
13 Statistical office	Are surveys, censuses, etc. streamlined into M&E needs? Is the role of the statistical office in M&E clear?
14 Line ministries	Are there M&E units in line ministries and semi-governmental institutions (parastatals), and are these properly relayed to central unit?

(continued)

Table 10.1. Continued

Topics	Questions
15 Decentralized levels	Are there M&E units at decentralized levels and are these properly relayed to central unit?
16 Link with projects	Is there any effort to relay with/coordinate with donor M&E mechanisms for projects?
IV. Capacity	
17 Problem acknowledged	Are current weaknesses in the system identified?
18 Capacity-building plan	Are there plans for remediation? Do these include training, appropriate salaries, etc.
V. Participation of actors outside government	
19 Parliament	Is the role of parliament properly recognized, and is there alignment with parliamentary control and oversight procedures?
20 Civil society	Is the role of civil society recognized? Are there clear procedures for the participation of civil society? Is the participation institutionally arranged or rather ad hoc?
21 Donors	Is the role of donors recognized? Are there clear procedures for participation of donors?
VI. Quality	
22 Effective use of M&E in APR	Is there a presentation of relevant M&E results? Are results compared to targets? Is there an analysis of discrepancies?
23 Internal usage of APR	Is the APR also used for internal purposes? Is it an instrument of national policy-making and/or policy-influencing and advocacy?

Note: Checklist used by Holvoet and Renard (2005, 2007) in their diagnosis of PRSP M&E in eleven SSA countries.
Source: See text.

10.5.4. Complementary donor-instigated M&E

Donors that try to put the harmonization and alignment principles into practice often engage in additional M&E exercises, with diverging degrees of coordination among themselves and/or with recipient systems. Rather than regarding these as temporary aberrations on the road to true alignment, they could be looked upon as interesting experiments from which lessons can be learnt for the second tier of a proposed twin-track approach. Some performance assessment frameworks (with varying degrees of alignment to the PRSP, APR, and policy matrix), (joint) sector reviews, and even some isolated donor M&E of programmes illustrate the road ahead. What is crucial is that such complementary M&E be well coordinated, tailored to the results of the diagnostic assessment of the recipient M&E, and adaptive to the changing quality of the latter. Different donors, confronted with different accountability needs imposed by their own constituencies, may engage in such complementary M&E to varying degrees. What is important is that there is proper coordination among donors and with the recipient M&E system. This starts with appropriate information sharing, but it can go much further.

These complementary M&E exercises should go beyond delivering particular products that satisfy immediate M&E needs. By involving national M&E supply- and demand-side actors where possible and appropriate, these exercises will function as learning-by-doing and capacity-building. The involvement of national actors also increases the probability that information generated from complementary M&E feeds into the recipient's M&E. Which actors should be involved in which kind of exercises depends upon the function—accountability or learning—being emphasized. Complementary M&E exercises currently performed suggest that donors do indeed involve national actors, without always respecting basic M&E principles. Joint-sector review (JSR) missions and related annual review meetings (ARMs), which may be conceived as periodic assessment exercises during implementation, are currently often used as complementary M&E to annual-sector progress reports. Positively, these missions are joint donor and heavily involve national stakeholders, including the implementing departments, central ministries (finance, planning), and, to a lesser extent, CSOs.

While not explicitly stated, the aim of the JSR and ARM is mostly twofold, at the same time serving an odd mixture of accountability and learning needs, involving a wide range of government and non-government actors. Some contributions to evaluation literature (see, for example, Lehtonen 2005) suggest that there might be ways to reconcile both functions. This will only be possible, however, if the trade-off need between both is well understood. It might be worth splitting JSRs into two separate exercises that explicitly address each of the functions. An evaluation of a government's performance, for example, will need to respect the principle of autonomy as much as possible. This implies the involvement of independent actors on the demand side, such as the auditor general's office, independent policy research institutes, evaluation associations, and independent CSOs. One could even argue that donors (or at least some departments in donor agencies) are themselves not independent enough to be involved in these accountability exercises.[23]

Additionally, accountability exercises demand careful preparation. In order to extrapolate findings from a limited sample, it is necessary to strengthen the external validity of the assessment by ensuring that the sample is sufficiently representative. On the other hand, learning necessitates zooming into and

---

[23] In one revealing interview, an auditor general confided that in his view donors did not really support him in his goal to undertake independent performance auditing, because they feared that what might come out would not please them.

analysing unexpected results, success stories, failures, or specific experiments, in the way services are delivered, for instance. Here external validity is obviously not such a major concern; on the contrary, internal validity should be optimized, so as to make credible conclusions about cause—effect linkages of the underlying programme theory. In order to ensure feedback for future policy-making and management, those responsible for policy and programme design and implementation need to be involved. The fact that the usefulness of these 'learning' exercises potentially extends beyond the particular programme, sector, or even country setting, while the costs of such 'impact evaluation' exercises are high, justifies considerable donor involvement, at least in terms of financial and technical inputs. In order to ensure that findings from such exercises are disseminated and used internationally, one might also think about joint donor responsibility in the elaboration of international databases and in doing prospective evaluation and meta-analysis summarizing what has been learned about a particular problem or policy, as well as what has not been learned and needs further research (see also Center for Global Development 2006).

Finally, there is a need for independent evaluation of the new aid paradigm itself, preferably led by independent (joint donor) evaluation departments, policy research institutes, or universities, so as to ensure the necessary independence and to lend credibility to the findings.[24] To increase feedback to national policies, it also makes good sense to involve representatives of different stakeholders. In order to be useful for future policymaking, such evaluation should distinguish between process and impact evaluation.[25] The former aims to assess whether all necessary ingredients that have been identified as necessary in the new aid paradigm have been implemented as foreseen and whether they are functioning as foreseen. Only when one is satisfied that the necessary ingredients of the new aid paradigm have been implemented is it possible to test the new aid paradigm itself and its underlying programme theory, by checking whether the predicted final outcomes for poverty reduction are being realized. Skipping the first essential phase of process evaluation mortgages any conclusion about the new aid paradigm.

---

[24] One of the most ambitious efforts aimed at assessing the new aid paradigm has been the recent Joint Evaluation of General Budget Support; see Chapter 11 of this volume by Michael Hubbard, as well as IDD 2006 for an overview of methodology and results. Another, more recent and ongoing, effort is the Evaluation of the Implementation of the Paris Declaration.

[25] This is exactly what is done in the Evaluation of the Implementation of the Paris Declaration which distinguishes among phase 1 (focus on actual implementation of the Paris Declaration, i.e., inputs and to the extent possible outputs) and phase 2 (focus on the contribution of the Paris Declaration to aid effectiveness and development results). For an overview of the methodology and results of phase 1, see Wood et al. (2008); results of phase 2 will be available by 2011.

10.6. Conclusion

The shift towards programme-based approaches requires that both donors and recipients review their M&E policies. Recipients are expected to expand and improve their presently embryonic M&E arrangements; donors are expected to harmonize and to wind down a major part of their own burdensome M&E mechanism and rely instead on recipient M&E systems. This implies a series of reforms that are technically daunting and politically sensitive, and maybe it is not surprising that progress so far has been limited. Changes in recipient systems are slow and concentrated on specific components of M&E systems, biased towards the more-technical and methodological components, including statistical capacities and data collection on poverty and MDGs. At the same time, there is a worrisome vagueness surrounding the overall M&E policy, particularly regarding the way the two basic principles of M&E, accountability and learning, are guiding the institutional and organizational set-up of M&E in countries that do not necessarily excel in transparency or accountability towards their own citizens. Donors have pushed reforms that conform to their own slimmed-down and somewhat biased vision of M&E, skewed towards public finance management (input level), recently combined with a vivid interest in sophisticated data-collections systems to capture the other end of the causal chain, that is, poverty and MDG follow-up. Regarding some of the more sensitive and difficult-to-manage issues they have been remarkably silent.

Donors have understandable difficulty in trying to escape from the 'chicken and egg' dilemma they are in. As long as a minimum recipient institutional capacity in terms of design, implementation, and evaluation apparatus is not installed and functioning, alignment to national M&E systems is difficult to defend, and donors are compelled to duplicate recipient M&E activities, with related demands on recipient systems. Donor reactions are, however, far from uniform. Some of the more enthusiastic followers of the new aid approach may be tempted to adopt a version of 'alignment' that puts almost all the responsibility for M&E on the recipient side, notwithstanding the glaring political, institutional, and technical weaknesses of partner countries. In fact, the donor discourse could lead to an unhelpful polarization of the positions on how to proceed with M&E reform. Is there, then, no intermediary position between, on the one hand, a principled handing over of M&E responsibilities to partner countries without even a prior assessment of the national system and the demand and supply pressures that shape it, and on the other hand, a continuation of non-harmonized and non-aligned donor M&E practices? This chapter has sought to contribute to filling this gap and has argued that there is room for fruitful intermediate solutions. It has proposed a pragmatic twin-track process approach, based on a combination of effective strengthening of both demand and supply sides of recipient M&E systems through coordinated and holistic diagnosis, capacity development, independent follow-up, and process conditionality, coupled with complementary externally steered M&E that rather than duplicating national efforts strives at bridging existing gaps in national M&E systems. While it will undoubtedly take much time and energy, it is possible to move towards broad-based national ownership of M&E, without ever fully eliminating the need for donor involvement.

References

3rd High-Level Forum on Aid Effectiveness (2008) <http://www.oecd.org/document/20/ 0,3343,en_2649_3236398_41201108_1_1_1_1,00.html>.

Bamberger, M. (1989) 'The Monitoring and Evaluation of Public Sector Programs in Asia: Why are Development Programs Monitored but not Evaluated?' *Evaluation Review*, 13: 223–42.

——(1991) 'The Politics of Evaluation in Developing Countries'. *Evaluation and Programme Planning*, 14: 325–39.

——(2000) 'The Evaluation of International Development Programmes: A View from the Front'. *American Journal of Evaluation*, 21: 95–102.

Bedi, T., A. Coudouel, M. Cox, et al. (2006) *Beyond the Numbers: Understanding the Institutions for Poverty Reduction Strategies*. Washington, DC: World Bank.

Bigsten, A. (2006) 'Donor Coordination and the Uses of Aid'. Göteborg University Department of Economics Working Papers in Economics 196. Göteborg: Göteborg University.

Booth, D. (2005) 'Missing Links in the Politics of Development: Learning from the PRSP Experiment'. Overseas Development Institute Working Paper 256. London: ODI.

——and H. Lucas (2002) 'Good Practice in the Development of PRSP Indicators and Monitoring Systems'. Overseas Development Institute Working Paper 172. London: ODI.

Boyle, R., D. Lemaire, and R. C. Rist (1999) 'Introduction: Building Evaluation Capacity'. In R. Boyle and D. Lemaire (eds), *Building Effective Evaluation Capacity: Lessons from Practice*. New Brunswick, NJ, and London: Transaction Publishers.

Center for Global Development (2006) *When Will We Ever Learn? Improving Lives through Impact Evaluation*. Report of the Evaluation Gap Working Group. Washington, DC: Center for Global Development.

Elbers, C., J. W. Gunning, and K. de Hoop (2007) 'Assessing Budget Support with Statistical Impact Evaluation'. Tinbergen Institute Discussion Paper TI 2007-075/2, VU University Amsterdam, Tinbergen Institute and AIID.

Evans, A., and E. Ngalwea (2001) 'Institutionalizing the PRSP Approach in Tanzania'. In D. Booth (ed.), *The PRSP Institutionalization Study: Final Report*. London: ODI.

——and A. van Diesen (2002) 'Tanzania's Poverty Monitoring System: A Review of Early Experience and Current Challenges'. Mimeo. London and Dar es Salaam.

GTZ-BMZ (Deutsche Geschellschaft für Technische Zusammenarbeit—German Federal Ministry for Economic Co-operation and Development) (2004) *National Monitoring of Strategies for Sustainable Poverty Reduction/PRSPs*, Vol. i. Eshborn: GTZ, Governance and Democracy Division, Mainstreaming Poverty Reduction Project.

Hauge, A. (2001) 'Strengthening Capacity for Monitoring and Evaluation in Uganda: A Results-based Management Perspective'. Evaluation Capacity Development Working Paper 8. Washington, DC: World Bank Operations Evaluation Department.

——(2003) 'The Development of Monitoring and Evaluation Capacities to Improve Government Performance in Uganda'. Evaluation Capacity Development Working Paper 10. Washington, DC: World Bank Operations Evaluation Department.

Holvoet, N., and R. Renard (2005) 'Putting the New Aid Paradigm to Work: Challenges for Monitoring and Evaluation'. University of Antwerp Institute of Development Policy and Management Discussion Paper 2. Antwerp: IDPM-UA.

————(2007) 'Monitoring and Evaluation under the PRSP: Solid Rock or Quicksand?' *Evaluation and Programme Planning*, 30: 66–81.

IDD (International Development Department) and Associates (2006) 'Evaluation of General Budget Support: Synthesis Report'. Birmingham: IDD and Associates.

IMF (International Monetary Fund) (2004) 'Report on the Evaluation of Poverty Reduction Strategy Papers (PRSPs) and the Poverty Reduction and Growth Facility (PRGF)'. Washington, DC: IMF Independent Evaluation Office.

——and International Development Association (2003) 'Poverty Reduction Strategy Papers: Detailed Analysis of Progress in Implementation'. Washington, DC: IMF and World Bank (IDA).

——and World Bank (2005) '2005 Review of the Poverty Reduction Strategy Approach: Balancing Accountabilities and Scaling Up Results'. Washington, DC: IMF and World Bank (IDA).

Kusek, J. Z., and R. C. Rist (2002) 'Building Results-based Monitoring and Evaluation Systems: Assessing Developing Countries Readiness'. *Zeitschrift für Evaluation*, 1: 151–8.

——and R. C. Rist (2004) *Ten Steps to a Results-based Monitoring and Evaluation System: A Handbook for Development Practitioners*. Washington, DC: World Bank.

Lavergne, R., and A. Alba (2003) *CIDA Primer on Programme-based Approaches*. Gatineau: CIDA (Canadian International Development Agency) Analysis and Research Division, Policy Branch.

Lehtinen, T. (2002) 'Measuring the Performance of EC Development Co-operation: Lessons from the Experiences of International Development Agencies'. European Centre for Development Policy Management Discussion Paper 41. Maastricht: European Centre for Development Policy Management.

Lehtonen, M. (2005) 'OECD Environmental Performance Review: Accountability (f)or Learning'. *Evaluation*, 11: 169–88.

Lucas, H., D. Evans, and K. Pasteur, with R. Lloyd (2004) 'Research on the Current State of PRS Monitoring Systems'. Institute of Development Studies Discussion Paper 382. Brighton: University of Sussex Institute of Development Studies.

McGee, R., and A. Norton (2000) 'Participation in Poverty Reduction Strategies: A Synthesis of Experience with Participatory Approaches to Policy Design, Implementation and Monitoring'. Institute of Development Studies Working Paper 109. Brighton: IDS.

——J. Levene, and A. Hughes (2002) 'Assessing Participation in Poverty Reduction Strategy Papers: A Desk-based Synthesis of Experiences in Sub-Saharan Africa'. Institute of Development Studies Research Report 52. Brighton: IDS.

Mackay, K. (1999) 'Evaluation Capacity Development: A Diagnostic Guide and Action Framework'. ECD Working Paper 6. Washington, DC: World Bank.

May, E., D. Shand, K. Mackay, et al. (eds) (2006) 'Towards the Institutionalization of Monitoring and Evaluation Systems in Latin America and the Caribbean'. Proceedings of a World Bank/Inter-American Development Bank Conference. Washington, DC: World Bank.

Mayne, J. (1999) 'Addressing Attribution Through Contribution Analysis: Using Performance Measures Sensibly'. Discussion Paper. Ottawa: Office of the Auditor General of Canada.

ODI (Overseas Development Institute) (2003) 'PRS Monitoring in Africa'. PRSP Synthesis Note 7. PRSP Monitoring and Synthesis Project. London: ODI.

——(2004) 'PRSP Annual Progress Reports and Joint Staff Assessments: A Review of Progress'. PRSP Briefing Note 9, PRSP Monitoring and Synthesis Project. London: ODI.

OECD-DAC (2003) *Harmonizing Donor Practices for Effective Aid Delivery*, Vol. i. Paris: OECD-Development Assistance Committee.

——(2005a) *Harmonizing Donor Practices for Effective Aid Delivery*, Vol. ii. Paris: OECD-Development Assistance Committee.

——(2005b) *Survey on Harmonization and Alignment*. Paris: OECD-Development Assistance Committee.

——(2007) *2006 Survey on Monitoring the Paris Declaration*. Paris: OECD-Development Assistance Committee.

——(2008) *2008 Survey on Monitoring the Paris Declaration; Effective Aid by 2010: What it Will Take?* Paris: OECD-Development Assistance Committee.

Palumbo, D. (1987) 'Politics and Evaluation'. In D. Palumbo (ed), *The Politics of Program Evaluation*. London: Sage Publications.

Picciotto, R. (2003) 'International Trends and Development Evaluation: The Need for Ideas'. *American Journal of Evaluation*, 24: 227–34.

Prennushi, G., G. Rubio, and K. Subbarao (2001) 'Monitoring and Evaluation Plus Annexes'. *PRSP Sourcebook*. Washington, DC: World Bank: 107–30 and 433–62.

Rist, R. C. (ed.) (1990) *Program Evaluation and the Management of Government: Patterns and Prospects across Eight Nations*. New Brunswick, NJ: Transaction Publishers.

Robb, C. (2002) Can the Poor Influence Policy? Participatory Poverty Assessment in the Developing World, 2nd edn. Washington, DC: World Bank and IMF.

Rossi, P. H., H. E. Freeman, and M. W. Lipsey (2004) *Evaluation: A Systematic Approach*, 7th edn. Thousand Oaks, Calif.: Sage.

SPA (Special Partnership with Africa) (2001) 'Conclusions of the Joint Meeting of the ECA PRSP Learning Group and the SPA Technical Group'. Addis Ababa, 7 Nov. <http://siteresources.worldbank.org/INTPRS1/Resources/Comprehensive-Review/spa4.pdf>.

SPA-6 Budget Support Working Group (2004) 'Survey of the Alignment of Budget Support and Balance of Payments Support with National PRS Processes'. Report by the BSWG co-chairs <http://spa.synisys.com/index.jsp?sid=1&id=1533&pid=1134>.

——(2006) 'Survey of the Alignment of Budget Support and Balance of Payments Support with National PRS Processes'. Report by the BSWG co-chairs, <http://spa.synisys.com/index.jsp?sid=1&id=1532&pid=1134>.

Valadez J., and M. Bamberger (1994) 'Organizational and Management Issues in Programme Evaluation'. In *World Bank, Monitoring and Evaluating Social Programmes in Developing Countries: A Handbook for Policymakers, Managers and Researchers*. Washington, DC: World Bank.

White, H. (2002) 'The Road to Nowhere? Results-based Management in Development Agencies'. Evaluating International Cooperation Think Tank No. 3. <http://www.oneworld.org/thinktank/evaluate/index.html>.

Wood, B., D. Kabell, F. Sagasti, and N. Muwanga (2008) 'Synthesis Report on the First Phase of the Evaluation of the implementation of the Paris Declaration'. Copenhagen. <http://www.undg.org/docs/9219/Synthesis-Report.pdf>.

World Bank (2002) '2002 Annual Report on Evaluation Capacity Development: 2002 Annual Report'. World Bank Operations Evaluation Department. Washington, DC: World Bank.

——(2003a) 'Toward Country-led Development: A Multi-partner Evaluation of the Comprehensive Development Framework'. Synthesis Report. Washington, DC: World Bank.

——(2003b) 'Participation in Monitoring and Evaluation of PRSPs: A Document Review of Trends and Approaches Emerging from 21 Full PRSPs'. World Bank Operations Evaluation Department. Washington, DC: World Bank.

——(2003c) 'A User's Guide to Poverty and Social Impact Analysis, Poverty Reduction Group (PRMPR) and Social Development Department (SDV)'. Washington, DC: World Bank. <http://www.worldbank.org/psia>.

——(2004) 'The Poverty Reduction Strategy Initiative: An Independent Evaluation of the World Bank's Support Through 2003'. World Bank Operations Evaluation Department. Washington, DC: World Bank.

——(2005) 'Enabling Capacity to Achieve Results'. 2005 Comprehensive Development Framework (CDF) Progress Report. Operations Policy and Country Service. Washington, DC: World Bank.

——(2007) 'Results-based National Development Strategies: Assessment and Challenges Ahead'. Washington, DC: World Bank.

11

Practical and Theoretical Implications of the Joint Evaluation of General Budget Support

Michael Hubbard[1]

11.1. Introduction

This chapter discusses implications for practice and theory of the Joint Evaluation of General Budget Support 2004–6 based on case studies in Burkina Faso, Malawi, Mozambique, Nicaragua, Rwanda, Uganda, and Vietnam,[2] and the separate evaluation study in Tanzania (Lawson et al. 2005). The evaluation was commissioned by a consortium of OECD-DAC based donors. The evaluation was preceded by the design of an evaluation framework, which was further developed during the evaluation studies. The evaluation framework is in the form of a logical framework with feedback effects. It sought to find out the effects which the partnership general budget support (PGBS) (via its inputs of finance, policy dialogue, conditionality, technical assistance, harmonization, and alignment) has had on collaborating governments, and particularly the services they deliver to the poor. The short duration of PGBS programmes to date, even in Uganda where they have been established since the mid-1990s, reduced the extent to which effects on services to the poor could be attributed

[1] The author is a team member of the evaluation study. Evidence and much analysis presented in the chapter are drawn from reports of the evaluation, particularly the Synthesis Report, which was compiled principally by Stephen Lister and Rebecca Carter (respectively team leader and research coordinator for the study). A draft of this chapter was presented to the UNU-WIDER Development Conference on Aid, 'Aid: Principles, Policies, and Performance', held on 16–17 June 2006 in Helsinki.

[2] The study was carried out by a consortium led by International Development Department, University of Birmingham. For synthesis and country reports from the evaluation, see <http://www.idd.bham.ac.uk/general-budget-support/> and <http://www.oecd.org/site/0,2865,en_21 571361_36507471_1_1_1_1_1,00.html>.

to PGBS, though PGBS is argued to have contributed to the expansion of education and health services (for example, in Tanzania).

Budget support as a form of aid takes a variety of forms. In the transition from colony to independence, it was used by the colonial power to close the budgetary gap in newly independent states (for example, 'grants in aid' to Uganda and Botswana) on a short-medium term basis. It has been used by individual donors and international financial institutions (IFIs) to help states carry out major, politically difficult reforms after economic crises (for example, Japanese assistance to southeast Asian states after the Asian financial crisis of 1996–7). It is used on a short-term basis to assist governments to provide humanitarian assistance after natural disasters (for example, Pakistan after the recent Himalayan earthquakes). It is also used on a longer term bilateral basis to support politically favoured regimes under military threat (for example, USA support to Israel and Egypt).

Partnership general budget support is longer term budget support with active policy dialogue and supporting capacity-building activities, designed to strengthen recipient government policy for poverty reduction. It emerged from the Heavily Indebted Poor Country (HIPC) Initiative of the late 1990s which sought to establish the common purpose of donors and government to reduce poverty in return for debt relief (for more on the historical background, see Chapters 2 and 4 in this volume by Finn Tarp and Machiko Nissanke respectively). The partnership approach of HIPC was in part a reaction to the often-confrontational experience with budget support for structural adjustment purposes in the 1980s and 1990s, particularly in low-income, aid-dependent states. PGBS is used as a tool for assisting committed political leadership to strengthen state functions and performance and get flexible resources to pursue desired policies: by providing a more reliable stream of funding through government and both demanding and enabling higher standards of performance from government systems; by rationalizing and simplifying donor demands on weak governments in line with the government's own objectives. To achieve these objectives, it sets up long-term communication and negotiation structures, and agreements regarding timetables of disbursements, performance levels, and joint funding by donors.

The evaluation analysed the content and effects of PGBS programmes in the case countries. This had to proceed by identifying PGBS programmes on a programme-by-programme basis since different donors and different countries use their own labels and categorize similar flows differently. This problem prevented the evaluation from carrying out in parallel an intended econometric study of the effects of budget support over a longer period.[3]

---

[3] The main international database on aid flows of different types (OECD-DAC's Creditor Reporting System) was found to lack clear definition of aid modalities and suffers from inadequate coverage of aid flows and unreliable categorization. Reliable multi-country quantitative analysis of programme aid flows and effects was found not to be possible with existing data. This emphasizes the need for aid categories to be internationally standardized and aid flows captured in an international database much more comprehensively and reliably.

The chapter first looks at the extent to which PGBS, on the evidence of the evaluation, stands up to common criticisms of the effects of aid on government in low-income, aid-dependent countries (section 11.2). A number of queries are then raised in section 11.3. In section 11.4, the chapter turns to its second main task of looking at what the findings of the evaluation contribute to understanding of the nature of PGBS. Section 11.5 concludes.

11.2. Charges against aid: how well does PGBS stand up to them?

A summary of the charges regarding the negative effects which aid can have on the recipient state would include:

- policy statements and policy realities may be driven further apart;
- donors may dictate an inappropriate policy agenda;
- domestic accountability may remain poor even though accountability to donors improves;
- government resource-management systems may be sidelined by putting resources through alternative channels (for example, project management units outside government);
- cost and waste in public services may increase;
- domestic public revenue collection may be reduced;
- opportunities for fraud may be increased;
- unnecessary management costs may be imposed on government by having to deal with multiple donors individually;
- aid raises resource availability risks to government through unpredictability of funding and donor short-termism;
- aid raises debt dependency, by expanding public expenditure commitments based on loans; and
- aid biases against vigorous private sector growth by expanding an unreformed public sector.

PGBS (partnership/poverty-reduction general budget support) is supposed to avoid the negative effects of other aid modalities, and to create benefits of wider and more secure collaboration between donors and governments, and among donors. Above all, it is supposed to help raise the capability of the state. We consider each of the main areas to which the charges above apply, but with a caution: the main differences observed were between countries, with great variation in the way PGBS is designed and managed. Also, in each country, PGBS as a mode of aid is evolving. Therefore it is dangerous to generalize specific effects of PGBS.

Other cautions: many effects noted are not of PGBS alone but of parallel initiatives by government and donors (for example, via OECD-DAC on harmonization and alignment). PGBS is presently the standard-bearer aid mode for a wider movement of change, of which sector programmes and projects with governments are increasingly part, where they are increasingly on-treasury and on-budget.

Charge 1: donors dictate policy; policy statements and realities may be driven further apart; domestic policy processes are weakened by donors

A hypothesis underlying PGBS is that more flexible resources enable more coherent policy. The country studies found evidence to support the following observations with respect to the effects of PGBS.

- The prospect of predictable funds to finance policies provided an incentive for policy review and development (for example, flexible and predictable funding for the budget in Rwanda encouraged governments to take risks in policymaking, being confident of the funding availability, such as implementation of public sector reform, and capitation grant for full fee-free basic education); in Uganda two of the policy moves that have had dramatic positive effects—universal primary education and the abolition of health care charges—were introduced unilaterally by the government of Uganda despite initial donor scepticism. The Tanzania evaluation found that GBS has enabled shifts in budget allocations, which indicated that the poverty-reduction strategy (PRS), with its stress on social services, was not a good reflection of political priorities (Lawson et al. 2005: para. 146).

- Making funds available through the regular planning and budgetary systems of government helped strengthen processes, gave sector agencies more incentive to compete for such funds, and increased coherence across public agencies (for example, financing a broader and more articulated set of sector policies in Burkina Faso's revised poverty-reduction strategy paper (PRSP) 2004).

- More coherent donor inputs to policy (this is a general effect of donor collaboration and coordination), plus more specific effects at sector level (for example, in Mozambique the PGBS working groups exposed sectors' progress to comparison and mutual learning, and increased pressure for change in sectors by making them part of the overall performance assessment framework rating).

- Increased transparency and participation: participation in policy processes is not strong in the case countries. However, better connecting of line ministries with central ones, particularly through medium-term budgeting, is an advance in many cases (for example, in Burkina Faso and in Rwanda, despite the difficulties with developing the medium-term expenditure/ budgetary framework (MTEF)).

251

- Technical assistance (TA) more focused on policy (for example, in Vietnam, PGBS with complementary TA projects helps strengthen policy design and implementation).

In sum, although there is plenty of evidence of donors trying to set policy agendas (for example, the criticisms of PRSPs and the Washington consensus—both of which inform donor thinking in PGBS), the evaluation found a correlation between overall PGBS effect in providing greater policy space and policy-making capacity to governments and the degree of PGBS penetration (duration, and relative importance and sophistication of dialogue arrangements). Thus, ironically, deeper involvement of donors in partnership arrangements with governments and other donors (joint-funding arrangements, agreed-performance assessment frameworks), characterized as 'government ownership with donor influence', is positively correlated with providing discretionary funding for government via PGBS.

Charge 2: domestic accountability remains poor even though accountability to donors improves

A hypothesis motivating PGBS is that accountability to donors shifts from concern with how their specific packages of resources are spent (as in projects) to focus on how well government manages resources through its planning, budgeting, and financial controls. Such better resource management by government is more transparent and worthy of challenge by parliament and society. Hence, domestic accountability should increase as a result of PGBS.
The country studies found that

- A strong effect of PGBS is in focusing donors on the quality of government systems. It has led to more (and more joint) analysis of public finance management (PFM) issues, and is beginning to lead to more coordinated and coherent TA (see Charge 3 below).

- Stronger links between policy and strategic-expenditure planning are needed to achieve accountability for results. Medium-term expenditure/budgetary frameworks are the tool for achieving this. But, creating MTEFs is not easy: it is not just a technical reform; it requires strong leadership on the government side to enforce expenditure limits and performance targets, and good management of public services. Uganda's head start in medium-term budgeting was the reason for its better scores across the range of PFM performance indicators than other case countries (credibility of the budget, comprehensiveness and transparency, policy based budgeting, predictability and control in budget execution, accounting and reporting).

- Weaknesses in the budgetary process are also inhibitions on democratic accountability (for example, as found in Mozambique: the fact that a large part of public expenditure is off-budget means it is not subject to either parliamentary scrutiny or external audit).

In sum, in none of the case countries was domestic accountability strong. Democratic accountability emerges from political processes as much as from better governance (for example, relatively strong parliamentary accountability in Rwanda, and political accountability in Vietnam within the ruling party). Though the effect was not strong, PGBS is arguably serving as a stimulus to debates over accountability (for example, civil society feeling cut out of donor–government processes, such as in Tanzania), providing better information on which accountability can be based, and helping to construct medium-term budgeting.

Charge 3: aid causes government resource-management systems to be sidelined by putting resources through alternative channels (for example, project management units outside government)

Another hypothesis motivating PGBS is that putting resources through government systems and demanding higher standards from them will improve their quality. PGBS should therefore help to counter negative effects on government capacity of other aid which bypasses government. The finding is that wherever PGBS has become established there are some positive effects on government's expenditure management systems, though these are only the beginnings from a still low base;[4] and there is greater alignment of aid with government planning and budget cycles. Non-PGBS modalities have also benefited from funds flowing directly into the budget as a whole, allowing a better balance between recurrent and capital expenditures; this also makes it easier for governments to provide the counterpart funds required by some donors' projects.

PGBS is by definition disbursed through, and therefore aligned with, government financial management and procurement systems; this accounts for many of the effects found. Much aid remains off-treasury and off-budget in most case countries—including aid provided by some of the same donors who participate in PGBS in the same country. Since performance in procurement was weak in most case countries, though improving, weakness of government system appears not to be the reason for slowness in getting on-budget; entrenched practices in sector programmes and projects, and the habit of sector ministries receiving direct payments from donors rather than from the budget, may rather be the reason. There is therefore the prospect of more aid coming on-budget as

---

[4] The evaluation estimated levels and trends of change for a variety of PFM indicators used by the Public Expenditure and Financial Accountability (PEFA) assessments and HIPC in the categories: PFM out-turns; credibility of the budget; key crosscutting issues: comprehensiveness and transparency; budget cycle; donor practices. While most levels were reported as weak or moderate, most trends were constant or rising.

practices change and central government exerts more budgetary authority. However, greater reliance by donors on government TA management, statistics, and analytic work is neither automatic nor immediately in prospect. Government leadership in aid coordination is usually limited, and even where it is stronger (for example, Uganda, Rwanda, Nicaragua, and Tanzania) does not yet include leadership in TA management. Collaboration in the analytic work on which donors rely (for example, expenditure and impact reviews) is rare—let alone reliance on government's own analytic work. The evaluation found some increase in reliance on government auditing and reporting, but little if any use of government analytic work. Difficulties in creating capacity, particularly in small countries, may be the cause: either high costs of setting up adequate services of this sort within government, or political obstacles to opening up public service employment sufficiently to skilled external candidates (which is a possible reason for the absence of government leadership in TA management), or to contracted services, or to developing such services on a regional basis. The Bretton Woods institutions lead the provision of analytic work, particularly in PFM.

Charge 4: aid can increase cost and waste in public services by putting money too rapidly into poorly managed services without reform

A hypothesis of the PRS approaches is that increased funding of essential social services reduces poverty. The charge is that aid can increase cost and waste in public services, by putting money too rapidly into poorly managed services without reform. The country studies found that state expenditure on social sectors—health and education, particularly—expanded as a proportion of gross domestic product (GDP) in response to HIPC and PGBS.[5] But expansion has been in quantity rather than quality of services, extending access to often low-grade services.

The tool for leveraging PGBS payments into increases in social expenditure has been 'pro-poor expenditures' (PPEs). The HIPC initiative in the late 1990s prompted the focus on PPEs, with the aim of ensuring that the poor benefit from debt relief. PRSPs have further raised the profile of the concept. The finding was that defining pro-poor expenditures has been useful in reorienting budgets towards underfunded programmes (for example, Uganda) or for tracking key expenditures and enhancing their predictability while budget systems are strengthened (Malawi and Mozambique). But raising the proportion of PPEs is not a tool that can easily be used more than once. Regarding quality, broad definitions of PPEs may insufficiently prioritize expenditures within sectors, while narrow definitions may be inadequate in a comprehensive

---

[5] In Nicaragua and Malawi where the experience of PGBS is very brief, HIPC Initiative is the sole cause of the rise in health and education spending.

strategy for poverty reduction. Thus, in the long run, PPEs may distract from the need for decision-making processes which deliver efficient expenditure allocations for the budget as a whole, and strong, comprehensive PFM systems.

In sum, PPEs are a blunt instrument and no substitute for strengthening the link between social services planning and medium-term budgeting. PPEs are not an efficient means to ensure that substantial increases in PGBS further reduce social poverty. This suggests the absorptive capacity for increased aid is limited to the pace at which services quality and the public finance systems funding the services can be improved; that in turn raises reform issues, including non-state provision of public services.

Charge 5: aid disrupts the public-finance accountability relation between taxpayers and government, and reduces public-revenue collection

Regarding revenue collection, revenue reforms in the case countries (particularly the move to set up independent revenue authorities) pre-dated or accompanied HIPC and PGBS, supported by projects and TA. There was no fall in the revenue/GDP ratio in the case countries during the PGBS period and in some cases it rose. In principle, further increases in PGBS could be linked to maintaining revenue/GDP, or even increasing it to a target level that would enable budget support to be phased out by a desired date, provided that desired GDP growth is maintained (Foster and Keith 2003).

Accountability problems tend to be less with revenue levels than revenue processes, owing to underperforming domestic institutions: for example, inadequate parliamentary scrutiny; predatory revenue collection by local governments; failure to prosecute revenue fraud owing to a weak criminal justice system. Arguably, GBS is a vital means for raising accountability by creating policy space through flexible funding for committed governments to improve such institutional functioning, and by raising capacity in PFM, as indicated above (Charge 2).

Charge 6: increased aid through government systems may increase opportunities for corruption

The assumption often is that programme aid, being less directly controlled by donors, is more open to fraud than is project aid. Although corruption in relation to PGBS was not a focus of the evaluation, no evidence was found that GBS is more prone to fraud than other aid instruments. The increased focus accompanying PGBS on improved fiduciary management of public funds may make it less so, though the improvements are slow and from very low levels. Much fraud is associated with construction contracts, and programme aid is less oriented to the capital budget than is project aid. Furthermore, aid agencies themselves as they move away from tied aid and towards budget support are less likely to attract charges of collusion in non-transparent contracts and in tax avoidance on imports.

Charge 7: unnecessary costs are forced on government by having to deal with multiple donors who impose conflicting demands, with uncertain disbursement of committed aid

An assumption motivating PGBS is the expectation that donor collaboration with government and with each other to support government budgets will reduce costs of dealing with multiple donors (harmonization and alignment) and increase predictability of disbursement. Country studies found that PGBS savings on costs stem from the built-in harmonization that it brings through donors working together. The difficulties of measuring transaction costs meant that the studies were not able to assess whether PGBS had resulted in overall changes. It was clear that PGBS transaction costs are substantial at the setup stage (costs of concentrated PGBS negotiation are significant); and may be lower than at the implementation stage, though this is less clear. Further, many of the increased costs accompanying PGBS—many of which arise from coordination and review meetings—may have long-term external benefits for greater coherence. An important observation is that the net effect of PGBS programmes on overall transaction costs must be to raise them as long as other forms of aid continue in parallel on a large scale.

A concern has been the emergence of performance assessment frameworks (PAFs) as separate donor-oriented mechanisms of accountability, proliferating multiple performance indicators. There is no doubt that these raise transaction costs both for donors and government and reduce ownership. The evaluation, extending the recommendations of the Paris Declaration, notes the opportunity and importance of:

- integrating PAFs into new generations of government operational strategies;
- linking PAFs more systematically to strategies for developing national monitoring and evaluation capacity; and
- linking central and sector dialogue and monitoring.

Regarding predictability of aid disbursements, each of the study countries had experience of programme-aid suspensions, and even in the case of mature PGBS relationships (Uganda and Mozambique) there are concerns in government about the extent to which disbursements by donors can be relied upon.[6]

---

[6] Predictability of direct budget support was estimated as weak in Malawi and Uganda and only moderate in Nicaragua and Vietnam, though improving in Uganda and Vietnam. And 'predictability in the availability of funds for commitment of expenditures'—a government rather than donor responsibility—was also mostly weak, though good in Vietnam and moderately in Burkina Faso and Uganda (IDD and Associates 2006: annex D).

However, PGBS has the advantage of providing a collective forum in which such problems have been addressed, even if not fully resolved. Positive changes include: timetables for PGBS reviews and deadlines for disbursements dictated by government's budget cycle, rankings of donor performance in budget support (SPA 2005), mutual accountability reviews (Mozambique), and revision by the International Monetary Fund (IMF) of its on-track/off-track signalling to reduce risks of donor overreaction.

The main risk remains broadly political: PGBS disbursements are particularly vulnerable to suspensions to register political protest, since they are direct transfers to government to carry out its everyday business, rather than emergency humanitarian aid, or projects in which commercial contractual commitments have been signed. Proposed ways of reducing the political vulnerability of PGBS include associating it more clearly with its budgetary uses—such notional ring-fencing might serve to protect it a little better, particularly where budget support is assigned to local governments for essential services, since local governments usually are not the cause of international political stand-offs.

Charge 8: aid does not effectively reduce unsustainable debt of poor countries

This charge is of continuing moral hazard and adverse selection in the aid industry; that HIPC, despite its innovations,[7] has not ended the 'debt-go-round' in which donors pretend to enforce conditions and recipients pretend to fulfil them; multilaterals continue to make risky loans to governments which cannot realistically service them, confident that bilaterals will provide debt relief if needed; the IMF still plays the contradictory role of gatekeeper and creditor, under pressure to reopen the gate virtually immediately after closing it. In this way the development banks and IMF provide a safety net for insolvent governments, at the expense of incentives to governments and themselves to manage resources well. Those making the charge (Easterly 2001; IOB 2003) cite decades of repeated debt relief which have not reduced indebtedness.

PGBS, emerging from the HIPC, consisting of loans as well as grants, is easily classified as part of this alleged global welfare arrangement for insolvent governments cum business generation for development banks and the IMF.

The crunch questions for PGBS are whether it is countering or reinforcing this alleged incentive to poor management of resources and debt, and whether it is encouraging economic growth better to enable the economy to use and service loans. On the first of these questions, the evaluation finds that PGBS is

---

[7] HIPC's innovations in debt relief included greater size, focus on creating debt sustainability for the most debt-ridden poor countries, coverage of debt stock as well as debt servicing, insistence that World Bank, IMF, and regional development banks should pay a portion of the debt relief themselves, plus commitment of recipients to PRSPs.

contributing positively to recipients' PFM systems, though progress is slow and uneven among countries. IFIs are also participating increasingly in PGBS structures for donor–government collaboration, including joint funding arrangements and performance assessment frameworks (Lawson, Gerster, and Hoole 2005), which makes rogue behaviour by donors less likely. PRSPs are also beginning to be altered by governments towards their own plans (for example, Vietnam and Mozambique). To the second question there is not such a confident defence, as is discussed below.

Charge 9: aid does not encourage the private sector sufficiently

The theory of GBS gives priority to governance institutions, with better-functioning governance institutions leading to greater investor confidence and growth (as in endogenous growth theory). The charge is that aid is now neglecting investments in infrastructure and reforms to promote private business. In doing so, it risks expanding an unreformed public sector, which competes for scarce skilled resources and capital. This is a charge levelled particularly against HIPC and against the content of current PGBS programmes, because of their orientation towards raising social sector spending.

PGBS can claim some credit for higher growth rates where instability in donor government relations had restricted investment; however, this effect is difficult to isolate since flows of budget support tend to accompany political change, particularly where this involves ending of civil hostilities, or regime change towards more open politics and trade. In these circumstances, there is a bounceback effect in investment and business activity, to which aid contributes. All of the PGBS evaluation case studies were in such countries, except Burkina Faso.

Large aid inflows can raise exchange values of domestic currencies, discouraging exports and foreign investment and encouraging imports, in 'Dutch disease' style. Given that in the case study countries PGBS has generally substituted for other aid rather than increased aid levels overall, this is a charge which does not immediately stick. However, the intention is to raise PGBS and overall aid levels (as in Monterrey commitments) in order to achieve the Millennium Development Goals (MDGs); therefore the potential rise in exchange values of recipient country currencies resulting from increases in aid is a pertinent concern. In Uganda and Tanzania, both with mature PGBS relations with donors, sterilization costs in the form of higher interest charges have been substantial in recent years. These result from open market purchases by the treasury in order to stabilize nominal exchange rates and reduce inflationary tendencies. The cause of the problem is not aid alone, since there are other inflows of foreign exchange (for example, investment, remittances, exports proceeds) but aid is a major factor. Collaboration with the IMF on this problem has resulted (for example, in Tanzania) in reduced sterilization of inflows, letting inflation rates creep up. The problem is partly one of small low-income economies with their own currencies, and small, shallow financial markets, which reemphasizes the potential benefits to be gained from greater regional integration in both trade and factor markets.

Summing up

The evaluation of PGBS has thrown light particularly on operational arrangements and how well they work. Earlier research, for example, Foster and Keith (2003), argued that GBS as a low-transaction-cost means of increasing aid flows could enable states with demonstrated ability to generate economic growth and maintain political stability to move more rapidly in reducing poverty, but did not examine operational arrangements in any detail. Allowing for cautions regarding its short period of operation and variation among countries, what the evaluation has demonstrated is that PGBS:

- can increase allocative efficiency in public spending, by providing flexible funds and enabling public priorities to be financed;[8]
- provides a focus on PFM which is enabling/encouraging other forms of aid to be brought on budget and/or on treasury;
- provides a forum of sufficient critical mass to: (i) enable flows of finance and rules of different donors to be consolidated; (ii) become increasingly influential in donor–government relations, involving most bilateral and multilateral donors and (in the most advanced cases) strong involvement of government; (iii) be able to evolve operational arrangements for PGBS, for example, reducing its unpredictability through timetabling disbursements and clarifying conditions in joint funding agreements and performance assessment frameworks; and (iv) be stable and long term in its outlook.

The evaluation found that PGBS can, at worst, plead neutrality to the charges above (in other words, it does no harm) and, at best has some positive impact (notably costs imposed by donors and discretion to government). The exception is its doubtful benefit to the private sector and growth.

11.3. Queries arising

Queries were raised with regard to:

- *Pro-poor expenditures*: efficiency and future viability. Do net benefits from PGBS hit a ceiling which it is difficult to break through? Raising pro-poor

---

[8] Defining allocative efficiency as publicly desired allocation of public resources/actual allocation, and operational efficiency as outputs of priority public services per unit inputs.

expenditures leveraged a step increase in social spending under HIPC and PGBS. But, this may not easily be repeated. There is no quick fix alternative to enabling central, sector, and local systems of government to work better together in budgeting, service provision, cash management, monitoring, and planning. This is an obstacle facing all aid modes and is therefore not an argument against PGBS.

- Marked expansions in aid to small countries risk 'Dutch disease' effects unless markets in foreign exchange, goods, services, and factors are deepened and widened; increased regional integration in trade, employment, and financial markets could reduce 'Dutch disease' effects.

- Tendency of PAFs to be separate from government strategy documents and to multiply indicators and conditions instead of streamline them.

- *Revenue/GDP*: is it high enough to keep social poverty at the desired level and achieve non-aid dependence within a politically acceptable timeframe? Or is it already too high to sustain needed growth?

- *Private-sector development and economic growth*: are they sufficiently encouraged by PGBS and by other components of the wider relationship between poor and rich countries, particularly trade?

- *Government systems that are not used by PGBS*: analytic work, aid coordination, and TA management. Tying PAFs increasingly into government plans and government data and monitoring systems is an important step.

A wider question which arises is: does PGBS take any predictable path? The only common element in entry conditions to PGBS was found to be political trust, which may or may not deepen. The operational arrangements for PGBS differ in terms of multilateral/bilateral leadership, donor–government working groups, degree of harmonization, approaches to disbursement, and conditionality. However, much of these differences may be because PGBS is a new way of working. There is some evidence of learning from what appeared to be more advanced collaborative arrangements (Mozambique, Uganda, Vietnam, and Tanzania), in which case greater convergence in PGBS operational arrangements might be observed in future. The flow of funds does tend to increase over time (compare Malawi and Nicaragua—where PGBS was just beginning—with Mozambique, Burkina Faso, and Uganda, with programmes several years old). And, most importantly, the benefits from PGBS were found to be greater and the operational arrangements better developed in the countries where PGBS was longer established.

But, the case studies do not provide evidence for confidently projecting these findings as a 'happy trend' in which there is increasingly productive collaboration until the recipient government is sufficiently able, and the country sufficiently wealthy, that PGBS is no longer required. First, political trust remains fragile at any stage of the PGBS relationship (for example, in Malawi and

Nicaragua it was fragile at the beginning of PGBS; in Uganda it became fragile after many years of PGBS). Second, there is no certainty that improvements in government capacity or economic growth can be continuously maintained by PGBS: the case studies found that even PFM systems, on which PGBS efforts are most heavily concentrated, though improved, are still very weak, while the effects of PGBS on economic growth are not clear. Third, the influence of PGBS is limited: it is only one influence among many on governments, with domestic and regional political considerations being far more important; and PGBS funds remain a minor flow of foreign exchange, even within aid flows. In sum, while PGBS in different countries might tread an increasingly similar path in terms of operational arrangements (that is, working groups, performance agreements, joint funding agreements, timetables, and so on), its future effects and continuity cannot easily be predicted, let alone taken for granted.

11.4. Understanding PGBS effects: entitlements, rules, hierarchy, club, and market

This section discusses the implications of the study findings for how we understand the nature of PGBS and behaviour of actors with in PGBS. A major finding of the evaluation is that PGBS has effects on longer term behaviour and relationships with government and other modes of aid, notably:

- the evidence of increased policy development by governments;
- the greater stability, longer term working arrangements, and leadership it tends to establish in donor–government relations; and
- the gravitational influence it has on other aid to government (sector programmes, projects), attracting them into PGBS forums, and encouraging their aid to be paid into treasury and to be reflected in the budget.

11.4.1. Entitlement

What type of innovation then is PGBS, that it has such benefits? It contains a strong element of entitlement.[9] Entitlements arise from current economic activity (trade, own production, employment), from past economic activity (savings) and from social relations (inheritance, rights to receive transfers) (Sen 1981: 2). It is this last source of entitlement—the right to receive transfers—which describes PGBS in the context of aid. PGBS is not a guaranteed, fixed transfer but establishes a joint understanding that, subject to

---

[9] 'Entitlement refers to the set of alternative commodity bundles that a person can command in a society using the totality of rights and opportunities that he or she faces' (Sen 1984: 497).

performance, transfers will be made. The right to receive transfers confers some degree of confidence that there will be a future stream of income in addition to the income currently received from that source. Entitlements to a future income are particularly valued as hedges against risk, in the manner that a 'put option' raises the asset value of a security held.[10] In this way, PGBS, through current non-earmarked transfers into treasury and through creating the confidence that they will be repeated in future, potentially makes for increased policy discretion for government both immediately and in the future: it encourages policies to be pursued that previously may not have been funded (for example, by projects), and also encourages policy development. These effects will not necessarily take place: that depends on priorities and the will of government leaders. But PGBS makes it easier to do so.

11.4.2. Coordination

The longer term commitment encourages creation of structures to manage the relationship, which become a fixed point towards which passing relationships (for example, short/medium term projects) or more specific relationships (for example, sector programmes) tend to gravitate: because that is where the longer term thinking is being done, and where the link to higher levels of government are stronger. Hence the evaluation found that PGBS forums increase in size as PGBS becomes more established, even tending to become unmanageably large (for example, in Mozambique). This is evidence of PGBS reducing coordination failure. Coordination failure lowers allocative efficiency, and typically stems from synchronization problems (poor timing), information problems (main actors having different information), and assignment problems (poor teamwork) (Milgrom and Roberts 1992: 90–2). The move to promote harmonization and alignment is designed to reduce coordination failures. PGBS, through both its inbuilt alignment (disbursing via government systems) and the gravitational pull of its structures on aid arrangements with lower mass (donors are keen to be part of more influential structures), reduces coordination failure.

11.4.3. Incentives

Entitlements which reduce future risk are recognized as having a greater effect on longer term behaviour than current income alone has, in the manner that 'permanent income' determines consumption spending. Positive effects are the stimulus to policy development and coordination, indicated above. The right to

---

[10] 'An option contract that gives the holder the right to sell a certain quantity of an underlying security to the writer of the option, at a specified price (strike price) up to a specified date (expiration date)'. Source of definition: <http://www.investorwords.com>.

receive future transfers also has potentially negative effects on behaviour—recognized in the monopoly model as inefficiencies, and in moral hazard as increased risk displacement onto the insurer once the contract is in place. Single transfers are much more likely to be free gifts (i.e., no strings attached) than are repeated transfers, because of the latter's greater cost and the stronger moral hazard effects of commitments to future transfers.

Therefore entitlements to future transfers tend to come packaged with rules which govern them. However, rules differ (for example, in content and means of enforcement) according to the operating environment, the nature of the entitlement, and nature of the organization through which the entitlement is provided. Before exploring differences in rules and their effects as they apply to PGBS, we need first therefore to set out the range of features of collaborations.

11.4.4. Hierarchy, club, and market

It is suggested, as set out in Figure 11.1, that there are three types of relation in organizations, in different mixes:[11]

- *market relations* are those in buying and selling, focused on the transaction, in which the rules are those governing commerce;
- *club relations* are those in collaborating for a primarily non-commercial purpose, in which rules are decided by club members to govern their behaviour towards each other and towards non-members;
- *hierarchy relations* are for control, in which the rules are decided by leaders of the hierarchy.[12]

One or other relation tends to be dominant in any one structure, and is usually the relation appropriate to the main purpose for which the structure exists, and by which it then tends to be labelled overall. Thus, a structure labelled *business firm* contains relations of hierarchy and club within it, but the market relation predominates in its behaviour. A bureaucracy contains market and club relations, but its primary function is decision-making in a hierarchical manner. A voluntary organization contains elements of hierarchy and market but club elements predominate. Predominance of one relation also characterizes relations between organizations.

---

[11] Building onto Williamson's concepts of markets and hierarchies (Williamson 1975) and inspired by Hirschman's (1970) analysis of dissent behaviour in organizations (exit, voice, loyalty).

[12] Different relations are appropriate to different operations of an organization: human resource management theory, learning from Japanese experience, stresses the importance of club relations among staff within the organization, while finance management stresses hierarchy, and strategic management stresses market.

Characteristics	Types of relations		
	Market	Club	Hierarchy
Objective	mutual benefit from exchange	common interest and purpose	given task to be accomplished
Focus	transactions	collaboration	control
Rules	commercial rules enforcing contracts	club rules relating to entry, conduct, entitlements, exit	decided by leaders
Entitlements	exchange value in the transaction	as set out in club rules	at discretion of leadership
Incentives	gain from the exchange	joint achievement	reward for success and punishment for failure
How uncertainty and risk are dealt with	hedging, insurance	participation, trust, transparency, information sharing	feedback of specific indicators to decision makers
Dissent behaviour	exit, sometimes preceded by voice	voice and loyalty, with exit as last resort	loyalty, then exit with voice

Figure 11.1 Types and characteristics of relations in organizations

Source: Author.

They are predominantly market or hierarchy when confined to the activity which is their *raison d'être* (for example, selling/buying books, enforcing/ paying taxes). But, when the activity is a common interest (for example, setting/maintaining safety standards in an industry, improving waste disposal in a locality), relations are predominantly club.[13]

---

[13] So-called 'hybrid organizations' are usually common interest collaborations among separate organizations and relations within them are therefore predominantly club in nature. Menard (2004) discusses the variety of 'hybrid organizations' and their behaviour.

Organizational structures are dynamic, and the relational element which is dominant may change as the purpose of the organization and/or its means of survival changes; for example, charities which effectively or formally become firms and vice versa. Figure 11.1 sets out a range of organizational relations (market, club, and hierarchy), then differentiates each according to its more detailed characteristics, identified here as objective, focus, rules, entitlements, incentives, approach to risk and uncertainty, and dissent behaviour.

In terms of the relations set out in Figure 11.1, how can PGBS be described? Lawson et al. (2003: 79) suggest that PGBS partnerships are a club in which uncertainties regarding the government's development agenda that is being supported require donors to have *voice* (influence) in return for which they accept limitations on *exit. Loyalty* in the relationship can be increased by better understanding each others' motivations, constraints, and risks. The observations of the PGBS evaluation and of the PAF study (Lawson, Gerster, and Hoole 2005) enable further light to be thrown on relations within PGBS arrangements:

- In donor–government relations PGBS aspires to be a club (joint commitment to PRS and so on) but is in weak states still often more of a hierarchy pretending to be a club.[14] Hierarchy is dominant owing to PRSPs not yet being fully owned, limited participation and 'voice' by government in constructing rules, lower levels of trust, and quick resort to punishment (usually suspension of disbursement)[15] by donors.

- PGBS operations have set up parallel structures to government (hierarchy with vertical integration) in the form of PAFs and annual progress reviews (APRs) which are separate from government's PRS and monitoring and evaluation systems—understandable where government systems are weak, but ironic since a major purpose of PGBS is to avoid parallel structures which sideline government systems; and a priority for integration into government plans and systems, as the evaluation recommends.

- Only where recipient governments have more capacity and commitment are club relations clearly evident in donor–government PGBS dealings. Uganda and Vietnam are examples: both have strong 'voice' and participation, both constructed their own PRS, insist on their own policy priorities, and challenge donors (including Vietnam going 'off-track' with IMF but its PGBS continuing).

---

[14] A PGBS arrangement which is predominantly 'club' in nature might also deliberately masquerade as 'hierarchy' for external appearance; for example, with regard to prior actions that are already a fait accompli but used for signalling to external stakeholders (for example, World Bank board) that they are exerting influence. Thanks to Stephen Lister for pointing this out.

[15] Suspension of disbursement is less than 'exit' (termination of relations) since the underlying aid agreement between country and donor usually remains in place.

- Among donors, club relations vary in strength. While there is strong desire to take part in PGBS meetings as important sources of information, participation ('voice' plus collaboration) is often confined to a smaller subgroup. It is sometimes regarded as a matter of chance whether or not there is effective leadership of the donor group. More generally, effective participation by government seems to be the crucial factor determining wider and deeper participation by donors.

Donors have different assumptions about how the PGBS relation with government should be conducted: some see more of a market orientation as appropriate; that is, a transaction-focused approach in which there is an exchange of funds against actions and results delivered on particular indicators; others want more of a club approach, emphasizing attention to process, information richness, and trends as the basis for judging progress. The latter requires a harmonized and aligned approach (that is, working together, using government systems as far as possible); the former, in principle, does not require harmonization among donors and relies entirely on government actions and systems— since payments are made on the basis of transparent performance-indicator achievements. This is notably the principle underlying the Millennium Challenge Account of the USA government, also recently favoured by the European Commission for budget support. To discuss this issue further we turn to look at rules more closely.

11.4.5. Rules

Rules fulfil different purposes according to the nature of the relation through which the entitlement is provided: in a hierarchy, rules help retain control; in a club they are a means for rebalancing the incentives changed by alterations in entitlement, seeking to raise incentives for positive effects and reduce negative incentives. Whatever the organizational character, rules must be appropriate to the particular operating environment and should be reviewed and changed as circumstances change. In sum, rules differ (for example, in content and means of enforcement) according to the operating environment (risk and uncertainty, flexibility), the nature of the entitlement, and the nature of the relation through which the entitlement is provided.

Figure 11.2 sets out the types of rules currently present in PGBS arrangements. The evaluation confirmed the expectation from contract theory that, owing to pervasive risk and uncertainty, PGBS, and PAFs in particular, currently resemble a 'relational contract' in design and operation. A relational contract 'specifies only the general terms and objectives of a relationship and specifies mechanisms for decision-making and dispute resolution' (Milgrom and Roberts 1992). Relational contracts are widely used when the contracted task is complex and/or the environment in which it is taking place has much risk and

Types of rules	Types of relations		
	Market	Club	Hierarchy
General rules	commercial rules enforcing contracts	club rules relating to entry, conduct, entitlements, exit	decided by leaders
Rules for basic payment	macroeconomic stability on-track	trend performance	prior actions
Rules for results oriented payments	performance related tranches, based on indicators		
Monitoring information: (what is monitored?) (what data?) (who monitors?)	specific agreed indicators, using agreed data and objective monitor	ideally government own indicators and data for plan and budget, monitored by government own team, supported and reviewed for quality	leaders monitor indicators they choose, collecting own data

Figure 11.2 Types of PGBS rules according to types of organizational relations

Source: Author.

uncertainty (for example, major engineering works). A relational contract partially/temporarily suspends market relations between principal and agent in order to allow them to work together in a club-like manner, that is, collaborative problem-solving for a common purpose. It is also an important means of building trust through teamwork in the face of uncertainty. A relational contract amounts to a commercial framework with broad parameters (time, cost, quality) within which club relations predominate as long as the overall parameters do not look like being upset. If they do, there is a switch to more commercial (market) behaviour to alter the task or put in place more

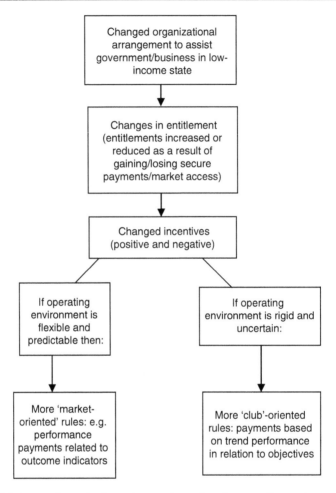

Figure 11.3 Appropriate rules for assistance depend on the operating environment

Source: Author.

appropriate parameters. In the case of PAFs the parameters are necessarily very broad and there is no formal commercial contract at its heart.

The resemblance of PGBS behaviour to behaviour in relational contracts—the mix of market and club behaviour, and the switching between the two as confidence in the relationship fluctuates—may clarify why rules within PGBS arrangements vary: among donors there are varying levels of confidence in the relationship and there is much uncertainty about response to incentives. Integrating PAFs into government plans, budgets, data and monitoring systems—strongly recommended by the evaluation and Paris Declaration—will help to unify rules.

Figure 11.3 illustrates the main point made above. It suggests that a change in organizational arrangements and resulting entitlement (for example, introduction of PGBS) in turn changes incentives and rules. The appropriate rules depend on the operating environment, which is characterized as either flexible and predictable (necessary inputs are readily available, prices are stable, transaction costs are low, key actors are free to make necessary changes) or rigid and uncertain (the opposite), or in between these extremes. The more flexible and predictable the operating environment, the more beneficially can market-oriented rules be used, since the incentive they provide can be responded to; and the more rigid and uncertain the operating environment the more appropriate are club rules, since performance incentives can less easily be responded to genuinely and may encourage fraud, and become a diversion from priorities. In none of the case countries could the operating environment be described as stable and flexible. Hence the recommendations of the evaluation regarding performance assessment frameworks:

- Take care that disbursement-linked conditions are kept to a minimum and are genuinely agreed with government.
- Ensure that performance assessment systems address all links in the results chain, so as to serve the management and monitoring of the implementation of strategies, as well as the monitoring of results.
- Decisions to increase or reduce levels of PGBS support should mainly be based on medium-term assessments of overall performance. (from Recommendation 7; IDD and Associates 2006: 6.54)

And the Paris Declaration states in this regard:

Work with partner countries to rely, as far as possible, on partner countries' results-oriented reporting and monitoring frameworks.

Harmonize their monitoring and reporting requirements, and, until they can rely more extensively on partner countries' statistical, monitoring and evaluation systems, [work] with partner countries to the maximum extent possible on joint formats for periodic reporting. (OECD-DAC 2005)

11.5. Summary and conclusion

This chapter has discussed implications for practice and theory of the Joint Evaluation of General Budget Support 2004–6 based on case studies in Burkina Faso, Malawi, Mozambique, Nicaragua, Rwanda, Uganda, and Vietnam. The chapter first looked at the extent to which general budget support, on the evidence of the evaluation, stands up to common criticisms of the effects of aid on government in low-income, aid-dependent countries. Allowing for much caution owing to the short period of partnership general budget support (PGBS) programmes in some countries, the finding is that there are small but positive impacts (notably reducing unnecessary transaction costs and increasing discretion of government—thereby raising allocative and operational efficiency). Net benefits are generally greater where PGBS programmes are longer established.

Areas of uncertainty regarding future effects are its uncertain overall contribution to the private sector and growth, its vulnerability to changes in political relations, and the limitations to raising 'pro-poor expenditure'—the main tool it has used to leverage increases in health and education spending; long-term improvements in access and quality of public services will rely on better planning, budgeting, and services management.

The chapter then considered how the evaluation results affect the way that PGBS is understood in theory. It first suggested that PGBS raises entitlements (by increasing confidence that there will be continuing flows of budget support) which can encourage policy development and stable donor–government collaboration structures, to which other shorter term aid arrangements gravitate, thereby reducing previous coordination failures. Relations in organizations were then classified as market, club, or hierarchy. Applied to PGBS coordination structures this suggests they are aspirant clubs, with hierarchical features strongest where PGBS is least established, and club features stronger where government is more capable and assertive.

Entitlements are accompanied by rules which attempt to raise positive incentive effects of the entitlement and reduce its negative incentive effects. In PGBS arrangements rules vary from hierarchical (for example, prior actions), through club-oriented (for example, assessment on medium-term trends) to market-oriented (performance payments related to achievement on specific indicators). The analysis of rules in relation to PGBS incentives and operating environments (on a spectrum from rigid and uncertain to flexible and predictable) concludes that fine tuning rules in more rigid and uncertain operating environments is counterproductive. In none of the case countries is the operating environment stable and flexible. Integrating PGBS performance assessment frameworks into government plans and monitoring systems will serve to unify rules.

A number of issues arise from the analysis. First, theory suggests that club relations should be predominant in PGBS arrangements, since they are based on apparent common interest and—in the usually rigid and uncertain operating environments of developing countries—the goals they set cannot easily be achieved by predominantly market or hierarchical relations between donor and recipient. There is evidence that more-successful cases of PGBS have stronger club features. Where government capacity is lower and government is heavily dependent on donors, PGBS relations are more hierarchic.

Second, PGBS success relies heavily on credible long-term commitments (that is, entitlements) positively affecting incentives. Positive effects were found to be investment in policy review, policymaking capacity, and public finance management. Potential negative effects of PGBS entitlement on incentives could be to divert government attention from domestic revenue and domestic accountability. But, the evaluation did not find evidence of these negative effects.

Third, the rules of engagement in PGBS agreements (timetables, performance indicators) reflect the underlying club nature of PGBS. The effectiveness of club relations depends heavily on credible commitments by the main parties. This is especially so in PGBS relations, given their wide scope (the whole of government policy to reduce poverty and improve governance) and the uncertainties facing each party. Asset specificity does not create a risk in PGBS arrangements, since there are no investments which rely on PGBS arrangements continuing.[16] Rather, the problem is extensive uncertainties for all main parties, including how to control incentive effects resulting from PGBS.

Uncertainties underlie the preoccupation of PGBS partnership arrangements with designing performance assessment frameworks. They also underlie the problem of too many performance indicators, and the search for ways to make PGBS less vulnerable to changes in donor priorities and political stand-offs. Attempts to shift PGBS rules towards a market basis (a small number of agreed outcome indicators which trigger/deny disbursements, without partnership working) have had to be scaled back to fixed plus variable tranches.

General budget support using market-type rules based on outcome indicators, with arm's-length relations, remains a prospect. As capacity of recipient governments rises—particularly in the quality of budgeting and monitoring—and donors make more reliable and predictable commitments, the operating environment for PGBS should become less uncertain, encouraging shifts towards more market-type rules.

References

Easterly, W. (2001) *The Elusive Quest for Growth*. Cambridge, Mass.: MIT Press.

Foster, M., and A. Keith (2003) *The Case for Increased Aid: Final Report to the Department for International Development*. Vol. i. *Main Report*. Chelmsford: Mick Foster Economics Ltd.

Hirschman, A. (1970) *Exit, Voice and Loyalty*. Cambridge, Mass.: Harvard University Press.

IDD (International Development Department) and Associates (2006) 'Evaluation of General Budget Support: Synthesis Report'. Birmingham: IDD and Associates.

IOB (Inspectie Ontwikkelingssamenwerking en Beleidsevaluatie) (2003) 'Results of International Debt Relief, 1990–1999, with Case Studies of Bolivia, Jamaica, Mozambique, Nicaragua, Peru, Tanzania, Uganda and Zambia'. IOB Evaluations 292. The Hague: IOB.

Lawson, A., D. Booth, A. Harding, et al. (2003) *General Budget Support Evaluability Study Phase 1: Synthesis Report*. Oxford and London: OPM/ODI.

---

[16] Asset specificity creates particular risks related to the investment, whereas uncertainty in PGBS relations stems from many different sources for different parties, and therefore takes many forms.

Lawson, A., D. Booth, M. Msuya, et al. (2005) 'Joint Evaluation of General Budget Support, Tanzania 1995–2004'. Dar es Salaam and London: Daima Associates/ODI.

——R. Gerster, and D. Hoole (2005) 'Learning from Experience with Performance Assessment Frameworks for General Budget Support: Synthesis Report'. Study commissioned and financed by Swiss State Secretariat for Economic Affairs (Seco) in the framework of the Joint Evaluation of General Budget Support undertaken by the OECD/OECD-DAC. Oxford and Berne: OPM/Seco.

Menard, C. (2004) 'The Economics of Hybrid Organizations'. *Journal of Institutional and Theoretical Economics*, 160: 345–76.

Milgrom, P., and J. Roberts (1992) *Economics, Organization and Management*. Boston, Mass.: Prentice Hall.

OECD-DAC (2005) 'Paris Declaration on Aid Effectiveness'. 2 March Paris: OECD.

Sen, A. (1981) *Poverty and Famines*. Oxford: Clarendon Press.

——(1984) *Resources, Values and Development*. Oxford: Blackwell.

SPA (Special Partnership with Africa) (2005) *Survey of the Alignment of Budget Support and Balance of Payments Support with National PRS Processes: Report by the BSWG Co-Chairs*. Washington, DC: Strategic Partnership with Africa.

Williamson, O. (1975) *Markets and Hierarchies*. New York: Free Press.

12

New Aid Modalities and Reporting Support for Child Rights: Lessons from Assessing Aid for Basic Social Services[1]

Eva Jespersen and Julia Benn

12.1. Introduction

A number of donors explicitly recognize the Convention on the Rights of the Child (CRC) as guiding their development policy. In reporting to the Committee on the Rights of the Child all donors are expected to provide data on their aid in direct support of children, but the Committee currently does not appear to apply a systematic approach to assess such efforts by donor countries. Also, parliamentarians and civil society in many countries take an interest in aid targeted to children. For international comparison, transparency, and accountability, it may therefore be desirable to have an internationally agreed approach for recording and assessing such donor efforts. However, the new aid architecture pulls in the opposite direction, in particular as aid is increasingly provided as budget support to the partner government.

This chapter presents some reflections on the use of the current reporting system—the OECD-DAC creditor-reporting system—and in interpreting the results with regard to aid in support of children's rights, as well as in support of other developmental objectives. It reviews the assessment of basic social services with respect to potential lessons. Section 12.2 discusses the new aid environment and the challenges this presents to existing aid-reporting systems, particularly from the perspective of international reporting on aid for children. Section 12.3 illustrates some of the challenges faced by the reporting system in capturing aid for specific purposes (in this case, basic social services) in light of

---

[1] The findings, interpretations, and views expressed in this chapter are entirely those of the authors. An earlier version of this paper has been released as Jespersen and Benn (2007). <http://www.unicef-irc.org/publications/pdf/iwp_2007_02.pdf>.

the changing aid modalities such as sector budget support. Section 12.4 presents some specific observations for the next steps of the initiative better to capture official development assistance (ODA) for children. Section 12.5 concludes.

12.2. Consideration on reporting ODA for children

12.2.1. Changing aid environment

The Convention on the Rights of the Child (hereafter referred to as the Convention or CRC) and the World Summit for Children (New York, September 1990) drew attention to the role of the international community in the co-operation and provision of adequate resources for advancing and accelerating the progress in realizing the human rights of every child. The modalities and orientation of development cooperation have undergone many changes since then. The growing concern for social development led to a number of thematic international conferences during the 1990s.[2] Greater appreciation for a 'human-rights-based approach' to development and a convergence among donors (and recipients) on the importance of poverty reduction also grew (see Chapter 5 of this volume by Graham Brown, Frances Stewart, and Arnim Langer for more on the human rights approach to aid).

Changes were also influenced by the untenable debt burden faced by many low-income countries, as well as by frustrations of the international community that the prevailing modes of development cooperation did not achieve anticipated results. Another round of meetings and agreements in the new millennium therefore focused on the modes of providing assistance[3] and the notion of a 'new aid architecture' with an emphasis on developing country 'ownership' and simplified and harmonized development assistance (see the related discussions in Chapters 2 and 4 of this volume by Finn Tarp and Machiko Nissanke respectively). At the same time, a host of other initiatives have emerged, and new players have come on the scene to advance international objectives when these were seen to be falling behind.[4] Returning

---

[2] For example, 1990 International Conference on Education for All (Jomtien); 1990 World Summit for Children (New York); 1992 International Conference on Nutrition (Rome); 1993 Conference on Human Rights (Vienna); 1994 International Conference on Population and Development (Cairo); 1995 World Summit on Social Development (Copenhagen); Fourth World Conference on Women, 1995 (Beijing); Millennium Summit, 2000 (New York).

[3] Monterrey International Conference on Financing for Development (2002); Rome High Level Forum on Harmonisation (2003); Marrakech Roundtable on Managing Development Results (2004); Paris Declaration on Aid Effectiveness (2005); World Summit (2005); High Level Panel on Operational Coherence (2006).

[4] 20/20 Initiative for Funding Universal Access to Basic Social Services (WSC), Education Fast Track Initiative, Global Alliance for Vaccines and Immunisation (GAVI), UNAIDS, Global Fund to fight AIDS, Tuberculosis, and Malaria (GFATM), etc.

components have been assessments of available international resources and the filling of estimated resource gaps for either the broad objectives of poverty reduction and sustainable development or more thematic/cross-cutting issues such as basic social services and education for all. The trend towards budget support for negotiated national government-'owned' (or, at least, -led) plans has been accompanied by a growth in global funds targeted to specific issues, which has also brought in the international private/philanthropic sector along-side traditional donors.

12.2.2. The CRC and international cooperation

The CRC integrates civil, political, economic, social, and cultural rights of children, and while addressed to state parties recognizes the primary responsi-bility of parents/caregivers and the role of civil society and the international community in its implementation. Article 4 states that

States Parties shall undertake all appropriate legislative, administrative, and other mea-sures for the implementation of the rights recognized in the present Convention. With regard to *economic, social and cultural rights*, States Parties shall undertake such measures to *the maximum extent of their available resources* and, where needed, *within the framework of international co-operation*. (emphasis added)

The Convention further emphasizes that 'particular account should be taken of the needs of developing countries' in addressing the rights of the child to education (Article 28) and to the highest attainable standard of health (Article 24). The Convention also highlights the child's right to social security (Arti-cle 25); public support for acquiring necessary nutrition, clothing, housing (Article 27); and thus a standard of living adequate for the physical, mental, spiritual, moral, and social development of the child (Article 27(1)). Further-more, it mentions the child's right to be heard and to participate on issues directly affecting his immediate situation (Articles 12–15), and acknowledges the child's right to be protected from economic, sexual, and other exploitation and abuse, trafficking, and to be shielded from all forms of violence (Article 19), with special emphasis in the context of armed conflict.[5] Not all of these issues fall directly within the purview of Article 4 on economic, social, and cultural rights but extend to civil and political rights. But, the spirit of the entire convention conveys international co-operation. Article 44 calls on state parties to report every five years to the Committee on the Rights of the Child (the Committee) on their implementation of the Convention. The Committee re-views reports and publishes concluding observations on the state party perfor-mance.

---

[5] The articles are mentioned to illustrate the levels at which development cooperation takes place. The list is by no means exhaustive and readers are encouraged to review the CRC.

An assessment of selected Concluding Observations made by the Committee suggests that, while commentary on financial resources in support of children has become more substantive in recent years, there appears to be no consistent methodology or guidance provided to state parties with regard to reporting on international cooperation or for the Committee to assess whether development cooperation in support of children has been steered by a human rights approach.

It is widely argued that stable, sustained high levels of broad-based (poverty-reducing) economic growth, peace and security, political stability, general investments in administrative, social, and economic infrastructure, and employment creation all contribute significantly to the advancement of children's rights by creating an environment in which direct investments in children are more productive. It can therefore be questioned whether it is feasible, or even meaningful, to 'single out' development cooperation directed at children or indeed within the spirit of the Paris Agenda on ownership. Such a task is increasingly difficult in light of the new aid modalities and the greater emphasis on promoting government ownership through joint planning and general budget support.

Yet, there are concerns in the child rights community (including within aid administrations) that any recently increased attention to children in development plans may lessen; that the new aid modalities may leave fewer opportunities to advance the child-rights agenda through technical cooperation, including with non-state actors, and through advocacy in areas of child protection such as juvenile justice, child labour, exploitation, and trafficking as well as in strengthening civil society and increasing awareness of the Convention at all levels of society. That said, aid for child rights outside social sectors by donors such as Sweden and Norway is to a considerable degree channelled through non-governmental organizations (NGOs) (discussed below), but there is also a fear that funding for programme-country NGO partners may be in decline.

By ratifying the Convention, donor and developing countries alike are, however, committed to some form of accountability, and questions can be asked about commonly agreed guiding principles. Furthermore, UNICEF Innocenti Research Centre (IRC) will release a study in 2009 on how donors seek to support and promote child rights in their development cooperation. The study is expected to focus as much on strengthening capacity for child rights advocacy among staff as on the direction of funds for specific activities. This could set some principles for the Committee in assessing the aid of individual donor State Parties.

We argue that some international comparable accountability for the allocation may still be desired. It should also be feasible—to a considerable degree—when bearing in mind the caveats to interpretation which are discussed in the following section. It may not, however, be meaningful to propose a system whereby support for activities benefiting children can be summarized into a single number to be compared against an aid target in support of children's rights. It is not feasible to link ODA to specific objectives within the child-rights agenda (for example, ODA in support of children's participation or aid supporting juvenile justice reform).

12.2.3. Assessing aid quantity, quality, and leverage

QUANTITY

The notion of shared responsibility to accelerate development in lower-income countries dates back to the first development decade in the 1960s. At that time, it was estimated that 0.7 per cent of gross domestic product (GDP) from developed countries could fill the resource gap that would enable GDP to grow by 6 per cent in the developing countries. Subsequently, the 0.7 per cent benchmark became the goal for aid from the developed world and was endorsed by the UN. Over the years it has become delinked from its original focus on capital accumulation, and is seen as the rich nations' measurement of support and burden-sharing in international development.

OECD-DAC member states report on their ODA according a set of agreed principles and rules (which define, inter alia, ODA and the ODA recipient countries and organizations). The rules ensure consistency in reporting over time and comparability of data between donors. In principle this ensures transparency and accountability in the assessment of development assistance vis-à-vis the international community and taxpayers in donor countries. The OECD reporting system, however, is 'exclusive' in the sense that one aid activity can be reported only against a single sector. Statistics of a 'qualitative nature' are collected for key cross-cutting themes in international development (for example, assistance explicitly targeted to improving gender equality) through the so-called policy-markers.

Based on national reporting the OECD calculates the share of ODA in each DAC member's gross national income (GNI) (earlier GDP), which is seen as a measure of overall burden sharing. However, the assessment of donor efforts to increase resources to specific sectors or themes cannot be based solely on ODA volumes. The targeting of aid also needs to be addressed. The usual practice is to examine aid trends within a sector as compared to total aid or total 'sector allocable' aid, which facilitates the identification of sector policies and priorities of the donor by excluding either unpredictable categories or those that are not entirely under the control of the aid administration and could not have been allocated in any case to the sector (see section 12.3). For example, in recent years, total ODA figures have included increasing amounts of debt relief, the calculation of which is not without controversy. Also, allocations to humanitarian assistance (including in-kind food aid) which are of great importance, may not reflect current development policy objectives or directions or may fluctuate considerably on an annual basis. However, as will be discussed later, if multilateral funding is excluded from the 'sector' or thematic funding, the assessment may lead to an underestimation of effort.

Assessment of ODA volumes is also carried out in the context of international conferences that evaluate, usually with some contention, the resource gaps in specific sectors or themes. Global estimates for resource requirements are usually based on 'best practices', incorporating effective and efficient approaches, and are intended to advance sustainable systems. Evaluations are, however, limited with regards to what role these estimates play in increasing ODA for particular purposes or whether they are instrumental in building a consensus around conference objectives. The continued attention to these types of projections suggests that they are important to the global debate.

Recent OECD reports on aid allocations to specific sectors or themes (for example, basic social services (BSS), HIV/AIDS, water supply, and sanitation) have pointed to the difficulty of incorporating activities in statistics data that address several objectives at the same time. Donors may use markers in their internal reporting systems to capture their aid allocations for specific priorities. However, counting the same activity against several priorities will bias the analysis of the extent to which donors' contributions are closing the identified resource gaps in general.

QUALITY

Estimating resource gaps and monitoring aid flows to assess progress are closely linked to the aid-effectiveness agenda—that is, issues of allocation among countries or their support of 'global public goods' (for example, new vaccines to fight malaria and HIV/AIDS); the absorptive capacity or potential of countries and/or government institutions to make good use of resources; the balance among interventions (textbooks, teacher training, and sanitation facilities in schools); coordination among different types of development partners (bilateral and multilateral donors, NGOs, and the partner government); the role of resources provided through international development finance and the private sector; and the more general question of the fungibility of aid. These challenges have given rise to the current debate about the channels of delivery, coordination, selectivity in the choice of partner countries, ownership, and so on that constitute the new aid architecture.

Another qualitative aspect that raises new challenges to the interpretation of ODA levels has to do with the integration of human-rights-based approaches to development cooperation. It is now commonly understood that to serve its purpose and achieve its objectives, design and supervision within aid activity must engage in a dialogue between 'the duty bearers' (the appropriate level of government and service providers) and the 'right holders' (those for whom the services are intended, including marginalized and vulnerable groups who may not be reached with systems targeted to the population in general). OECD-DAC is currently discussing the integration of human rights and development.[6] Participating UN agencies at the Stamford meeting in May 2003 adopted guiding principles for human-rights-based approaches to programming. However, determining whether an activity has been developed and is carried out through a human-rights-based approach introduces a new set of challenges for aid assessment. It suggests that an agreed set of assessment criteria should be part of the regular qualitative peer reviews of member countries' aid programmes carried out by the DAC.

LEVERAGING AND MULTIPLE DELIVERY CHANNELS

Leveraging—using allocations or policy analysis to attract other allocations/ actions for shared objectives—is an important part of development co-operation whether implemented through traditional partnerships or new modalities such as budget support (the previous chapter by Michael Hubbard (Chapter 11) has a detailed discussion on budget support). Donor governments support development cooperation through a wide range of partners to leverage/contribute to development at different levels of society, including government institutions, civil society, and NGOs. They take advantage of the expertise, access, and focus of specialized multilateral organizations (ILO, WHO, UNESCO) or operational agencies (UNICEF, UNDP, WFP, UNFPA) as well as NGOs that may also be specialized or have a particular operational approach/reach. Funding for these partners is either in the form of general support for their mandates (core funding for multilateral organizations and framework agreements with NGOs), funds-in-trust, or contributions to specific projects and programmes in line with the donor's development objectives (the latter two are recorded in DAC statistics as multi-bilateral aid). Delegated co-operation is a relatively new channel of aid delivery. Rather than select a multilateral/UN or NGO partner, the 'sleeping partner' allocates resources towards a country or an objective by designating another DAC member to act and negotiate on its behalf. This may give the donor a higher profile with the partner country than would be the case with an international partner.

Leveraging has also been raised in the context of public—private partnerships— initiatives to mobilize private resources both locally and internationally for development purposes. Relatively large private contributions to specific initiatives, such as the Global Fund to fight AIDS, Tuberculosis, and Malaria (GFATM) and the Global Alliance for Vaccines and Immunization (GAVI), have brought about new structures in development cooperation. These can be seen as vertical

---

[6] OECD GOVNET mandated the Human Rights and Development Task Team to work towards an action-oriented policy paper; a related workshop on integrating human rights into development was held on 19 Oct. 2005.

programmes challenging—or complementing—the current trend towards budget support. Efforts are at least being made to integrate the assistance from these programmes into sector programmes and poverty-reduction strategy papers (PRSPs).[7] As the following analysis will show, GFATM, for example, appears to have been successful in mobilizing and directing funds towards the HIV/AIDS crisis. However, education aid which does not have corporate sponsor(s) has also increased. Both areas have been the subject of recent conferences and high-visibility initiatives.

Such multi-layered development co-operation with an increasing number of players—and increased attention to harmonization and quality, including aid guided by a human-rights approach—poses demands on the compilation and interpretation of ODA statistics for specific purposes. Core funding of multilateral and non-governmental partners is a good example. Data are available on these contributions as well as increasingly on the activities subsequently financed. Statistical presentations occasionally depict these as being part of a donor's aid for a specific purpose (imputed amounts)—for example, for HIV/AIDS or education. However, a proliferation of such statistics can easily inflate the public's perception of total ODA.

MULTIPLE REPORTING OBLIGATIONS, MULTIPLE REPORTING SYSTEMS

Reporting systems are expected to produce data that enable the quality, quantity, and leveraging of aid to be assessed concurrently. There is a pull in opposite directions: the Paris agreement between donors and developing countries, supported by much of the economic development research community and vocal civil society advocates, asks donor governments to provide more-or-less unconditional support for partner governments or to channel funds as cash transfers to multilateral and NGO partners. Yet, at the same time, taxpayers, media, and other stakeholders in international development are asking for evidence of strong financial commitment to specific human-development objectives.

In practical terms, reporting systems serve several objectives. Foreign affairs ministries and development cooperation agencies report to parliament (or in the case of a multilateral agency to its board of governments). They are increasingly requested to indicate results on key objectives (as viewed by the general public/media—for example, addressing street children and trafficking) while also showing support for the Paris Agenda. It is interesting to see that one of the strongest donor advocates for budget support, DFID, was asked to give Parliament sectoral breakdowns for aid delivered as budget support. Since 2004, the

---

[7] The impact on assessment of aid of the health aid pact launched in Sept. 2007 as an initiative by the UK Prime Minister Gordon Brown with a number of multilateral organizations, including the World Bank, and bilateral donors (Canada, France, Germany, and Norway) to coordinate aid programmes at the country level, is not yet clear.

department has applied a methodology whereby budget-support expenditure is attributed pro rata to the ODA-eligible parts of the recipient government's budget. The focus on ODA-eligible expenditure explicitly excludes elements such as defence. It is intended to promote greater transparency on how each country receiving British aid uses it (for more detail, see UNESCO 2005: 190). The same rationale is sometimes evident in aid-activity descriptions (for example, a donor reporting on its contribution to the World Bank-managed Afghanistan Reconstruction Trust Fund is required to highlight its preferences for support to education, public administration, and livelihood and social security). Donor governments report annually to the DAC on aid using a series of classifications that intermingle the purposes and modalities of aid and policy outcomes. Donors are also called on to produce increasingly detailed accounts of activities for specific sectors or objectives for various international events or conventions, which usually have specific reporting obligations. The requirement to report every five years on 'international cooperation' in support of the CRC is an example.

As each development theme has its particular specificities, there is a tendency to launch new initiatives to track financial flows. One such new initiative is 'monitoring financial flows for child health at global and country levels' (sponsored, among others, by USAID). It develops and tests methodologies for tracking expenditures on child health, including ODA from major international donors, with the aim:

• to 'help raise global awareness' of the gap between expenditures and the funding needed to achieve the child-survival objectives embodied in the MDGs;
• to encourage greater and more-efficient national and international investment for child survival; and
• to hold stakeholders at all levels accountable.

Importantly, the initiative concludes that OECD-DAC's creditor reporting system (CRS) database should constitute the basis for global ODA tracking, and that it will require improved project descriptions by all reporting agencies and better reporting by multilaterals (Powell-Jackson et al. 2006). Also, this initiative may run up against the Paris Agenda objectives.

The multi-type donor structure and expectations and demand of accountability by private contributors have led to parallel reporting systems. Some of these initiatives have sought to capture intra-sector ODA allocations—for example, to health within a wide range of activities, including research and development. This begs the question whether separate systems/surveys of individual donors can provide information that is of a comparable quality and comprehensiveness to justify going beyond the OECD system, and suggests that alternative estimates be used only as 'ballpark' indications. Operating within the OECD-DAC system makes it possible to complement reporting categories with word searches and collective reflection on how to capture contributions from 'complementary' activities. It should be acknowledged that the OECD-DAC system has evolved from a system that reflects development cooperation priorities of the 1970s, including categories detailing interventions in areas that are of less focus in today's aid orientation. However, the implementation of a marker system does extend the opportunities of analysis, as does the increased opportunity of word searches at project level. These developments suggest that DAC might seek to capture some of the private NGO flows in the CRS format, on a voluntary basis, or that DAC donors should seek to enhance their activity-specific reporting with descriptors to make word searches easier and to allow easy reference back to the DAC-supported system in the interest of accountability.

12.3. Aid for basic social services

This section illustrates some of the factors that need to be considered in order to assess aid for cross-cutting development concerns, such as universal access to basic social services (BSS).[8] The concept of BSS pertains to the provision of services in education, health (nutritional and reproductive), and clean water supply and adequate sanitation at the primary or basic level. Within a broader supportive environment, these services are necessary to promote the survival, protection, and development of children, as articulated in the Convention.

12.3.1. Origin of the concept 'basic social services'

The concept of 'basic social services'[9] was put forward by UNDP, UNESCO, UNFPA, UNICEF, and WHO as part of the so-called 20/20 Initiative which was promoted in the declaration of the World Summit on Social Development (WSSD) in Copenhagen in May 1995.[10] Based on global estimates of resource requirements to meet social development goals, most notably those set at the 1990 World Summit for Children, and the essential health service packages (World Bank 1993), the agencies calculated the resource gap to be US$30–40 billion annually during the 1990s. They further proposed, as a guiding principle, that developing countries strive to allocate 20 per cent of their public expenditures to support these services, appropriately balanced to maximize synergy. The donor community would, in return, meet the gap in funding,

---

[8] The analysis in section 12.3 is shaped by the analysis undertaken by the OECD; see OECD (2006).

[9] The origin and basis for the initiative is elaborated in Parker and Jespersen (1994).

[10] The World Bank joined in a subsequent revision prepared for the WSSD+5 in Geneva in 2000.

which, it was argued, could be met by earmarking 20 per cent of each donor's total aid budget to BSS, along with a steady progress towards the 0.7 per cent ODA goal.[11] DAC members agreed to revise the CRS sector classification to allow aid earmarked to basic social services to be identified separately. The first analysis of member states' support for BSS was prepared by OECD-DAC for the 2000 Geneva Summit, which took stock, at mid-decade, of the WSSD agenda. This indicated that donors were on average allocating 14 per cent of 'sector allocable' ODA to basic social services.[12] Reviews by UNDP and UNICEF for the 1998 Hanoi Conference on the 20/20 Initiative had indicated that developing countries had on average allocated the same level of public spending to these services.[13] Subsequent reviews of aid flows have shown increases in allocation for basic social services.

From the outset, the 20/20 Initiative was met with widespread scepticism: the initiative was seen as placing too much emphasis on resources while ignoring the importance of a strong institutional context—which was, in turn, countered by arguments that effectiveness, efficiency, and synergy were integral to the proposed approach. Furthermore, it should be seen as a necessary but not sufficient part within a greater context (20 per cent for BSS and 80 per cent for the rest).

In the current perspective, it may be considered that the initiative failed to link the BSS concept directly to the CRC and its objectives of 'highest attainable level of health' and 'of education'. Furthermore, the focus was on supporting public services that directly advance good health and good education for all. It did not include what is commonly understood as social safety nets/protection/welfare systems, which are necessary for the protection of children from harm and abuse. Nor, perhaps intentionally, did it include humanitarian assistance. Thus, to assess the ODA in support of the realization of children's rights, it is necessary to consider reporting under a wider set of aid categories. Section 12.4 reviews the experience of two donors.

12.3.2. Trends in ODA and aid to basic social services since 1995

Total ODA has increased steadily from 1997 onwards in real terms, and since 2001 also as a percentage of GNI.[14] The Monterrey Conference in 2002 led to

---

[11] The date by which universal access should be achieved is somewhat obscure. The WSC goals were set for 2000 but the population and development resource needs were extended to 2015.

[12] As is discussed in section 12.2, the assessment of priority to BSS is currently calculated against sector allocable ODA, suggesting in effect that this share should be somewhat higher than the share in total ODA to bridge the estimated resource gap.

[13] UNICEF and UNDP with contributions from the World Bank and United Nations Population Fund (UNFPA); see UNICEF (1998).

[14] Unless otherwise noted, commitment data have been used (showing direction and intent of the aid programme). Efforts are increasing by DAC members to report actual expenditures to the OECD. See discussion in Annex to Jespersen and Benn (2007).

further increases in ODA: sector-allocable aid grew from an average of US$36 billion in 2001–2 to US$45 billion in 2003–4 (constant 2004 prices).[15] Debt relief almost doubled during the same period (from US$7 billion to US$13 billion). But, despite statements from many bilateral donors to that effect, there are no significant increases in general budget support (included in the category 'general programme assistance'). Multilateral aid (that is, contributions by DAC members to the core budgets of multilateral organizations) increased only slightly over the period. Sector-allocable aid can be broken down into four main categories: social infrastructure and services, economic infrastructure and services, production, and multisector aid. Aid to 'social infrastructure and services' has been increasing throughout the last decade (Figure 12.1) and most of the rise in 2003–4 is attributed to this category. Support to education has remained relatively stable, whereas health and population/reproductive health sectors have attracted more funding, in particular to combat HIV/AIDS. Nevertheless, the largest increases have taken place in the

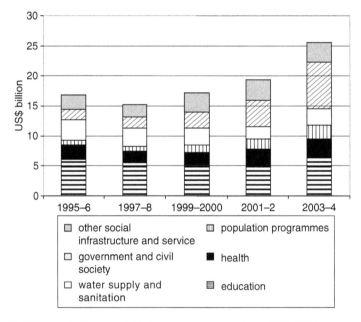

Figure 12.1 Bilateral ODA to social infrastructure and services, 1995–2004, commitments (constant 2004 prices)

Source: OECD/DAC.

[15] Sector-allocable ODA consists of ODA with the exclusion of humanitarian assistance, aid related to debt cancellation, general programme assistance (including budget support), and core funding for multilateral organizations.

government and civil society sector in the fields of security and peace building and support to general government administration. Aid for economic infrastructure and services has been declining, except during 2004, which reflects the start-up in the reconstruction of Iraq.

Basic social services sectors have benefited from an overall increase in sector-allocable aid. Bilateral ODA commitments to BSS more than doubled between 1995 and 2004 (from US$3.2 billion in 1995–6 to US$7.1 billion in 2003–4) (Figure 12.2). Growing steadily until 2000, there was a major increase in 2002 in aid to basic health and population/reproductive health, which is partly explained by the creation of the GFATM[16] with initial commitments from donors amounting to US$700 million in 2002, and in 2004 in aid to basic education. The addition to basic education may reflect the revitalization of the goals of Education for All in Dakar (April 2000) and the Fast Track Initiative Catalytic Fund. The trend in aid to BSS sub-sectors is increasing across all DAC donors. Detailed analysis shows, however, that the 'jumps' are due to a few relatively large commitments, subsequently benefiting a limited number of recipient countries (cf. OECD 2006).

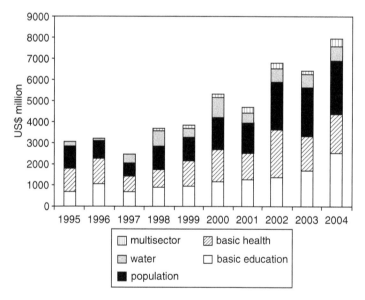

Figure 12.2 Bilateral ODA to basic social services, breakdown by sub-sector, 1995–2004, commitments (constant 2004 prices)

Source: OECD/DAC.

[16] From 2003 onwards contributions to GFATM have been recorded as multilateral aid.

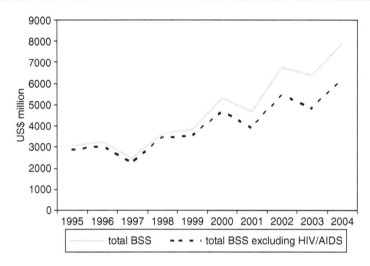

Figure 12.3 Bilateral ODA to basic social services, excluding HIV/AIDS, 1995–2004, commitments (constant 2004 prices)

Source: OECD/DAC.

Because the increase in ODA for HIV/AIDS has been so considerable, it is of interest to review the basic social service assistance that excludes these allocations. Figure 12.3 shows that the trend still increasing, albeit more modestly.

Examination of the data on aid directed to BSS confirms the upward trend if considered against the sector-allocable ODA. This is also evident when measured against the proposed 20 per cent target, as Figure 12.4 illustrates. As a share of total bilateral sector-allocable ODA, aid to basic social services peaked at 18 per cent in 2002 and is currently 16 per cent on average. If contributions to multilateral organizations are taken into account, the share is almost 20 per cent.

It is interesting to note that although the key champions for basic social services and the 20/20 Initiative had faded by 2000,[17] the upward trend in aid to BSS continued. Much of this is explained by the fact that many of the goals targeted by the Initiative were integrated and reconfirmed as the goals of the Millennium Declaration of the Millennium Summit in New York, September 2000.[18]

---

[17] An editorial in the *Lancet* (11–17 Dec. 2004: 2071–4) also argued that UNICEF, by increasingly directing its attention to other areas of the child rights agenda, has given less attention to child survival and development.

[18] The Millennium Declaration and the MDGs omit the goals regarding reproductive health that were set at the 1994 Cairo Conference and reaffirmed at the Beijing Conference on Women and Development.

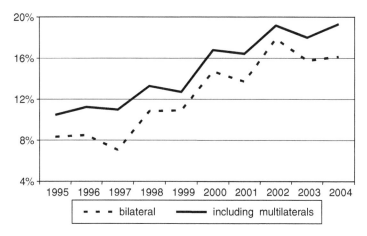

Figure 12.4 Share of aid to basic social services, 1995–2004, bilateral aid and total aid (including imputed amounts for multilaterals) (2004 prices)

Source: OECD/DAC.

12.3.3. Changes in modalities for support to BSS

The data on aid to BSS relate to projects and programmes which have basic social services as their main purpose. Aid to BSS channelled through sector programmes, sector budget support, or pooled funding is captured only when these focus entirely on basic services (such as the education-sector development programme in Bangladesh) or if a donor reports commitments at the component level. This, however, is usually not the case. Sector programmes reported at a more general level (such as the health-sector strategic plan in Mozambique) are not captured. The obvious point of interest that arises is the size of the share of aid delivered in the form of sector-wide approaches to education, health, or water. These contributions are separately identified in the CRS through a 'sector programme flag'.[19]

As part of the general review on the reporting of sector programmes in the CRS, DAC members were requested to verify the commitments they had made to education, health, and water supply and sanitation in 1995–2004. The DAC Secretariat provided each member with a list of possible sector programmes, resulting from a text search on words such as 'sector

---

[19] Sector programme aid is defined as comprising 'contributions to carry out wide-ranging development plans in a defined sector such as agriculture, education, transportation, etc.'. The directives further specify that 'assistance is made available "in cash" or "in kind", with or without restriction on the specific use of the funds, but on the condition that the recipient executes a development plan in favour of the sector concerned'. Sector budget support as such is not defined in the current directives, but falls under the definition of sector programme aid.

reform', 'sector support', 'swap', 'pooled fund', or 'budget support'. Descriptions of all activities valued over US$10 million were also reviewed. Members were then asked to go through the list, indicate the activities which were indeed sector programmes (as defined in the directives) and the amount estimated to be spent on BSS.

As Table 12.1 shows, aid extended in the form of sector programmes has been increasing over the last five years, but still constitutes only a minor share of total aid to education, health, and water supply and sanitation. Furthermore, the bulk of the programmes in these sectors have been recorded as BSS and are thus captured in the standard aid statistics on BSS, as Figure 12.5 illustrates.[20] In 2003, 11 per cent of the allocations to BSS were within sector

Table 12.1. Commitments for sector programmes in education, health, and water, 2000–4, US$ millions (constant 2004 prices)

	2000	2001	2002	2003	2004
Australia	—	—	—	—	—
Austria	—	—	3.8*	0.7*	2.0*
Belgium	—	9.1	26.1	8.9	22.8
Canada	—	—	—	70.2	130.8
Denmark	61.9	—	131.8	78.5	382.0
Finland	—	—	—	44.6	35.2
France	—	—	—	10.1*	33.7*
Germany	n/a	n/a	n/a	n/a	n/a
Greece	—	—	—	1.1	—
Ireland	—	—	—	21.8	26.0
Italy	—	—	10.2	—	—
Japan	—	—	—	—	7.7
Luxembourg	—	—	—	—	—
Netherlands	74.0	27.2	351.5	80.8	287.6
New Zealand	—	—	—	7.7	16.3
Norway	—	27.5	33.7	160.3	56.2
Portugal	—	1.9	2.9	0.9	4.1
Spain	—	—	—	4.2	—
Sweden	25.0	—	46.1	222.4	50.0
Switzerland	—	—	—	52.8*	1.6
United Kingdom	—	—	—	829.6	385.7
United States	—	—	420.2	82.5	650.1
EU	569.9	396.0	229.4	471.5	300.5
Total DAC	730.8	461.8	1,255.7	2,148.6	2,392.4
Memo: Total aid to education, health, water by DAC members	12,421.0	11,257.1	13,184.2	15,089.3	17,721.0

Note: * = data to be amended. For France, only the French Development Agency (AfD) has provided corrected data.

[20] About three-quarters of the total amount of sector programmes in education and health in 2000–4 were classified under purpose codes 112xx and 122xx, respectively; 60 per cent of sector programmes in water supply and sanitation were classified under code 14030.

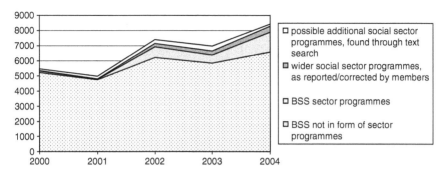

Figure 12.5 Bilateral aid to BSS in 2000–4 and wider social sector programmes (education, health, water supply, and sanitation), US$ millions (2004 prices)

Source: OECD/DAC.

programmes, and 17 per cent in 2004. Finally, to obtain an indication of the maximum amount of BSS aid, data on 'possible social sector programmes' for members that have not yet responded to the Secretariat are included to indicate the upper limit of aid to BSS.

While the review on the reporting of sector programmes is still incomplete, it is already possible at this stage to conclude that standard statistics do capture the quasi totality of DAC members' bilateral aid to BSS over the period 1995–2004.

12.4. Issues to consider in the development of a schematic approach for capturing ODA for children

A small but growing number of smaller donors explicitly recognize the CRC as the guide to their development policy, including Austria, Belgium, Norway, and Sweden. The development-assistance policies of Norway and Sweden, for example, are both guided by strategies to promote and protect the human rights of children.

- The child-rights strategy of Norway focuses on health, education, participation, and protection; special mention is also made of children affected by armed conflict, the role of children in peace building, and violence against children. (Norway's Ministry of Foreign Affairs 2005)
- Sweden's strategy focuses assistance in support of child rights on health, education, social reform, and disadvantaged children (particularly child labourers, children with disabilities, children subjected to sexual exploitation, children affected by HIV/AIDS, by war, armed conflicts, and refugee situations, and children in institutions) (GoS 2001).

The aforementioned forthcoming UNICEF IRC study on donors and child rights also considers how some of the big donors that are not explicitly guided by child rights, but none the less have children as explicit concerns, support the realization of child rights in developing countries. Some of the areas of focus in Norway and Sweden conform with the DAC statistical definition of aid to BSS while others appear to apply to, and are frequently recorded in, the sectors 'government and civil society' and 'other social infrastructure and services'. Norway's and Sweden's internal recording systems (used for reporting to the CRS) permit the tagging of activities specifically identified by these donors as being directed towards children as main beneficiaries. Therefore, a review of their data can indicate the codes under which child-centred aid (protection and participation, children affected by war, refugee children) is likely to be found. An initial examination of the data for Sweden shows that over half of total aid targeted to children was for education and health/ population. But, child-centred aid is also being delivered through human rights activities, and social and welfare services, a large share of which is earmarked for programmes on HIV/AIDS mitigation. In the case of Norway, aid targeted to children, although more widely spread, was nevertheless focused on education, health/population, and activities classified as support to human rights, strengthening civil society, and social/welfare services. In both cases, highlighting activities as being geared for children may suggest no more than the fact that children (often also women) are among the targeted beneficiaries, whether in connection with mine clearance or supporting juvenile justice systems advocated by the CRC.

It remains to be determined whether additional non-BSS activities targeted to children could be captured through data information on the channel of delivery (searching for agencies such as UNICEF, Save the Children).[21] Based on such a review, a shortcut approach could then be proposed for identifying the sectors where major geared-for-children activities appear most frequently or should be most substantively classified. At this stage, it is nevertheless possible to conclude that the following areas would need to be considered in a systematic approach to identify aid specifically targeted to children.

---

[21] The internal systems of Norway and Sweden permit the estimation of this total through a specific field (policy-marker) identifying activities targeted to children. However, it is important to note that there may be considerable variations within the agencies and between the countries on how the marker is used. These variations, plus the fact that not all donors have such a marker, would seem to imply that it is not advisable to attempt international comparisons of ODA for specific child-centred activities beyond aid to basic social services. By utilizing the distinct child policy-markers, it is nevertheless possible to review child-centred activities for an understanding of the nature of the support and the channels of delivery (e.g., multilateral agencies, Save the Children, churches). This can in turn contribute to suggestions for 'key search words' for donors who do not have specific markers.

12.4.1. Aid to BSS

BSS was conceived to identify basic services for children and their families, as articulated at the major international conferences in the early 1990s. To capture ODA for children as defined by the CRC (under 18 years), it could be considered to add (to aid for BSS) aid for lower secondary and even higher secondary education (vocational training directed at those under 18).

12.4.2. Sector-wide approaches targeted specifically at basic services

Donors have stated that support for basic services in the social sectors is increasingly, or significantly, undertaken through participation in co-ordinated donor support for government-sector initiatives, either through the coordination and harmonization of efforts (sector-programme support (SPS)/sector-wide approaches (SWAPs)) or through direct budget support to the sector (basket/pooled funding/budget support). Some sector initiatives are directly targeted to basic services, while others support reforms and development of entire sectors. Sector programmes targeted at basic services are reported under the relevant basic services codes.[22]

12.4.3. Other sector-wide approaches

It is widely argued that sector reform/development programmes contribute to the fundamentals of long-term sustainable development, including improvement of services at the basic level and thus these should be counted in their entirety as support for BSS.

12.4.4. Pro-rating of regular resource contributions through other development agencies

Donors also channel some part of their support for basic social services and assistance directly targeted to children through the multilateral system and possibly particularly outside the BSS area. Multi-bilateral assistance is captured in the CRS. By contrast, support provided as regular resources to agencies that deal with social services or children is not part of bilateral sector-allocable ODA. Such aid can be included in the statistics using the method of pro-rating. It is important to do so, as otherwise donors' efforts to support BSS and children will be underestimated.

Much assistance within the child-rights agenda, particularly outside the BSS, appears to be channelled through framework agreements with national NGOs or organizations in the partner countries. These agreements outline the broader

---

[22] The review of reporting on sector programmes in the CRS confirmed this.

objectives of social development or promotion of children's rights that can be attained through a variety of activities across countries. In such cases, donors' reporting to the CRS relate to the framework agreements but not the activities financed within the agreements. Information on the use of funds is obtained by the donor agencies from the NGOs ex-post.

12.4.5. Other ODA targeted directly at children

It is recognized that many CRC concerns can best be understood and implemented in terms of operational approaches (human rights-based approaches to programming) although they also have validity in their own right, as is shown by the focus areas of Norway and Sweden. While a system of international comparison of ODA efforts in direct support of children cannot identify qualitative differences among programme interventions within a given sector,[23] it could be used to track a number of activity areas that are frequently identified as child protection and child-rights promotion. These include areas such as combating child labour, child soldiers, exploitation and abuse, and promotion of the participation and, more generally, the human rights of children. Some of these activities are also prominently linked to humanitarian assistance. Assistance directed at children outside BSS is likely to be found in such categories as 'government and civil society', and 'other social infrastructure and services' (and in humanitarian assistance). However, these categories are also used for support for activities that are general in nature or targeted at other categories of beneficiaries, and direct support to children may constitute only a small share of the total. Based on the proposed methodology, Table 12.2 details the data on aid targeted to children within education, health, and water supply and sanitation sectors by Sweden and Norway. Aid to BSS captured through standard statistics make up 40 per cent to 50 per cent of the aid targeted to children.

The current limited analysis of child-targeted aid suggests that donors who are explicitly committed to advancing the child-rights agenda allocate a considerable proportion of their efforts outside the social sectors that are traditionally associated with children. Many activities are classified as human rights and support to civil society.[24] A further analysis should examine whether this assistance is targeted directly at advancing child-rights, protecting children, or have children among the beneficiaries. The analysis could also shed light on the channels of delivery to show how the international community in practice endeavours to reach children. According to a preliminary view, multilateral agencies and a combination of local and selected international NGOs are the key players in these efforts. This in turn suggests that donors seek out these

---

[23] For example, whether primary education development is child-centred or not.
[24] Note that it has been possible to track assistance for the demobilization of child soldiers only from 2005 onwards.

Table 12.2. Estimates of ODA in direct support of children within education, health, and water supply and sanitation sectors, commitments by Norway and Sweden, 2003–4

	Norway		Sweden	
	2003	2004	2003	2004
A Aid to basic social services	197	141	189	150
Basic education	120	76	44	59
Basic health	69	52	103	90
Basic drinking water & basic sanitation	4	2	43	1
Multisector aid to basic social services	4	11	0	0
Of which sector programmes targeted specially at basic services	52	26	190	48
B Secondary education	2	6	5	1
C Other sector programmes (in education, health, water supply & sanitation	60	0	87	14
Of which estimated allocations for basic services	n/a		82	12
D Pro-rating of multilateral contributions[1]	152	227	106	201
Total	351	374	382	364

Note:
[1] Including World Bank, regional banks, UNICEF, UNFPA, UNAIDS.
Source: OECD/DAC.

particular partners because these are known to advocate human-rights-based approaches and have recognized track records for stimulating sustainable change in these areas. Further qualitative examination will enable clearer understanding of such decision processes.

12.5. Concluding remarks

There has been a clear upward trend in ODA for basic social services during the past decade as a proportion of total sector allocable ODA and more modestly in real terms. Increased aid for HIV/AIDS has been a significant factor in the overall increase. The delivery of aid in general and to the social sectors is changing. Budget support, sector programmes, and special grant-giving programmes such as GFATM have become more prevalent as instruments of harmonization and recognition of the lead roles and responsibilities of governments in programme countries. These changes affect children, albeit possibly less so than initial appearances may suggest. Aid plays an important role in bridging resource gaps, stimulating reforms, and resource mobilization by partner governments. However, issues such as the often short-term nature of aid commitments, a lack of absorptive capacity in the programme country, and the growing service deficit (growing number of school-age children or HIV infected children who are not receiving services) result in persistently high resource and capacity gaps as suggested by the slow progress towards the Millennium Development Goals.

Awareness of and commitments to the child-rights agenda have grown among donors and considerable aid may be flowing to areas of child protection and to child-rights promoters. These activities may be less affected by the new aid modalities as bilateral donors appear to be providing much assistance through NGOs and the multilateral system. Aid to children outside basic social services is currently difficult to assess.

The analysis for this chapter suggests the desirability of a system better to track such aid in order to assess impact, draw lessons, and stimulate policy discussions with programme countries and with the Committee on the Rights of the Child. Ultimately, however, donors also need consistently to apply a child and general human rights approach in their development assistance, in negotiations of budget support, programme assistance, humanitarian programmes, and in choice of development partners. Better assessment of ODA can support such reflections but not replace political will and dialogue.

References

Government of Sweden (GoS) (2001) 'The Rights of the Child as a Perspective in Development Co-operation'. Stockholm: Government Communication 2001/02:186. <http://www.regeringen.se/content/1/c4/10/92/cdced638.pdf>.

Jespersen, E., and J. Benn (2007) 'International Support for the Realisation of Children's Rights: Aid Modalities and Accountability in Reporting, and a Review of Aid for Basic Social Services'. Innocenti Working Paper 2007-02. Florence: UNICEF Innocenti Research Centre. <http://www.unicef-irc.org/publications/pdf/iwp_2007_02.pdf>.

Ministry of Foreign Affairs of Norway (2005) 'Three Billion Reasons: Norway's Development Strategy for Children and Young People in the South'. Oslo: Ministry of Foreign Affairs.

OECD (2005) 'Paris Declaration on Aid Effectiveness'. High-Level Forum, 28 Feb.–2 Mar. Paris: OECD.

——(2006) 'CRS Aid Activities for BSS 1999–2004' and 'OECD International Development Statistics Online Databases'. <http://www.oecd.org/dac/stats/idsonline>.

Parker, D., and E. Jespersen (1994) '20/20: Mobilizing Resources for Children in the 1990s'. UNICEF Staff Working Paper 12. New York: UNICEF.

Powell-Jackson, T., J. Borgi, D. Mueller, et al. (2006) 'Countdown to 2015: Tracking Donor Assistance to Maternal, Newborn and Child Health'. *Lancet*, 368: 1077–87.

UNESCO (2005) 'EFA Global Monitoring Report 2005'. <http://portal.unesco.org/education/en/ev.php-URL_ID=35939&URL_DO=DO_TOPIC&URL_SECTION=201.html>.

UNICEF (1990) *Convention on the Rights of the Child*. World Declaration and Plan of Action from the World Summit for Children. New York: UNICEF.

UNICEF-UNDP (1998) 'Country Experiences in Assessing the Adequacy, Equity and Efficiency of Public Spending on Basic Social Services'. Paper prepared for the 20/20 Initiative Meeting, 27–9 Oct., Hanoi.

World Bank (1993) 'Investing in Health: World Development Report 1993'. Washington, DC: World Bank.

Part V

Managing Aid Flows

13

'Big Push' versus Absorptive Capacity: How to Reconcile the Two Approaches

Patrick Guillaumont and Sylviane Guillaumont Jeanneney

13.1. Introduction

Two opposing views seem to dominate the present aid debate: the 'big push' thesis and the absorptive capacity concern. The 'big push' is supported in particular by Sachs (2005) and is based on the poverty trap concept, while the absorptive capacity concern collects in a manifold concept several opposing views to the first approach. On the one hand, there is the United Nations' *mot d'ordre*, 'doubling aid to reduce poverty by half', and, on the other hand, the reviving scepticism that aid will not be absorbed usefully. *The End of Poverty*, by Jeffery Sachs (2005) faces the *White Man's Burden* by William Easterly (2006a). Incidentally, the term 'big push' does not appear in the index of Sachs' book but then neither is 'absorptive capacity' found in the Easterly index. The concept 'big push' listed in the Easterly index refers to the 'legend of the "big push"', and 'absorptive capacity' in the Sachs index makes reference to the statement: 'Limited absorptive capacity is not an argument against aid. It is the very reason that aid is needed!'

These two opposing views are not really new and paradoxically have common roots. One author, Paul N. Rosenstein-Rodan, may even appear as a major contributor both to the 'big push' theory and to the absorptive capacity concept applied to foreign aid. He first argued for the idea of increasing returns, for a 'big push', in 1943. During the 1950s he was joined by other development pioneers, in particular Nurkse (1953), who underlined the need for balanced growth to break the vicious circle of the supply and demand of capital. In 1961, Rosenstein-Rodan presented a comprehensive use of the absorptive capacity concept to measure the capital needs of the developing countries, based on the famous proposal by Millikan and Rostow (1957) to allocate aid according to capacity (once domestic savings were taken into account). Nurkse himself referred to the limitations of aid's absorptive capacity for investment, as did most of the main works on development economics in the 1950s. These limitations were first acknowledged in the International Bank for Reconstruction and Development's (IBRD) Fourth Annual Report in 1949 (see Guillaumont 1971 for a historic survey).

Why did absorptive capacity and the 'big push' not appear as contradictory half a century ago as they do today? First, both concepts are founded on the idea that low-income countries face structural obstacles to growth, which are reflected in the absorptive capacity and which require massive investment in interdependent sectors to be resolved. Second, aid today is likely to increase significantly: absorptive capacity then becomes a kind of warning against the risk of waste, whereas in the past it was a criterion for mobilizing more aid. Fifty years ago the main criticism of aid was not presented in this context. Coming from rather extreme and opposite political positions, whether liberal or radical, criticism was targeted at the support given through aid either to enlarging states or to non-democratic regimes and corrupted bourgeoisies. Currently, opposition is somewhat different. The main argument for doubling aid is not simply to fill a financial gap, but to push countries out of the stagnation trap which will be impossible to escape otherwise (without, however, any clear statistical link between the size of the needed push and requirements for aid). The criticism then is an attack against the idea of a trap and its 'big push' corollary. Other critical opinions or reservations—mostly with regard to the notion of absorptive capacity—are intended to highlight all the reasons why increased aid is likely to be useless, wasted, or even harmful. Consequently an increase in aid would not lead to a 'big push' or the subsequent escape from poverty.

In this context, the notion of absorptive capacity of external aid has been used in connection with several different, at times contradictory, meanings. We can identify four main meanings:

- The first is the 'pipeline' effect; disbursement constraints or disbursement slowness, evidenced by a low rate of utilization of credits or a long lag between commitments and disbursements.

- The second meaning refers to possible macroeconomic problems associated with large aid inflows (disbursements): these include in particular the loss of competitiveness through real currency appreciation ('Dutch disease' effect) and the recently debated effects of aid volatility.

- The third and more classical meaning of absorptive capacity is a sharp decrease (or possibly a cancellation) in the marginal return of aid beyond a certain point in terms of growth when analysed at the macro level, in terms of projects or specific expenditures when analysed at the micro level. This is the 'decreasing returns' effect.

- Finally, a fourth meaning should be added, which is the 'socio-political approach', or the weakening of institutions induced by aid or a lack of social assimilation.

In this chapter we examine whether absorptive capacity, according to each of these four meanings, represents a justifiable reason for rejecting the proposal of a large increase in aid to help poor countries to leave the underdevelopment trap, subject to the existence of such a trap. To do so we consider the following points and related questions:

- *The poverty trap hypothesis*: fact or fiction? We argue this is a probability for many countries, particularly the least-developed countries (LDCs). Consequently, increased aid for these states is important.

- *Disbursement constraints and short-term bottlenecks*: why is there an under-utilization of credits? Reforming the aid procedures is needed to overcome these constraints.

- *Macroeconomic difficulties*, including the loss of competitiveness and macroeconomic volatility: to what extent is there the risk of 'Dutch disease'? What is needed here is a focus on both productivity and the stabilizing impact of aid.

- *Decreasing returns*: why are they decreasing more or less quickly? We argue that the decrease is slowed down in vulnerable countries, which makes these nations a priority in aid allocation.

- *Institution weakening*: how can it be avoided? We believe that it can be avoided to a large extent with performance-based conditionality.

13.2. The underdevelopment trap: not the rule, but a risk for many—particularly the LDCs

The possibility that low-income countries may be locked in a trap of poverty or underdevelopment and that moving out of the trap is unlikely to occur without a significant aid boost can be considered as the underlying principle of the UN Millennium Project and of the Report of the Commission for Africa initiated by Tony Blair. It is also the basis of the related proposals to find new and additional development resources, such as the International Finance Facility. However, the underlying principle has recently been challenged in several studies, some rather sophisticated and academic, others rather polemical. The issue is actually extensive and quite complicated. Without going into details of the debate, we take a look at the main arguments of the recent critique. These appear twofold: (i) there are neither analytical nor empirical grounds for the existence of a trap; (ii) neither is there evidence of aid being a factor likely to support the 'big push' (out of the trap). In spite of the critique, our conclusions support the importance of an aid-supported 'big push'.

13.2.1. Truncated criticism of the concept of a low-level equilibrium

The concept of a poverty trap at the macro level, developed in the 1950s in particular by Leibenstein (1954) and Nelson (1956), has recently been revitalized. Sachs et al. (2004) re-examine three sources of a trap: a low-level stable equilibrium, namely increasing returns, the saving income function, and the fertility-income function. The two first factors have been debated in particular by Kraay and Raddatz (2005), who argue that the functions do not conform to such conditions that could lead to a trap. Their scepticism seems to be endorsed by the 2005 *Global Monitoring Report* (World Bank 2005), 'In general... neither macroeconomic nor microeconomic evidence tends to support the existence of such traps'. Easterly's criticism in his book (2006a) and in a recent review paper (2006b) has been more radical. A purely empirical argument has been added to the analytical scepticism and can be summarized as follows: the number of countries that forty or fifty years ago were low income but that have been able to grow significantly and to move up from this low level is not negligible. Thus, a low level of income by itself is not a stable equilibrium or a trap, a fact which cannot be contested.

The point is that many countries, which were initially considered as low income, have remained poor and they share certain common structural characteristics, suggesting that the combination of these characteristics creates conditions conducive to low-level equilibrium. In Guillaumont (2009), we identify these in the persistently low-income-per-capita countries as the combination of a relatively low level of human capital and a high vulnerability to exogenous shocks. These two structural handicaps interact which makes sustained growth rather unlikely for logical reasons not rejected by econometric tests. Furthermore, these factors—in addition to the low level of income per capita—are precisely the same elements that the UN uses to identify the LDCs. It would then appear that a group of nations, corresponding roughly to the present LDCs, can be considered to constitute the future's most likely low-income countries. Briefly stated, not all low-income countries are trapped, but some clearly are and these are the LDCs. More precisely we find that:

• While there is no absolute convergence among all developing countries, two clear regimes of absolute convergence exist, the non-LDCs and the LDCs (at a significantly lower level, and leading to a lower steady state).

• Over a long (thirty-year) period, differences in income per capita perspectives among developing countries are rather well explained by three factors that correspond to the LDC identification criteria: in addition to the initial level of income per capita, the two variables reflecting structural handicaps—an economic vulnerability index and an index of human capital weakness, both expressed in logs—are significant negative factors. This means that they reflect an obstacle to growth or the possibility of a trap, all the more so because of their interaction (quite weaker results are found with the linear specification).

Of course, there can be other interpretations of the logic behind the notion of an underdevelopment trap (see, for instance, Berthélemy 2006), but it seems necessary to look at the structural specificities or initial conditions of countries that have been poor and remained poor for long periods.

13.2.2. The misuse of aid effectiveness literature to deny the possibility of a 'big push'

Another argument that has been used to play down the possibilities of a 'big push' supported by high aid inflows for moving countries out of the trap is in the mitigated results of cross-country regressions on aid effectiveness (see, for example, Chapter 2 of this volume by Finn Tarp). First, the results are not as ambiguous as is often argued, although the aggregate concept of aid has such a heterogeneous content (including humanitarian aid) that it makes it difficult to obtain very strong results. As we see later, positive results on aid effectiveness (possibly contingent on specific factors) have been found to be robust in external assessments (see Roodman 2004, for instance, on Hansen and Tarp 2001, and on Guillaumont and Chauvet 2001, and on Burnside and Dollar 2004). In particular, we argue that aid is efficient in promoting growth in countries that are vulnerable to exogenous shocks (Guillaumont and Chauvet 2001; Chauvet and Guillaumont 2004; 2009). We note that in a recent sceptical survey of aid–growth regressions referred to by opponents to the 'big push'-cum-aid, the authors (Rajan and Subramanian 2005b) omit consideration of the vulnerability factor of aid effectiveness.

Second, it is debatable that none of the low-income countries that have been able to emerge were supported by large, or even transitory, inflows of external aid. The most successful aid process is precisely the type that leads to self-sustained growth, and ultimately to a weaker aid–growth relationship. It seems that present econometric studies have not adequately addressed the time sequence of this relationship. Historical perspective is needed, which we can obtain by reviewing Korea, Mauritius, Thailand, Indonesia, and Tunisia— the countries that over the past decades have emerged or are now emerging. At the beginning of their growth period, these countries received significant inflows of aid which have subsequently and quite normally decreased during periods of growth.[1] For instance, the average aid-to-gross domestic product (GDP) ratio has decreased in Korea from 6.3 per cent in the 1960s to 0.1 in the 1980s, and in Tunisia from 8.1 per cent in the 1960s to 1.5 per cent during 1990–2003. Let us look at the few LDCs which were upgraded by the UN from the LDC status after they had experienced a certain degree of growth—Botswana in 1994, Cape Verde and the Maldives in 2004 (albeit with postponed implementation of the decision). They had all received an initially high level of aid which then declined, suggesting that countries locked into a trap can escape with the help of the international community. For instance, in Botswana the aid-to-GDP ratio has decreased from 18.8 per cent in the 1980s to 1.9 per cent in 1990–2003.[2] But, it should be remembered that not all of these countries were LDCs with the severest initial conditions, particularly with regard to human capital, a fact which made it easier to move up. These conditions, particularly human capital, could have been supported by prior aid. If the aim of aid inflows is to lead to sustained growth, it is worthwhile to facilitate the progress by changing the preconditional requirements of a possible take-off.[3]

13.3. Disbursement constraints: a need to reform procedures

Disbursement constraints constitute the first difficulty of absorbing more aid. The problem of the lag between commitments and disbursements has been considered for many years (Guillaumont 1967: 146–71) but curiously has not led to many studies, even though quantitative analysis can be easily applied. Complaints by recipients (and at times by donors) about the large gap between cumulative commitments and disbursements, the so-called 'pipeline', are becoming more and more frequent. The rate of under-utilization of credits, in fact, is in some cases very high, leading to scepticism about the possibility of recipients being able to use significantly higher amounts of aid. The reasons behind this under-utilization may lie in the circumstances of the receiving countries, such as low administrative capacities or weak transportation infrastructure, as well as the non-fulfilment of conditions attached to disbursement. However, with these facts in mind, Svensson (2006: 13) observes: 'a strong bias towards "always" disbursing committed funds to the ex ante designated recipient, or project, irrespective of the recipient government's performance ... and the conditions in other potential aid recipient countries (projects).'

---

[1] In India, owing to size, the aid-to-GDP ratio has always been low. However, after adjustment for the size factor, it also appears to have been significant, then declining.
[2] In Cape Verde it has decrease from 37 per cent in the 1980s to 16 per cent in 2000–3 and in the Maldives from 14 per cent to 3.7 per cent.
[3] More generally the issue of evaluation is counterfactual, as usual. It is always difficult to say what would have happened without aid in very poor countries.

Here the risk is excess spending under budget pressure rather than disbursement lags. But, disbursement lags may also result from the inadequacy of aid modalities to adjust to recipient circumstances. 'Aid fragmentation', or the multiplicity of aid sources in a country, each with different procedures, forms, and disbursement conditions, becomes a greater problem when the country is small with low administrative capacities. Donors are inclined to target support for the reinforcement of the recipient's administrative capacities rather than modify their own behaviour (de Renzio et al. 2004). This is a valuable but long-term process, as is the improvement of transport facilities and infrastructure which also makes the disbursement of project aid easier. Identifying and tackling such bottlenecks will stay on the agenda for a long time. The solution is to search for more appropriate procedures. However, to quote Heller:

Donor intentions and goals still deviate substantially from the reality of donor assistance practices. Current approaches with respect to the goals for harmonization, alignment, and predictability are still far short of the professed objectives and aid recipients have reasons to be uncertain about how long it will take for these gaps to be closed. Moreover, it must be daunting for LDCs to catalogue both the number of donors with which they must work, as well as the multiplicity of their objectives, modalities of operation, underlying criteria for aid levels, and conditionalities and terms of aid. (Heller 2005: 26)

It is why, in addition to considerations of alignment, ownership, and predictability (we revert to these later), the Declaration of the Paris Forum on Aid Effectiveness in 2005 underlines the need for the 'harmonization' of procedures and coordination of donors, and defines related indicators. But, progress since 2005 has been extremely slow, as shown by the *2008 Survey on Monitoring the Paris Declaration* (OECD 2008).[4]

Given the difficulties of the harmonization process, it is possible that more radical reform might be needed. This could, as we show later, consist of adopting an outcome-based conditionality, thus meeting both the concerns of disbursement lags and disbursement incentives, and eliminating bias from either source.

13.4. Macroeconomic drawbacks from higher aid inflows: are they real?

We now assume that not only commitments but also disbursements are significantly increased, albeit with some possible delay. Disbursement lags postpone the risk of macroeconomic drawbacks which we examine next. Two kinds of problems have been extensively considered in recent literature (Killick 2004; 2005; White 2005; Foster and Killick 2006; Killick and Foster 2007; O'Connell,

---

[4] Indicators 9 and 10.

Adam, and Buffie 2008). One is the risk resulting from an appreciation of the real exchange rate; the second risk, likely to reinforce the first, is associated with the volatility of aid flows. These two risks, while not negligible, are often over-estimated, and deserve, at the very least, adequate assessment with regard to some basic economic principles.

13.4.1. Real exchange rate concern: will increased aid induce a loss of competitiveness?

There are a number of studies that point to the risk of real exchange rate appreciation after the scaling-up of aid flows; by authors based at the International Monetary Fund (IMF) and the World Bank,[5] and from the academic aid literature.[6] It is argued that increased aid inflows generate the 'Dutch disease' effect through a real exchange rate appreciation, with a subsequent loss of competitiveness in the tradable sectors, harming exports as well as competitive import substitution. Aid can induce this effect, either through higher domestic prices of non-tradables in a fixed exchange rate regime, or through the appreciation of the nominal exchange rate in a regime of floating rates. The empirical evidence on the occurrence of 'Dutch disease' seems to be weakening (see, for instance, some studies in Berg et al. 2005). Gupta, Powell, and Yang (2006) present a sample of econometric studies which illustrate the contradiction among the results. Some authors find a positive link between aid inflows and real exchange rate (for example, Kasekende and Atingi-Ego 1999 for Ghana) while others observe a negative link. Even the influential paper by Rajan and Subramanian (2005a), which argues that aid has a negative effect on the share of labour-intensive and tradable industries, only suggests that this may be due to a real appreciation. The hypothesis is not tested, nor is consideration given to possible effects on other tradables, such as agriculture, and tradable services, which may be particularly important in small and highly aid-dependent developing countries.

Why is there so little evidence? In the short run, the increase in the price of non-tradables occurs only if productive capacity in the non-tradable sector is fully utilized. If there is under-utilized capacity, for instance, owing to disguised urban unemployment, the supply elasticity may be relatively high. In the long run, real appreciation will occur after a sustained higher aid level only if it is not compensated by an increase of productivity in the non-tradable sector, as Heller (2005) argues in recommending the use of aid to favour such an increase, which in reality is not easy. Moreover, in the longer run, an increase in productivity in the tradable sector is likely to compensate the effect on competitiveness of a

---

[5] See Arellano et al. (2005); Heller (2005); Rajan and Subramanian (2005a, 2005b); World Bank and IMF (2005, 2006); Foster and Killick (2006); Gupta, Powell, and Yang (2006).

[6] See Gunning (2004); Adam (2005); Bevan (2005); Adam and Bevan (2006).

possible rise of the non-tradable price. According to the Balassa-Samuelson theorem, if income growth per capita that is higher than in the rest of the world involves appreciation of the real exchange rate, then the 'big push' should lead to a similar effect. Thus, there cannot be a 'big push' without real appreciation—if aid succeeds in supporting the 'big push', it would cause the real value of the currency to appreciate. Appreciation is no longer a problem, it is a reflection of the strategy's success.

These arguments have strong implications for economic policy. In the short run, macroeconomic management of increased aid inflows may help to prevent an over-rapid rise of non-tradable relative prices, although sterilization of reserves can be only a transitory and partial solution (Heller 2005). More important is to consider the uses of aid as well as of public domestic resources. It is necessary to maintain a balance between aid allocated to productive sectors and aid to social sectors. Aid to increase the health and education of children will indeed increase productivity, but only in the long term. Using aid to improve infrastructure is an important factor for increasing absorptive capacity (Agénor et al. 2006). Briefly stated, aid that strives to promote balanced growth also needs to be balanced.

13.4.2. Threaten of aid volatility: is aid destabilizing or stabilizing?

Aid volatility has become a very fashionable topic and is one of the favourite arguments to illustrate the dangers of a rapid increase in aid. Aid, if volatile, might be a source of macroeconomic instability and all the more so the higher the level of aid.[7] This can be a way of highlighting absorptive capacity. Aid may indeed appear volatile, but that does not mean it is destabilizing, nor is it likely to be so if its level is increased.

Next we summarize the conclusions of ongoing research partly presented in Guillaumont (2006) and Chauvet and Guillaumont (2009). The first issue is to choose a second monetary flow which is relevant for the comparison of aid volatility, usually tax revenue, in order to examine the effect of aid instability on public budget stability or national income. Because the concern is with macroeconomic vulnerability, it is preferable to compare aid fluctuations (or cycle) with the exports of goods and services, the aggregate of which is the most likely to be affected by exogenous shocks. Tax revenues, like national income, are influenced by the overall impact of exports, and also by aid. Moreover, all aid flows are not channelled through the public budget, a fact that makes it important to consider the volatility of the different types of aid (Fielding and Mavrotas 2005).

---

[7] Lensink and Morrissey (2000); Pallage and Robe (2001); Rand and Tarp (2002); Buliř and Hamann (2003, 2005); Eifert and Gelb (2005).

In comparing total aid (net) to (goods and services) export fluctuations (measured in various ways), Guillaumont (2006) and Chauvet and Guillaumont (2009) come to the four following conclusions.

(i) Over thirty years (1970–99), the average level of aid volatility for a large sample of developing countries has been approximately the same as that of exports but half the export volatility level for the African subsample. Measured on 8-year sub-periods with a cycle component with regard to a trend drawn from a Hodrick-Prescott filter, both aid and export volatilities on average are equivalent to 8.8 per cent for the whole sample, while they are 5.9 per cent (aid) and 11.2 (exports) for the African sub-sample.[8]

(ii) Criticism of aid volatility may be misplaced if aid has a compensatory profile, which could be consistent with the finding that aid is more effective in more vulnerable countries (see above). As previously argued for real exchange rate appreciation, aid volatility could be a solution rather than a problem. From that perspective, it is not the volatility of aid per se that should be criticized, but rather its pro-cyclicality. With regard to exports, pro-cyclicality appears not to be the rule—not even in the majority of cases, as is sometimes asserted. The pro-cyclical character of aid is measured by the correlation between the 'cycle' of aid (that is, its deviation from its trend) and the 'cycle' of exports. Using the Hodrick-Prescott filter and considering more than 100 developing countries over the period 1970–99 (broken down into 8-year sub-periods which produced 465 sub-period observations), country correlation between the cycle of net aid disbursements and the cycle of exports of goods and services appears to be negative almost as often as positive (222 cases versus 243). A similar balance is found for the African sub-sample. This means that aid is counter-cyclical nearly as often as it is pro-cyclical. Furthermore, in the majority of cases the correlation coefficients on which the comparison is based are not significant.[9]

(iii) Measuring counter- or pro-cyclicality is less relevant than determining whether aid inflows are stabilizing or destabilizing with regard to total aid plus export flows. Pro-cyclical aid can still be stabilizing if its volatility, expressed in relative terms, is lower than the volatility of exports. There may also be opposite and paradoxical cases where aid is countercyclical and destabilizing, when its volatility is significantly higher than that of exports, depending on the relative levels of aid and exports.[10] What is the real picture? To assess the stabilizing character of aid, we consider an index corresponding to the difference between

---

[8] This conclusion is akin to that of Sunday Khan who shows that export income of CEMAC countries is about five times more volatile than aid flows (Khan 2006).

[9] At a 15 per cent threshold.

[10] The arithmetic condition is that the absolute value of the ratio of the relative cycles of exports and aid exceeds one by twice the ratio of exports to aid.

the instability (volatility) of exports and that of the aid plus export flows. If the difference is positive, aid is stabilizing; if negative, aid is destabilizing. Generally, aid had a stabilizing impact, more during the 1990s than during previous periods: the average impact is positive and equal to 18 per cent of the average value of the instability of exports (28 per cent for the African sub-sample). In the majority of cases where aid was pro-cyclical, it was then stabilizing. When aid was countercyclical, it was, as expected, generally but not always stabilizing. On the whole, aid had a destabilizing effect in less than one-tenth of the cases. Figure 13.1 demonstrates that the stabilizing impact of aid (measured by the difference between the two instabilities) is all the more important the higher the aid-to-GDP ratio, and is not significantly influenced by the level of aid volatility.

(iv) In the future, if aid amounts grow substantially, the potential stabilizing or destabilizing impact with regard to exports will be higher, but the risk of a destabilizing impact will remain low since in the case of pro-cyclicality it is conditioned by a level of volatility higher than that of exports.

Given that exports are not the only exogenous source of instability, it is also relevant to examine whether aid contributes to reducing or enhancing growth

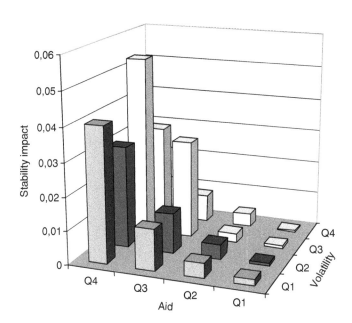

Figure 13.1 Stabilizing impact of aid with regard to exports, based on aid-to-GDP ratio and aid volatility

volatility, once the influence of the traditional structural factors of this overall volatility is taken into account. Using a GMM estimator with five-year average observations, and applying initial income per capita, exports-to-GDP ratio, and export volatility as control variables, it appears that the aid-to-GDP ratio has a significant negative impact on growth volatility (aid-to-GDP ratio and income per capita instrumented)[11] (Chauvet and Guillaumont 2009). Even if aid has on average had a rather stabilizing outcome in the past, some policy lessons can be drawn to avoid the destabilizing effect of higher aid levels in the future. On the donor side, the principle of conditionality is itself a potential instability factor, and all the more so once donor policies are harmonized (Heller 2005). However, the move towards a more gradual conditionality, generated through an output-based conditionality, may lower the risk of aid instability since the assessment of results or outcome is less dichotomous than that of policy measures implementation. Moreover, better transparency in the criteria of aid allocation may render aid more predictable and then facilitate the domestic management of aid flows.

Finally it is argued that aid can be used more extensively as insurance to smooth public and private incomes in the face of export instability or other shocks. As we have explained elsewhere, solutions do exist that can be built on a contractual basis involving the international community, recipient-country governments, and producer groups respecting market trends (Guillaumont and Guillaumont Jeanneney 2003: 353–67; Guillaumont et al. 2005). Notably, they include grant disbursement and/or debt service adjustment in response to price shocks, and support to domestic insurance schemes targeted to agricultural producers. On the recipient side, higher aid dependency needs a cautious management of the domestic fiscal space. The government has to be able to maintain some flexibility in public expenditures and to save some potential for domestic borrowing. It may also find it appropriate to accumulate a certain level of foreign reserves that are likely to be used to smooth the impact of aid inflows.

13.5. Decreasing returns: occurring more slowly in vulnerable countries

Absorptive capacity, in the usual meaning, is associated with decreasing returns. There may be decreasing returns of aid, as with any other factor. However,

---

[11] Aid volatility added alone to the regression does not change the result and is not significant. When a multiplicative variable (aid ratio × aid volatility) is added, it appears significantly positive, suggesting a threshold beyond which an increase of the aid to GDP ratio may become a factor of macroeconomic instability. But this last result is not very robust, as it can be expected, since the impact of aid volatility differs from one country to the next, depending on proper counter-cyclicality.

decreasing returns do not exclude increasing returns below a specific aid level, consistent with the 'big push' hypothesis. An additional analytical difficulty comes from the fact that the turning-point is likely to differ among recipient countries, depending on the specific characteristics and circumstances of each nation. Here we focus on their structural vulnerability since in our previous works this has appeared to constitute a significant factor of aid effectiveness. We rely on both macro and micro evidence to argue that vulnerability influences the profile of aid's marginal returns.

13.5.1. Lessons from growth regressions: is the 'big push' justified by vulnerability?

The test of the decreasing marginal returns of aid has been an important part of the debate on aid–growth relationships. In growth regressions both the aid variable and its squared value are included as explanatory variables, with positive and negative coefficients expected respectively. This specification involved not only a decreasing marginal impact of aid on growth, but also that an aid increase beyond a certain level is detrimental to growth (inverse U curb). The turning-point could be construed as a measurement of absorptive capacity. Conversely, if the coefficients are respectively negative and positive, or only significant and positive for the squared term, it is an argument in favour of the 'big push'.

The estimation, including the aid term and its squared value, was run initially by Hadjimichael et al. (1995) with reference to absorptive capacity constraints, and has since become common practice (Burnside and Dollar 2000; Collier and Dollar 2001, 2002; Hansen and Tarp 2000, 2001; Lensink and White 2001). Results vary considerably, with the squared term being either significantly negative or insignificant. The results depend, as clearly documented by Hansen and Tarp, on whether another non-linearity is introduced in the model through a multiplicative term of aid.

In earlier studies on the influence of vulnerability on aid effectiveness (Guillaumont and Chauvet 2001; Chauvet and Guillaumont 2004), non-linearity was introduced through a multiplicative term (aid × vulnerability index), but without the aid squared term. Results suggest that aid is more effective in more vulnerable countries; or, in other words, the negative impact of vulnerability is dampened by aid. A more recent paper focusing on Africa (Chauvet and Guillaumont 2006) comes to a similar conclusion, with the instability of goods and services exports as the only measure of vulnerability. This allows us to assess the stabilizing impact of aid examined above. Regressions are run on a sample of thirty-eight African countries for six five-year periods (with GMM and additional instrumentation of aid). Controlling for aid ratio and export instability levels, we obtain a significant positive impact on growth of either the multiplicative variable (aid × export instability) or the indicator of the stabilization impact of aid (the difference between the instability of exports and the instability of the aggregate flow (export + aid)). In these specifications, the marginal effectiveness of aid does depend on vulnerability, but not on the aid level. It suggests that if there were a turning-point based on the aid level (evidenced by a significant coefficient of squared value of aid) this point would be eliminated by higher vulnerability.

To test simultaneously the existence of two successive turning-points which correspond, first, to a minimum amount of aid *below which it is no longer effective* (an approach to the 'big push'), and second, to the level *beyond which it becomes ineffective* (a measure of the absorptive capacity), it might be conceivable to estimate the growth regression with not only the aid variable and its squared value, but also its cubic value, expecting the coefficients to be respectively negative, positive and negative, and the returns at the two turning-points being successively increasing and decreasing. Then the two approaches could be reconciled. However, this specification is not very appropriate: there is no reason to expect negative marginal returns instead of nil returns below the first threshold, or even beyond the second one. This is why it seems better to look for thresholds which empirically differentiate aid growth relationships according to the level of aid. This has been done by Gomanee, Girma, and Morrissey (2003). They find that aid beyond 2 per cent of GNP becomes effective in contributing to growth and there is no evidence of diminishing returns to aid afterwards. But, by using annual growth data, these authors may be capturing short-term rather than long-term aid effects. Moreover, the threshold is assumed to be the same for all countries, but it is likely that aid effectiveness thresholds depend on the specific circumstances of recipient countries.

13.5.2. New micro evidence from project evaluation confirming the impact of vulnerability

The ambiguous results of growth regressions regarding aid-effectiveness thresholds may be due to some extent to the heterogeneity of aid aggregates, including projects, budget support, debt relief, technical assistance, and so on. For this reason it is useful to consider a more homogeneous set of aid inflows (for instance, a set of projects) and to analyse whether their results depend on the total amount of aid as well as the specific features of recipient countries. If our assumption holds that aid's marginal returns are influenced by the vulnerability of countries, this should be reflected at the micro level, as we will now see.

A working paper by Guillaumont and Laajaj (2006) considers the results of an evaluation of World Bank projects conducted by the Bank's Independent Evaluation Group. In this database the outcome of projects is measured on a six-scale notation ranging from very unsatisfactory to very satisfactory. This makes

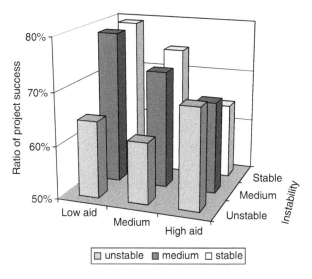

Figure 13.2 Slower decreasing returns of World Bank projects when exports are more unstable

it easy to examine if the rate of success is influenced by the level of aid in the recipient countries and if this relationship depends on their economic vulnerability. We surmise that the rate of success decreases when the total amount of aid received by the country increases, but to a lesser extent in the highly vulnerable countries. This view is confirmed by Figure 13.2, which represents the average project success according to the combined levels of export instability and aid-to-GDP ratio. The success rate[12] has been broken down into nine groups. 'Low aid' corresponds to a third of the projects carried out in countries receiving aid at less than 1 per cent of GDP (the lowest level of ODA); 'high aid' to the top third (receiving aid exceeding 8 per cent of GDP). Thus, 'medium aid' went to the intermediate group; each group was similarly subdivided into the upper-, middle-, and lower-third groups of projects, according to the export instability of the countries, weighted by the exports-to-GDP ratio.

As can be seen, the average success rate for low-aid-level countries is 15 points higher in a stable country. However, in stable countries, this rate decreases sharply when the level of aid increases, suggesting a limited absorptive capacity. On the other hand, in the most unstable countries, the success rate does not clearly decrease as it is the highest in the most-generously aided countries; moreover, in the most-aided countries, the average success of projects is the greater the more unstable the country. Some econometric estimations confirm these relationships. Following Kaufmann and Wang (1995); Isham, Kaufmann, and Pritchett (1997);

---

[12] A project is considered successful if it has been rated at least moderately satisfactory.

Isham and Kaufman (1999); and Levin and Dollar (2005) we estimate the factors determining the success of World Bank projects, but we do not aggregate project data at the national level so that the regressions are run at the micro level, with an observation for each project. Since the outcome of the projects is measured on a six-scale notation, our econometric model is an ordered logit. It combines factors related to the characteristics of the project (sector, IDA or IBRD conditions, and so on) and to the circumstances of the country (income per capita, level of education, quality of institutions, and so on) (as well as year dummies). Our specific concern is to test the influence of the other, following variables:

- the total aid-to-GDP ratio, to identify possible decreasing (or increasing) aid returns (variable introduced also by Levin and Dollar);
- the volatility of exports, which can induce an unstable environment likely to be harmful for the fulfilment of projects;
- one variable multiplicative of the two previous ones, consistent with our previous finding at the macro level (with Chauvet) that aid dampens the negative effects of external shocks.

We expect the success of projects to decline as the total amount of aid increases and as the recipient country faces external shocks (export instability), while the impact of the interactive (multiplicative) variable (aid × instability) becomes positive.[13] The results of the base regression do not reject our hypotheses. The success of projects decreases less in the more-unstable countries, a finding that emphasizes the need for aid in vulnerable countries. Another finding concerns the role of education in the success of projects. The rate of success is positively influenced by the level of education, but a low educational level dampens the negative impact of aid size on the success of projects. When a multiplicative variable of aid and education is introduced in the model, it appears to have a significant negative impact. This should not be surprising: aid has a knowledge content that makes its marginal impact higher the lower the level of education (similar finding in Gomanee, Girma, and Morrissey 2003).

---

[13] In this model the success of project, which is directly estimated, is found to be decreasing since the coefficient of the aid value received by the implementing country is negative. Then if the outcome of projects is declining when the total amount of aid increases and if it is lower when the recipient country faces external shocks (export instability), the positive expected impact of the interactive (multiplicative) variable (aid × instability) means, as in the growth model, that aid dampens the effect of instability. In the aid–growth model aid lowers the negative impact of instability even if there are constant returns, in the success-of-project model the decrease of aid project outcome is slowed down by instability.

Considering that both vulnerability and low human capital are factors of slower decline of aid effectiveness and that these two characteristics in conjunction with a low level of income are the criteria identifying the LDCs, this suggests that the function of success of projects may differ between LDCs and other developing countries. While vulnerability and lack of human capital have a negative impact on the average project success, they can moderate the possibility of failure, or even increase the chances of success when aid levels increase, which does not preclude such a decline beyond a certain level of aid. This means that they extend the limits of absorptive capacity. We then estimated a success-of-project model where the explanatory variables are the aid-to-GDP ratio, its squared value, and a dummy variable for LDCs, introduced both additively and multiplicatively of the aid ratio and its squared value.[14] The results are illustrated Figure 13.3. In the non-LDC developing countries, the outcome of projects is generally higher than in LDCs, but declines when aid increases (the turning-point of approximately 17 per cent aid ratio is not empirically relevant since countries reach this level of aid only in less than 1 per cent of the cases). In LDCs the average rate of success increases when the aid-to-GDP ratio increases, at least below the threshold estimated at around 25 per cent in the estimation corresponding to Figure 13.3, and does not decrease quickly beyond the threshold (25 per cent of cases beyond this point). Clearly, even if the LDCs have a lower average rate of success, they show increasing returns to aid and higher absorptive capacity. A final but no less intriguing result of the previous estimations is that institutions do not appear to be significant factor in the success of projects.

13.6. Weakening institutions: towards performance-based conditionality

The relationship between aid and institutions of the recipient countries has been examined in the literature from three different angles. First, in the aid-effectiveness literature, institutions (and policy) have been presented as a crucial factor of effectiveness (in the World Bank paradigm of assessing aid—for example, Burnside and Dollar (2000, 2004) and Collier and Dollar (2001, 2002)), a factor that is strongly debated, as is well known. Second, the impact of institutions on inter-country aid allocation has been analysed and debated, both as a positive issue and as a normative issue in particular with the aim to assess the selectivity of donors (Amprou, Guillaumont, and Guillaumont Jeanneney 2007). Third, the effect of aid on the quality of policies and institutions has for a long time been a matter of concern and is now of topical interest, as it could significantly limit

---

[14] The variables corresponding to the identification of LDCs, income per capita, vulnerability, lack of human capital are excluded.

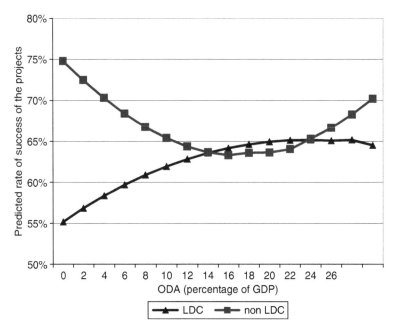

Figure 13.3 LDCs: initial handicap but higher absorptive capacity

absorptive capacity. Relying on earlier studies on this last issue, we try to see how aid can be prevented from weakening the institutions of recipient countries.

13.6.1. The institutional dimension of absorptive capacity

Is aid dependency weakening domestic institutions which are now considered an important factor of economic growth? Several potential negative effects of large aid inflows on institutions have been identified, mainly the detrimental impact of aid on private saving, on state revenue, and the consequences on the account-ability of public management (or the link between the state and the civil society).

The first analytical attack against foreign aid that has been largely debated on empirical grounds (Griffin 1970; Papanek 1973) was the crowding-out effect of aid on savings. A common conclusion at the aggregate level is that even if aid has a short-term negative impact on savings, it nevertheless increases invest-ment and thus contributes through a higher income to a long-term increase of the saving ratio (Guillaumont 1985: 295–307). The crowding-out effect was founded on two basic assumptions linked to policy and institutions. First, aid was assumed to dominate the better investment opportunities, discouraging private savings and investment. It would thus exert an institutional effect on the financial system, the deepening of which would be reduced. Whether this

314

effect resulted from aid or from other sources of external finance is not known and has not been extensively investigated.

The second crowding-out effect, related to fiscal revenue, has been examined in more detail, both through cross-section and country case studies. However, results are mitigated, as is noted in the survey by Moss, Pettersson, and van der Walle (2006). Even if the literature frequently finds a negative relationship, it raises several questions. The first is due to the heterogeneity of aid flows and tax receipts, with each tax group inducing specific responses to each aid type. Gupta et al. (2004) suggest that grants, but not loans, have a negative effect on total tax revenue, while Mavrotas (2005; who also considers the effects on the different kinds of public expenditure) argues to the contrary, 'in Uganda the government did not reduce its tax effort following additional disbursements of different types of foreign aid'. A second problem is related to aid endogeneity. Aid and fiscal receipts are linked by reciprocal relations and may be influenced by common factors while the instrumentation of the aid variable is often unsatisfactory. Finally, and most importantly, studies focused on the short-term impact of aid inflows do not capture the long-term institutional effects.

With regard to long-run effects, two opposite views exist. On the one hand, the concern over aid dependency leads to underlining the risk that the state is over-dependent on foreign aid and is thus accountable to foreign donors instead of the national population or civil society. From that perspective, the crowding-out of fiscal revenue is considered to be a factor of weak accountability, since governments do not need to maintain their legitimacy to collect revenue (Moss, Pettersson, and van der Walle 2006). However, it is not certain that tax collection is always an aspect of democracy and institution-building, as the heavy taxation of African agriculture in the 1970s and thereafter has shown. On the other hand, increased aid can be considered as a transitory impulse that generates a pump-priming effect which will reduce the requirement for aid itself. A good example is given by tax policy: if aid enables a country to reduce high and distortionary taxation, it will help to remove the obstacle to growth and possibly lead to larger amounts of public revenue in the future (Gunning 2004).

Other factors are the more detrimental effects of aid on institutions and these are mainly due to the way in which aid is delivered. There is indeed a sociopolitical dimension to absorptive capacity but it comes from aid modalities to some extent. This may seem paradoxical since larger and larger portions of aid are devoted to budget support, which is conditioned by policy reform. Traditional conditionality has been strongly criticized. In particular it has been argued that it was inefficient due to the common interest of the partners to act as if it was efficient (Collier et al. 1997). This criticism has found expression in the hypothesis by Burnside and Dollar (2000) that aid has no effect on policy.

It has been challenged not only in cross-section studies (see, for instance, Chauvet and Guillaumont 2004),[15] but also more significantly by the African case studies by the World Bank (Devarajan, Dollar, and Holmgren 2001) and by Berg (2003) and Tarp (2003). It is difficult not to acknowledge that the intense policy dialogue between donors and recipient governments has sometimes been successful in generating significant policy decisions or institution reforms.

Furthermore, the crucial issue of ownership, already raised during the initial criticism of conditionality (Killick 1998), seems to remain unsolved. The pressure of donors to 'obtain' policy measures and reforms and the commitment of recipient countries to be accountable to external agents have resulted in governments and civil servants in these countries becoming distanced from full responsibility for their actions. Moreover, they are less inclined to justify their action except by their external commitments. 'The hypothesis here is that large aid flows fundamentally alter the relationship between government, elites and local citizens' (Moss, Pettersson, and van der Walle 2006). This lack of ownership and accountability to citizens is enhanced by the weight of donor advice, presence, missions, and own agenda, as stressed by Berg in his posthumous paper (2003).

13.6.2. Why a performance-based conditionality is an answer to aid dependency

Faced with the sociopolitical limits to absorptive capacity, the usual donor response is to consider that the main source of difficulties is the weak administrative capacity, which needs to be enhanced. Reinforcement of capacities has thus been a goal of aid, well-reflected in the share of technical assistance provided. A future increase of aid should then justify further advances in this direction. It is a reasonable principle. However, it has at times been implemented in an inefficient manner. A common practice is to set up autonomous agencies in order to attract the best civil servants, with possibly higher wages after appropriate training, and to avoid administrative inertia. It is a short-term search for efficiency, and often triggers discouragement within traditional administration. Policy that aims at reducing the number of civil servants but compensating the remainder with better pay (possibly after appropriate training) has a longer-term focus, although it may be politically difficult.

The analysis of the drawbacks of aid dependency calls for deeper reform in aid practice (see Chapter 11 of this volume by Michael Hubbard). In previous papers, we have argued in favour of an outcome-based or performance-based conditionality for budget support instead of conditionality that is based on the

---

[15] Tests do not reject the hypothesis that policy is improved by aid when quality is weak, which leads to aid effectiveness being negatively influenced by previous policy (and positively by the current one).

adoption of policy changes (Collier et al. 1997; Adam et al. 2004). Performance would be measured as much as possible in terms of ultimate objectives, such as reduced child mortality or knowledge acquisition by children. To quote:

performance conditionality allows for better ownership of reforms, since the choice of instruments would reside with the country; it avoids arbitrary judgement on multiple heterogeneous economic policy measures; it facilitates gradual and progressive support according to the degree of progress of performance relative to outturns; and by eliminating the scope for discordant conditionality, it supports better coordination between donors. (Adam et al. 2004: 1064)

Although the principle of this proposal has not met with strong criticism, the likelihood of its implementation by a significant number of donors appears rather limited. Even the European Union, which has taken the pioneering initiative for reform in that direction, has gone only half way, as the retained conditions refer to intermediate indicators related to policy instruments (ibid.). The main obstacles to full implementation of a performance-based conditionality are twofold. One is the lack of trust in the capacity and will of the recipient countries, which create a vicious circle since capacities will not develop fully without ownership. The second and probably more important hindrance is the weight of habit within aid agencies. Full performance-based conditionality would involve a dramatic change in agency jobs, which would be devoted to monitoring and assessing the progress of countries based on a few ultimate development indicators, taking into account the impact of exogenous factors, independent of policy.

Furthermore, it may not be possible to undertake such reform in countries which have merely a minimal state or in the continually failing states. At least temporarily, increased aid inflows should be delivered more directly through technical assistance and projects implemented in particular through civil society organizations (Cohen et al. 2006; EGDI 2006); these efforts should bypass the failing states (Chauvet and Collier 2005).

13.7. Conclusion: how to reconcile the two approaches

In this chapter we have neither rejected the relevance of the 'big push' nor denied the existence of serious limitations to absorptive capacity, but assert that both require further analysis. The limitations to absorptive capacity do not imply that the 'big push' should be abandoned; on the contrary, the 'big push' seems to be needed to remove these obstacles. However, this becomes feasible only if aid policies are consistently designed. Our general conclusion on the reconciliation of the two approaches is that absorptive capacity is heavily dependent on aid itself, or on its very modalities. The 'big push' and absorptive capacity approaches cannot be reconciled without reforming aid as its amount increases. From that perspective, the following main lessons can be drawn.

First, it is necessary to balance the utilization of aid between directly productive activities and social services in order to avoid a transitory loss of competitiveness. Second, schemes that promote the use of aid as insurance against exogenous shocks should be enhanced because they lower the risk of 'Dutch disease' and contribute to a faster and more equitable long-term growth. Third, owing to the higher marginal impact of aid in vulnerable countries and in particular the LDCs, where the need for a 'big push' is the most obvious, priority should be given to these countries in aid allocation. Finally, performance-based conditionality should, as much as possible, be substituted for the traditional policy-based one in order to cope with several absorptive capacity limitations, of which the sociopolitical element is the most important. An aid-supported 'big push' will not be effective without a new ownership of policy by the recipient countries.

References

Adam, C. S. (2005) 'Exogenous Inflows and Real Exchange Rates: Theoretical Quirk or Empirical Reality?' Paper presented at the IMF Seminar on Foreign Aid and Macroeconomic Management, 14–15 Mar., Maputo.

——and D. Bevan (2006) 'Aid and the Supply Side: Public Investment, Export Performance and Dutch Disease in Low-income Countries'. *World Bank Economic Review*, 20: 261–90.

——G. Chambas, P. Guillaumont, et al. (2004) 'Performance-based Conditionality: A European Perspective'. <http://publi.cerdi.org/ed/2003/2003.06.pdf>. Repr. *World Development*, 32: 1059–70.

Agénor, P.-R., N. Bayraktar, E. Pinto Moreira, and K. El Aynaoui (2006) 'Achieving the Millennium Development Goals in Sub-Saharan Africa: A Macroeconomic Monitoring Framework'. *World Economy*, 29: 1519–47.

Amprou, J., P. Guillaumont, and S. Guillaumont Jeanneney (2007) 'Aid Selectivity According to Augmented Criteria'. *World Economy*, 30: 733–63.

Arellano, C., A. Buliř, T. Lane, and L. Lipshitz (2005) 'The Dynamic Implications of Foreign Aid and its Volatility'. International Monetary Fund Working Paper 05/119, Washington, DC: IMF.

Berg, A., M. Hussain, S. Aiyar, et al. (2005) 'The Macroeconomics of Managing Increased Aid Inflows: Experiences of Low-income Countries and Policy Implications'. Mimeo. Washington, DC: IMF.

Berg, E. (2003) 'Augmenter l'efficacité de l'aide: une critique de quelques points de vue actuels'. *Revue d'économie du développement*, 4: 11–42.

Berthélemy, J.-C. (2006) 'Clubs de convergence et équilibres multiples: comment les économies émergentes ont-elles réussi à échapper au piège du sous-développement?' *Revue d'économie du développement*, 1: 5–44.

Bevan, D. L. (2005) 'An Analytical Overview of Aid Absorption: Recognizing and Avoiding Macroeconomic Hazards'. Paper presented at the IMF Seminar on Foreign Aid and Macroeconomic Management, 14–15 Mar., Maputo.

Bulíř, A., and A. J. Hamann (2003) 'Aid Volatility: An Empirical Assessment'. *IMF Staff Papers*, 50: 64–89.

————(2005) 'Volatility of Development Aid: From the Frying Pan into the Fire?' International Monetary Fund Working Paper 06/65. Washington, DC: IMF.

Burnside, C., and D. Dollar (2000) 'Aid, Policy and Growth'. *American Economic Review*, 90: 847–68.

————(2004) 'Aid, Policies and Growth: A Reply'. *American Economic Review*, 94: 781–4.

Chauvet, L., and P. Collier (2005) 'Policy Turnarounds in Failing States'. Mimeo. Oxford: Centre for the Study of African Economies.

——and P. Guillaumont (2004) 'Aid and Growth Revisited: Policy, Economic Vulnerability and Political Instability'. In B. Tungodden, N. Stern, and I. Kolstad (eds), *Toward Pro-Poor Policies: Aid, Institutions and Globalization*. Oxford, New York, and Washington, DC: Oxford University Press/World Bank.

————(2006) 'Aid Volatility and Growth Again: When Aid Volatility Matters and When to Does Not'. *Review of Development Economics*, 13(3): 452–63.

Cohen, D., S. Guillaumont Jeanneney, and P. Jacquet (2006) 'La Politique d'aide au développement de la France: introduction générale'. In D. Cohen, S. Guillaumont Jeanneney, and P. Jacquet (eds), *La France et l'aide publique au développement*. Paris: Le Conseil d'Analyse économique.

Collier, P., and D. Dollar (2001) 'Can the World Cut Poverty in Half?: How Policy Reform and Effective Aid Can Meet the International Development Goals'. *World Development*, 29: 1787–802.

————(2002) 'Aid Allocation and Poverty Reduction'. *European Economic Review*, 46: 1475–500.

——P. Guillaumont, S. Guillaumont Jeanneney, and J. W. Gunning (1997) 'Redesigning Conditionality'. *World Development*, 25: 1399–407.

de Renzio, P., D. Booth, A. Rogerson, and Z. Curian (2004) 'Incentives for Harmonisation and Alignment in Aid Agency'. Overseas Development Institute Working Paper 248. London: ODI.

Devarajan, S., D. Dollar, and T. Holmgren (eds) (2001) *Aid and Reform in Africa: Lessons from Ten Case Studies*. Oxford: Oxford University Press for the World Bank.

Easterly, W. (2006a) *The White Man's Burden: Why the West's Efforts to Aid the Rest Have Done So Much Ill and So Little Good*. New York: Penguin Press.

——(2006b) 'The Big Push Déjà Vu: A Review of Jeffrey Sachs's *The End of Poverty: Economic Possibilities for Our Time*'. *Journal of Economic Literature*, 44: 96–105.

EGDI (Expert Group on Development Issues) (2006) 'The Politics of Service Deliveries in Democracies: Better Access for the Poor'. Expert Group on Development Issues. Write-up from Workshop, 27–8 Apr., Stockholm.

Eifert, B., and A. Gelb (2005) 'Improving the Dynamics of Aid: Towards More Predictable Budget Support'. World Bank Policy Research Department Working Paper 3732. Washington, DC: World Bank.

Fielding, D., and G. Mavrotas (2005) 'The Volatility of Aid'. WIDER Discussion Paper 2005/06. Helsinki: UNU-WIDER.

Foster M., and T. Killick (2006) 'What Would Doubling Aid Do for Macroeconomic Management in Africa: A Synthesis Paper'. Overseas Development Institute Working Paper 264. London: ODI.

Gomanee, K., S. Girma, and O. Morrissey (2003) 'Searching for Aid Threshold Effects'. University of Nottingham Centre for Research in Economic Development and International Trade Research Paper 03/15. Nottingham: CREDIT.

Griffin, K. (1970) 'Foreign Capital, Domestic Savings and Economic Development'. *Bulletin of the Oxford University Institute of Economics and Statistics*, 32: 99–112.

Guillaumont, P. (1967) 'L'Aide au développement en Afrique de l'Ouest: schéma d'analyse in OCDE'. *Progrès social et croissance économique*. Paris: Centre de développement.

——(1971) *L'Absorption du capital*. Paris: Éditions Cujas.

——(1985) *Economie du développement*, Vol. iii. *Dynamique internationale du développement*. Paris: Presses Universitaires de France.

——(2006) 'Macroeconomic Vulnerability in Low-income Countries and Aid Responses'. In F. Bourguignon, B. Pleskovic, and J. van der Gaag (eds), *Securing Development in an Unstable World* (Annual Bank Conference in Development Economics, Europe). Washington, DC. IBRD/World Bank.

——(2009) *Caught in the Trap*: *Identifying Least Developed Countries*. Paris: Economica.

——and L. Chauvet (2001) 'Aid and Performance: A Reassessment'. *Journal of Development Studies*, 37: 66–87.

——and S. Guillaumont Jeanneney (2003) 'Dampening Price Shocks'. In P. Collier and I. Bannon (eds), *Natural Resources and Violent Conflict*. Washington, DC: World Bank.

————P. Jacquet, et al. (2004) 'Attenuating through Aid the Vulnerability to Price Shocks'. In F. Bourguignon, P. Jacquet, and B. Pleskovic (eds), *Economic Integration and Social Responsibility*. Washington, DC: World Bank.

——and R. Laajaj (2006) 'When Instability Increases the Marginal Effectiveness of Aid Projects'. World Bank Policy Research Department Working Paper 4034. Washington, DC: World Bank.

Gunning, J. W. (2004) 'Why Give Aid?'. Paper presented at the 2nd AFD-EUDN Conference, 'Development Aid: Why and How?' 25 Nov., Paris.

Gupta, S., B. Clements, A. Pivovarsky, and E. Tiongson (2004) 'Foreign Aid and Revenue Response: Does the Composition of Foreign Aid Matter?' In S. Gupta, B. Clements, and G. Inchauste (eds), *Helping Countries Develop: The Role of Fiscal Policy*. Washington, DC: IMF.

——R. Powell, and Y. Yang (2006) *The Macroeconomic Challenge of Scaling Up Aid to Africa: A Checklist for Practitioners*. Washington, DC: IMF.

Hadjimichael, M. T., D. Ghura, M. Muhleisen, et al. (1995) 'Sub-Saharan Africa: Growth, Savings and Investment, 1986–93'. International Monetary Fund Occasional Paper 118. Washington, DC: IMF.

Hansen, H., and F. Tarp (2000) 'Aid Effectiveness Disputed'. *Journal of International Development*, 12: 375–98.

————(2001) 'Aid and Growth Regressions'. *Journal of Development Economics*, 64: 547–70.

Heller, P. S. (2005) 'Pity the Finance Minister: Issues in Managing a Substantial Scaling Up of Aid Flows'. *World Economics*, 6: 69–110.

IMF (International Monetary Fund) (2005) 'The Macroeconomic of Managing Increased Aid Inflows: Experiences of Low-income Countries and Policy Implications'. International Monetary Fund Policy Development and Review Department, 8 Aug. Washington, DC: IMF.

Isham, J., and D. Kaufmann (1999) 'The Forgotten Rationale for Policy Reform: The Productivity of Investment Projects'. *Quarterly Journal of Economics*, 114: 149–84.

——and L. H. Pritchett (1997) 'Civil Liberties, Democracy, and the Performance of Government Projects'. *World Bank Economic Review*, 11: 219–42.

Kasekende, L. A., and M. Atingi-Ego (1999) 'Uganda Experience with Aid'. *Journal of African Economies*, 8: 619–49.

Kaufmann, D., and Y. Wang (1995) 'Macroeconomic Policies and Project Performance in the Social Sectors: A Model of Human Capital Production and Evidence from LDCs'. *World Development*, 23: 751–65.

Khan S. (2006) 'The Volatility of Resource Inflows and Economic Growth in CEMAC Countries'. Research report. Ottawa: North–South Institute.

Killick T. (1998) *Aid and the Political Economy of Policy Change*. ODI. London: Routledge

——(2004) 'Politics, Evidence and the New Aid Agenda'. *Development Policy Review*, 32: 5–29.

——(2005) 'Don't Throw Money at Africa'. *IDS Bulletin*, 36: 14–19.

——and M. Foster (2007) 'The Macroeconomic of Doubling Aid to Africa and the Centrality of the Supply Side'. *Development Policy Review*, 25: 167–92.

Kraay, A., and C. Raddatz (2005) 'Poverty Traps, Aid, and Growth'. World Bank Policy Research Department Working Paper 3631. Washington, DC: World Bank.

Leibenstein, H. (1954) *The Theory of Economic-Demographic Development*. Princeton, NJ: Princeton University Press.

Lensink, R., and O. Morrissey (2000) 'Aid Instability as a Measure of Uncertainty and the Positive Impact of Aid on Growth'. *Journal of Development Studies*, 36: 30–48.

——and H. White (2001) 'Are There Negative Returns to Aid?' *Journal of Development Studies*, 37: 42–65.

Levin, V., and D. Dollar (2005) 'Sowing and Reaping Institutional Quality and Project Outcomes in Developing Countries'. World Bank Policy Research Department Working Paper 3524. Washington, DC: World Bank.

Mavrotas, G. (2005) 'Aid Heterogeneity: Looking at Aid Effectiveness from a Different Angle'. *Journal of International Development*, 17: 1019–36.

Millikan, M. F., and W. W. Rostow (1957) *A Proposal: Key to an Effective Foreign Policy*. New York: Harpers and Brothers.

Moss, T., G. Pettersson, and N. van der Walle (2006) 'An Aid–Institutions Paradox? A Review Essay on Aid Dependency and State Building in Sub-Saharan Africa'. Center for Global Development Working Paper 74. Washington, DC: CGD.

Nelson, R. (1956) 'A Theory of Low-level Equilibrium Trap in Underdeveloped Economies'. *American Economic Review*, 46: 894–908.

Nurkse, R. (1953) *Problems of Capital Formation in Underdeveloped Countries*. Oxford: Basil Blackwell.

O'Connell S. A., C. S. Adam, and E. F. Buffie (2008) 'Aid and Fiscal Instability'. Centre for the Study of African Economies Working Paper WPS/2008/18. Oxford: CSAE.

OECD (2008) *2008 Survey on Monitoring the Paris Declaration: Effective Aid by 2010? What it Will Take*. Development Co-operation Directorate (DCD/DAC)

Pallage, S., and M. A. Robe (2001) 'Foreign Aid and the Business Cycle'. *Review of International Economics*, 9: 641–72.

Papanek, G. F. (1973) 'Aid, Foreign Private Investment, Savings and Growth in Less-Developed Countries'. *Journal of Political Economy*, 81: 120–30.

Rajan, R. G., and A. Subramanian (2005a) 'What Undermines Aid's Impact on Growth?' IMF Working Paper 05/126, Washington, DC: IMF.

——(2005b) 'Aid and Growth: What Does the Cross-country Evidence Really Show?' International Monetary Fund Working Paper 05/127. Washington, DC: IMF.

Rand, J., and F. Tarp (2002) 'Business Cycles in Developing Countries: Are They Different?'. *World Development*, 30: 2071–88.

Roodman, D. (2004) 'The Anarchy of Numbers: Aid, Development and Cross-country Empirics'. Center for Global Development Working Paper 32. Washington, DC: CGD.

Rosenstein-Rodan, P. N. (1943) 'Problems of Industrialization of Eastern and South Eastern Europe'. *Economic Journal*, 53: 202–11.

——(1961a) 'Notes on the Theory of the Big Push'. In H. S. Ellis and H. C. Wallich (eds), *Economic Development for Latin America*. New York: St Martin's Press.

——(1961b) 'International Aid for Underdeveloped Countries'. *Review of Economics and Statistics*, 63: 107–32.

Sachs, J. (2005) *The End of Poverty: Economic Possibilities for Our Time*. London: Penguin Book.

——J. W. McArthur, G. Schmidt-Traub, et al. (2004) 'Ending Africa's Poverty Trap'. *Brookings Papers on Economic Activity*, 1: 117–239.

Svensson, J. (2006) 'Absorption Capacity and Disbursement Constraints'. Paper presented at the Third AFD/EUDN conference, 'Financer le développement: les défis d'un doublement de l'aide'. 14 Dec. 2005, Paris.

Tarp, F. (2003) 'Review of S. Devarajan, D. Dollar, and T. Holmgren, *Aid and Reform in Africa*'. *Journal of African Economics*, 10: 341–53.

White, H. (2005) 'The Case for Doubling Aid'. *IDS Bulletin*, 36: 9–13.

World Bank (2005–6) *Global Monitoring Report*. Washington, DC: World Bank.

14

Aid and Rent-driven Growth: Mauritania, Kenya, and Mozambique Compared

Richard M. Auty

14.1. Introduction

The 'resource curse' literature suggests that within immature political systems high rent elicits political contests for its capture that can deflect rent deployment from wealth creation (through the provision of public goods and maintenance of incentives for efficient investment) into patronage channels that distort the economy, reduce investment efficiency, and trigger a growth collapse in the absence of reform (Auty 2007). This chapter identifies the 'resource curse' as a subset of a wider 'rent curse' that can be caused by foreign aid and contrived rent as well as by natural resources. It conceptualizes foreign aid as a geopolitical form of rent that along with natural resource rent and contrived (government-monopoly) rent is one of three key sources of rent in low-income countries.

Natural resource rent is defined here as the surplus revenue from a resource-based activity after deducting all production costs, including a risk-related return on investment. It may be regarded as a gift from Nature, because in theory it can be taxed by governments from resource-based activity without impairing incentives to produce. Contrived rent is derived by governments changing relative prices through crop marketing boards, the exchange rate, trade policy, licensing, and credit usually to favour one interest group over another.[1] It is associated with a relatively high share of government

---

[1] Crowson (personal communication) correctly notes the three 'rent' streams are more accurately defined as supernumerary government revenue, that is, revenue in excess of normal levels. But even the acronym SGR is cumbersome, so 'rent' is used in this sense hereafter.

expenditure in gross domestic product (GDP) and high levels of import protection. Within this context, foreign aid potentially shares the unearned or 'windfall' characteristic of natural resource rent, although aid tended to become more effective through the 1990s as donors appreciated how aid could be deployed for political patronage (Collier 2006).

The rent from natural resources in developing countries has typically comprised between one-tenth and one-fifth of GDP through the 1990s (Auty 2001: 11 and 131) and 2000s (World Bank 2006: 26–7). Contrived rent can be of similar magnitude (Krueger 1992: 61) and in recent decades the scale of geopolitical rent relative to GDP in many low-income countries has matched that of natural resource rent (Svensson 2000), taking the *total* rent within the economy from one-fifth to one-third of GDP, and more. The management of a revenue stream on such a scale, which is detached from the economic activity that generates it, and is also fungible, would challenge the stability of even mature political economies.

The economic literature suggests that a high rent/GDP ratio can facilitate economic development if the rent from resource exports is used to boost capital formation and if the associated foreign exchange is deployed to enhance capacity to import the capital goods required to build a modern economy. But, the potential economic benefits will only accrue if the rent is deployed effectively—that is, by a developmental political state, which after Lal (1995: 310–27) is one that has both sufficient autonomy to pursue a coherent economic policy and the aim of maximizing social welfare. In the absence of such a political state, rent is likely to feed patronage networks and destabilize the political economy (Collier and Hoeffler 2006).

Since the mid-1970s high *natural resource* rent in the developing economies has been linked with economic growth collapses (Lal 1995; Sachs and Warner 1995). The emerging theory of rent cycling posits that rent extraction and deployment in low-income countries deeply impacts government incentives and the development trajectory (Auty 2007). It shows that high rent elicits political contests for its capture, which within immature political states deflect government effort into redistributing rent at the expense of promoting wealth creation. The resulting rent allocation distorts the economy, reduces investment efficiency, and increases vulnerability to shocks that trigger a growth collapse in the absence of economic reform, which rent beneficiaries resist. The growth collapses in many developing economies through the 1970s and 1980s (Figure 14.1) are rooted in the misallocation of rent that was facilitated by fashionable post-war development theories that advocated intensified state intervention in the economy, but overestimated the integrity of political states (Auty 2001). Policies to override markets were frequently captured by vested interests and used to boost rent-seeking in ways that could be sustained for longer periods and with larger cumulative impacts in high-rent (resource-rich) countries than in low-rent countries.

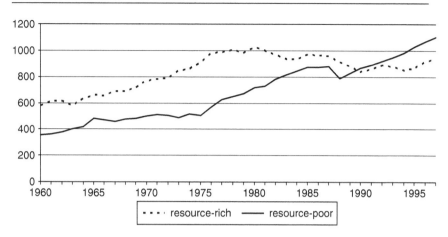

Figure 14.1 Median GDP per capita (constant 1995 US$) resource-rich and resource-poor developing countries

Source: Auty (2001: 5).

Foreign aid increased sharply through the 1980s to help revive the collapsed economies. Although Gomanee, Girma, and Morrissey (2005) and Karras (2006) estimate that each 1 per cent rise in the aid/gross national product (GNP) ratio raises per capita GDP growth by 0.14 per cent to 0.25 per cent,[2] the provision of *geopolitical* rent to revive collapsed resource-rich economies invariably disappointed (Svenssen 2000). The literature disputes whether the modest outcome is because rent feeds corruption (Boone 1996; Leeson 2007), causes political instability (Islam 2005), or triggers 'Dutch disease' effects (Rajan and Subramanian 2005). This chapter argues that all three 'causes' are symptoms of the destabilizing political competition that aid can trigger in immature political states as a large and potentially fungible form of rent.

In assessing the efficiency of foreign aid during the period 1971–90, Boone (1996) finds that it did not increase the investment rate in recipient countries, but went mostly into boosting consumption and expanding the scale of government. Nor did this increased consumption benefit the poor in any of the three different types of political state that Boone analysed (autocratic, oligarchic laissez-faire, and egalitarian). Hodler (2007) also finds that increased aid is likely to expand rent-seeking activity. Burnside and Dollar (2000) seek to refine

---

[2] More specifically, Karras (2006) finds for 71 countries during 1960–97 that an increase in aid equivalent to 1 per cent of GDP raises the PCGDP growth rate by 0.14 to 0.26 per cent, irrespective of policy effects. Similarly, Gomanee, Girma, and Morrissey (2005) report a 0.25 per cent increase in per capita GDP growth from a 1 per cent rise in the aid/GNP ratio for twenty-five sub-Saharan African countries during 1970–7. However, aid must help to restructure the economy to achieve self-sustaining GDP growth.

the gloomy conclusion that *the elite capture foreign aid*. They argue that although aid has no discernible effect on countries with maladroit policies it has a strong positive effect on countries pursuing sound policies regarding fiscal balance and trade openness. Burnside and Dollar (2000) receive little support, however, from subsequent research (Hansen and Tarp 2001; Islam 2005; Rajan and Subramanian 2005; see also Finn Tarp's contribution to this volume (Chapter 2) on the aid-effectiveness debate). Islam (2005) finds that although sound policies are a necessary condition for growth they are not sufficient in the absence of political stability, which is required to encourage investment. In the *absence of political stability*, aid is likely to be dissipated in unproductive consumption, much as Boone describes. Svensson (2000) confirms that for countries with weak political institutions, increases in foreign aid exacerbate corruption because much of the aid feeds rent-seeking activity. Collier and Hoeffler (2005) warn that aid is more likely to be dissipated through rent-seeking in democracies with weak political accountability than in autocratic political states.

Rajan and Subramanian (2005) identify a third channel for aid's adverse impact: they find that domestic *expenditure of overseas aid within the public sector triggers 'Dutch disease' effects* that constrain labour-intensive manufacturing growth (whereas expenditure of private sector remittances does not).[3] This finding echoes that of Bevan, Collier, and Gunning (1987) that windfall natural resource rent is less likely to be saved and also invested effectively when it is concentrated on governments than when it is diffused across many economic agents. Similarly, Gelb et al. (1988) demonstrate that the concentration of the 1974–8 and 1979–81 oil windfalls on governments led to over-rapid domestic absorption of the rent that triggered 'Dutch disease' and rent-seeking, which depressed economy-wide investment efficiency.

The three identified 'causes' of malfunctioning aid are interlinked: rents trigger contests that feed corruption, destabilize policy, and cause over-rapid rent absorption (amplifying 'Dutch disease' effects, that is, distorting the economy). This is not the case for all forms of aid, however, so the argument must be further nuanced: if foreign aid flows are disaggregated, some forms are less prone to political capture. For example, Collier (2006) finds that since the 1980s foreign aid outcomes have improved in sub-Saharan Africa compared with the earlier oil rent outcomes. He attributes this to a learning curve that has directed aid into economies that demonstrate the capacity to use it effectively and also into applications that are subject to public accountability. Collier suggests that whereas oil rent lowers the share of government revenue from taxation, which is scrutinized, relative to 'sovereign' revenue that is not scrutinized, foreign aid may be subject to adequate scrutiny if it is channelled to: technical assistance; projects that are subjected to competitive tender;

---

[3] Mahon (2007) also reports that remittances are deployed more effectively than aid in southern Mexico.

programmes managed by governments with proven records of effective deployment; and forgiveness of debt that can never be serviced. Mavrotas and Ouattara (2006) also qualify the differential impact of aid modalities: they report with reference to Côte d'Ivoire during 1975–99 that increased *programme* aid boosts investment (that can be monitored) and also lowers government consumption, whereas higher *project* aid boosts government consumption (as do technical aid and food aid) but shrinks investment. Ostrom et al. (2002) draw upon the literature on institutions to suggest policies to sustain favourable aid outcomes.

This chapter applies rent-cycling theory to the post-colonial development trajectories of Mauritania, Kenya, and Mozambique in order to distinguish the conditions under which geopolitical rent is detrimental to sustained economic recovery from those where it is beneficial. The theory sets rent in its broad development context. Its high-rent staple trap model explains why many developing economies came to require foreign aid and the preconditions that the aid stream encountered. The chapter finds that aid can reinforce the inertia of rent-seeking and retard economic restructuring but argues that the selective deployment of aid as part of a dual-track reform strategy can improve outcomes. The chapter proceeds by introducing rent-cycling theory in section 14.2. The theory is then applied to analyse why streams of geopolitical rent were counterproductive in Mauritania and Kenya in sections 14.3 and 14.4, respectively. Section 14.5 explains the mainly beneficial outcome of rent deployment in Mozambique. Section 14.6 sets out policy implications.

14.2. High-rent and low-rent political economy models

Rent-cycling theory posits that the scale of the rent profoundly affects government incentives and the development trajectory (Auty 2007). Low rent encourages governments to invest in public goods and maintain efficiency incentives in order to create wealth that they can tax, because that is their principal source of income. Low rent thereby aligns the interests of the elite with those of the majority poor. The resulting incentives to create wealth foster a reliance on markets and nurture a virtuous economic circle because the economy follows its comparative advantage, which in the absence of scope for commodity exports in low-rent economies lies in competitive labour-intensive manufactured exports. Low-rent economies therefore conform to the competitive industrialization model, which is set out below because it provides a useful counterfactual with which to analyse the high-rent staple trap model, which follows. In low-rent economies, early competitive industrialization quickly eliminates surplus rural labour, which then boosts real wages that in turn stimulates investment in skill-intensive and capital-intensive manufacturing (the shaded column in Figure 14.2). The rapid expansion of skills caps the remuneration of

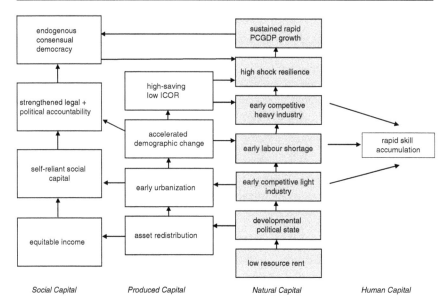

Figure 14.2 Low rent and the competitive industrialization model
Source: Auty (2007: 572).

skilled workers while the elimination of surplus labour puts a floor under the wages of the poor to yield a relatively egalitarian income distribution as well as sharply rising incomes.[4]

Early industrialization also triggers a virtuous socio-political circle because it entails early urbanization that accelerates passage through the demographic cycle, which lowers the dependent/worker ratio so the share of saving and investment in GDP rises faster earlier. Just as important: the higher investment is efficiently applied because of the economy's exposure to global competition so it drives rapid per capita GDP growth, which historically has conferred a seven-year doubling rate on per capita incomes. The high rate of economic growth brings rapid social change as new political groups emerge, which strengthen three key sanctions against antisocial governance to promote incremental democratization as (i) entrepreneurs protect their investment by lobbying for property rights and the rule of law (Li, Li, and Zhang 2000); (ii) unsubsidized urbanization strengthens civic voice (Isham et al. 2005); and (iii) early government reliance on taxing income, profits, and expenditure rather than trade spurs demand for accountable public finances (Ross 2001). Table 14.1 traces the effects of low rent for the three commonly identified types

[4] Congdon Force and Olsson (2007) model how high rent motivates elites to extract rent by weakening property rights while low rent strengthens property rights to foster wealth creation.

Table 14.1. Evolution of political accountability under political states with differing autonomy and aims

Autonomy of state	Basic aims of state	Critical features	Rent pattern	Strength of sanction against anti-social governance		
				Political accountability	Social capital	Rule of law
Low rent incentives						
Benevolent autocratic nation builder	Secure rapid GDP growth to sustain compact elite + build social unity	Low rent; external threat; poor have low opportunity cost	Low rent siphoning; efficient diffuse rent raising + dispersal	Weak; but predation curbed by priority for social unity	Bonding social capital dominant; slow expansion of bridging + linking	Nominal; elite dispense justice, at times arbitrarily
Diffuse factional oligarchy	Expand elite to deter policy capture and sustain rapid GDP growth	Low-rent; intra-elite (land/ethnic/army) rivals; rapid equal GDP growth	Low diffuse rent extraction for public goods + (skewed) wealth creation	Moderate: growing parliament power v. executive	Competitive urbanization builds autonomous linking + bridging social capital	Strengthening legal protection; common law fairer > civil law
Consensual factional democracy	Growth then equity via providing basic social entitlements	Low rent; middle class growth saps elite + shrinks poor	Diffuse extraction + dispersal for growth > redistribution	High: independent parliament + second chamber	Autonomous linking + bridging social capital; risk of Olson effects	Legal independence cuts transaction costs + risk
High-rent incentives						
Predatory autocratic dictator	Maximize elite rent siphoning through force if necessary	High rent; violent predation; staple trap trajectory	Point rent extraction by elite slows GDP growth	None: power held by violence, which only elite contest	Weak: intense elite rivalry; poor have bonding social capital	None: elite controls by force; poor rely on custom
Concentrated factional oligarchy	Dominant faction captures policy to sustain rent + power	High rent; unequal asset share; staple trap trajectory	Point extraction but some public goods benefit mainly elite	Minimal; puppet legislature run by oligarchy;	Dependent on elite; repressed civic associations	Skewed to favour elite > poor
Polarized factional democracy	Capture policy to benefit tribal clients even if slows long-term GDP growth	Democracy polarized on tribal lines; retarded GDP growth	Rent extraction + skewed distribution to tribal clients > GDP growth	Fragile: parliament liable to wild policy swings + some dictator risk	Polarized civic associations feed polarized democracy	Judiciary subject to capture + biased to tribal clients

Note: Moving down the table, political accountability strengthens incrementally and endogenously under low rent (spawning developmental political states). It is retarded in the presence of high rent (favouring non-developmental political states), but after a growth collapse exogenous democratization can occur abruptly if neighbourhood effects are accommodating.
Source: See text.

of political state: the incentives from low rent elicit an autocracy that is benign rather than predatory; an oligarchy that is self-liquidating (as early competitive industrialization drives rapid social change that proliferates competing interest groups able to form alliances to check policy capture by any one faction); and a democracy that is consensual (reflecting public satisfaction with policies that bring rapid socio-economic gain).

In contrast to the virtuous low-rent trajectory, high rent increases the ratio of 'sovereign' revenue relative to tax revenue and sparks political contests to capture the rent that deflect government effort into revenue distribution at the expense of promoting wealth creation, *an outcome that foreign aid can perpetuate*. High rent confers immediate (often personal) gain on governments whereas the benefits from wealth creation are deferred and may therefore accrue to the government's successors. The high-rent incentives render an autocracy likely to be predatory rather than benign (Table 14.1); whereas an oligarchy will remain concentrated because, as explained below, structural and social change are retarded compared with the low-rent competitive industrialization model; and a democracy will be polarized rather than consensual because the high-income inequality associated with resource-rich economies polarizes political parties between income redistribution and the status quo, so that change in government brings major changes in policy that deter investment.

High rent incentivizes governments to cycle more rent through patronage channels and to rely less on markets than low rent economies do. This deflects the high-rent economy from its comparative advantage, which reduces investment efficiency so economic growth slows, presaging a growth collapse in the absence of reform. The high-rent economy also omits the labour-intensive stage of early competitive industrialization, with three adverse consequences (the shaded column in Figure 14.3). First, industrialization is not only retarded but also capital-intensive so it fails to absorb surplus rural labour so that income inequality widens. The resultant social tensions encourage governments to subsidize employment by using rent to protect infant industry and over-expand the bureaucracy. Second, entrepreneurial talent is misallocated because lobbying for government favours is more remunerative than investing in productive activity. Third, lagged industrialization retards urbanization and delays passage through the demographic cycle so the dependant—worker ratio remains high and consumption continues to absorb a high share of GDP.

The resulting distortion of the economy lowers the efficiency of capital so that economic growth decelerates. The economy also becomes vulnerable to shocks because the growing demand for rent from the subsidised sector eventually outstrips the rent supply either because commodity prices fall or else long-term structural change shrinks the relative size of the primary sector within GDP. But, rent-recipients resist economic reform because it extends competitive markets that constrain the rent recipients' scope to capture rent,

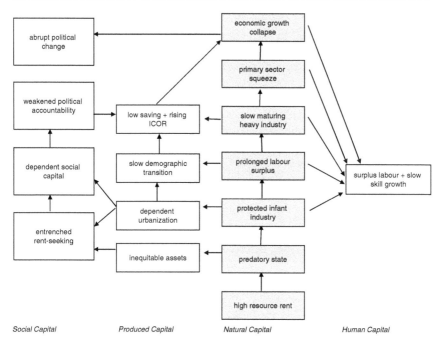

Figure 14.3 High rent and the staple trap model
Source: Auty (2007: 573).

so governments find it easier politically to extract the returns to capital and labour from the primary sector as well as the rent. This depresses incentives in the primary sector and creates a staple trap of growing dependence upon a primary sector that is weakening. In this way the high-rent development trajectory renders the economy vulnerable to shocks and a growth collapse. Recovery is protracted, partly because the cumulative misallocation of investment causes all forms of capital to run down and partly because the inertia of rent-seeking causes rent-recipients to exert their political muscle to oppose market reform because it shrinks their rent-extracting opportunities.

Finally, the high-rent staple trap also retards political maturation by undermining all three sanctions against antisocial governance as: first, entrepreneurs lobby government officials for favours instead of pushing for competitive markets, property rights, and the rule of law; second, rent cycling feeds a dependent social capital that relies on state favours, which mutes civic voice; and third, commodity rent displaces personal taxation, blunting demands for public accountability. Basically, growth collapses occur in high-rent economies because the rent encourages governments to prioritize political aims at the expense of economic ones so markets are repressed and rent cycling acquires a powerful inertia. Rent cycling theory argues that the potentially adverse effects will be heightened in the presence of statist development policies, concentrated rent streams, and ethnic tension (Auty 2008).

This chapter uses rent-cycling theory to evaluate foreign aid as a rent stream. The next three sections apply the theory to each of the case studies to explain the growth collapses that triggered external assistance and how that assistance impacted on their political economies. Mauritania experienced unusually high rent dependence from independence in 1960 and shows how a large increase in foreign aid from 1974 helped perpetuate distortion of the political economy by feeding rent-seeking, easing pressure for reform, and retarding economic restructuring. A shorter expansion of aid in Kenya through the 1980s also disappointed, but aid in Mozambique through the 1990s proved effective.

14.3. Sustained high geopolitical rent and 'Dutch disease' in Mauritania

Since independence, Mauritania has generated a rent stream of around one-third of GDP, and since 1974 mostly from geopolitical rent (Table 14.2). In 1960, barely 2 per cent of Mauritania's one million inhabitants were urbanized, three-quarters being herders scattered across one million square kilometres of arid land and one-quarter being farmers beside the Senegal River (Cour 2004). A new iron-ore mine gave a one-off boost to per capita income in the 1960s that faltered and by 1974 mineral rent peaked at one-third of GDP, and mining generated two-thirds of modern sector income and 80 per cent of exports. In that year foreign aid quadrupled to one-quarter of gross national income (GNI) to help Mauritania adjust to the 1973 oil shock. Aid persisted at that level for three decades, with minor fluctuations even as mineral rent attenuated sharply (Table 14.2). Subsequently, a fishing agreement with the EU conferred quasi-rents that were worth 8 per cent of GDP by the early 2000s. Mauritania's

Table 14.2. Foreign aid flows, 1960–2004 (aid percentage GNI): Mauritania, Kenya, and Mozambique

	Mauritania	Kenya	Mozambique
1960–4	3.1	6.4	n/a
1965–9	6.7	4.7	n/a
1970–4	10.1	3.8	n/a
1975–9	32.9	4.7	n/a
1980–4	26.9	6.8	5.8
1985–9	24.8	8.9	26.2
1990–4	25.0	13.6	48.4
1995–9	22.4	5.2	32.5
2000–4	20.1	3.7	29.5

Source: World Bank (2008).

unusually large and sustained rent stream has, however, been associated with weakly monitored public finances, sizeable economic distortion, and a prolonged growth collapse.

After independence, the Mauritanian elite maintained power by channelling the rent through a clientelistic system. A *nominal* democracy was suspended in 1978 but restored in 1993 as a consequence of International Monetary Fund (IMF) conditionality. Nevertheless, the government established by a military coup in 1984 ruled for two decades and won three elections during 1993–2003 with over two-thirds of the vote by using public office to co-opt tribal leaders and fracture the opposition. The regime rapidly rotated office holders so that short tenure encouraged maximum rent siphoning, which some estimates put at one-quarter of public revenue. The elite exploited both foreign aid and the IMF as sources of rent. For a decade prior to 2004, the government secretly ran off-budget expenditures substantially in excess of those reported to the IMF. In 2005, the national accounts had to be revised to determine how the economy had actually performed. One consequence of such rent cycling is that Mauritania's governance indices in Table 14.3 are little better than those of Malawi, a country with less than half its per capita GDP. In addition to feeding corruption, Mauritania's rent-driven clientelism engendered a dependent form of social capital that looked to the government and the extended family for sustenance. Poor relatives migrated from the countryside and expected their wealthier urban relatives to provide for them until they found a government job or other employment.

Mauritania's rent cycling has strongly distorted the economy, thereby squandering the potentially strong contribution of irrigated agriculture to the country's early economic growth. The share of agriculture in GDP declined (Table 14.4), although stagnant per capita GDP (Table 14.5) might be expected to stabilize its share. The IMF (2005a) estimated that agriculture still employed more than half the workforce in 2004 but generated only 16 per cent of GDP, barely half the size expected for a country at Mauritania's level of development while manufacturing was two-thirds the size expected. Moreover, only half the herding subsector's 12 per cent of GDP was commercialized while cropping generated a meagre 4 per cent of GDP, only one-quarter of which was commercial, although cropping employed three-quarters of the rural workforce. Yet, Mauritania's 150,000 irrigable hectares, if integrated with improved livestock management and road access to markets, could lift agriculture's share of GDP above the expected one-third level.

The economic distortion reflects the fact that the large aid-dominated rent stream eased pressure for economic reform until rising foreign debt necessitated IMF help in the 1990s.[5] The resulting prolonged rural neglect denied most

[5] When external debt was twice GDP and debt service absorbed one-quarter of export earnings (World Bank 2008).

Table 14.3. Index of institutional quality, 2006: Mauritania, Kenya, Mozambique, and regional comparator countries

Country	PCGDP (US$ PPP 2006)	Voice + accountability	Political stability	Effective governance	Regulation burden	Rule of law	Graft	Overall index
Malawi	703	−0.31	+0.02	−0.85	−0.64	−0.46	−0.74	−2.98
Mozambique	739	−0.06	+0.52	−0.30	−0.49	−0.59	−0.57	−1.49
Ghana	1,247	+0.37	+0.23	+0.05	−0.09	−0.13	−0.12	+0.31
Zambia	1,273	−0.34	+0.29	−0.74	−0.56	−0.61	−0.78	−2.74
Kenya	1,436	−0.18	−1.09	−0.69	−0.21	−0.98	−0.97	−4.12
Lesotho	1,438	+0.25	+0.16	−0.27	−0.62	−0.25	−0.05	−0.78
Nigeria	1,853	−0.78	−1.99	−0.96	−0.89	−1.27	−1.29	−7.18
Mauritania	1,890	−0.95	−0.29	−0.64	−0.24	−0.43	−0.60	−3.15
Cameroon	2,043	−1.42	−0.22	−0.89	−0.69	−1.02	−0.94	−5.18
Angola	4,435	−1.25	−0.51	−1.20	−1.20	−1.29	−1.14	−6.59
Swaziland	4,709	−1.10	−0.14	−0.70	−0.52	−0.69	−0.47	−3.62
Namibia	4,820	+0.39	+0.83	+0.13	+0.16	+0.17	+0.16	+1.84
South Africa	9,087	+0.60	−0.07	+0.78	+0.68	+0.24	+0.56	+2.79
Botswana	12,744	+0.57	+1.23	+0.74	+0.48	+0.63	+0.81	+4.46

Source: World Bank (2007).

Table 14.4. Structural change: Mauritania, Kenya and Mozambique, 1960–2004

	1960–4	1965–9	1970–4	1975–9	1980–4	1985–9	1990–4	1995–9	2000–4
Mauritania									
PCGDP (US$ 2,000)	206.9	239.4	298.7	330.9	348.2	310.3	311.2	339.2	366.6
PCGDP (US$ 2,000)	206.9	239.4	298.7	330.9	348.2	310.3	311.2	339.2	366.6
Agriculture (percentage GDP)	43.1	31.1	31.2	29.3	31.6	29.2	28.1	25.1	20.4
Industry	24.8	38.2	35.4	30.6	24.4	29.5	30.1	30.5	30.3
Manufacturing	n/a	n/a	n/a	n/a	n/a	12.6	11.5	10.4	9.0
Services	32.0	30.7	32.7	40.1	44.0	41.2	41.8	44.3	49.3
Kenya									
PCGDP (US$ 2,000)	228.4	311.1	341.2	324.9	317.2	353.0	363.4	360.3	343.3
Agriculture (percentage GDP)	39.4	35.6	34.2	37.1	33.3	31.8	29.5	27.5	17.5
Industry	17.0	18.8	20.4	19.6	19.9	18.9	18.4	16.5	18.9
Manufacturing	9.7	11.4	12.1	11.8	12.2	11.7	11.2	10.8	13.0
Services	43.6	45.6	45.4	43.3	46.8	49.3	52.0	56.0	63.6
Mozambique									
PCGDP (US$ 2,000)	n/a	n/a	n/a	n/a	130.06	133.1	150.9	182.9	241.2
Agriculture	n/a	n/a	n/a	n/a	34.8	44.6	32.5	35.2	26.6
Industry	n/a	n/a	n/a	n/a	29.7	19.9	19.2	20.7	28.6
Manufacturing	n/a	n/a	n/a	n/a	n/a	n/a	8.4	11.2	14.8
Services	n/a	n/a	n/a	n/a	35.6	29.2	48.3	44.8	44.9

Source: World Bank (2008).

Table 14.5. Output growth: Mauritania, Kenya and Mozambique, 1960–2004

	1960–4	1965–9	1970–4	1975–9	1980–4	1985–9	1990–4	1995–9	2000–4
GDP growth (per cent/year)									
Mauritania	10.5	6.3	4.1	1.2	1.0	3.4	3.2	4.1	5.2
Kenya	3.9	7.2	8.9	5.4	2.8	5.7	1.6	2.7	1.2
Mozambique	n/a	n/a	n/a	n/a	–6.0	5.6	2.6	8.5	7.4
PCGDP growth (per cent/year)									
Mauritania	8.0	3.8	1.7	–0.4	–1.4	1.1	0.7	1.2	2.7
Kenya	0.7	3.8	5.2	1.6	–1.0	2.2	–1.2	0.2	–0.8
Mozambique	n/a	n/a	n/a	n/a	–8.3	4.5	0.9	6.1	5.2
PCGDP (2000 $ PPP)									
Mauritania	n/a	n/a	n/a	1665	1602	1484	1548	1699	1760
Kenya	n/a	n/a	n/a	983	1026	1061	1100	1049	988
Mozambique	n/a	n/a	n/a	n/a	613	558	646	770	1020
Crop output index[1]									
Mauritania	48.4	52.4	35.4	37.9	44.2	79.5	77.4	114.5	91.6
Kenya	27.0	32.3	38.6	49.5	51.7	67.4	75.6	92.4	97.0
Mozambique	67.1	74.6	89.6	77.0	72.1	65.7	64.2	95.1	101.8

Note:
[1] 1999–2001 = 100.

Source: World Bank (2008).

Mauritanians the opportunity to acquire the assets and skills required to take advantage of a market economy. In addition to imposing sizeable welfare losses, the rent-cycling policy that sustained low rural incomes repressed domestic purchasing power, which in the early stages of economic development should stimulate local supply of basic manufactured goods and services (Mellor 1976). Moreover, Mauritania's remarkably low *commercial* farm output cut the sector's capacity to supply inputs for agro-processing, which is also a key feature of early industrialization.

The corollary of rural neglect is an over-expanded urban sector dominated by the capital city Nouakchott, which houses one-third of the population and generates three-fifths of GDP (Cour 2004), mainly by cycling the rent. Large private trading monopolies and inefficient state-owned water and electricity companies were permitted to skim rent from the urban economy at the expense of domestic private producers whose margins were shrunk by high-cost water and intermittent power as well as by expensive transport that reflected a haulage monopoly, unpaved arterial roads, and the inefficiency of Nouakchott port. The monopolies also dominated bank credit at the expense of small private firms whose perceived 'high risk' elicited interest rates of 20 per cent or more. The trading monopolies reserved domestic markets for imports like German dairy products and Dutch onions, even when local products were cheaper. Summarizing, Mauritania's legacy of prolonged rent deployment, dominated by foreign aid, is one of corrupt rent cycling; acute economic distortion; low incomes; and limited skill accumulation. These are inauspicious preconditions for managing an oil boom projected to generate an extra 25 per cent of GDP annually in public revenue during 2007–16.

14.4. Geopolitical rent retards Kenya's competitive industrialization

Failure to sustain GDP growth and thereby complete the demographic transition saw Kenya's population expand sixfold during 1948–2004 and transform Kenya from a resource-rich economy into a resource-poor one (World Bank 1963, 2008). Between 1960 and 2005 per capita cropland declined from 0.42 hectares to only 0.14 (World Bank 2008). Rent-cycling theory predicts that in the absence of sizeable productivity gains, declining per capita crop rent will strengthen incentives to diversify the economy into competitive manufacturing, as in Mauritius after it exhausted its land frontier in the 1960s. Yet, although at independence in 1963 the Kenyan economy had already developed a sizeable export-oriented manufacturing sector upon which to build, industrial competitiveness subsequently regressed. This section argues that rent from agriculture initially subsidized this regression and then foreign aid (Table 14.3) inadvertently helped to extend it.

The Kenyan elite initially supported open trade to facilitate export production from the large landholdings they acquired from white settlers at independence; a policy which also constrained rent-seeking. However, in 1968 the elite amended the law in order to acquire urban manufacturing and importing businesses (Bates 1983), activities that were already major sources of contrived rent elsewhere in sub-Saharan Africa (Bigsten 1993). This triggered a drift into protectionist policies that shifted the internal terms of trade in favour of manufacturing and against agriculture. Sharpley and Lewis (1990: 206–41) estimate that by 1984, subsidies to manufacturing comprised 60 per cent of its value added (7 per cent of total GDP) and absorbed 28 per cent of the previous twenty years' growth in farm output. The share of exports in manufacturing output regressed to 10 per cent by the early 1980s compared with 40 per cent in the mid-1960s. A coffee boom during 1976–9 conferred extra rent equivalent to 8 per cent of GDP annually (Cuddington 1989) which the Kenyan government extracted through crop-marketing boards, leaving farmers with only one-third of world prices to cover their costs (World Bank 2003: 44). Other crops subject to state predation like maize and sugar also lost viability whereas less-regulated crops like tea and horticulture did not.

When the coffee boom faded, public expenditure and external debt proved unsustainable and Kenya's economic growth collapsed: the rate of per capita GDP growth, which averaged 2.8 per cent annually during the 1960s and 1970s, fell to 0.3 per cent during the 1980s and –0.5 per cent in the 1990s (Table 14.5). Despite the growth collapse and intensifying pressure on natural resources, the economy failed to diversify into competitive manufacturing (Table 14.4) because rent-seekers undermined IMF-backed economic reforms. Increased aid facilitated rent-seeking by allowing the successor to Kenya's founding president (who died in 1978) to maintain a political coalition of smaller tribes in the western rift valley (Ndegwa 2003). The new leader shored up his coalition by drawing on geopolitical rent, which more than doubled to average 11.4 per cent of GNI annually during 1986–95, peaking at 13.6 per cent in the early 1990s (Table 14.2). Both government officials and businessmen siphoned away geopolitical rent through scams, including one that recycled four hundred million dollars through fictitious mineral exports (*Economist* 2006). Aid did raise per capita GDP slightly but it was also associated with a halving in agriculture's share of GDP (Table 14.4) whereas economic reform might be expected to re-expand it.

In the mid-1990s, donors responded to Kenyan corruption by cutting aid to 4 per cent of GNI, causing incomes to dip. The long-serving government was still re-elected in 1997, however, albeit with barely two-fifths of the vote, courtesy of a fractured opposition. The preceding increase in aid was associated with a continued lag in economic restructuring, extending the resulting loss in welfare. The World Bank (2003: 29) estimates that Kenya's mean per capita GDP growth during 1960–2000 of 1.5 per cent is 3.5 per cent slower than the high-performing Asian economies although Kenya's lower per capita income implies

its underlying growth potential was 1.5 per cent *higher* than the Asian economies. Even after the ruling party lost power in 2002 to a fifteen-party coalition
that captured two-thirds of the vote, the welfare underperformance seemed
likely to persist due to rent-seeking inertia. When donors expanded aid to
encourage economic reform the new government muted its attacks on corruption and reverted to rent cycling to maintain its unwieldy political coalition
(Ndegwa 2003).

14.5. Targeting geopolitical rent on wealth creation in Mozambique

Geopolitical rent has been deployed more effectively in Mozambique than in
Mauritania and Kenya. The restructuring of the Mozambique economy after it
had been distorted by a failed experiment with central planning and years of
civil strife attracted unusually high flows of foreign aid, which averaged 42.4 per
cent of GNI annually during 1987–2004 (Table 14.2). Aid lifted Mozambique's
investment rate to almost 50 per cent of GDP, more than double the expected
level, and expanded import capacity, removing a severe constraint on growth
(de Sousa and Sulemane 2003). It was associated with a sustained economic
recovery from the mid-1990s, once civil strife ended (Table 14.4). Aid is also
linked with a revival of democracy and creditably high indices of governance
for a country with Mozambique's per capita income (Table 14.3). These outcomes may reflect the scrutiny of public expenditure by a credible political
opposition and the increasing donor preference for tighter monitoring.

The restoration of democracy produced two relatively evenly matched political parties that drew support from the rival contestants in the civil war, so
unlike Mauritania and Kenya the opposition was not fragmented and initially
at least presented a credible threat to the ruling party. In addition, donors
targeted aid at investment, which they could more effectively monitor than
boosting either general budget support or current consumption. The investment drew on surplus domestic labour and was import-intensive. Adam and
Bevan (2003) find that aid directed at import-rich infrastructure limits 'Dutch
disease' effects by boosting the productivity of private sector activity.

The deployment of targeted aid within a contested polity may also explain
why Mozambique's stabilization policy succeeded in the late 1990s. Successful
stabilization, boosted by generous tax exemptions, elicited a large inflow of
foreign direct investment (FDI) into capital-intensive projects, notably a US$2.2
billion aluminium smelter. Fears that the scale of investment would feed 'Dutch
disease' effects proved unfounded because it too was import-intensive and
during the construction phase 1999–2003 the real exchange rate fell from 76
per cent of its 1990 value to 60 per cent (IMF 2003: 27). But, the foreign
investment created few long-term jobs and boosted urban growth, mostly in

the far south of the country. Although agriculture sustains 80 per cent of the workforce and grew at 6.6 per cent annually during 1996–2004, its share of GDP declined as heavy industry and tourism grew faster (IMF 2005b: 7). Nevertheless, the rate of rural poverty fell from 71 per cent in 1996 to 55 per cent in 2003, paralleling the national drop, which the IMF (2005b: 12–13) attributes to rapid GDP growth, improved market access for some farmers, and broad-based advances in education and health.

Adam and Bevan (2003) warn, however, that aid targeted at infrastructure amplifies income inequality because it benefits urban households more than rural households. The resumption of rapid per capita GDP growth in Mozambique did not boost domestic consumption proportionately. This is partly because the withdrawal of geopolitical rent channelled much of the extra output into debt service and exports rather than into consumption (personal communication 2003, Alan H. Gelb). But, it also reflects a long-standing urban policy bias. Mozambique's central planning initially stressed heavy industry and large-scale agriculture at the expense of peasant farming, and even before the FDI inflow agriculture generated a share of GDP 8 per cent lower than expected for an economy at Mozambique's level of development, whereas industry's share was 9 per cent more than expected (Tarp et al. 2002: 12). As in Mauritania, many farmers in Mozambique lacked market access and so could not take advantage of economic improvements. Although the fraction of smallholders engaging in markets doubled from 1996 to 2005, the ratio remained at barely one-quarter (IMF 2005b: 12).

Farmers need all-weather tertiary roads if they are to emerge from subsistence production and capture the productivity *and* environmental gains from crop specialization (Tiffin and Mortimore 1994).[6] Yet, government and donors in Mozambique concentrated transport investment on primary roads (Tarp et al. 2002: 108), which bridge space between cities, rather than open it up for development. Continued rural neglect lies behind the fact that 60 per cent of Mozambique's population remain illiterate, one-third lack access to health care, and one-eighth are HIV positive. Moreover, weak tax enforcement leaves Mozambique taxation at 12.5 per cent of GDP, half the target level, but similar to other regional aid recipients like Uganda and Rwanda (IMF 2005b: 34). Unfortunately, Mozambique government officials began to rely on aid to substitute for domestic public revenue, which they siphoned away for personal gain (Hanlon 2004). The country's graft index deteriorated from –0.39 to –0.57 during 1996–2006, whereas rising incomes should have improved it (World Bank 2007). An attempt to strengthen local ownership of the aid programme by consolidating aid within the overall budget risks feeding rent-seekers rather than strengthening overall policy coherence, especially as declining political support weakens the main opposition party.

---

[6] In Mozambique, the penalty arising from high marketing costs ranges from 25 per cent of revenue for maize to 80 per cent for cassava and other basic food crops (Tarp et al. 2002).

As aid and donor influence wane, sustained development in Mozambique requires the mainly rural electorate to cohere in resisting policy capture by rent-seeking urban interests. As in Mauritania, the economic case for supporting the rural economy is strong: a simulation (Tarp et al. 2002: 76–85) finds that as aid shrinks the strongest growth potential lies in agriculture because it is less adversely affected by the associated cuts in public investment and import compression than either the construction or urban services sectors. Agriculture also promotes labour-intensive growth and acquisition of simple business skills (IMF 2005b: 16).

14.6. Conclusions

Rent-cycling theory explains how high rent can deflect government incentives into rent cycling at the expense of sustained wealth creation by distorting the economy, lowering investment efficiency, and increasing vulnerability to shocks and growth collapses. The higher the rent the longer that maladroit rent deployment continues and the greater the distortion of the political economy. The provision of foreign aid to restructure collapsed economies risks perpetuating the distortion of the political economy if it functions as a stream of geopolitical rent. The literature suggests that, like natural resource rent, foreign aid can feed corruption, distort the economy through 'Dutch disease' effects, and help perpetuate a growth collapse.

Mauritania and Kenya experienced growth collapses linked to maladroit rent cycling, driven initially by mineral rent and crop rent, respectively, but subsequently sustained by increased geopolitical rent. Rent-cycling theory suggests that growth collapses eventually self-correct because they accelerate the onset of resource scarcity, which motivates governments to create wealth and that shifts incentives and the development trajectory of low-rent economies into competitive labour-intensive industrialization. This did not occur in either Mauritania or Kenya because when their growth collapses triggered sharp increases in foreign aid, rent-seekers treated it as an additional source of rent. Their experience shows how the inertia of rent-seeking can cause the foreign aid that is deployed to revive distorted economies to perpetuate rent-seeking, economic distortion, and growth collapses *in the presence of weak sanctions against antisocial governance and of a fractious society.*

The Mozambique case suggests, however, that geopolitical rent can be beneficial where: (i) donors target investment (rather than current consumption and/or budgetary support, which are more fungible) and monitor it and also encourage institutions for transparent macro policy and public finances; and (ii) a credible pro-reform political opposition coheres to hold the government to account. Two factors behind Mozambique's superior outcome are the learning curve of aid donors and the fact that the risk of renewed civil strife helped reinforce the democratic check on the government, at least initially.

Rajan and Zingales (2006) warn, however, that institutional reform may not be sufficient to promote development in the absence of supportive political constituencies. Rent-cycling theory explains why reformers need to build political constituencies to back their policies. It suggests that a dual-track strategy (espoused by successful economies as varied as China, Malaysia, and Mauritius) can limit the damaging inertia of rent-seeking by weaning the economy off patronage-channelled rent distribution and into market-guided wealth creation. Track one stimulates a dynamic market economy that imposes minimal immediate costs on the elite while building a political lobby in favour of economy-wide reform. Track two promotes reform of the rent-driven (usually urban) economy, but slowly, in recognition of the political risk to reforming governments if they tackle vested interests head-on from the outset. In all three case studies analysed here, a dual-track strategy would strengthen the rural constituency and unlock its important contribution to early economic development, not least as a political check on urban rent-seeking, provided ethnicity does not fragment the rural vote.

References

Adam, C. S., and D. L. Bevan (2003) 'Aid, Public Expenditure and Dutch Disease'. CSE Working Paper 184. Oxford: Oxford University Department of Economics.

Auty, R. M. (ed.) (2001) *Resource Abundance and Economic Development*. Oxford: Oxford University Press for UNU-WIDER.

——(2007) 'Patterns of Rent-extraction and Deployment in Developing Countries: Implications for Governance, Economic Policy and Performance'. In G. Mavrotas and A. Shorrocks (eds), *Advancing Development: Core Themes in Global Economics*. Basingstoke: Palgrave Macmillan for UNU-WIDER, 555–77.

——(2008) 'Political Economy of African Mineral Revenue Deployment: Angola, Botswana, Nigeria and Zambia Compared'. Elcano Working Paper 28/2008. Madrid: Real Instituto Elcano.

Bates, R. H. (1983) *Beyond the Miracle of the Market: The Political Economy of Agrarian Development in Kenya*. Cambridge: Cambridge University Press.

Bevan, D., P. Collier, and J. W. Gunning (1987) 'Consequences of a Commodity Boom in a Controlled Economy: Accumulation and Redistribution in Kenya'. *World Bank Economic Review*, 1: 489–513.

Bigsten, A. (1993) 'Regulations versus Price Reforms in Crisis Management: The Case of Kenya'. In M. Blomström and M. Lundahl (eds), *Economic Crisis in Africa: Perspectives on Policy Responses*. London: Routledge.

Boone, P. (1996) 'Politics and the Effectiveness of Foreign Aid'. *European Economic Review*, 89: 22–46.

Burnside, C., and D. Dollar (2000) 'Aid, Policies and Growth'. *American Economic Review*, 90: 857–68.

Collier, P. (2006) 'Is Aid Oil? An Analysis of Whether Africa Can Absorb More Aid'. *World Development*, 34: 1482–97.

——and A. Hoeffler (2005) 'Democracy and Resource Rents'. Global Policy Research Group Working Paper 016. London: Economic and Social Research Council.

————(2006) 'Testing the Neocon Agenda: Democracy in Resource-rich Societies'. Mimeo. Oxford: University of Oxford Department of Economics.

Congdon Force, H., and O. Olsson (2007) 'Endogenous Institutional Change after Independence'. *European Economic Review*, 51: 1896–921.

Cour, J.-M. (2004) 'Première esquisse de maquette démo-économique de la Mauritanie et de la Wilaya du Guidimagha'. Nouakchott: World Bank.

Cuddington, J. (1989) 'Commodity Price Booms in Developing Countries'. *World Bank Research Observer*, 4: 143–65.

de Sousa, C., and J. Sulemane (2003) 'Explaining African Growth Performance: Case of Mozambique'. Mimeo. Maputo.

The Economist (2006) 'Caught in the Act' (28 Jan.): 61–2.

Gelb, A. H., et al. (1988) *Oil Windfalls: Blessing or Curse?* New York: Oxford University Press.

Gomanee, K., S. Girma, and O. Morrissey (2005) 'Aid and Growth in Sub-Saharan Africa'. *Journal of International Development*, 17: 1055–105.

Hanlon, J. (2004) 'Do Donors Promote Corruption? The Case of Mozambique'. *Third World Quarterly*, 25: 747–63.

Hansen, H., and F. Tarp (2001) 'Aid Effectiveness Disputed'. *Journal of International Development*, 12: 357–98.

Hodler, R. (2007) 'Rent Seeking and Aid Effectiveness'. *International Tax and Public Finance*, 14: 425–41.

IMF (International Monetary Fund) (2003) 'Ex-post Assessment of Mozambique's Performance Under Fund-supported Programs'. Washington, DC: IMF.

——(2005a) *Islamic Republic of Mauritania: Selected Issues and Statistical Appendix*. International Monetary Fund Report 05/00. Washington, DC: IMF.

——(2005b) *Republic of Mozambique: Selected Issues and Statistical Appendix*. International Monetary Fund Report 05/311. Washington, DC: IMF.

Isham, J., L. Pritchett, M. Woolcock, and G. Busby (2005) 'The Varieties of Resource Experience: How Natural Resource Export Structures Affect the Political Economy of Economic Growth'. *World Bank Economic Review*, 19: 141–64.

Islam, M. N. (2005) 'Regime Changes, Economic Policies and the Effect of Aid on Growth'. *Journal of Development Economics*, 41: 1467–92.

Karras, G. (2006) 'Foreign Aid and Long-Run Economic Growth'. *Journal of International Development*, 18: 15–28.

Krueger, A. O. (1992) *Political Economy of Agricultural Pricing Policy*. Baltimore, Md.: Johns Hopkins University Press.

Lal, D. (1995) 'Why Growth Rates Differ: The Political Economy of Social Capability in 21 Developing Countries'. In B. H. Koo and D. H. Perkins (eds), *Social Capability and Long-run Economic Growth*. Basingstoke: Macmillan.

Leeson, P. T. (2007) 'Escaping Poverty: Foreign Aid, Private Property and Economic Development'. *Journal of International Economics*, 51: 437–61.

Li, S., S. Li, and W. Zhang (2000) 'The Road to Capitalism: Competition and Institutional Change in China'. *Journal of Comparative Economics*, 28: 269–92.

Mahon, J. (2007) *Revenue and Regimes*. Williamstown, Mass.: Williams College.

Mavrotas, G., and B. Ouattara (2006) 'Aid Disaggregation and the Public Sector in Aid-recipient Economies: Some Evidence from Côte d'Ivoire'. *Review of Development Economics*, 10: 434–51.

Mellor, J. W. (1976) *The New Economics of Growth*. Ithaca NY: Cornell University Press.

Ndegwa, S. (2003) 'Kenya: Third Time Lucky?' *Journal of Democracy*, 14: 145–58.

Ostrom, E., C. Gibson, S. Shivakumar, and K. Andersson (2002), 'Aid Incentives and Sustainability: An Institutional Analysis of Development Cooperation'. Evaluation Study 02/01. Stockholm: Sida.

Rajan, R. G., and A. Subramanian (2005) 'What Undermines Aid's Impact on Growth?' International Monetary Fund Working Paper 05/126. Washington, DC: IMF.

——and L. Zingales (2006) 'The Persistence of Underdevelopment: Institutions, Human Capital or Constituencies?'. National Bureau of Economic Research Working Paper 12093. Cambridge, Mass.: NBER.

Ross, M. (2001) 'Does Oil Hinder Democracy?' *World Politics*, 53: 325–61.

Sachs, J. D., and A. M. Warner (1995) 'Economic Reform and the Process of Global Integration'. *Brookings Papers on Economic Activity*, 1: 1–118.

Sharpley, J., and A. Lewis (1990) 'The Manufacturing Sector in the Mid 1980s'. In R. C. Riddell (ed.), *Manufacturing Africa*. London: James Currey.

Svensson, J. (2000) 'Foreign Aid and Rent-seeking'. *Journal of International Economics*, 51: 437–61.

Tarp, F., C. Arndt, H. T. Jensen, et al. (2002) 'Facing the Development Challenge in Mozambique: An Economy-wide Perspective'. International Food Policy Research Institute Report 126. Washington, DC: IFPRI.

Tiffin, M., and M. Mortimore (1994) 'Malthus Controverted: The Role of Capital and Technology in Growth and Recovery in Kenya'. *World Development*, 22: 997–1010.

World Bank (1963) *The Economic Development of Kenya*. Baltimore, Md.: Johns Hopkins University Press.

——(2003) *Kenya: A Policy Agenda to Restore Growth*. Washington, DC: World Bank.

——(2006) *Where Is the Wealth of Nations?* Washington, DC: World Bank.

——(2007) *Estimates of Governance Quality*. Washington, DC: World Bank.

——(2008) *World Development Indicators 2008*. Washington, DC: World Bank.

Index

Abbott, Phil 20 n.
ABCD paradigm 313
absorptive capacity 8, 10, 14, 21, 45, 191, 200,
  255, 278
  'big push' versus 297–322
  lack of 183, 293
  limited in using aid productively 68 n.
accountability 13, 47, 112, 209 n., 213, 214,
  216, 223, 224, 225, 226, 230, 231, 234, 236,
  237, 239, 240, 243, 256, 271, 273, 277, 282,
  314, 328, 332
  commitment to some form of 276
  democratic 253
  downward 235
  enhancing 212
  expectations and demand of 281
  financial 238 n.
  furthering vis-à-vis local populations 48
  lack of 134, 316
  mutual reviews 257
  poor 250, 252
  strong 253
  vital means for raising 255
  weak 315, 326
  see also PEFA
Accra Agenda for Action (2008) 224
Aceh 171 n.
Acemoglu, D. 210
ACP (African, Caribbean and Pacific)
  countries 80
ActionAid 175
Adam, C. S. 38, 47, 48 n., 49, 80, 214 n., 304,
  317, 339, 340
Addis Ababa principle 237
Addison, T. 5, 7, 8 n., 9 n., 10, 65 n., 179 n.
adjustment loans 31
  see also structural adjustment
administrative capacity 139
Afghanistan 33 n., 57, 133, 159, 180
  interim administration (2001) 173
  malaria endemic in 153
Afghanistan Reconstruction Trust Fund 281
Africa 21, 43, 46, 307, 309, 316
  China a significant donor in 163

colonial penetration 156
conflicts in 129
crisis hit 30
economically successful states 208
enthusiasm for development 57
ethnic groups regionally concentrated 104
failed projects 20
fiscal contracts 213 n.
heavy taxation of agriculture 315
mortality rates 153
one of the safest capitals in 165
per capita income 158 n.
policy agendas 11
PRSPs 131
unsuitable cases for standard Bretton Woods
  lending 172
  see also ACP; CEMAC; Commission for Africa;
  SPA; sub-Saharan Africa; also under various
  country names
African Development Bank 72
Afro-Americans 95, 96
age classification 103
Agency for International Development (US) 59
agriculture:
  heavy taxation of 315
  irrigated 333
  labour-intensive growth promoted 341
  share of GDP 333
  smallholder 131
aid allocation 33–4, 46, 78, 90, 106, 116, 117,
  136, 139, 140, 141, 305
  basic approach in 48
  behaviour of donors 39
  CPIA/selectivity-based 65, 66–74, 75, 76, 79,
  80
  creating star performers by engineering 64
  criteria for 40, 153, 308
  discriminatory 47
  endogenous 36
  governance indicators to justify 210
  impact of institutions on 313
  non-developmental considerations strongly
  influence 199
  normal considerations governing 97

Lightning Source UK Ltd.
Milton Keynes UK
UKHW022148020822
406747UK00003B/153

9 780199 580934